Ideal Government
and the Mixed Constitution
in the Middle Ages

Ideal Government
and the Mixed Constitution
in the Middle Ages

James M. Blythe

PRINCETON UNIVERSITY PRESS

PRINCETON, NEW JERSEY

Copyright © 1992 by Princeton University Press
Published by Princeton University Press, 41 William Street,
Princeton, New Jersey 08540
In the United Kingdom: Princeton University Press, Oxford

Library of Congress Cataloging-in-Publication Data

Blythe, James M., 1948–
Ideal government and the mixed constitution in the
Middle Ages / James M. Blythe.
p. cm.
Includes bibliographical references and index.
1. Political science—History. 2. Constitutional history.
3. Middle Ages. I. Title.
JA82.B59   1992   320'.09'02—dc20   91-21104

ISBN 0-691-03167-3

This book has been composed in Linotron Galliard

Princeton University Press books are printed
on acid-free paper and meet the guidelines for permanence and
durability of the Committee on Production Guidelines for
Book Longevity of the Council on Library Resources

Printed in the United States of America

1   3   5   7   9   10   8   6   4   2

*To those who helped and encouraged me
during the long years of my graduate work
and the four years since then that I spent
working on this book:*

Sheila Martin, *my mother* Ann Blythe, *my
aunts* Charlotte Horton *and* Sara
Nancarrow, *and my brother* Richard
Blythe; *and to those who died before I
finished: my father* Donald Blythe, *my aunt*
Gwen Brace, *and my uncle* Richard
Horton.

Thanne kam ther a kyng: Knyghthod him ladde;
Might of the communes made hym to regne.
And thanne cam Kynde Wit and clerkes he made,
For to counseillen the Kynge and the Commune save
. . .

The Kynge and the Commune and Kynde Wit the
thridde
Shopen lawe and leute—ech lif to knowe his owene.
—William Langland, *The Vision of Piers Plowman*
(c. 1380)

It had been, it seems, a splendid constitution full of
senates and committees and checks and balances and
other things delightful to the political theorist. "If it
was that fine," said Stanford, "why didn't it last?" "It
lasted six hundred years, signor," said Graziella, "and
when it was quite worn out and would not work at
all any more, it was exported, of course, to the
United States of America."
—Sarah Caudwell, *Thus Was Adonis Murdered* (1982)

CONTENTS

PREFACE

So MANY HISTORIANS have written on the mixed constitution that it is disconcerting to come across ignorance of its origins in Greek thought and its importance in early modern England. But such is displayed in a 1987 letter to the American Historical Association's *Perspectives*. The author writes: "The basic idea of a mixed type of government with a divided power arrangement, of checks and balances between three branches, of fragmented sources of power, adopted by the [American Constitutional] Convention in 1787 was not originated by its delegates; it was the brain-child of Niccolo Machiavelli in 1517."[1]

If it were not for the self-righteousness with which the author dismisses the poor clods (if any) who imagine that John Adams concocted the mixed constitution all by himself, I would not bother to dredge up his letter now, for I doubt that the misconception it betrays or the one that it castigates are common ones among historians. But this shows that even the more well-known aspects of this venerable theory deserve to be still more widely known. And even among those who know a lot about it there is another common misconception—that after the ancient Greeks and Romans had done with the theory it disappeared, except possibly for a few freakish references here and there, until the glorious Florentines recovered Polybius in the early sixteenth century. After that the theory took off, but its roots in the modern world are always traced back to Polybius.

Not everyone, of course, takes such an extreme view. Many medieval historians have discussed some aspects of the mixed constitution in Thomas Aquinas and John of Paris. Brian Tierney has taken this somewhat further and suggested that a detailed study of medieval mixed constitutionalism would be rewarding. But no one has yet tried to show in detail that the theory flourished in the Middle Ages and that the modern development of it owes at least as much to Aristotle and the medieval tradition as it does to Polybius. That is what my book attempts to do.

The letter previously quoted concludes, "None of this is new. It is time for the public to be informed and perceptions discontinued that do not conform to reality." Indeed.

Two scholars have been especially influential in current discussions of Renaissance and Early Modern political theory, particularly as applied to Republicanism: Quentin Skinner and J.G.A. Pocock. Since some readers have interpreted my book as directed against their (in many ways very dif-

---

[1] A. J. Pansini, in *Perspectives*, December 1987, p. 10.

ferent) conclusions, it may be prudent to clarify my position at the outset.
I do not mean it as a backhand compliment to say that the research of both
has been of great help to me and that their contribution has been immense.
And while I disagree with each of them on various points, my disagreements usually have more to do with what they leave out—usually medieval,
or scholastic, or non-Italian influence—than what they include. In a few
areas, however, I find that each to varying degrees misinterprets or misrepresents medieval Aristotelian thought.

Although I accuse them of underestimating the contribution of medieval
Aristotelians to republican thought, I should say at once that both these
authors acknowledge medieval and Aristotelian sources far more than most
other Renaissance and Early Modern historians. Skinner, for example, ably
refutes the influential scholar of Florentine civic humanism, Hans Baron,
on this very point. But each also distinguishes sharply between Italian republicanism and Northern monarchism. No one can deny that in the High
and late Middle Ages Northern Italy teemed with independent cities ex-
perimenting with all manner of governmental arrangements from fairly
broadly-based—in their own view, democratic—republics to tyrannies,
while monarchy dominated in Northern Europe, but what is more important, I think, is that in both places theorists, drawing from a common Tho-
mist-Aristotelian political ideology, argued for a diffusion of governmental
powers. It is simply not enough, as Skinner tends to do, to treat Thomas
Aquinas (sometimes classed with the Italians), Engelbert of Admont, Nicole Oresme, and John of Paris, to name only a few, as monarchists and
contrast them with purported Italian republicans such as Ptolemy of Lucca
and Marsilius of Padua. All of these writers in fact shared certain concepts
of limited government, even though each phrases his ideas somewhat differently because of specific political experiences and contingencies (which
are, of course, important in themselves). It is this underlying consensus
and its contribution to theories of mixed constitutions that is the subject
of this book.

My book falls within the category of "history of ideas," a field Skinner
criticizes with some very cogent arguments—that it assumes a possibly
nonexistent consistency of meaning of words, that it ignores an author's
development over the years, that like "textualism" it leads to pulling ideas
out of context and making what were unimportant remarks of the author
central and leads to the fallacy of accusing an author of failing to solve or
treat an issue, as if what interests us today is what should interest anyone
in any period. These points are perhaps all too true for many scholars and
worth stressing, but also not, I think, points with which most serious historians of ideas would disagree. Nor do I think Skinner would deny the
importance of the history of ideas. His procedure, as he outlines it, is to
study the history of ideologies, focusing on the normative vocabulary avail-

able to those involved and coming thereby to a better grasp of the connections between theory and practice. He continues, "My main reason, however, for suggesting that we should focus on the study of ideologies is that this would enable us to return to the classic texts themselves with a clearer prospect of understanding them."[2] What he in effect does propose, and what he executes ably in his work, is a history of ideas informed by an understanding of historical change and of all those external and internal factors that result in a given text while at the same time avoiding the "contextualist" fallacy of going from historical conditions and normative vocabularies to determinism.

Whether I live up to this standard is a question for the reader. I admit that at times I do elevate scattered comments to a greater prominence than the medieval or Early Modern author would approve. But I believe that this is justified in trying to show how an idea is transmitted and developed so long as one does not distort the author's meaning. As Pocock writes, "Any text may be an actor in an indefinite series of linguistic processes."[3] And I must also admit to being occasionally disappointed that medieval writers were not always as interested in the mixed constitution as I am. But I hope that I am conscious of the issues raised by Skinner and especially that I am sensitive to the mentality of medieval writers. I try always to be aware of the relationship of theory and practice and to place the medieval theories within a political context, but I realize that there is much more to be done within this area. In the future I hope to write more on this subject.

While Skinner and I (in my more limited area) have somewhat of the same goals, I am really trying to do something quite different from Pocock. Like Skinner, Pocock is interested in vocabularies, but in a different way. He wants to show how the development of republican ideals reflected and responded to a variety of concerns of humanist thought. Certainly this is true and Pocock is to be commended for showing this development in a way never before attempted. In doing this, however, he is not so much concerned with demonstrating the detailed historical development of ideas, by which humanists and others adopted concepts and structures from people with whom they had relatively few common concerns. But this is exactly what I am trying to do, and in so doing I am not in general attacking Pocock's thesis, although inevitably there are some points on which I do disagree. One of these has to do with the relationship of medieval and Renaissance thought. Comparing the late medieval English lawyer John Fortescue with Florentine humanists such as Salutati and Bruni, Pocock refers to a radical break in outlook. While this is true in some ways,

---

[2] Quentin Skinner, *The Foundations of Modern Political Theory*, vol. 1, p. xiii.

[3] J.G.A. Pocock, "The Concept of a Language and the *métier d'historien*: Some Considerations on Practice," p. 31.

Pocock tends to overlook the continuing existence and influence of Scholastic thought well into the Early Modern era. This is a phenomenon that Skinner does discuss.

Pocock insists on the persistence and reappearance in various periods of the Aristotelian tradition, and in general on the predominance of this tradition over the specific Polybian ideas (which of course in themselves represent one aspect of the Aristotelian tradition). But he is careful to point out that in any particular case it is questionable to ascribe direct influence to the *Politics,* and even more to ascribe it individually or collectively to the medieval Aristotelians.[4] Further, Pocock's methodology, as John H. Geerken points out, is more synchronistic than causal and historical—Pocock generally rejects causal and historical arguments and is concerned more with structures of relationships across time than with development through time.[5] Thus his pronouncements concerning an early modern synthesis of Polybian and Aristotelian thought are interesting (and ultimately, I believe, true) yet hardly conclusive in themselves.

Furthermore, he often seems to contradict his perception concerning the persistence of the Aristotelian tradition and the importance of the Middle Ages by insisting on a radical break in the Renaissance and thereby minimizing the medieval contribution. For example, the transition from the Christian world view, which, in his opinion, excluded temporal history and centered criteria for good government in the universal order, to the Aristotelian domain of particularity and contingency began, he feels, only with the civic humanism of the fifteenth century.[6] Despite other profound disagreements this accords with Hans Baron's view that no significant criticism of monarchy or appreciation of the Roman Republic appeared before this time.[7] In short, in Pocock's view, the later theory of the mixed constitution may be traced to the confluence of vague Aristotelian ideas which somehow found their way into the mentalities of fifteenth- and sixteenth-century intellectuals and to the Polybian analysis of Roman society. I, however, try to show specific lines of influence of medieval thinkers.

Finally, a note on my translations. In the text I have used English almost exclusively, except in a few cases where it was necessary or where common usage favors the Latin—for example, Aquinas's *Summa Theologiae* instead of *Summary of Theology.* I have tried to translate consistently certain key words used by the medieval writers, even if this leads to occasional awkwardness. Certain of these are obvious (although certain translators do not

---

[4] J.G.A. Pocock, *The Machiavellian Moment: Florentine Political Theory and the Atlantic Republican Tradition*, p. 67.

[5] John H. Geerken, "Pocock and Machiavelli: Structuralist Explanation in History," pp. 309–18.

[6] Pocock, *Machiavellian Moment*, p. 8.

[7] Hans Baron, *The Crisis of the Early Italian Renaissance.*

seem to think so); for example, *regalis* and *monarchicus* are distinct Latin words that to some medieval authors mean very different things and they should be translated as "regal" and "monarchical" respectively. For others the actual translation is more arbitrary; for example, there are many words that mean approximately "government" and verb forms meaning "to govern." For convenience, I give here a list of the equivalents I have chosen:

regimen = government; *regere* = to govern

principatus = rule; *principari* = to rule; *princeps* = ruler

politia = polity; *politicus* = political

dominium = dominion; *dominatio* = dominance; *dominari* = to exercise dominion, dominate

regula = regulation; *regulare* = to regulate

gubernatio = governance; *gubernare* = to exercise governance, guide; *gubernator* = governor

imperium = command; *imperare* = to command

moderamen = direction

ducatus = leadership; *dux* = leader

mandatum = mandate; *mandare* = to mandate

praeesse = to have precedence

praesedere = to preside

praeficere = to place in authority

praecipere = to order

regnum = kingdom; *regnare* = to reign; *regalis* = regal; *rex* = king

Especially problematical is translating *princeps* as "ruler," since this word commonly is taken to mean "prince," and frequently does mean just what we would expect, that is, a single ruler. On the other hand, in medieval Aristotelian thought it more frequently refers to the ruling element in a government, whether it be a monarch or a group of citizens. The tension is especially acute in Nicole Oresme. In this case I felt that general usage and consistency were most important so long as the reader is aware of the situation. In a few cases I have put the meaning "prince" in brackets where "ruler" really seemed inadequate. For the same reason I have sometimes put "duke" or "doge" in brackets after "leader" and "imperium" after "command." Another problem is that the word *servus* can mean either "slave," "serf," or "servant" and *dominus* "master," "lord," or simply "owner." Aristotle obviously wrote about slaves and masters, but the medieval writer could easily have misunderstood his intent. In these cases, again to preserve consistency, I have translated these words as "lord" and "servant," but the reader should know that this is not exactly what Aristotle had in mind and that for medieval people there were also other overtones.

A slightly different problem arises from the word that Moerbeke translated correctly as "city." Aristotle wrote almost exclusively about cities, for him the most common political unit. Obviously this did not match much of medieval experience, but the medieval Aristotelians continued to write about *cities* and by this word meant not only or even usually a literal city, but a polity in general.

ACKNOWLEDGMENTS

FIRST AND FOREMOST I would like to thank Brian Tierney of Cornell University, who first suggested that I study the mixed constitution, who guided me through my doctoral dissertation, and who since then has helped me with suggestions and by reading and criticizing my work. I am also grateful to two other Cornell Professors—James John and John Najemy—who with Tierney supervised my doctoral work and have always been available to help me. I would also like to thank Professor David Robey of the University of Manchester, who although he does not know me at all kindly prepared for me a transcription of parts of Henry of Rimini's *Treatise on the Four Cardinal Virtues* and photocopied parts of Lorenzo de' Monaci's *Chronicle*, neither of which I could obtain here.

PART 1

The Mixed Constitution

Chapter 1

INTRODUCTION

THERE HAS RARELY if ever been a government absolute in practice. A ruler or ruling group has always to consider the interests and actions of the ruled, if only to repress them, and generally it must limit its own desires in order to survive for long. Yet the history of civilization has been the history of the domination of one class or another over those with no direct power. From this reality, and from the observation that allowing one group to prevail most often leads to oppression, or that every group has something to offer society or has a right to participate, has come the idea of the mixed constitution, which in its most common form combines the rule of a king, the aristocrats, and the common people. It is an idea midway between Marxism, which finds no tolerable basis for class collaboration, and the dominant Western form of capitalism, which pretends that class distinctions do not exist and has so managed to inculcate this view in its native subjects that it is able to rule for the moment under cover of "democracy."

This idea of the mixed constitution has enjoyed a long and varied career. In its widest sense it can be found in the written records of political activity in practically every period of Western history. Its earliest intimations may be discerned in the works of Homer, the poet of a Greece barely emerging from the post-Mycenean "Dark Ages"; its lineaments were sketched by several of the early Greek writers: Tyrtaeus, Solon, Thucydides, and Isocrates; its details were elaborated and the theory brought to its full fruition in Greece by Plato and Aristotle. Much later, the Greek hostage Polybius carried the theory to Rome where he saw the confirmation of its virtues in the success and prosperity of that city. Cicero represents the culmination of this tradition, and its last significant theoretician in the classical period.[1] Then the death of the Republic and the triumph of a new autocracy stifled for a time expressions of political participation. Likewise, neither the well-known indifference of the early Christians to the form of any government not representing the direct and personal rule of the messiah, nor the trans-

---

[1] For studies of the mixed constitution in antiquity see G.J.D. Aalders, "Die Mischverfassung und ihre historische Dokumentation in dem *Politica* des Aristoteles" and *Die Theorie der Gemischten Verfassung im Altertum*; E. Braun, "Die Theorie der Mischverfassung bei Aristoteles"; T. A. Sinclair, *A History of Greek Political Thought*; Kurt Von Fritz, *The Theory of the Mixed Constitution in Antiquity: A Critical Analysis of Polybius' Political Ideas*; and Paula Zillig, *Die Theorie der gemischten Verfassung in ihrer literarischen Entwickelung in Altertum und ihr Verhaltnis zur Lehre Lockes und Montesquieus über Verfassung*.

formation of this attitude for a slightly later generation into gleeful support
of the Empire's power to purify the earthly kingdom by the elimination of
heretics was conducive to interest in theories of mixed government.

During the early Middle Ages none of the important classical texts was
available in Latin, and although the comments of several writers and a
number of Germanic and feudal customs and institutions seem compatible
with mixed government, no theoretical development or independent statement of the theory took place. Later, the theory of the mixed constitution
became a central fixture of early modern political thought. Fifteenth- and
sixteenth-century Florentines, for example, wrote about Venice as a mixed
constitution, and reformed their government to imitate it. By the sixteenth
century many educated Englishmen, parliamentarians in particular, came
to think of their government in the same way—with a monarchic king, an
aristocratic House of Lords, and a democratic House of Commons. This
process culminated in the formal acceptance of the mixed constitutional
model by Charles I in 1642—even though his move was only a desperate
and unsuccessful attempt to avert a civil war. The United States Constitution was consciously modeled after the mixed constitution described by
Polybius and was to include a monarchical president, an aristocratic Senate, and a democratic House of Representatives, each of which was to act
as a check for the other two.[2] J.G.A. Pocock writes of the tradition of
thought on the citizen and the republic growing ultimately from the
thought of Aristotle and says that it "can almost be called the tradition of
mixed government."[3] "Almost," Pocock writes, because he intends not
only the development of the idea of the mixed constitution, but also the
unfolding of the whole complex of concepts clustered about the natural
involvement of the citizen as a political and social animal in the affairs of
the community and the perception of this community and an active civil
life as having value beyond their Augustinian role in the repression of vice
and the promotion of order. Although the mixed constitution per se and
the active participation of the citizen are at most complementary conceptions, they are inexorably bound in Pocock's mind because he perceives the

---

[2] For treatments of the early modern development of the mixed constitution see Corinne
Comstock Weston, *English Constitutional Theory and the House of Lords, 1556–1832*, "Begin-
nings of the Classical Theory of the English Constitution," "The Theory of Mixed Monarchy
under Charles I and After," and, with Janelle Renfrow Greenberg, *Subjects and Sovereigns: The
Grand Controversy over Legal Sovereignty in Stuart England*; Michael Mendle, *Dangerous Positions: Mixed Government, the Estates of the Realm, and the Answer to the XIX Propositions*; Zillig,
Theorie der gemischten Verfassung; Robert Eccleshall, *Order and Reason in Politics: Theories of
Absolute and Limited Monarchy in Early Modern England*; M.J.C. Vile, *Constitutionalism and
the Separation of Powers*; John William Allen, *A History of Political Thought in the Sixteenth
Century*; S. P. Chrimes, *English Constitutional Ideas in the Fifteenth Century*; and Gilbert Chinard, "Polybios and the American Constitution."

[3] Pocock, *Machiavellian Moment*, p. 67.

necessity of implementing participation with due regard for all the various legitimate claims of groups to rule, such as number, wealth, virtue, and power—that is, something quite like Aristotle's conception of distributive justice.

As it will be the subject of the bulk of this book and the remainder of the introduction, I have purposely left out of account in this brief summary the development of the theory in the High and late Middle Ages. As with so many other classical ideas, the common conception used to be that except for a brief and unimportant reference here and there, the mixed constitution was neglected until Renaissance luminaries rescued it from the oblivion imposed by rigid medieval people uninterested in "new" ideas. In this case, they say, the impetus was the translation of the sixth book of Polybius's *Histories* into Latin in the early sixteenth century.

But as all serious historians now realize, most Early Modern ideas have their roots in the Middle Ages—though in the case of each idea the old concept usually prevails until someone comes along and actually digs up these roots; and even then nonmedieval historians frequently lapse into their old world view.

The translations of Aristotle's *Ethics* and *Rhetoric* in the early thirteenth century and most forcefully and directly William of Moerbeke's Latin *Politics,* which appeared around 1260, introduced the ideas of the mixed constitution, of the citizen, and of participation in government, among many others, into the medieval world. This development stimulated a huge outpouring of commentaries and other treatises attempting to understand and assimilate Greek political thought.[4] But most of the political ideas of Plato, Polybius, Cicero, and the minor classical writers remained unknown for several more centuries.

Aristotle's works were thrust upon a world that on the surface could scarcely differ more from ancient Greece. The one, everywhere but in Northern Italy, comprised several feudal and incipient national monarchies as well as two other monarchical institutions, the Roman Catholic Church and the Roman Empire, each of which claimed universal scope and authority. The other comprised a plethora of independent city-states governed only infrequently by a monarch. The one traditionally based itself on

---

[4] Aristotle, *Ethicorum Nichomacheorum libri decem*; *Ars Rhetorica*; *Politicorum libri octo cum vetusta translatione Guilelmi Moerbeke* (henceforth, *Politics*). For a listing of the huge number of medieval commentaries on Aristotle, see Charles H. Lohr, "Medieval Latin Aristotle Commentaries." For discussions of commentaries on the *Politics* and other medieval works closely related to it, see Ferdinand Edward Cranz, *Aristotelianism in Medieval Political Theory: A Study of the Reception of the Politics*; Jean Dunbabin, "The Reception and Interpretation of Aristotle's Politics" and "Aristotle in the Schools"; Martin Grabmann, "Die mittelalterlichen Kommentare zur Politik des Aristoteles" and "Studien über den Einfluss der aristotelischen Philosophie auf der mittelalterlichen Theorien uber das Verhältnis von Kirche und Staat"; and Conor Martin, "Some Medieval Commentaries on Aristotle's *Politics*."

lordship as a proprietary arrangement; the other, in theory, on government as an expression of the aspirations of the citizens as a whole and existing for the common good of all. Consequently, the one confused office and person; the other strictly separated them. The one perceived forms of government as fixed and God-given; the other, as mutable and subject to the desires of the citizens.

Yet the enthusiasm with which thirteenth-century philosophers and theologians greeted the *Politics* suggests that forces were already at work within medieval society that were more compatible with Aristotelian thought than is immediately apparent. During the twelfth and thirteenth centuries cities were reasserting their importance, in Northern Italy actually coming to resemble in some ways the Hellenic *polis*, or city-state, which gave its name to the general term used both by the Greek and medieval writers for a particular constitutional arrangement or a particular state—polity.[5] At the same time representative bodies were emerging, although obviously not for the same purpose in the national monarchies as in the ancient *ecclesiae*. In addition, buttressed by the newly rejuvenated Roman Law, corporate bodies were redefining the relationship between head and members with implications for both Church and state and the unitary concept of a universal Church encompassing the two swords of spiritual and temporal power was beginning to crumble. Finally, feudal monarchy itself was not absolute, but based on a balance of power between the king and his vassals. By the early thirteenth century, before the translation of the *Politics*, notably in the writings of the English lawyer Bracton, and with respect to the Church in the works of the canonists,[6] there were some remarkable formulations of the basis of monarchy which, while ignorant of the terminology of classical mixed constitutional theory, nevertheless display an affinity with it. In short, by the time the *Politics* became available, political reality in Europe no longer matched traditional political theory. And this was as true in the Northern monarchies as in the Italian city-republics. Aristotle provided a coherent body of political thought that enabled medieval writers to bring theory to the defense of the new realities.

The first few generations to address themselves to the problems posed by the *Politics*: represented first and foremost by Thomas Aquinas; then those influenced by him such as Giles of Rome, Peter of Auvergne, Ptolemy of Lucca, Engelbert of Admont, and John of Paris; and finally a number of fourteenth-century writers such as Marsilius of Padua, William of Ockham, Bartolus of Sassoferrato, Jean Buridan, and Nicole Oresme, faced

---

[5] For the development of the Northern Italian cities and their influence on political theory, see Skinner, *Modern Political Theory*; J. K. Hyde, *Padua in the Age of Dante* and *Society and Politics in Medieval Italy*; Nicolai Rubinstein, "Marsilius of Padua and Italian Political Theory of his Time"; and R. Witt, "The Rebirth of the Concept of Republican Liberty in Italy."

[6] See, for example, Brian Tierney, "The Canonists and the Medieval State."

the difficult yet intriguing problem of adapting Aristotle's ideas to their contemporary reality. They were not conscious of the contradictions—they asked not, "How can we twist Aristotle to our purposes?" but, "What can Aristotle have meant?"

It is my purpose to address the approach and thought of the first few generations toward the question of the best political arrangement, to see how they imposed their concerns and values on Aristotle, and, conversely, how Aristotle molded their modes of thought. It is the primary goal of this book to show that for the most part these writers came to accept a mixed constitution, usually involving a king limited by the body of citizens, as the best form of government, and that even those who did not go as far consciously or unconsciously incorporated elements of mixed constitutional theory into their ideal government. Their conclusions resulted from a complex interplay of factors: from their medieval world outlook, from their own political experience and observation, and from their assimilation of classical theory and medieval commentaries on it. On the one hand, they forced Aristotle into service to defend existing governments, on the other they squeezed existing governments into Aristotelian molds. This interplay perhaps explains why few writers actually used the words *mixed constitution* extensively. Supporting the national monarchies of the day, they were reluctant to use a new term and preferred rather to discuss restraints on a king's power.

For these reasons, the new and varied political theory that emerged diverged from both Aristotelian and Christian Augustinian thought. Aristotle's ideas about politics, like those on philosophy and theology, clashed with traditional Christian beliefs. Paul and, especially, Augustine had presented government as a consequence of sin. If Adam had not fallen, they argued, dominion of one person over another would never have been necessary or desirable, but since people are now evil and sinful their evil actions must be forcibly repressed. God instituted kings for this purpose, they concluded, and even tyrannical rulers must be obeyed as instruments of God's will. In contrast, Aristotle confronted medieval thinkers with a systematic theory of the origin of political authority from the natural impulses of people to congregate and rule themselves on their own behalf. Further, he set as a primary task of his work the determination of the ideal government,[7] something not an issue in the Early Medieval period, and to this end he proposed several classifications of rule in which monarchy played a limited role, at most equal to alternate forms.

It was Aristotle's classification and questioning of the forms of govern-

---

[7] In the last paragraph of the *Ethics* (10.9.1181b.20–25), which serves as a prologue to the *Politics*, Aristotle puts forth the investigation into the best constitution as one of the purposes of his work.

ment combined with the volatile European political condition and the strained relationship between Church and state (which were still largely perceived as two aspects of the same Christian society) that forced a reconsideration of the purpose and form of government. The problem of the medieval political theorists was to combine and assimilate, refute, or smoothly ignore the varying viewpoints: government as coercive and imposed versus government arising from the conscious and cooperative activity of people, government as absolute and eternal versus government as a pragmatic solution to specific problems, government with no place for participation versus government based on the will and participation of the citizens. In trying to reformulate their understanding of medieval society in Aristotelian terms, thirteenth- and fourteenth-century thinkers reshaped the whole tradition of Western political theory.

My secondary purpose is to relate medieval political thought to the later flourishing of theories of the mixed constitution. There are actually two separate questions here, relating to two separate periods of development: What relationship do the thirteenth- and fourteenth-century theories have to the late fourteenth- and fifteenth-century ideas of those like Jean Gerson and Pierre d'Ailly who advocated a mixed constitution for the Church and John Fortescue who labeled the English system a "regal and political kingdom?" And, what relationship do they have to the early modern ideas of the mixed constitution in Italy, England, and the United States?

In the first case the influence can be clearly demonstrated, although the relevance to the mixed constitution is problematic because there is far from universal agreement that John Fortescue, for one, advocated anything resembling a mixed constitution. The second case is far more difficult and controversial, especially since the later theories are frequently couched in Polybian terminology. Many, perhaps most, of the modern students of this development are convinced that Polybius was the only significant source, that the Scholastic Aristotelian component was negligible, and that the purely Aristotelian elements were derived either from the works of Aristotle himself or his classical followers.[8] In contrast, I argue that the rediscovery of Polybius spurred and shaped an already developing vital tradition but was in no way responsible for its existence.

Brian Tierney, who has discussed both the continuity of medieval and

---

[8] Francis D. Wormuth, *The Origins of Modern Constitutionalism*, pp. 7, 22, for example, compares the seventeenth-century theory of the mixed constitution with that of Polybius and concludes: "It is of course to Polybius that later ages owe the conception." The same is assumed by most who wrote about later mixed constitutional theories, such as Chinard, "Polybios"; Vile, *Constitutionalism*, pp. 36–37; Weston, *House of Lords*, chap. 1, and "Mixed Monarchy," p. 426; Stanley Pargellis, "The Theory of Balanced Government," p. 39; and Donald W. Hanson, *From Kingdom to Commonwealth: The Development of Civic Consciousness in English Political Thought*, pp. 246–50.

later political thought and the mutual influence of the ecclesiological and secular theorists, has analyzed the relationship between medieval mixed constitutional ideas and canonistic and corporate doctrine. Against Pocock, he argues convincingly that the theory of the mixed constitution developed as much in ecclesiastical as in secular writing.[9] In particular, he shows that two biblical models for the mixed constitution—that of the Jews under Moses and the Apostolic Church—first developed by Thomas Aquinas and John of Paris, were influential with the conciliarists of the fifteenth century and with later secular mixed constitutional writers in the sixteenth and seventeenth centuries. Their theories, he writes, fuse the revived ancient mixed constitution with medieval ideas of corporate rule.[10] The use of ancient sources by the later writers, he argues, obscures the actual medieval origin of their ideas. He stresses that the modern idea of the collegiate sovereignty of king, Lords, and Commons, or of pope, cardinals, and General Council had little to do with the ancient *polis*.[11]

Tierney's argument is persuasive but incomplete. He discusses Thomas Aquinas's mixed constitutional theory, mentions its appropriation by John of Paris, and then leaps forward to the conciliar movement and later thought. I wish to extend the discussion to other political theorists of the intermediate period, and also to show more fully the relationship of medieval and classical thought. In so doing, I hope to refute those who regard Thomas Aquinas's and John of Paris's comments on the mixed constitution as isolated statements, and who assert that mixed constitutional thought played no significant role in medieval political theory, let alone that medieval ideas of the mixed constitution influenced those of the seventeenth and eighteenth centuries.[12]

[9] Brian Tierney, *Religion, Law, and the Growth of Constitutional Thought*, pp. 3, 82, 87–91; and "Aristotle, Aquinas, and the Ideal Constitution," pp. 4–5.

[10] Tierney, *Religion*, pp. 3, 82.

[11] Tierney, *Religion*, pp. 104–5.

[12] John B. Morrall, *Political Theory in Medieval Times*; Skinner, *Modern Political Theory*; and Walter Ullmann, *A History of Political Thought: The Middle Ages*, do not mention the mixed constitution as such in this period at all. Charles McIlwain, *Constitutionalism: Ancient and Modern* and *The Growth of Political Thought in the West*, thinks that there was no idea of the mixed constitution before the sixteenth century, that in the medieval period only Marsilius of Padua had any idea of limited monarchy, and that even he accepted limits only in emergencies (*Growth*, pp. 308, 330, 332, 354–61). Dunbabin, "Aristotle," pp. 67, 72–73, argues that all medieval writers supported absolute monarchy and that Thomas's "mixed constitution" was simply a way to avoid public dissatisfaction and not a way to curb royal power. Wormuth, *Origins*, pp. 30–36, 51, thinks that the idea of the mixed constitution is alien to medieval political thought and that with few exceptions, medieval writers favored absolute kingship. Georges de Lagarde, *La Naissance de l'esprit laïque au déclin du Moyen âge*, states that all the commentators present the *Politics* as an apology for hereditary monarchy. Some, of course, do agree that medieval political thought generally favored limited government, but even they have very little to say directly about the mixed constitution. Foremost among these are R. W.

Before proceeding I must clarify what I mean by *mixed constitution*, since this term has been used in many ways and for many purposes. To say first what it is not, it is not identical to a balance or separation of powers, as is often assumed.[13] A government is balanced or characterized by checks and balances if the various organs of government act as mutual restraints. It has separation of powers if the various organs have differing functions. Neither of these is an essential ingredient of a mixed constitution, although each may be, and often has been, connected to it by making the governmental agencies represent or actually incorporate the one, the few, and the many, as in Polybius's interpretation of the Roman Republic or John Adams's view of the American Constitution.

Such restrictive definitions are responsible for the failure of some historians to find medieval antecedents for Early Modern mixed constitutional thought. Donald Hanson's analysis of England illustrates this problem: he would assert that before the seventeenth century all thought that appears to be related to the mixed constitution, for example, in Bracton and Fortescue, is really something quite distinct called "double majesty." His definition of mixed constitution incorporates all of the confusion previously noted with respect to the conflation of the various theories. To qualify as a mixed constitution there must be a conscious embodiment of the idea that the best government is a combination of the virtues of monarchy, aristocracy, and democracy, each of which must be separately institutionalized and have different functions. The result, Hanson adds, is a balance of powers. With such restrictions it is not surprising that Hanson has trouble finding theoreticians of the mixed constitution. Not only does he equate the mixed constitution, separation of powers, and checks and balances, but also he demands that the mixed constitution take the best parts from each simple constitution and insists on the identification of certain constitutional forms with certain class interests. Doubtless all of these trends come

---

and A. J. Carlyle, *A History of Medieval Political Theory in the West*, see especially vol. 5, pp. 52, 68, 75, 129, who argue that all medieval tradition incorporated the idea of limited government. Michael J. Wilks, *The Problem of Sovereignty in the Later Middle Ages*, pp. 15–16, 431, in principle accepts the importance of continuity of mixed constitutional theory, but has little to say about it. He also connects limited government with belief in a body of fundamental law (p. 153) and with nominalist philosophy (pp. 18–119), with which I cannot completely agree. Thomas Gilby, *Principality and Polity: Aquinas and the Rise of State Theory in the West*, p. 294, writes about Aquinas's mixed constitution and goes to the other extreme from those who see no continuity, in identifying this form with a nineteenth century constitutional monarchy. Thomas Molnar, "The Medieval Beginnings of Political Secularization," p. 165, also takes a peculiar position. He regrets that Aquinas, John of Paris, William of Ockham, and the other medieval Aristotelians, in separating the ruler and the people by giving each a role, and in eliminating the spiritual authority of the king, destroyed the old unitary Christian society.

[13] See, for example, Pargellis, "Balanced Government," where the balanced government and mixed constitution are casually identified.

together in the seventeenth and eighteenth centuries, which is Hanson's point, but with all these restrictions almost no ancient or medieval author could be classified as a supporter of the mixed constitution. Even Polybius could be fit in only with difficulty, and Aristotle not at all.[14]

I prefer to begin with a definition wide enough to include all thought that explicitly concerns itself with the mixed constitution—something I feel that Hanson's definition does not, nor does any definition that focuses on the ends of a mixed constitution. In this way all the variations can be treated as part of the long development of a single idea and not as isolated phenomena. From the very beginning the mixed constitution was associated with the division of the political community into the one, the few, and the many, and at many times these groups were associated with the simple forms of monarchy, aristocracy, and democracy. A mixed government in its broadest sense, then, is any one in which power is shared by at least two of these groups, or one in which there is a combination of two or more simple forms of government. The sharing or combination may be accomplished institutionally or by incorporating procedures thought to characterize various forms. An example of the former would be the rule of king and parliament, of the latter an aristocratic property qualification combined with a democratic selection by lot.

There are two other concepts, originally introduced but not stressed by Aristotle, that came to be very closely related to mixed constitutional ideas in the Middle Ages—those of regal and political rule. Sometimes Aristotle referred to the six simple forms of government, the three just mentioned together with their corruptions, and sometimes to four kinds of rule: regal, political, despotic, and economic. It seems to me that he is not thereby presenting alternate classificatory schemata, but rather distinguishing two very different ways of looking at government. For this reason I call monarchy and the other simple types *forms*, and regal, etc. *modes*. Forms have to do with the particular groups possessing power, modes with the way power is exercised. Political and regal rule are over a free people; in the former the citizens rule and are ruled in turn, in the latter one person with full power rules alone. Despotic rule is over a slave people for the benefit of the master. A mistranslation of a key passage in the Latin *Politics* erroneously suggested that Aristotle intended both regal and political rule to refer to a king, in the first case ruling according to his will or according to laws taking their origin and authority from him alone, and in the second ruling according to laws made by the citizens as a whole. This presentation, unlike Aristotle's, suggests a complete separation of modes and forms, so that, for example, there could be political monarchy if a king ruled by law

[14] Hanson, *Kingdom to Commonwealth*, p. 217.

or regal aristocracy if the good ruled by their own will. Thus, political rule itself becomes suggestive of a mixed constitution.

Interest in these modes was spurred by the efforts of kings and popes to centralize their authority, to establish themselves as regal monarchs over the feudal barons and bishops, both groups that continually asserted their right to bind the monarch and tried to use the same theory to their advantage. It also was spurred by an ambiguity in Roman Law, which had itself been revived and begun to be intensively studied a century and a half before the recovery of the *Politics*. On the one hand Roman Law treated the people as the ultimate source of law, but on the other it gave all power to the emperor: "What pleases the ruler [prince] has the force of law." And the *lex regia*, by which the people had supposedly handed over its authority to the emperor, was controversial. Could the people do this permanently? Could they do it at all? What were the implications for governments other than the empire?

With these factors in mind, I am ready to look at the development of ideas of mixed government with especial regard to the place of medieval thought, both as it transformed classical theory and as it served as the basis for later ideas. All the medieval Aristotelian political theorists addressed themselves to the question of the best government that was presented to them in the *Politics*. They discussed the specific theory of the mixed constitution as an optimal form only occasionally, but in commenting on the best form of government these writers used concepts drawn from Aristotle and the Roman Republic and related these concepts to the governments with which they were familiar. Their theories influenced later and more specific presentations of mixed and ideal government and thereby a whole tradition of political thought. This is the development I will now outline, after first taking a look at the theory in classical and early medieval times.

Chapter 2

THE MIXED CONSTITUTION IN ANTIQUITY AND THE EARLY MIDDLE AGES

THE MIXED CONSTITUTION IN GREECE BEFORE ARISTOTLE

High and late Medieval writers had really very little ancient political theory available to them. Aristotle's *Politics* was not translated until 1260, Cicero's *De Republica* was known mainly through its citations by Augustine, and the political works of Polybius, Plato, and others were unknown until the Renaissance. So, although I must say something of ancient and early medieval theory, I need go into detail only about Aristotle, because of his importance to the Middle Ages, and Polybius, because of his central position in Renaissance and Early Modern mixed constitutional theory. Surprisingly, I have found that some medieval writers actually come closer to Polybius, whom they did not know, than to Aristotle.

There is no surviving discussion of which of several governmental forms was considered best before the mid-fifth century B.C.E. But as early as the ninth century, Homer, in his *Iliad*, describes the Greek military force in a way that suggests the mixed constitution, with the monarchical leader Agamemnon restrained by the nobles and, to a lesser degree, by the entire Greek camp. In fact, none of the governments described in the *Iliad* or *Odyssey* is absolute.[1]

Up through the Middle Ages Sparta was the prime example of a mixed constitution, and Tyrtaeus as early as the seventh century B.C.E. treats it as such in reality, if not in name. He writes, but without elaboration, that the participation of the kings, the assembly of elders, and men of the people assured the good order of that city. A few decades later the Athenian politician Solon denied the equality of the people and nobles, but wanted both to have a role in government and stressed the importance of the consent of all citizens to it. Both writers imply that there is a benefit and justice in a sharing of power.[2]

In the fifth century, Hippodamus, whom Aristotle calls "the first person

[1] Sinclair, *Greek Political Thought*, p. 11. See also Sinclair's descriptions of Ithaca, Troy, and mythical Scheria. One could argue that in practice this is inevitable, but here it is treated as the normal course of events.

[2] Sinclair, *Greek Political Thought*, p. 24; Zillig, *Theorie der Gemischten Verfassung*, p. 11.

not a statesman who made inquiries about the best form of government,"[3] and, more importantly Herodotus, began to classify and evaluate the various possibilities for government. Hippodamus recognizes three classes: the skilled workers, the farmers, and the soldiers. He wants all to be eligible for all offices, and he accords full citizenship to all, but envisions no actual mixing of the government. Herodotus, in his account of the debate of the Persians over what form of government to adopt after the overthrow of pseudo-Smerdis—a debate that led to the crowning of Darius as king—anticipates much of later Greek political theory: the classification of governments into good and bad forms of monarchy, aristocracy, and democracy; the association of the rule of the one, few and many with particular constitutional forms; the assumption that each form has good and bad aspects; and the idea that officials should be answerable for their acts. However, he does not mention mixing the various forms.[4]

Thucydides, in the late fifth century, was the first to refer to mixing explicitly. Writing about how Theramenes replaced the oligarchic "Four Hundred" in Athens with the "Five Thousand," which included all who could furnish themselves with arms, he comments: "This government during its early days was the best which the Athenians enjoyed within my memory. For, the mixture of the oligarchs and people was moderate."[5] This is a mixing, however, only in the sense that the wide representation was democratic, but the property requirement and the law that no one could receive pay for office were oligarchic. There is still only one ruling class. The result is close to what Aristotle later calls a "middle class polity."[6] A few years later Xenophon puts the same ideas into the mouth of Theramenes in his *Hellenica*.[7]

Isocrates went much further, although probably under the influence of his contemporary, Plato. He mentions the institutional mixing of Athens,

[3] Aristotle, *Politics*, 2.8.1267b21–1268a29. Hippodamus's theory is known only from the account in the *Politics*.

[4] Herodotus, *Histories*, vol. 1, 3.80–83; see also the accounts in Sinclair, *Greek Political Thought*, pp. 36–39 and Aalders, *Theorie der Gemischten Verfassung*, pp. 27–28. What Herodotus calls oligarchy—the rule of a few best—Aristotle calls aristocracy, but he retains the word *oligarchy* to refer loosely to the rule of any few, good or bad.

[5] Thucydides, *The Peloponnesian Wars*, vol. 1, 8.97. The second sentence is my translation of "μετριά γὰρ ἥ τε ἐσ τοὺς ὀλίγους καί τοὺς πολλους ἐγένετο." Jowett's "oligarchy and democracy were duly attempered" did not seem adequate. See also Aalders, "Mischverfassung," pp. 202–4; *Theorie der Gemischten Verfassung*, pp. 23–28, and Zillig, *Theorie der Gemischten Verfassung*, pp. 16–18. J.H. Oliver, "Praise of Athens as a Mixed Constitution," argues that Thucydides' version of Pericles' "Funeral Oration" can be interpreted as a paean to the mixed constitution.

[6] Aristotle also saw the arms-bearing group as the basis for his "polity," which he also often described as a mixture of oligarchy and democracy, e.g., at *Politics* 2.6.

[7] Xenophon, *Hellenica*, vol. 2, 2.3.45. See also Aalders, "Mischverfassung," p. 203; and Zillig, *Theorie der Gemischten Verfassung*, pp. 17–20.

his ideal, and Sparta. Athens is a mixture of aristocracy and democracy since the magistracy is chosen from the wealthy but is answerable to the people. On the other hand, in the *Evagoras* he describes the government of one man (King Evagoras of Cyprus) as itself being compounded of various forms:

> In general, he fell in no respect short of the qualities which belong to kings, but choosing from each kind of government the best characteristic, he was democratic in his service to the people, political in the administration of the city as a whole, an able general in his good counsel in the face of dangers, and tyrannical in his superiority in all these qualities.[8]

The compound is internal to the king; his regime has a democratic aspect, for example, not because the people have any role in government, but because the king serves their interests.[9] Isocrates never asks what is best absolutely, but refers only to the arrangements in particular places. He is not theoretically sophisticated, but his attitude reflects the general tendency of late fifth- and early fourth-century Greek thought, when there was a marked turn to questions of expediency in government, a tendency from which Plato, and later Aristotle, were not exempt.[10]

With Plato we come to the first writer to give any kind of detailed and theoretical treatment to the mixed constitution, although it is not his ideal form, which is usually an aristocracy of guardians or philosopher-kings. In his early works Plato analyzes various kinds of government but always retains the perfect aristocracy as best. But his experience in later life of trying to establish a stable government in Syracuse led him to consider the mixed constitution more fully. In his final (unsuccessful) plan Plato envisioned three kings representing monarchy, thirty-five guardians as an aristocratic element, and a democratic citizens' assembly. His intent was to effect a compromise that would satisfy the various factions struggling for control.[11]

[8] Isocrates, *Oration* 9.46. The translation has "statesmanlike" for πολιτικὸς and "princely" for τυραννικὸς; another manuscript has μεγαλοφον, which means "haughty" or "proud," but princely seems a distortion in either case.

[9] See Aalders, *Theorie der Gemischten Verfassung*, p. 37, and "Mischverfassung," p. 205. See also Zillig, *Theorie der Gemischten Verfassung*, pp. 20–25. In some ways this suggests Walter Burley's view of Edward III.

[10] Sinclair, *Greek Political Thought*, pp. 7, 121, 136. Identifying the ideal state in Greece had always been a practical question: founders of the many new cities established from the eighth century on by colonists from other cities employed experts in government to draw up constitutions for them.

[11] Sinclair, *Greek Political Thought*, p. 184. Greek political theorists seem to have no difficulty in accepting multiple monarchs. The explanation is that each king has independent powers to act alone in certain areas; although other kings might have restraining powers, the multiple kings do not act as a group. In this spirit, many theories of the mixed constitution point to the two consuls of Rome and the two kings of Sparta as monarchical elements.

This plan is reflected in his last political work, *The Laws*. There he argues that since only the ideal ruler can remain uncorrupt, all great powers should be mixed. In this regard he praises Sparta, but gives three somewhat different accounts of its constitutional structure. In his first account, he approves the mixture of the three good forms of government:

> A god, who watched over Sparta, seeing into the future, gave you two families of kings instead of one; and thus brought you within the limits of moderation. In the next place, some human wisdom mingled with divine power, observing that the constitution of your government was still too feverish and excited, tempered your inborn strength and pride of birth with the moderation which comes of age, making the power of your twenty-eight elders equal with that of the kings in the most important matters. But your third savior, perceiving that your government was still swelling and foaming, and desirous to impose a curb on it, instituted the Ephors, whose powers he made to resemble that of magistrates elected by lot; and by this arrangement the kingly office, being compounded of the right elements and duly moderated, was preserved and was the means of preserving all the rest.[12]

The key word of this passage is *tempering*. The problem is one of not allowing any group to possess enough power to impose its will. There is no question here of combining the good qualities of the various forms of government: the only purpose for allowing any but the ideal rulers a share of power is to prevent one imperfect group from dominating another when the ideal is not possible. Plato sees the development in Sparta as a gradual mixing of elements over time: the original monarchy being vested in two individuals was from its inception already somewhat balanced, but the later additions of an aristocratic body of elders and a democratic assembly were necessary to provide still more checks on the powers first of the kings and then of the kings and elders. The moderation which this mixture of elements produced was responsible for the lasting quality for which all Greeks had long admired Sparta. Ultimately this is Plato's reason for his defense of a mixed constitution: practically it is the most stable and will be able to provide more just and harmonious conditions for its citizens.[13]

A few paragraphs later Plato asserts that there are only two "mother

[12] Plato, *The Laws*, pp. 691–93.

[13] Plato's comment about the moderation of the monarchy has led Glenn R. Morrow, *Plato's Cretan City: A Historical Interpretation of the Laws*, p. 539; and following him Aalders, *Theorie der Gemischten Verfassung*, p. 39, to talk of a mixture not of the whole state, but only of the monarchy or, rather, the executive. This does not seem reasonable to me, not least because there was no real conception of separation of powers into legislative, executive, and judicial in Greek political thought. Plato no doubt uses the expression because it is customary to call a polity with a king a kingship regardless of other constitutional arrangements. This usage persists throughout the Middle Ages. Writers often label a state that they have described as a mixed constitution "monarchy."

forms of states" that give rise to all the others—monarchy and democracy. To be well-governed a city must have a measure of both. As examples of states that have successfully done this he gives Sparta, Crete, and the former governments of Athens and Persia. The emphasis here is on moderation, but also on the way that such a constitution will bind the people to it and make them more willing to defend it. The aristocratic element of the previous passage seems to be missing. Aalders answers this by claiming that for Plato the difference between monarchy and aristocracy is irrelevant since they are based on the same principle. But this equivalence is really only true of the ideal aristocracy and monarchy. What Plato is trying to do is to describe the common features of several moderate regimes, and he finds that they share the authority of monarchy and the freedom of democracy in such a way that neither the power of the one group nor the licence of the other is allowed to progress unchecked. This does not mean that they cannot have different constitutional arrangements; for example, in his description of the old Persian constitution he includes an informal aristocratic element: "And if there was any wise man among them, who was able to give good counsel, he imparted his wisdom to the public; for the king was not jealous, but allowed him full liberty of speech, and gave honour to those who could advise him in any manner."[14]

Finally, in yet another description of Sparta, Plato comments that it (and Crete as well) seems equally, from different perspectives, to be a tyranny, a democracy, an aristocracy, and a monarchy. As such, it is superior to the six simple forms, in which there are no citizens, but only men subject to a ruling group.[15] Later writers often repeated this idea that a mixed constitution would look like each of its components from different angles.

In summary, Plato recognizes three levels of acceptable government. The first, his ideal and the only true government, is the absolute rule of those who understand what is to be done and understand the will of God. Failing the best, no one group has a valid claim to rule permanently. The best that can be done is to preserve a modicum of freedom, stability, and harmony. This implies the balance of the mixed constitution. If even that is impossible we must settle for a government that at least abides by the law and to which the subjects consent—this implies either (in decreasing order of acceptability) monarchy, aristocracy, or good democracy. By the end of his life Plato, while never giving up hope for his ideal state, had learned from his experiences how much success in the construction of polities depends on external circumstances beyond the control of the lawgiver,[16] and he was more inclined to accept secondary forms.

[14] Plato, *Laws*, p. 694.
[15] Plato, *Laws*, pp. 712–13.
[16] Sinclair, *Greek Political Thought*, p. 191.

ARISTOTLE

Aristotle's views on the mixed constitution were the only ones available in Latin during the later Middle Ages. It was his work that influenced the discussions in that period of the mixed constitution, of power relationships within the family, of classification of types of rule, and of the distinction between regal and political rule. The summary of Aristotle's views, then, is the first step toward understanding later medieval political theory, as well as toward answering the question of Aristotle's and the medieval Aristotelians' possible influence on Renaissance and Early Modern mixed constitutionalism.[17]

Aristotle does not present a totally coherent analysis of the types of polity and does not definitively choose one as best. He uses contradictory classifications and uses the word *best* in several, often undistinguished, senses: that which is absolutely or ideally best, that which is best for certain people or in certain circumstances, and that which is best for most people at most times. He reproaches earlier theorists for failing to consider the practicalities and instead focusing only on the ideal. These factors complicate the determination of Aristotle's sympathies, and, indeed, modern authorities are divided on the question.

Aristotle classifies government in several different ways. Most often he uses a variation of the sixfold schema, found previously in Herodotus and Plato. He distinguishes monarchy, aristocracy, and polity—confusingly using here the general term for a specific form of government, which others had called "good democracy"—by whether the one, the few, or the many hold power and separates them from their degenerate forms of tyranny, oligarchy, and democracy by whether the ruling group rules for the common benefit or for its own private benefit.[18] Although he writes about the virtue of a king, the wisdom and virtue of the aristocrats, and the freedom of the many, he almost always thinks of these six forms as based solely on the number of rulers. Almost as frequently he uses another traditional schema that describes all polities as either oligarchic or democratic depending upon whether the rich or poor is the ruling class.[19] Oligarchies are harder and more despotic, democracies softer and more remiss in disci-

---

[17] In this section I will try to coordinate two approaches: I am interested in discussing what Aristotle had to say, and at the same time I want to indicate what the medievals actually had to work with. Therefore, I will be using the Moerbeke translation, but I will point out any relevant discrepancies between this and the original *Politics*.

[18] Aristotle, *Politics*, 3.7.1279a. Aristotle uses a similar schema in the *Ethics*, 8.10.1160a–b, there also calling polity "timocracy," and adding a property qualification for it—however, this restriction does not come through in the Latin.

[19] Aristotle, *Politics*, 4.4.1291b. He calls monarchy a type of oligarchy, 4.10.1280a34.

pline.[20] Aristotle uses these two schemata throughout the *Politics*, and he makes no effort to reconcile them. Finally, in the *Rhetoric* Aristotle uses a fourfold classification of polities: monarchy, aristocracy, oligarchy, and democracy. In this schema each form can be either good or bad.[21]

Sometimes Aristotle distinguishes between these forms of rule and what I have called modes of rule; the former referring to the size and motivation of the ruling class, the latter to the way it exercises power. In the first chapter of the *Politics*, Aristotle reproaches Plato for separating political, regal, economic, and despotic rule solely on the basis of the size of the community, as if, he says, there were no difference between a large household and a small city.[22] Although he never concretely defines these terms, he generally associates political rule with alternation of office among a free and equal people, regal rule with the absolute rule of one man over a free but unequal people, and despotic rule as absolute rule over an inferior people who are naturally slaves. Both political and regal rule are for the benefit of the subjects, despotic rule only incidentally so. Economic rule is a general name for the rule of a family, and so is not, properly speaking, a mode at all. In fact, particular family relationships exemplify the other modes of rule: the rule of master over slave is despotic, the nuptial rule of man over wife is political, and the paternal rule of father over child is regal.[23]

What does Aristotle favor? There are several possible answers. Although Aristotle rarely mentions kingship, there is some justification for the claim of most medieval writers that Aristotle held it to be the most perfect constitution. "It is necessary," he writes, "that that which is a transgression of the first and most divine [polity] is the worst. But kingship . . . exists on account of the manifold excellence of the king, and tyranny, being the worst is most distant from polity."[24] This monarchy is best only if the king

---

[20] Aristotle, *Politics*, 4.3.1290a.

[21] Aristotle, *Rhetoric*, 1.8.1365b–1366a.

[22] Aristotle, *Politics*, 1.1.1252a.

[23] Aristotle, *Politics*, 1.3, 5, 6, 7, 12; 3.4.1277b; 3.6.1278b. See also James Blythe, "Family, Government, and the Medieval Aristotelians." Moerbeke's translation of Aristotle's distinction of regal and political power (1.1.1252a) caused some of the most serious misunderstanding of Aristotle by the medieval writers. Aristotle wrote that in a political regime rule is κατὰ μέρος, according to the principles of the science, that is, citizens hold offices in turns, according to the rules established for this. Moerbeke translated this passage to read that someone rules politically when, according to the rules of the discipline, one is *secundum partem* both ruler and subject. This could easily be construed to mean that in some things a single man ruled and in others not; this misunderstanding was frequent in the Middle Ages. The phrase about "rules" suggested to Thomas Aquinas that a political ruler ruled by law, a regal ruler not. For some relevant texts see McIlwain, *Growth of Political Thought*, app. 2, pp. 398–403, and further discussion following.

[24] Aristotle, *Politics*, 4.2.1289a, b: "Necesse enim eam quidem quae primae et divinissimae transgressionem, esse pessimam. Regnum autem . . . propter multam excellentiam regis esse; et tyrannidem, pessimam existentem, plurimum distare a politia." Here he is using the term

is godlike compared to everyone else—justice then demands that he rule absolutely, not in part.[25] These same considerations would apply to the absolute rule of any group, especially of a few—it would be just if and only if this group qualitatively excelled the rest, but unlike Plato, Aristotle does not really expect that such a one or such a group will ever exist.[26]

Since Aristotle does not expect the conditions for ideal absolute government to exist, he must look to other factors for constructing the best polity in the real world. In common with all Greek theorists writing after the debacles of the fifth century, Aristotle was intent on a moderate, just, and stable polity, but to a much greater degree than the others he was conscious of the class structure of his society. A mixed constitution, which would give a part to the various social classes, would be a solution guaranteeing stability. In a way Aristotle revived the earlier Greek idea of the mixture of classes and only secondarily of constitutional forms. His emphasis is on proportional equality and distributive justice and not at all on a balance of power among the classes.

It would be unjust, according to Aristotle, for any individual or group —even the best one—to rule alone and thereby oppress the others. If the few, however good, rule, then most people will be dishonored because they will have no opportunity to rule; if one person alone rules it is even worse. For this reason Aristotle concludes that the many may have a better claim

---

polity neither as the rule of the many for the common good nor as the generic name, but as a synonym for the best form. Monarchy, in Aristotle's opinion, is the most primitive form of city government, and therefore in a sense the most natural. For this reason, he writes, all men say that the gods are ruled monarchically, for they liken the lives of gods to their own (1.2.1252b). Moerbeke translates the word βασιλίαν as *regnum* (see, e.g., 3.14, 4.2), a reasonable choice, but one that makes it easy for some, especially those ignorant of ancient Greek political divisions and geography, to think that by *regnum* Aristotle meant what they did—a large national monarchy.

[25] Aristotle, *Politics*, 3.17.1288a, 1284a. "Ei autem qui tantam excellentiam habet . . . relinquitur solum obedire tali et dominium esse, non secundum partem sed simpliciter." Aristotle's comparison of the king's virtue to that of his subjects contrasts with Plato's emphasis on the intrinsic virtue necessary for such an office. On the surface Aristotle seems to be saying, and most critics have agreed, that the ruler's virtue must exceed the sum of the virtue of all the rest in the state. E. Braun, "Die Summierungstheorie des Aristoteles," gives this as one example of what he calls Aristotle's *Summierungstheorie*, that if one group's qualities in sum exceed those of another group it has a stronger claim to rule. But R. G. Mulgan, "A Note on Aristotle's Absolute Ruler," p. 66, argues convincingly that Aristotle means that the king and his subjects are not on the same scale of virtue; if they possessed the same kind of virtue they could be compared, and on that basis the subjects would be entitled to a share, however small, of the rule. But Mulgan argues that the kingly rule discussed here is an absolute rule according to the will of the king. This does seem to be what Aristotle means—in the previous chapter (2.16.4–15) he treats absolute kingship as the only true form of monarchy, and law as appropriate only when there is rule among equals (by this he means proportionate, not absolute, equality).

[26] Aristotle, *Politics*, 7.14.1332b.

to rule than the best, and he even considers that the collective wisdom of the many may be greater than that of the wise alone.[27] And yet every class that possesses a quality that can contribute to the purpose of the government, that is, to the common good, has a just claim to rule. This is the principle of proportionate equality as contrasted to an unjust strict numerical equality of all, which would be a pure democracy that would fulfill the claims only of the common people.[28]

What qualities are relevant for political power? Aristotle mentions nobility, wealth, freedom, justice, virtue, and number. In any one of the simple constitutions, the class embodying one of these attributes will dominate and therefore the best constitution must be mixed. An equitable balance of elements, Aristotle writes, preserves cities.[29] A polity cannot endure unless all parts of the city wish it well, and this cannot happen unless each has a fair share in rule.[30] For solving these problems, Aristotle praises Solon's Athens and Sparta, the latter of which is stable because it satisfies everyone: the king has honor, the good rule in the Gerusia, and the people in the Ephorate.[31] In short, the end result of distributive justice is the mixed constitution: he writes that the better mixed a constitution is, the longer it will last. And the more elements a constitution contains, the better mixture it will be.[32]

These are the primary reasons that a mixed constitution is good, but on occasion Aristotle does suggest another—the uniting of the good characteristics of the society's constituents. He implicitly endorses this with his idea that a polity is best if it gives a share of power to classes with qualities relevant to government and condemns it when he describes tyranny as a mixture of extreme oligarchy and democracy suffering from the bad aspects of both.[33] This is also why he cites Solon's comment that just as a mixture

[27] Aristotle, *Politics*, 3.11.1281a, b. Aristotle means this at least partially as an answer to those (like Plato) who argue that experts are most capable of rule. He points out that in many things the consumer is best able to evaluate the product. The same holds true for the government of a city (3.11.1282a).

[28] Aristotle, *Politics*, 3.13.1282b–1283a.

[29] Aristotle, *Politics*, 3.13.1283a, b; II.2.1261a. See also Barker, *Political*, p. 480 and R. G. Mulgan, *Aristotle's Political Theory*, p. 82. Mulgan feels that Aristotle's account of distributive justice and distribution of power (1289a31) looks forward both to the ideal rule of those who have truly achieved the good life and also to the theory that the mixed constitution is second best, i.e., best in reality. By "balance" he does not mean the later sense of checks and balances, but rather the equitable proportion of each element.

[30] Aristotle, *Politics*, 3.11.1281a.

[31] Aristotle, *Politics*, 2.9.1270b. Aristotle makes similar remarks about the Cretan and Carthaginian constitutions, both of which he commends, albeit with some criticism (2.10–11.1271b–73b).

[32] Aristotle, *Politics*, 4.12.1297a. Cf. 5.7.1307a and 2.6.1266a5.

[33] Aristotle, *Politics*, 3.12.1282b–1283a; 5.10.1310b. "Ex duobus malis composita et transgressiones et peccata habens quae ab ambabus politiis."

of pure and impure food is more digestable than pure food alone, mixing the rule of the multitude with that of the few produces a better polity.[34]

If the absolute monarchy or aristocracy is best ideally, but the mixed constitution in reality, what does Aristotle mean when he calls the "middle-class polity" the best choice for most cities, the "best natural constitution of a city," and "the most secure of the imperfect forms?"[35] Is it a form of mixed constitution?

A mixed constitution represents a middle course between extremes, and so in a way does the middle class polity. Virtue itself is a mean, according to Aristotle, and those of moderate wealth are, in general, in his opinion, more reasonable and virtuous, having neither the rich's tendency to violence nor the poor's inability either to submit or rule. They do not envy the rich, nor are they envied by the poor. And those in the middle are most nearly equals.

The mixed constitution is stable, and so too is the middle-class polity. It, and only it, can protect against sedition effectively, and, in general, a large middle class decreases factionalism and acts as an umpire among the other classes.[36]

This might seem rather weak but for the fact that Aristotle explicitly links the two. It is while he is talking about the middle-class polity, for instance, that he comments, as if the connection were obvious, that the better a polity is mixed the longer lasting it will be. And he consistently treats the middle-class polity as a mean between democracy and oligarchy. But what can he mean? Ernest Barker argues that the middle class is itself a mixture of rich and poor, and that therefore its government is a mixed constitution, although certainly not in the usual sense of the term. Instead of having several constitutions juxtaposed but distinct, the middle-class polity would have several constitutions and social classes fused into a single entity.[37] This interpretation accords with what Aristotle wrote about mixtures in his scientific works.[38] From Aristotle's point of view one way

---

[34] Aristotle, *Politics*, 3.11.1281b.

[35] Aristotle, *Politics*, 4.11.1296a37; 4.11.1295a, b; 5.1.1302a.

[36] Aristotle, *Politics*, 4.12.1296b–1297a.

[37] Barker, *Plato and Aristotle*, p. 480.

[38] For Aristotle on physical mixture see Richard Sharvy, "Aristotle on Mixtures." Although Aristotle occasionally treats as a mixture the mere mingling of diverse components (such as with dry ingredients, *Topics*, 4.2.122b.31), he usually means something more. In *De Generatione et Corruptione*, 1.10, he even wonders whether mixture is possible; if each element continues to exist and is unaltered there is no real mixture, but if either is destroyed there is also no mixture since at least one of the components no longer exists. Sharvy derives five axioms on mixture from Aristotle's writing:

   Axiom 1: The two parts must be originally distinct.
   Axiom 2: They must be able to be separated, i.e., the ingredients persist potentially.
   Axiom 3: A true mixture is homeomerous, i.e., made up of like parts which are like the whole, just as any part of water is water.

of mixing is to take the mean of the two things to be mixed: the middle class is exactly this mean of rich and poor.[39]

William Bluhm defies the consensus that the mixed constitution and/or the middle-class polity represents the second best form for Aristotle. He argues that the middle-class polity is Aristotle's ideal form and thinks that it is this Aristotle describes in books 7 and 8 of the *Politics*, which most have interpreted as a perfect aristocracy.[40] Many of Bluhm's arguments seem cogent to me; in particular, he makes a number of strong arguments based upon the structure of the *Politics*, something that has always troubled analysts of that work.

Aristotle does imply at one point that the middle-class polity is best absolutely, although not necessarily in any one particular situation.[41] He also says that this polity falls short of the ideal,[42] but Bluhm argues that by this he means only that there still remain a few rich and a few poor. In the ideal polity described in 8.1 there is only a single class—the middle class—since all extremes have been absorbed. Bluhm argues that the state of these final books is not aristocracy in the usual sense of rule by a few since all the citizens are depicted as having the capacity to rule and be ruled. It is a regime of virtue, and in that sense an aristocracy, but it is a polity in that the many dominate.[43] There is no real conflict between Bluhm's descrip-

---

Axiom 4: Two things can mix only if they act reciprocally on each other, and this requires that their matter be similar.

Axiom 5: There must be a balance between the active powers of the various ingredients, e.g., a drop of wine in a barrel of water is not a mixture since the form of the wine is lost.

All of these seem relevant to the idea that I have been propounding of the mixed constitution as a fusion rather than a balance. Axiom 2 is appropriate for the usual mixed constitution, but apparently not so much so for the middle-class polity—except as one may be able to say that rich and poor exist potentially in it and may even reemerge if the harmony of the state is broken. Axiom 5 could be taken as support for Braun's *Summierungstheorie* of monarchy, since if the monarch's virtue so outweighs the sum of that of the remainder of the people, a mix may be impossible.

[39] Aristotle, *Politics*, 4.9.1294a. Mulgan, *Aristotle's Political Theory*, p. 106, argues that although this polity is moderate it is not a mixture—although there might be a mixture of democratic and oligarchic principles there is no balance of rich and poor but a constitution in which the middle class dominates. He also assumes that there must be a balance, a separate institutionalization of the elements. But Aristotle nowhere insists on these as requirements for a mixed constitution.

[40] William T. Bluhm, "The Place of the Polity in Aristotle's Theory of the Ideal State," p. 752. His final arguments are more doubtful. He claims that Aristotle was consciously using a Platonic framework of the ideal political order in order to discredit it. We are asked to regard Aristotle's comments in favor of kingship as mere empty words. I see no justification in the *Politics* itself for such an argument.

[41] Aristotle, *Politics*, 4.11.1296b; Bluhm, "Place of the Polity," p. 749.

[42] Aristotle, *Politics*, 4.11.1295a25.

[43] Bluhm, "Place of the Polity," pp. 751–52.

tion of this ideal polity and that of Barker and Mulgan. But what I think Bluhm has realized and the others have not is that the perfect aristocracy represents the highest form of middle-class polity, in which the mixture of rich and poor has been truly completed.

Thus, Aristotle, like Plato, recognized three levels of acceptable government, but beyond this their thinking is radically different. Aristotle has two ideal polities, both at the highest level. The first, absolute monarchy or aristocracy, is somewhat similar to Plato's ideal, but Aristotle never really expects or wants this to occur since it would preclude the citizenship of the many. The second ideal is the perfect middle-class polity or political aristocracy in which all would participate,[44] which is a model to which other polities can aspire.

Below these, at the second level, are the other mixed constitutions, less successful attempts to achieve distributive justice and equity with respect to the claims of all the classes. Aristotle viewed the mixed constitution as a mixture of classes more than as a mixture of forms. As long as classes existed there could never be a perfect polity, since the perfectly valid claims of one class would inevitably oppose those of another, but these mixed constitutions could approach the ideal.[45]

At the third level are the three good, simple constitutions. They are good in that they somewhat promote the community's interests, but they fall short of true justice and are easily corrupted. Nevertheless, for Aristotle they may be best for a certain place, people, or time that is not suited for a better form.

Finally, unlike Plato, Aristotle is willing to consider the preservation of governments that are not even minimally acceptable, but may be better than any reasonable alternative. Much more than Plato he is concerned with practical politics—how can a people have the best government that is possible for them?

GREECE AND ROME AFTER ARISTOTLE

Surprisingly, it turns out that Polybius owed more to Plato for his ideas than to Aristotle. In fact, it is probable that he knew Aristotle's views, if at all, only through the teachings of his followers and critics. One of these, who influenced both Polybius and Cicero was the fourth-century B.C.E.

---

[44] In his recognition of the value of the many in the ideal and in the secondary constitutions, Aristotle is in direct opposition to Plato. Plato may give a role to the many under the demands of practical necessity, but he never found any inherent virtue in the multitude.

[45] Here again Aristotle is at odds with Plato, who thought that in the absence of the ideal the best one could do was to patch together something to preserve order as well as possible.

peripatetic Dicaearchus of Messene.[46] Although none of his work survives, his views can be pieced together from the comments of others. Cicero may be reproducing the gist of his *Tripoliticus* when he writes:

> Of the three forms kingship is to my mind by far the best, but better still would be something balanced and harmonized out of all three best kinds of republic. For it is agreed that there should be in a state a certain royal and authoritative element, a second element assigned to and dependent on the influence of leading men, and thirdly a number of matters reserved for a decision of the people according to their will. Such a constitution has firstly a considerable degree of equality, without which free peoples can not long go on, and secondly stability whereas these other [unmixed] forms too readily degenerate into their corresponding bad forms.[47]

Dicaearchus emphasizes the mixture of three elements as the key fact in a mixed constitution, something not so clearly specified by his predecessors. In addition, he hints at separation of powers, since certain matters are reserved for the different elements, and he suggests that the mixed constitution combines the good points of the simple forms.

In Dicaearchus (and Plato before him) because the elements of the mixed constitutions remain separate institutionally there was an incipient balance of powers; stability results from the direct tempering effect of each on the other. Aristotle, on the other hand, wanted truly to fuse not only the principles but also the classes so that harmony would result from the mixture, rather than from the tension among the elements.[48]

The mixed constitution of Polybius (c. 200–120 B.C.E.) bears a noticeable resemblance to that of Dicaearchus. In book 6 of the *Histories*, where Polybius outlines his theory, he gives the usual sixfold classification of constitutions, and asserts that the best is the one that combines all three good elements.[49] Like Plato, and unlike Aristotle, he distinguishes the good from the bad forms not because of their adherence to the common good, but because of their voluntary character (generally identified with election) and the fact that they are established according to reason and according to law.[50]

Two aspects of Polybius's writing set him apart from his predecessors:

---

[46] See, e.g., Aalders, *Theorie der Gemischten Verfassung*, pp. 72–82; Sinclair, *Greek Political Thought*, pp. 250–52; and Zillig, *Theorie der Gemischten Verfassung*, pp. 48–49.

[47] Marcus Tullius Cicero, *On the Commonwealth*, p. 169; cited in Sinclair, *Greek Political Thought*, p. 251.

[48] For an opposing argument see Sinclair, *Greek Political Thought*, p. 251.

[49] Polybius, *The Histories of Polybius*, 6.3. His classification is slightly different from Plato's. Plato used the same word, *democracy*, for both the good and bad forms of the rule of the many. Polybius calls the good form democracy and the bad form ochlocracy, i.e., "mob rule."

[50] Polybius, *Histories*, 6.4.

the theory of the cycle of constitutions and the development of the idea of checks and balances. He had begun his studies to try to explain why the Roman government was so successful, and he ended by discovering what he thought to be the general laws of the historical development of society: "But in all polities we observe two sources of decay existing from natural causes, the one external, the other internal and self-produced. The external admits of no certain or fixed definition, but the internal follows a definite order."[51]

Polybius believes that all polities go through a cycle of seven stages: despotism, kingship, tyranny, aristocracy, oligarchy, democracy, and ochlocracy. The ultimate result of the last stage is a new despotism and a new beginning of the cycle. Understanding this process cannot change the cycle, but "if a man have a clear grasp of these principles he may perhaps make a mistake as to the dates at which this or that will happen to a particular constitution, but he will rarely be entirely mistaken as to the stage of growth or decay at which it has arrived or as to the point at which it will undergo some revolutionary change."[52]

Is there anything we can do to escape this cycle? Ultimately, Polybius would say no; every polity must degenerate at last, but certain governments are longer lasting than others, either by the accident of their particular development or by conscious design.[53] The problem with the simple constitutions is that they are quickly transformed into their opposites; if unchecked the power inherent in the ruling element in each easily becomes absolute. The question of how to prevent the concentration of too much power in any agency or class is at the center of Polybius's thought, but not of Aristotle's. If, either fortuitously or deliberately, the monarchic element, the noble class, and the people can somehow check and balance each other,

---

[51] Polybius, *Histories*, 6.57.

[52] Polybius, *Histories*, 6.4–10. Polybius is ambiguous with respect to despotism, an apparent seventh polity added to the six he has defined. As he describes it it is similar to that of Aristotle's despotism—it is rule over unfree people and not according to their will, but is naturally occurring, right when it does occur, and not to be confused with tyranny. It seems to be a type of kingship that becomes moderated "by the aid of art and adjustment" (Polybius's words) to true kingship. The result is that monarchy goes through a nonperfect stage before true monarchy appears. But he also presents aristocratic and democratic forms as only growing to their most perfect stages over time, although he does not dignify their different phases with names nor suggest that at any time they are over unfree or unwilling people. Polybius further obscures the issue by listing despotism along with oligarchy and ochlocracy as the three perversions, and thus in some way linking it with tyranny. See Von Fritz, *Mixed Constitution*, p. 45 and, for an opposing argument, Sinclair, *Greek Political Thought*, p. 273, n. 1.

[53] A common view is that the cycle of constitutions in Polybius applies only to the simple forms. See, e.g., Sabine and Smith's introduction to Marcus Tullius Cicero, *On the Commonwealth*, p. 59. But Polybius brings up the Roman constitution in the context of his discussion of the cycle of constitutions and says that it illustrates his position (*Histories*, 6.9).

they may be prevented from degenerating—not perhaps forever, but much longer than usual. Sparta is his example of the artificially constituted mixed constitution, and Rome of the naturally occurring one.

Sparta, designed by Lycurgus, escaped the initial development of Polybius's cycle—it came into existence with aspects of all the good constitutions already in place. Lycurgus understood the perils of simple constitutions, and therefore

> combined together all the excellencies and distinctive features of the best constitutions, that no part should become unduly predominate, and be perverted into its kindred vice; and that each power being checked by the others, no one part should turn the scale or decisively outbalance the others; but that by being accurately adjusted in exact equilibrium, the whole might remain long steady like a ship sailing close to the wind. The royal power was prevented from growing insolent by fear of the people, which had also assigned to it an adequate share in the constitution. The people in their turn were restrained from a bold contempt of the kings by fear of the gerousia.[54]

How different this description is from that of Aristotle on the same subject! In addition to the balance of the different forces here is the idea of taking the best features of each. Further, there is no concern here about the justice of the arrangement, only its utility. Good and stable as this constitution is it cannot escape the inevitable cycle; the elements eventually will be pulled toward their opposites, and the polity will eventually collapse into mob rule. Such fatalism is also missing from Aristotle.

In contrast to the one-man institution of the Spartan constitution, the Roman Republic evolved naturally over a period of time, which suggested to Polybius the analogy of biological growth and decay.[55] As each element grew it was checked before it could degenerate: the monarchic consuls by the senate, the aristocratic senate by the democratic power of the people. In this way the natural decay was arrested.[56] Because the mixed constitution here arose naturally Polybius considers it the best example for study.[57] He also seems to imply that such natural development makes for a better and more stable government. The harmony of the structure is illustrated by the fact that (as Plato and Aristotle had said about Sparta) no one, not even a citizen, could say whether it is monarchic, aristocratic, or democratic.[58]

The interaction between the mixed constitution and the cycle of govern-

---

[54] Polybius, *Histories*, 6.10.

[55] Polybius, *Histories*, 6.10; Von Fritz, *Mixed Constitution*, p. 90. As a biologist, Aristotle also was prone to organic metaphors.

[56] Polybius, *Histories*, 6.11–18.

[57] Polybius, *Histories*, 6.10.

[58] Polybius, *Histories*, 6.11.

ment is evident in Polybius's treatment of the Punic wars. Although both Rome and Carthage had mixed constitutions, they were in different stages of their development: at Carthage the people were the dominant element, whereas at Rome the aristocratic element was at its zenith. This is why Rome won.[59] Polybius implies that the mixed constitution is best when the best men are most prominent (following in this, as in much else, Plato's opinion of the multitude); he lacks the confidence in the many sometimes displayed by Aristotle, and joins them to the constitution not for their wisdom, but for their ability to restrain the other classes.[60]

Cicero, the last major mixed constitutional theorist of classical times, was most directly influenced by Polybius, but he also knew the work of Plato, Aristotle, Dicaearchus, and especially Panaetius.[61] His *On the Commonwealth* was lost from the early Middle Ages until the nineteenth century, except for snippets in the writings of Augustine and other early Christian writers, none of whom refers to the mixed constitution.

Like Aristotle and Panaetius, but unlike Polybius, Cicero begins from the lack of justice in any of the simple polities. Monarchy and aristocracy slight the many, but democracy fails to reward merit.[62] Still, he finds value in all three—monarchy for the love of the king for his subjects, aristocracy for its wisdom, and democracy for its freedom.[63]

Like Polybius, Cicero discusses a cycle of constitutions, but believes that there are several possible cycles.[64] The mixed constitution differs in that it is potentially exempt. It can develop naturally or by design, but if it is ever properly established the republic becomes, at least with respect to internal pressures, eternal.[65] For Cicero, as for Polybius, the mixture is institu-

---

[59] Polybius, *Histories*, 6.51.

[60] A few years after Polybius, Panaetius, a philosopher of the so-called Middle Stoa, proposed, like Polybius, an institutionally balanced arrangement, but incorporated Aristotle's idea of distributive justice. See Francis Devine, "Stoicism and the Best Regime"; Sinclair, *Greek Political Thought*, pp. 275–77, and Aalders, *Theorie der Gemischten Verfassung*, pp. 82–84. Although the Stoics are often associated with the mixed constitution (see, e.g., Barker, *Plato and Aristotle*), in fact, it was only those of the Middle Stoa who actually were sympathetic to it. The early Stoics had complete contempt for any kind of government, and the later Stoics such as Seneca and Marcus Aurelius were staunch supporters of monarchy. One of these last, Dio Chrysostom, included a critique of the mixed constitution in his writing. He compared it to a ship trying to find land with sailors, pilot, and owners all acting at cross-purposes while no one was looking out for the common good (discourse 34, "The Second Tarsic Discourse," 16; see also Devine, "Stoicism," p. 335).

[61] See Aalders, *Theorie der Gemischten Verfassung*, pp. 109–16; Zillig, *Theorie der Gemischten Verfassung*, pp. 59–61.

[62] Cicero, *On the Commonwealth*, 1.27.

[63] Cicero, *On the Commonwealth*, 1.35.

[64] For a chart of Cicero's possible constitutional pathways see Sabine and Smith's introduction to the *On the Commonwealth*, pp. 57–60.

[65] Sabine and Smith point out, correctly, that the problem is that Cicero is trying to show

tional.[66] He sees the mixing as good in itself since it assures distributive justice and provides a combination of the good points of each of the simple forms. His emphasis is not on this, however, but on the moderate nature of the result. As the middle of the road government that prevents the abuses of each of the simple forms, Cicero's mixed constitution is in the spirit of Aristotle's middle-class polity, as is his idea of the mixed constitution not only as a mixture of constitutional elements but also of classes. In general, Cicero's theory has a much more strongly ethical bias than does Polybius's.[67]

Thus, while Cicero's ideas are quite different from Polybius's, on one major point they agree. This is why, perhaps, Cicero has the reputation of being a Polybian: the harmony of the mixed constitution is assured because of the perfect balance of powers. But for Cicero the perfect polity reflects the order of the universe as it is described in Scipio's dream.[68] This metaphysical addition suggests why for Cicero the mixed constitution could persist forever, while for Polybius, as a purely pragmatic, earthly construction, it was ultimately doomed.

With Cicero we come to the last important figure in the classical theory of the mixed constitution. There is some subsequent discussion of it in the Greek world,[69] but except for a few words in Tacitus it will be a much later period before it is once more taken up in the West.

THE EARLY MEDIEVAL PERIOD

The Christians of the later Western Roman Empire had little interest in the theory of the mixed constitution, and soon even the term was lost. No

---

how Rome developed naturally into a mixed constitution and cannot fit this into Polybius's scheme because of his own view of Roman history. But they think, incorrectly, that Cicero is trying unsuccessfully to unite two unconnected aspects of Polybius's theories—that Polybius did not mean the cycle of constitutions to apply to the mixed constitution. In fact, it is Cicero who tries to take the mixed constitution out of the cycle. See Sinclair, *Greek Political Thought*, p. 274, who, however, thinks incorrectly that the inevitability of the cycle makes the mixed constitution an impossibility for Cicero. See Aalders, *Theorie der Gemischten Verfassung*, p. 114.

[66] Like Polybius, Cicero favors an aristocratic bias to the mixed constitution. He admits that Sparta and Carthage were mixed constitutions, but denies that they were well-tempered: he writes that as long as one man is king there will be a monarchic bias to the constitution—it will in fact be a monarchy even if it is not so in name (*On the Commonwealth*, 2.23; see Von Fritz, *Mixed Constitution*, p. 144). This is in contrast to Polybius's thought that Carthage has a democratic bias, and ignores the fact that there were two kings at Sparta.

[67] See Aalders, *Theorie der Gemischten Verfassung*, p. 114. In this Aalders contradicts his earlier argument that mixing is in itself not good.

[68] Cicero, *On the Commonwealth*, 6.9–26.

[69] See Aalders, *Theorie der Gemischten Verfassung*, pp. 120–28, and Zillig, *Theorie der Gemischten Verfassung*, pp. 64–66.

Latin texts on the subject have survived from this period. Of the works of the Latin Fathers only Augustine's *City of God*, written in the early fifth century C.E., to my knowledge, even makes mention of Aristotle's sixfold classification of government. Discussing Cicero's *On the Commonwealth*, Augustine relates Scipio's argument that a commonwealth exists where there is a just government, whether power rests with a monarch, a few aristocrats, or the whole people. If the rulers are unjust, Scipio continues, the commonwealth perishes, and monarchy becomes tyranny, aristocracy oligarchy, and the rule of the people collective tyranny.[70] In elucidating Cicero's criterion for a just ruler, Augustine also mentions the idea that good government exists for the common benefit of its subjects; the ruler must consider the advantage of the people and not his own.[71] Even though Cicero supported a mixed constitution, neither Augustine nor any other of the Latin patristic writers mentions it.

The idea that the unjust king who works for his own good is a tyrant is one that the early medieval period preserved; Isidore of Seville (560?–636), the author of the universally known *Etymologies*, mentions this with approval and traces the etymology of king (*rex*) from the word for ruling (*regendo*), which in turn he derives from the word for doing rightly (*recte faciendo*).[72] This definition does not in itself obligate the king to obey the law, but in practice the medieval king was so bound, and by the twelfth century it is a standard feature of monarchical theory. Pope Gregory the Great (540?–604) had already expressed this idea; he characterized the tyrant as one who oppresses the people and destroys the laws.[73]

In this early period Isidore alone writes about kingship in a way that suggests the mixed constitution. Law, he writes, is something that pertains to the whole people; therefore, for validity it must be sanctioned by the nobles and by the common people.[74] The sanctioning to which Isidore refers quite likely was the sanction of custom, which of course allows no active role for the people in lawmaking. Nevertheless, the statement is reminiscent of mixed constitutional ideas, and Thomas Aquinas quotes it with approval.

The Germanic kingship that prevailed in Western Europe after the invasions of the fifth and sixth centuries and the collapse of Roman rule was quite different from classical monarchy. It evolved out of the *comitatus*, the warrior bands, that formed themselves around charismatic leaders. The relationship between ruler and ruled was a personal and contractual one;

[70] Augustine, *De Civitate Dei*, 2.21.

[71] Augustine, *Epistolae*, 104.7.

[72] Isidore of Seville, *Etymologiae*, 9.3.

[73] Gregory the Great, *Moralia in Job*, 41, col. 1006.

[74] Isidore of Seville, *Etymologiae*, 5.4. "Lex est constitutio populi, secundum quam maiores natu simul cum plebibus aliquid sanxerunt."

although the leader might claim divine sanction, his authority was never absolute, and it depended upon the voluntary submission of the nobles. As an expression of custom, law was above society; it could be discovered or restated, but the king, like all others, was bound to it, and above all the king's function was to guard and protect the law.[75]

In addition, Germanic kingship gave rise to the idea that authority was divided in the community. Having as it did its origins in the *comitatus*, the relationship between king and nobles tended to be organized around military service and land granted for such service. This was the relationship that led to and defined feudalism, a system that developed and reached its height in the tenth to twelfth centuries, and fostered the feeling that other areas were outside the competence of the king and remained with the rest of the community (which generally meant the great men).[76] Donald Hanson calls this the doctrine of double majesty and stresses that it was an outlook shared by both king and nobles. The great men are the king's companions, and as in the *comitatus* the leader is chosen by them.[77] It is only in the late thirteenth century, he argues, that hereditary kingship became the rule, while ideas of absolute kingship did not become common until after the Middle Ages.[78] So although the Greek *polis* and the Germanic kingdom are very different, they share certain conceptions congenial to the mixed constitution.

In the century preceding the translation of the *Politics*, as feudalism with its personal associations gave way more and more to national kingdoms based on social concepts of power and office exercised for the good of the community, many of the concerns that were to occupy later thinkers began to emerge as subjects of political thought, for example the common good and the limitation of kingship. Law continued to be supreme, but began to be transformed from something above people, an expression of custom or natural law, to something that could be legislated. Writing just before the translation of the *Politics*, for instance, Henry of Bracton, famous for his maxim, "the king is beneath God and the law," grounds all valid law in counsel and consent, in a way that suggests the joint power of the one, the few, and the many in a mixed constitution:

> But it would not be absurd to call the English laws laws, although they are unwritten, since whatever should be justly defined and approved by the coun-

[75] See, e.g., Morrall, *Political Theory*, p. 16; and Carlyle and Carlyle, *Medieval Political Theory*, vol. 1.

[76] See, e.g., Wormuth, *Modern Constitutionalism*, p. 32.

[77] Hanson, *From Kingdom to Commonwealth*, pp. 42, 53.

[78] Hanson, *From Kingdom to Commonwealth*, p. 78. See McIlwain, *Growth of Political Thought* and Carlyle and Carlyle, *Medieval Political Theory*, vol. 1, for examples of early medieval attitudes.

sel and consent of the magnates and by the common agreement of the republic, with the authority of the king or prince leading, has the strength of law.[79]

Another passage in the same work, the famous "Addition concerning Charters" strongly states the purpose of the king's court in restraining the actions of the king:

> The king has a superior, namely God. Likewise the law through which the king was made. Likewise his court, namely the counts and barons, because the counts are called as it were allies of the king, and he who has allies has a master. And therefore if the king were without a bridle, i.e., without law, they ought to put a bridle on him unless they themselves with the king should be without a bridle. And then the subjects would shout . . .[80]

This passage was not in Bracton's original draft and may not be authentic, but it was written at about the same time.[81] Again we see the tripartite division of power, though admittedly the people are not given any role except in an emergency, and even the aristocracy only if the king abandons the law.

I have cited Bracton because his formulations are so similar to those of the theorists who were soon to be influenced by Aristotle's *Politics*. But he is by no means unique. These issues were in the air, and we can find them in commentaries on canon and Roman Law, in evolving corporate theory, in the formation of the various city-states of Northern Italy, in the development of national monarchies, and in the writings of political theorists. Aristotle provided a new vocabulary for the expression and debate of these issues and the concepts for a gradual transformation of the idea of political relationships. He provided a rationalization for the political realities of the time and emboldened reformers to do what they wanted to do anyway. It is only in these senses that we can speak of an "Aristotelian revolution." Now, finally, I may turn to the main subject of this book: the vast array of Aristotelian political writing in the century or so after the translation of the *Politics*.

ARISTOTELIAN POLITICAL LITERATURE AFTER 1260

The recovery of Aristotle's political ideas took place in the context and at the end of the medieval rediscovery of the entire body of Aristotle's writ-

[79] Henry of Bracton, *De Legibus*, 2.19. See also Brian Tierney, "Bracton on Government," pp. 306, 315; Gaines Post, "A Romano-Canonical Maxim 'quod omnes tangit' in Bracton," pp. 245–46; and Ewart Lewis, "King above Law? 'Quod Principi Placuit' in Bracton," p. 255.

[80] Henry of Bracton, *De Legibus*, 2.110.

[81] See Tierney, "Bracton," pp. 310–12; Ernst Kantorowicz, *The King's Two Bodies*, pp. 49–52; and Fritz Schulz, "Bracton on Kingship," pp. 174–75.

ings beginning in the early twelfth century. Most of these came by way of the Arabs and were translated together with Arab and occasionally Jewish commentaries. The *Politics* differed in that it had not been translated into Arabic and so could not be translated into Latin until a Greek edition of it became available after the Fourth Crusade (when also many of Aristotle's other works first became available in their original language). Thomas Aquinas convinced his friend William of Moerbeke, a Flemish cleric, one of the few Western Europeans to have a command of Greek, and later the archbishop of the Greek city of Corinth, to translate the *Politics* and correct the existing translations of other Aristotelian works using the new Greek manuscripts. William completed his work on the *Politics* around 1260. The lack of Arabic or Jewish commentaries (not to mention the alienness of the subject, in contrast with philosophy or logic) made it more difficult to understand, but at the same time left it more adaptable to medieval conditions. Because of its difficulties, its position as a latecomer, and the nature of its contents, which stood outside the usual interests of Scholastic writers, the *Politcs* at first attracted only a limited group of interested and mostly interconnected scholars, the majority of whom were associated, at least for a time, with the University of Paris. I correctly called medieval Aristotelian political literature "vast," but in comparison with works on Aristotelian logic, metaphysics, and natural philosophy it is actually quite small.

Four distinct kinds of medieval work are based on the *Politics:* the commentaries, the Questions, the comprehensive independent political treatises, and other miscellaneous writings.[82] The earliest responses to the translations of all of Aristotle's works were commentaries on the literal meaning and intentions of the text. Authors of these generally cited a short passage and then paraphrased it, adding their own comments to make the meaning clear and only occasionally to distinguish their own opinion. This was especially true of the *Politics*, commentators on which had to contend not only with the new ideas but also with William of Moerbeke's difficult Latin, which incorporated dozens of neologisms and grecisms—words with which they were utterly unfamiliar, such as *democracy*, *aristocracy*, and even *politics*. Albertus Magnus (1193?–1280), his student, Thomas Aquinas (c. 1225–74), and his student Peter of Auvergne (1240s–1304), who completed Thomas's commentary, were the first commentators, and they were all masters at the University of Paris. In the fourteenth century Walter Burley (1275–after 1344), who studied philosophy at Paris, and Nicole Oresme (c. 1320–82), a master at Paris, are the most prominent of the commentators, although Oresme is really in a category of his own. Writing more than one hundred years after the translation of the *Politics* and at the

---

[82] This is essentially the classification of Cranz, *Aristotelianism*, pp. 4–5.

request of the French king, he felt free to comment beyond the literal meaning, and some of his glosses are small treatises in themselves.[83] Although scholars continued to write commentaries through the early modern period, it is usually that of Thomas and Peter that circulated with the text and thus became essentially the standard gloss. This is true even after Moerbeke's version was replaced by the more accurate and elegant ones of Leonardo Bruni and other humanists in the fifteenth and sixteenth centuries.

One step removed from the limitations of the commentary form were the Questions. These organized the contents of a whole book of Aristotle into a series of questions, for which the authors gave arguments for and against possible answers and came eventually to conclusions of their own. This did leave more room for independent thought, but for the most part the Questions also kept very close to the order, content, and conclusions of the text. Here also the analysis often centered around the literal meaning of words. In addition to his commentary Peter of Auvergne also wrote Questions on the *Politics*, as did Jean Buridan (late 1200s–c. 1370), the teacher of Nicole Oresme at the University of Paris.[84]

Most interesting are the independent treatises which based themselves on Aristotle and attempted to be comprehensive studies of political science, but are not closely bound to the text of the *Politics*. Thomas Aquinas started and his student Ptolemy of Lucca (1236–1327) completed a treatise entitled *On the Government of Rulers*. Giles of Rome (c. 1243–1316), who probably attended Thomas's lectures in Paris, and Engelbert of Admont (c. 1250–1331), one of the few early writers not directly connected with the University of Paris, each wrote treatises of the same name. Like Peter of Auvergne's commentary, Ptolemy's treatise carried with it Thomas Aquinas's authority since most readers believed that Thomas wrote the whole of both works. John of Paris (c. 1250–1304) and Marsilius of Padua (c. 1275–after 1342), both from the University of Paris, wrote *On Royal and Papal Power* and *The Defender of Peace* respectively. Although both works were intended for more specific purposes, namely to oppose the theory of papal power in secular matters, they are best classified with this species since they each develop a coherent and general political theory.[85] En-

---

[83] Albertus Magnus, *Commentarium in Octo Libris Politicorum Aristotelis*; Thomas Aquinas, *In Libros Politicorum Aristotelis Expositio*; Walter Burley, *Expositio in octo libros Politicorum Aristotelis*; and Nicole Oresme, *Le Livre de Politiques d'Aristote*. Peter of Auvergne's completion of the unfinished commentary of Aquinas (Books 3.7–8) is contained in the edition of Aquinas's commentary cited. He actually began his commentary with book 3.1, and the additional material may be found in *The Commentary of Peter of Auvergne, the Inedited Part*.

[84] Peter of Auvergne, *Questiones super Politicum*; Jean Buridan, *Questiones super Octo Libros Politicorum Aristotelis*.

[85] Thomas Aquinas, *De Regimine Principum ad Regem Cypri*. This comprises books 1–2.4.5 of the entire *De Regimine Principum*, which Ptolemy of Lucca completed. Giles of Rome, *De*

glebert, though in some sense an outsider, was a follower of Thomas Aquinas and was well acquainted with John of Paris's work—in fact, he was chosen to draft the official church reply to John's attacks.

The political views of these writers were widely known. Even if few other writers directly attempted a comprehensive treatment of political science, many did use or at least refer to the ideas developed by those who did. Many works were influenced by the *Politics* and its scholars, including some of the other writings of men to whom I have already referred, that are not solely about political theory, but rather are most concerned with contemporary events, philosophy, or theology. I mention only a few that bear on the theory of best government—Thomas Aquinas's *Summa Theologiae*, Giles of Rome's *On Ecclesiastical Power*, Engelbert of Admont's *On the Providence of God, Mirror of Moral Virtues,* and *Treatise on the Rise, Progress, and End of the Roman Empire*, Ptolemy of Lucca's *A Short Determination of the Rights of the Empire* and *Hexameron*, Peter John Olivi's "On the Renunciation of Pope Celestine V," Dante Alighieri's *On Monarchy*, William of Ockham's *Diologue* and *Eight Questions on the Power of the Pope*, and Bartolus of Sassoferrato's "Treatise on the Government of a City."[86]

Medieval Aristotelian political theory flows from Thomas Aquinas—it is with him my study must begin.

Regimine Principum Libri III; Engelbert of Admont, *De Regimine Principum*; John of Paris, *Tractatus de Potestate Regia et Papali*; Marsilius of Padua, *Defensor pacis*.

[86] Thomas Aquinas, *Summa Theologiae*; Giles of Rome, *De Ecclesiastica Potestate*; Engelbert of Admont, "De providentia Dei," *Speculum virtutum moralium*, and *Tractatus de ortu, et progressu statu et fine Romani Imperii*; Ptolemy of Lucca, *Determinatio Compendiosa de Juribus Imperii*, and *Exameron*; Peter John Olivi, *De renuntiatione papae Coelestini V*; Dante Alighieri, *Monarchia*; William of Ockham, *Dialogus* and *Octo quaestiones de potestate papae*; and Bartolus of Sassoferrato, "Tractatus de regimine civitatis."

PART 2

Thomas Aquinas
and His Successors

Chapter 3

THOMAS AQUINAS

THOMAS AQUINAS (c. 1225–74) is the most important philosopher and theologian of the High Middle Ages. He was born near the town of Aquino, just south of the Papal States, the son of minor but wealthy nobles. His parents sent him at the age of five as an oblate to the Benedictine monastery of Monte Cassino for his education, with the expectation that he would eventually become abbot. Their plans were foiled when, as a student at the University of Naples, Thomas decided to join the Dominican order. His family imprisoned him for a year to prevent it, but eventually they let him go. He studied under Albertus Magnus in Paris and Cologne, and returned to Paris to earn his Master's degree and be admitted to the University of Paris faculty in 1256. After 1259, for the rest of his short life, Thomas wrote and taught successively at Naples, Orvieto, Rome, Viterbo, and again at Paris and Naples. In late 1273 he possibly had a stroke that left him unable to write, and a few months later, on his way to the Council of Lyons, died either of illness or as the result of wounds suffered when he hit his head on a tree along the road. A large man who spoke few words, his fellow students in Cologne called him "the dumb ox," but his written profundity eventually earned him sainthood in 1323 and, in 1557, the title "Angelic Doctor."

Firmly believing that faith and reason cannot contradict each other, Thomas set himself the task in his two greatest works, *Summa Theologiae* and *Summa Contra Gentiles*, of reconciling the Greek philosophy of Aristotle with Christian revelation. Most of Aristotle's works were available in the universities before Thomas's time, but he is possibly the earliest medieval writer to use Aristotle's *Politics*,[1] and he is certainly the most important for political theory as a whole. He is the giant whom later thinkers will interpret, bend to their own purposes, or, less frequently, refute. It is largely through Aquinas that the Aristotelian ideas of humans as social and political animals, of the citizen as one who participates in government, of the classification of government by the number and quality of its rulers, of the mixed constitution, and many other concepts entered the medieval mi-

---

[1] Opinion is divided as to whether Thomas's commentary on the *Politics* was written before or after that of Albertus Magnus. Recently, consensus seems to favor an earlier date for Thomas.

lieu, and future thought is as much shaped by his peculiar interpretations of these ancient principles as by Aristotle's ideas themselves.

Yet, his political theory is sufficiently ambiguous to allow him to be cited by different scholars as an advocate of absolute monarchy, limited monarchy, republicanism, and mixed constitutionalism.[2] As Brian Tierney notes, "We sometimes think of Thomas as a great synthesizer. . . . When one studies his political theory and ecclesiology the first impression is just the opposite. Thomas seems fascinatingly original but quite incoherent."[3] In many places Thomas exalts kingship, and calls it the best government for

[2] McIlwain, *Growth of Political Thought*, pp. 329–33, treats him as a pure monarchist. John D. Lewis and Oscar Jaszi, *Against the Tyrant*, concur. Gerald Phelan, in his preface to Thomas Aquinas, *On the Governance of Rulers*, pp. 3–26, takes a similar position, but leaves the way open for limitation of the monarchy by the people. Morall, *Political Theory*, pp. 78–79, and Dunbabin, "Aristotle in the Schools," p. 72, also think that Thomas opts for an absolute king, and see no conflict between this and Thomas's support for the mixed constitution, election, and consent. Others agree that Thomas favored monarchy, but a monarchy limited by the community, and they generally interpret the mixed constitution as just such a limited monarchy. Gilby, *Principality and Polity*, p. 294, goes so far as to equate Aquinas's mixed government with a nineteenth century constitutional monarchy, and Gabriel Bowe, *The Origin of Political Authority*, treats Thomas as a sort of constitutional democrat. Etienne Gilson, *The Christian Philosophy of St. Thomas Aquinas*, pp. 329–30, also favors such an explanation. See also W. H. Greenleaf, "The Thomasian Tradition and the Theory of Absolute Monarchy." Marcel Demongeot's, *Le Meilleur régime politique selon saint Thomas*, a pioneering sixty-year-old study that is still the only full-length examination of Aquinas's ideal state, is extremely valuable and clearly argued, although it is marred by several methodological flaws. He feels that Aquinas wanted to combine the principles of all the good forms of government and preserve them in the mean by tempering them with each other. Tierney, "Aristotle, Aquinas" and *Religion, Law*, also writes of taking principles from each, but identifies the principles somewhat differently and distinguishes Aquinas's theory more completely from ancient conceptions of the mixed constitution. Hanson, *From Kingdom to Commonwealth*, pp. 241–43, feels that Thomas hedges on the question of monarchy and gives neither the king nor the people ultimate authority—the result is a purely medieval conception of "double majesty." According to Wilks, *Problem of Sovereignty*, p. 125, both the people and God must come together in order to establish any complete political community. Aquinas's mixed constitution is a combination of Aristotle's regal and political types of rule in his own peculiarly medieval interpretation of them as being both forms of monarchy (pp. 19–20, 202). Ewart Lewis, "Natural Law and Expediency in Medieval Political Theory," p. 151, maintains that Thomas held that natural law can be said to sanction any arrangement if and only if it is useful to the common good. Otto Gierke, *Political Theories of the Middle Ages*, p. 151, n. 165, points out that Thomas attributes sovereignty sometimes to the people and sometimes to the prince depending upon the particular constitution. Gilby, *Principality and Polity*, p. 251, also insists that the only essential for Thomas is that the regime be for the common good, that he was not dogmatic about form. George H. Sabine, *A History of Political Theory*, p. 274, concurs, adding that Aquinas seemed to have no general theory of the derivation of authority. Finally, Henry Myers and Herwig Wolfram, *Medieval Kingship*, fail to find any coherence in Thomas's theory. They think that Thomas was unable to settle on any one form, and consequently cannot choose among several "best" governments.

[3] Tierney, "Aristotle, Aquinas," p. 1.

man. Unlike God's, however, the king's power should be "tempered" so as to remove the opportunity to tyrannize. The counsel of the wise is natural and essential, and their authority can even be seen as superior to that of a king. This can be taken as an argument for aristocracy. In other places Thomas suggests that ultimate authority rests with the whole people, so perhaps democracy is the best solution. In a number of places Thomas advocates as best the mixing of all the good simple forms of monarchy, aristocracy, and democracy. Finally, he sometimes suggests that the best form of government is a function of the particular people, place, and conditions.[4]

Because these statements all were written near the end of a relatively short writing career, it is unlikely that the diversity is explainable as the development over the years of Thomas's own opinion. How, then, can it be explained? Was Thomas simply unable in any coherent manner to fuse the alien and admittedly already somewhat contradictory Greek doctrines with dominant medieval political thought and reality? Was he unsure himself how mankind should best be ruled? Or is there an underlying conception that can unify all these statements?

I believe that there is such a conception, that Thomas consistently supported a theory of mixed constitution. I do not believe, however, that any of the interpretations of modern scholars adequately reflects his thought.[5] There is no real indication in Thomas's writings or accounts of his life of what particular experiences or observations predisposed him to mixed constitutions. Unfortunately, he is a frustrating writer who gives no contemporary examples of his political theories—in fact, the only even marginally historical government he mentions is that of the ancient Jews under Moses. But there are many aspects of his experience that could well have led him in the direction he eventually took. He came from a family of nobles, some of whom chaffed under the powerful Emperor Frederick II's restriction of their ancient liberties. His own Dominican order enjoyed a constitution

---

[4] E.g., Thomas Aquinas, *De Regimine Principum*, 1.1, 1.2, 1.5, 1.9; *Summa Theologiae*, 1.103.3, 1–2.90.3, 1–2.91.4, 1–2.95.4.ad 3, 1–2.95.4.ad 3, 1–2.105.1, and 1–2.105.2; *Summa Contra Gentiles* 3.1.81.

[5] I will restrict myself to those works actually written by Aquinas, and of those primarily the following: *Summa Theologiae*, and the initial portions of the *De Regimine Principum* (1.1–2.4.5) and the *In Libros Politicorum Aristotelis Expositio* (hereafter, *Commentary*), 1.1–3.6. Two common methodological flaws in the use of the *Commentary* are the assumptions that all of Thomas's portion represents his own thought, and that it is valid to cite even those portions of it not written by him. Many passages in the early commentaries on the *Politics* are pure paraphrase, which makes it difficult to separate the commentator's opinion from Aristotle's. Further, it is not legitimate to ascribe the views of Peter of Auvergne (who continued the *Commentary*) to Thomas, especially if, as I feel, they often disagree. While we must be very careful in our use of the *Commentary*, it is useful for the definitions of terms, which we may assume will have the same meanings in other works.

that was in all respects mixed, and Thomas actually wrote a treatise defending the Dominicans in the conflict between secular and mendicant masters in the 1250s.[6] He lived for some time in a France governed by St. Louis, whose power was limited by the nobility, and that was in the process of developing representative and restraining institutions, such as *parlements* and eventually the Estates General.[7] And he traveled in Northern Italy, where he would have encountered various forms of republican government that suggested mixed constitutions to quite a few of the medieval Aristotelians. Jeremy Catto proposes that Thomas was far from an academic in relation to politics and shows that through his family and professional connections he was deeply concerned with the events in Southern Italy. His family was split between the Angevines and Hohenstaufens; Catto sees Thomas's comments on monarchy as supportive of Charles of Anjou and his political writings as being among many Italian contributions to practical politics, in a class with works by John of Viterbo, Brunetto Latini, Dante, and Machiavelli.[8] All of these factors probably had some effect, although the degree and importance of each is a matter of speculation.

Mixed constitutions are normally thought of as mixtures of monarchy, aristocracy, and democracy. This way of thinking occurs also in Thomas, but another way of classifying regimes is equally important in his work—the distinction of what I have called modes of rule: regal, political, and despotic. Aristotle tended to dwell on his sixfold schema, but the distinction between regal and political rule became of great significance during Thomas's period, in part because of an ambiguous translation by Moerbeke and a consequent misunderstanding by Thomas. The phrase "regal and political" has attracted great attention because of its use by the fifteenth-century writer Fortescue in his description of the English state. He claimed to have gotten the idea from Aquinas, but although some effort has been made to determine the source, relatively little interest has been shown in Thomas's use of the words.[9]

Aristotle denigrates the theory that a household and a city differ only by the number of subjects. At this point he adds: "When one governs it is regal, when one in turn governs and is governed according to the rules of the science, it is political."[10] "Rules" in this context is clearly meant to refer

[6] Jeremy Catto, "Ideas and Experience in the Political Thought of Thomas Aquinas," p. 10, suggests that it was this conflict that started Thomas thinking about kinds of society.

[7] Demongeot, *Meilleur régime*, p. 205, suggests that Louis provided a model for Thomas's mixed constitution.

[8] Catto, "Ideas and Experience," pp. 15–20.

[9] See Felix Gilbert, "Sir John Fortescue's 'Dominium Regale et Politicum,' " pp. 88–97, for a convincing argument that the source was Ptolemy of Lucca's portion of the *On the Government of Rulers*.

[10] Aristotle, *Politics*, 1.1.1252a.15f. "καὶ πολιτικὸν δὲ καὶ βασιλικὸν ὅταν μὲν αὐ τον ἐφεστήκῃ, βασιλικόν, ὅταν δὲ κατὰ τοὺσ λόγουσ τῆς εἰστήμης τῆς τοιαύτης κατὰ

to the regulations and procedures of the polity governing the rotation of offices.

Moerbeke chose to render κατὰ μέρος (in turn) by *secundum partem* (in part), and to translate the whole passage as follows: "When one has precedence it is regal; when according to the rules of the discipline one is in part both ruling and subject it is political."[11] It is easy to see the misunderstanding possible: one person seems to be ruler in both regal and political regimes. What, then, are the "rules"? Well, they must be the laws which compel the ruler and make him in part a subject. This is exactly how Thomas construes the passage:

> For when one person has precedence simply and over all things, it is called a regal government. But when according to the rules of such a science that one presides in part, that is, according to laws posed through the political discipline, it is a political government; as it were the one rules in part, as regards those things in that one's power; and in part the one is a subject, as regards those things in which that one is subject to law.[12]

It is clear that the definitions Aquinas gives here are to be taken as the proper ones, since a few paragraphs before he said almost exactly the same thing in an unambiguous context, making it even more apparent that he is referring to one ruler in either case and that the "laws" are the statutes of the polity. Rule in a city, he writes, can be one of two kinds: regal or political. "The government is regal when that one who rules has full power. It is political when that one who has precedence has power restrained according to some laws of the city."[13]

Aquinas does recognize that political rule at least normally requires the

μέρος ἄρχων καὶ ἀρχόμενος, πολιτικόν." These words, I think, are to be understood as purely explanatory of the words *political* and *regal* that Aristotle has just used. A paraphrase would then be: There is more than a quantitative difference between a master, a head of a family, and a political or regal ruler in a city (and by these words I mean the following). The next words, "these things are not true" would then apply only to the alleged qualitative congruence of a city and a household. This meaning is conveyed by the translation of Benjamin Jowett in *The Basic Works of Aristotle*. For the opposite opinion, see the translation by T. A. Sinclair, *Aristotle's Politics*.

[11] Aristotle, *Politics*, 1.1.1252a.15f. "Quando quidem ipse praeest, regale, quando autem secundum sermones disciplinae talis secundum partem principans et subiectus, politicum."

[12] Thomas Aquinas, *In Libros Politicorum*, 1.1.15. "Quando enim ipse homo praeest simpliciter et secundum omnia, dicitur regimen regale. Quando vero secundum rationem talis scientiae in parte praesidet, idest secundum leges positas per disciplinam politicam, est regimen politicum; quasi secundum partem principetur, quantum ad ea scilicet quae eius potestatem subsunt; et secundum partem sit subiectus, quantum ad ea in quibus subiicitur legi."

[13] Thomas Aquinas, *In Libros Politicorum*, 1.1.13. "Civitas autem duplici regimine regitur: scilicet politico et regali. Regale quidem est regimen, quando ille qui civitate praeest habet plenarium potestatem. Politicum autem regimen est quando ille qui praeest habet potestatem coarctatam secundum aliquas leges civitatis."

interchange of rulers and ruled, and, strangely, he himself in places glosses the very words *in partem* misunderstood in 1.1 to explain that such an alternation occurs. Aristotle writes: "[In political rule] it is worthy that they rule in part."[14] Aquinas comments: "Then it seemed worthy that certain ones rule for one part of the time, and others at another time.[15] The basis for this alternation is the fundamental equality of the citizens; if such equality exists it is not just that one should dominate. This is a conviction that Aquinas, following Aristotle, repeats on numerous occasions. In this situation, there is no natural difference among the rulers, but only a fortuitous one of the actual time during which each holds an office.[16]

These are two rather disparate conceptions: is it of the essence of political rule that it is limited by law or that the rulers be changed, or must both occur? Aquinas gives two examples, one from human society and the other from nature, in which political rule exists where there is one permanent ruler. The rule of a husband over his wife is political because it is bound by the laws of matrimony; consequently, the husband lacks full power. The relationship, Thomas asserts, is analogous to the situation in which a rector rules according to the statutes of his city. The wife never takes her turn as ruler because the equality necessary for alternation is lacking; the man is naturally and permanently superior, and, as a result, naturally rules. The inequality is so obvious to Aristotle and Aquinas that they sum up the situation by observing that when rulers change the new ones take on the honors and appurtenances of rule, but a woman can never become a man or a man a woman.[17]

The other example, again based on natural superiority is more difficult to understand and even more provocative in its formulation. Aristotle states baldly that unlike the soul, which rules despotically over the body, the intellect rules desire by a political and regal principate. Aquinas attempts to clarify this: "Political and regal rule applies to free people whence they can contradict in some things, and similarly sometimes desire does not follow reason. This diversity results from the fact that the body cannot

[14] Aristotle, *Politics*, 3.6.1279a.10. "Secundum partem dignificant principari."
[15] Thomas Aquinas, *In Libros Politicorum*, 3.5.389. "Tunc enim dignum videtur quod in una parte temporis quidam principentur, in alia vero alii." See also 1.10.153.
[16] Thomas Aquinas, *In Libros Politicorum*, 1.5.90, 1.10.153–54, 2.1.183, 3.5.389.
[17] Thomas Aquinas, *In Libros Politicorum*, 1.10.152–3. "Vir principatur muliere politico principatu, idest sicut aliquis qui eligitur in rectorem civitati praeest . . . sed vir non habet plenarium potestatem super uxorem quantum ad omnia, sed secundum quod exigit lex matrimonii: sicut et rector civitatis habet potestatem super cives secundum statuta . . . [est] secundum naturam; quia semper quod est principalius in natura principatur . . . Sed masculus est naturaliter principalior femina . . . ergo naturaliter masculus principatur feminae. . . . Sic ergo patet quod politicus principatus permutatur de persona in personam: sed hoc non contigit in principatu maris ad feminam: non enim qui est mas postea fit femina, aut e converso; sed semper manet eodem modo."

be moved except by the soul, and therefore it is totally subject to it, but the desire can be moved not only by reason, but even by the sense, and it is not totally subject to reason."[18]

If both political and regal rule are over free people and both allow contradiction to some extent and the rule of one element permanently, then what is the distinction? Why is the rule of reason over desire both political and regal? One explanation suggests itself. *Political* has one of two meanings: either it is a general term for the human government of free people (in which sense all the six nondespotic forms are political), or it is the type of rule distinguished from regal rule by its relation to law. Thomas is aware of these two meanings; in fact, both Aristotle and Thomas introduce the passage under discussion with the comment that both political and despotic rule can be found in the human animal.[19] If this distinction is foremost in Thomas's mind, what he probably means is this: the soul rules the body despotically, but within the soul (which is free and therefore must be ruled by a species of political rule) the reason rules regally over the desire. This reading would eliminate the need to explain a rule both regal and political (in the second sense of *political*). The phrase is suggestive in retrospect, because of its use by Fortescue, but I do not think that Thomas had any kind of dual rule in mind. He uses the phrase because Aristotle does, not because it has any special significance for him. That Aristotle intended the same meaning is problematic, but not, I think, unlikely.

These two examples show that neither eligibility of a large number of citizens to rule through alternation nor the term of office of the rulers is the essential element of the distinction between political and regal rule, for in both cases political rule exists in a monarchical environment with an unchanging monarch. Political and regal modes of rule are not necessarily related to the extent of popular participation, the number of rulers, or the size of the community. These are a function of the actual institutions, which are secondary considerations. Aquinas interprets these terms analogically: regal rule is like that of a king who rules absolutely, political rule is like that of a polity in which a king rules according to laws established by the whole community. Aristotle's sixfold schema (which is based on the number of rulers) is simply the list of forms in which the modes of rule can be exercised in a city. Thus, it is quite possible to have political or regal monarchy, aristocracy, or democracy.[20]

[18] Thomas Aquinas, *In Libros Politicorum*, 1.3.64. "Principatu politico et regali qui est ad liberos, unde possunt in aliquibus contradicere et similiter appetitus aliquando non sequitur rationem. Et huiusmodi diversitatis ratio est, quia corpus non potest moveri nisi ab anima, et ideo totaliter subiicitur ei; sed appetitus potest moveri non solum a ratione, sed etiam a sensu, et ideo non totaliter subiicitur ratione."

[19] Thomas Aquinas, *In Libros Politicorum*, 1.3.64. See also 1.5.90 obj. 2."

[20] Of the modern authors only Demongeot and Wormuth discuss regal and political rule

Thomas is forced to this abstraction. Aristotle sees things in the light of the Greek polity with wide participation; Aquinas must preserve the terminology but assimilate it to the medieval kingdom. For him a monarchy is a normal state of affairs, and unconsciously he adapts Aristotle's terminology to the situation with which he is familiar. So, for him the number or transience of rulers is an accidental quality of rule, although it can be profitable to discuss it in these terms. The essence of the distinction is whether rule is absolute or according to law.[21]

In his *Commentary* Thomas paraphrases Aristotle's definition of the six forms of polity without embellishment.[22] Aristotle's hesitation as to whether number is a proper or accidental characteristic of the forms of rule is concerned solely with aristocracy and polity; Thomas never doubts that the rule of one defines and is essential to monarchy.[23] Nor does he ever deny that monarchy is the best form of government. Almost all his arguments for this are derived from metaphysical considerations of the order of the universe, the virtue of unity, and the image of the king as the embodiment of reason.[24] This is at variance with Aristotle, who conceded only

---

to any extent, and both misunderstand the concept. Demongeot, *Le Meilleur regime*, treats it as a minor classification brought forth incidentally to the more essential one of monarchy, aristocracy, oligarchy, and democracy. He identifies regal government with monarchy and political with the republic. Wormuth, *Modern Constitutionalism*, p. 31, feels that most medieval writers forced to choose among Aristotle's despotic, regal, and political (which he translates as "constitutional") rule could only pick regal. He is making the same error as Demongeot in assuming that monarchic and regal rules are the same. Wormuth thinks that when Thomas refers to a "free people" he is distinguishing despotic and regal rule, when in fact the distinction is between despotic and regal or political rule. This misapprehension leads to his difficulty over the relationship of king to law.

[21] Thomas Aquinas, *In Libros Politicorum*, 1.1.15. Even the absolute ruler is not entirely free from the law. Commenting on the Roman Law precept "the ruler [prince] is free from the law," Thomas guts it of most of its force. The ruler, he says, is exempt from its coercive power since the coercive power of the law comes only from the authority of the ruler. Therefore, rulers are exempt only in the sense that no one is competent to judge them. But with respect to the directive force of the law rulers are subject to the law by their own will (*Summa Theologiae*, 1–2.96.5ad 3). See also *Summa Theologiae*, 1–2.90.1.

[22] Thomas Aquinas, *In Libros Politicorum*, 2.7.242. The use of this schema explains sufficiently, I think, why Thomas does not often use the term *polity* in the sense of good rule of the many, but rather *democracy* for both the good and bad forms. Demongeot's explanation that Thomas recognized the polity as a mixed and not a simple form seems strained (*Le Meilleur règime*, p. 37).

[23] Aristotle, *Politics*, 3.8; *In Libros Politicorum*, 3.6.396–8.

[24] The rule of one is inherent in the very nature of both nature and man. In all things ordained to a single end there is some one element that rules the rest (*De Regimine Principum*, 1.1): "Every natural governance is governance by one. In the multitude of bodily members there is one which moves them all, namely the heart; and among the powers of the soul one power presides as chief, namely the reason. Even among bees there is one king and in the whole universe there is one God, maker and rector of all things" (*De Regimine Principum*,

that monarchy would be best if there existed one of supreme virtue (an unlikely occurrence in his view). Far from making analogies to the natural order of things, he implied that man projected his own predilection for and experience with kingship as the primitive form of government onto the community of the gods.[25]

But for the medieval mind this analogy with nature was obvious and decisive. Virtue was a prerequisite for the true king, but not the principal justification for the continuance of his office. The primary intention of a ruler, in society or nature, must be the promotion of unity or peace, and it is the ruler who is the cause of unity: "For, it is clear that several cannot be the cause of unity or concord, except so far as they are united. Furthermore, what is in itself one is a more apt and a better cause of unity than several things united. Therefore, a multitude is better guided by one than by several."[26]

Thomas also gives several practical reasons for monarchy, among them being that although tyranny is the worst of governments, it stems more often from the rule of many than from monarchy, that experience shows that places ruled by many almost always are torn apart by dissension, but that where there is a king there is peace, and that since it is more likely that one of many will turn from the common good than one alone, it is more expedient to be ruled by one.[27]

Next it must be shown that Thomas's conception of monarchy allows other powers coordinate with or restraining that of the king. Even *On the Government of Rulers*, which consistently praises monarchy, sounds a moderating note. In his discussion of tyranny, Thomas suggests three means of avoiding this evil. All presuppose some sort of authority residing in the community.

The first suggests that election of the monarch pertains to at least one segment of the community, and can be used to promote to office only those who are of such character as to make tyranny unlikely.[28] Although

---

1.2). Aquinas often makes a specific comparison of the king to God and the soul (*De Regimine Principum*, 1.9, 1.12).

[25] Aristotle, *Politics*, 1.2.1252b.24.

[26] Thomas Aquinas, *Summa Theologiae*, 1–1.103.3. "Unitatis autem causa per se est unum. Manifestum est enim quod plures multa unire et concordare non possunt, nisi aliquo modo uniantur. Illud autem quod est per se unum, potest convenientius et melius esse causa unitatis, quam multi uniti. Unde multitudo melius gubernatur per unum quam per plures." This insistence on the necessity of the unity of the ruler to provide unity in society does not strictly require monarchy. The same point and emphasis is made, for example, by Marsilius of Padua with quite a different conclusion (*Defensor pacis* 1.17). For him, unity can be sufficiently provided by the concentration of authority in the ruling body, which may include the entire collection of citizens.

[27] Thomas Aquinas, *De Regimine Principum*, 1.2, 1.5.

[28] Thomas Aquinas, *De Regimine Principum*, 1.7. "Primum autem est necessarium ut talis

his example of this, the first Jewish kings, shows that this selection may pertain to supernatural agency and not to the human population, his intention is clearly that in the absence of direct divine intervention the task falls to the people.[29]

Another caution is that there should be provision for the situation in which a king is transformed into a tyrant.[30] The method is vague; Thomas warns about the dangers of revolt and advises obedience and restraint in all but the most intolerable situations. In no case should private action be condoned; an attack upon tyranny can be the prerogative only of the "public authority," something Thomas never identifes with any kind of actual institution. Parliamentary bodies had not yet developed to the point where they were the obvious solution, but Thomas felt that there should be some remedy and that this remedy could not be an individual one as others, such as John of Salisbury, had suggested.[31] All his emphasis is on legality; he writes not of the best arrangement, but of what can be done given the actually existing institutions. If the multitude has the right to choose its king, it has the right to depose him, for the king has broken his pact with his subjects; that is, to govern for the common good. But if a higher authority has the right to provide a king then it is his responsibility to remove the tyrant.

This brings me to the third and most important of the means Thomas advocates to avoid tyranny. The proper selection and necessary deposition of kings in no way contradicts the notion of regal rule, although it is perhaps alien to its spirit. It is quite possible to say that the people select their king who then rules by his own will, that is, by the law which he makes, unless he should violate his trust. But Thomas makes the stronger statement that the governance of the kingdom should be so arranged that the

---

conditionis homo ab illis, ad quos hoc spectat officium, promoveatur in regem, quod non sit probabile in tyrannidem declinare."

[29] He shows preference for election over heredity in several places, for example, *In Libros Politicorum*, 2.16.334.

[30] Thomas Aquinas, *De Regimine Principum*, 1.6. "Demum vero curandum est si rex in tyrannidem diverteret, qualiter posset occuare."

[31] Thomas Aquinas, *De Regimine Principum*, 1.6. "Videtur autem magis contra tyrannorum saevitiam non privata praesumptione aliquam, sed auctoritate publica procedendum." Richard Regan, "Aquinas on Political Obedience and Disobedience," p. 84, makes the suggestion that perhaps this support for a public authority reflects not only a preference for constitutional monarchy, but also an historical consciousness that an institution of this sort was in the process of evolving. The examples Thomas gives both pertain to the Roman Empire and show the difference between a free and a subject people. The Roman Senate was able to depose and execute a tyrannical emperor and to revoke his laws, and likewise the emperor could replace a local king under his jurisdiction. In human society, he asserts, no one can properly exercise coercion (which is the essence of law) except through public authority, and the one to whom public power is entrusted must use it within the bounds of justice (*Summa Theologiae*, 2–2.66.8).

opportunity to tyrannize be removed and that the king's power should be so tempered that he cannot easily become a tyrant.[32] What can he have meant? The word "tempering" is especially provocative. Certainly something beyond power of deposition or the moral strength of custom is meant. It suggests that the king's power be limited or controlled by other governmental institutions so that it cannot exceed what is proper. This interpretation is supported by many previous comments in which he implies that government pertains to a free people as a whole who delegate it or part of it to the monarch—but he always leaves open the possibility of a king representing the interests of the people but not being directly responsible to it.[33]

Thomas is an unswerving champion of the law. He would like to derive this law from the people either as legislator or as the bearer of custom. But because of his misinterpretation of Aristotle's definition of regal and political rule, he feels he must leave the way open for a ruler acting by his own will alone. Even so, he tries to hedge in the regal king with all sorts of restrictions which in fact bring him close to what he calls one who rules politically. Thomas has two choices: he can either reject regal kingship or he can assimilate it to political kingship and try to gloss over the differences. Because of his commitment to monarchy as a principle of the universe he perhaps feels that he cannot reject it in its pure form out of hand (especially since God rules regally if this word has any meaning at all). On the other hand, he cannot really eliminate the differences. Later writers such as Giles of Rome were not troubled by the same enthusiasm for law, and could unabashedly accept regal rule; Ptolemy of Lucca, on the other hand could complete the identification of regal monarchy and despotism and reject both.

In the *Commentary* Thomas is more explicit about what he means by the word "temper," and confirms our suspicions that he was thinking of a mixed constitution in the recommendations of *On the Government of Rulers* for avoiding tyranny. Thomas comments on Aristotle's mention of the "opinion of some" that the best government is a mixture of monarchy, oligarchy, and democracy: "The reason is because one government is tempered from the admixture of another, and less material is given for sedition if all have a part in the rule of the city, namely if the people dominates in something, the powerful in something, and the king in something."[34] The

---

[32] Thomas Aquinas, *De Regimine Principum*, 1.6. "Deinde sic disponenda est regni gubernatio, ut regi iam instituto tyrannidis subtrahatur occasio. Simul etiam sic eius temperetur potestas, ut in tyrannidem de facili declinare non posset."

[33] The coercive power that is necessary for law is vested in the whole people or in one who has care of the whole people (*Summa Theologiae*, 1–2.90.4). See also 1–2.90.4 and 1–2.97.3ad 3.

[34] Thomas Aquinas, *In Libros Politicorum*, 2.7.245. "Quidem dicunt optimum regimen civi-

implication is the same as in *On the Government of Rulers* with respect to the king. The addition of the other coordinate powers ensures that his rule is more temperate; that is, that because of the restraining influence of the others, he will be unable to tyrannize. We find here that the mixture also works the other way: the excesses possible from the rule of the few and the many, that is, extreme oligarchy and democracy, are mutually prevented by the tempering influence of the other powers and that such an arrangement undermines sedition.

While these are all practical reasons for the mixed constitution, in two passages of *Summa Theologiae* Thomas suggests that it is best in more fundamental ways. In both cases he advances original ideas, in one case linking the mixed constitution to the teachings of the Church fathers, in the other to the Bible and God's will. First, in a discussion of law he implies that it is only in a mixed government that we can speak of law in its proper sense. He notes that human law, being framed by the one who governs, is relative to the form of government. In a monarchy there are constitutions of princes, in an aristocracy *senatus consulta*, in an oligarchy praetorian law, and in a democracy *plebiscita*. He concludes, "There is something mixed from these, which is the best and from this comes *lex*, 'which the elders sanction together with the plebs,' as Isidore says."[35] In other words, in an unmixed state there is the law of this or that group; in a mixed state there is law simply speaking. This is the first time that anyone attempted to assimilate the early medieval ideas of Isidore with the mixed constitution of Aristotle. Isidore presumably meant to refer to the hereditary nobility, that is, the senatorial aristocracy, by the words *maiores natu*, and for him they were a natural element of rule, but he does not mention the mixed constitution at all—this is entirely Thomas's reading.

In his fullest discussion of the best government Thomas makes an even more compelling argument for mixed government: it is the form given by

---

tatis est quod est quasi commixtum ex omnibus praedictis regiminibus. Et huius ratio est, quia unum regimen temperetur ex admixtione alterius, est minus datur seditionis materia, si omnes habent partem in principatu civitatis; puta si in aliquo dominetur populus, in aliquo potentes, in aliquo rex." Aristotle used the terms *democracy* and *oligarchy* rather generally as rule of the people and the few, and not always as the bad forms of the sixfold classification. Thomas follows him here.

[35] Thomas Aquinas, *Summa Theologiae*, 1–2.95.4.3. "Et secundum hoc distinguuntur leges humanae secundum diversa regimina civitatum. Quorum unum . . . est regnum, quando scilicet civitas gubernatur ab uno: et secundum hoc accipiuntur constitutiones principum. Aliud vero regimen est aristocratia . . . et secundum hoc sumuntur responsa prudentium, et etiam senatus consulta. Aliud regimen est oligarchia . . . et secundum hoc sumitur ius praetorium, quod etiam honorarium dicitur. Aliud autem regimen est populi, quod nominatur democratia: et secundum hoc sumuntur plebiscita. . . . Et etiam aliquod ex istis conmixtum, quod est optimum: et secundum hoc sumitur lex 'quam maiores natu simul cum plebibus sanxerunt,' ut Isidorus dicit." The reference to Isidore of Seville is to *Etymologia*, 5.4.

God to his chosen people. He begins by mentioning two general principles of good government. The first is that "all should have some part in rule, for by this the peace of the people is preserved, and all love such an order and guard it."[36] His reason for giving all a share is practical; each will be content if this is the case. He does not really think that the average person has something to offer since he is neither (except accidentally) virtuous or wise. Thomas never takes up Aristotle's views on the collective wisdom of the whole multitude, and there is no reason to think that he shares them.

Nevertheless, he does insist that all should in some way share in government. This raises an obvious question. Monarchy, even regal monarchy if a virtuous enough man exists, is a good, even the best form of government, as Thomas himself says in the same passage in which he insists on universal participation. If one king is to have all power, how can all share? The only solution is to consider any political office, of which there must be many in even the most absolute monarchy, to embody a share of rule. In this way there would always be at least a small group of people who could be said to participate in rule. Is it the case, then, that a regal monarchy is in fact a mixed government of monarchy and aristocracy? No, for a distinction can be made between officials performing their duties at the institution of and subject to the king, and those who have an independent right to existence.[37] Even though the mixed constitution cannot preserve in its full purity any of its constituent parts, it cannot be meaningfully mixed unless each part subsists in some way in the mixture.

After saying that all should have a part, Thomas goes on to give another factor to be considered in setting up a right ordering of society—the form of government.

> Although there are various species of these, as Aristotle reports . . . the principal ones are the kingdom, in which one rules according to virtue; and aristocracy, that is, the power of the best, in which some few rule according to virtue. Whence the best order of rulers is in some city or kingdom, in which one is placed in authority according to his virtue who has precedence over all, and under him are some ruling according to virtue; and nevertheless such rule pertains to all, because they can be chosen from all and they are chosen by

---

[36] Thomas Aquinas, *Summa Theologiae*, 1–2.105.2. "Circa bonam ordinationem principum in aliqua civitate vel gente, duo sunt attendenda. Quorum unum est ut omnes aliquam partem habeant in principatu: per hoc enim conservatur pax populi, et omnes talem ordinationem amant et custodiunt."

[37] Mario Grignaschi, "La definition du 'civis' dans la scholastique," p. 85, considers somewhat the same problem in relation to citizenship. Aristotle's and Thomas's definition of a citizen as one who shares in the power of a city is really only satisfactory, as Aristotle himself admits, in a government with a broad basis of rule. Again, the only way to reconcile the idea of "citizen" with that of a "free subject" of a monarchy is by considering any office a *principatus*.

all. Such is the best polity, well-mixed from kingdom, insofar as one has precedence over all, and aristocracy, insofar as many rule according to their virtue, and from democracy, that is from the power of the people, insofar as princes can be chosen from the people, and election of princes pertains to the people.[38]

One cannot ignore the difference between the beginning and the end of this passage. There are many forms of government; the best are monarchy and aristocracy; therefore, the best government is a blend of monarchy, aristocracy, and democracy. Both monarchy and aristocracy are based on the principle of virtue; the only difference is the quantitative one of the number of rulers. Why, then, are both desirable? Although the phrasing (they are the best, therefore their combination is best) suggests that he also expects that since these are the best forms of government their combination will unite the good qualities of each, it must be repeated that Aquinas does not give separate qualities to each, and that his primary interest must be in the tempering effect.[39] But why democracy at all? Its inclusion is not the result of the second consideration (the forms of government) but of the first (everyone should have a share). There is no necessary virtue connected with the people, but there is something to be gained by making it feel a part of the government. Its role is restricted to the election of the king and aristocrats, so it is excluded from real participation in an Aristo-

[38] Thomas Aquinas, *Summa Theologiae*, 1–2.105.1. "Cuius cum sint diversae species, ut Philosophus tradit in III Politicis, praecipuae tamen sunt regnum, in quo unus principatur secundum virtutem; et aristocratia, idest potestas optimorum, in qua aliqui pauci principantur secundum virtutem. Unde optima ordinatio principum est in aliqua civitate vel regno, in qua unus praeficitur secundum virtutem qui omnibus praesit; et sub ipso sunt aliqui principantes secundum virtutem; et tamen talis principatus ad omnes pertinet, tum quia ex omnibus eligi possunt, tum quia etiam ab omnibus eliguntur. Talis enim est optima politia, bene commixta ex regno, inquantum unus praeest; et aristocratia, inquantum multi principantur secundum virtutem; et ex democratia, idest potestate populi, inquantum ex popularibus possunt eligi principes, et ad populum pertinet electio principum."

[39] Another view is that Thomas devised the mixed constitution to combine the unity of monarchy, the wisdom of aristocracy, and the liberty of democracy. See, e.g., Tierney, "Aristotle, Aquinas," p. 4. The only relevant passage in the works of Aquinas comes in his discussion of distributive justice (*Summa Theologiae*, 2–2.61.2): "And therefore in distributive justice more is given from the common goods as the individual holds more principality in the community. This principality is assessed in an aristocratic community according to virtue, in an oligarchic according to wealth, in a democratic according to liberty, and otherwise in others." It is difficult to see any necessary connection of this description of what various regimes consider important with a mixed government, except that as a mixture of the types it will naturally incorporate some of the qualities of each. But this is a different matter from the statement that Thomas's first concern was "uniting in one government the excellence proper to each simple regime" (Tierney, "Aristotle, Aquinas," p. 4). It is only in the *Summa Contra Gentiles* (3.1.81) that Thomas relates wisdom to government at all in enjoining the appointment of many wise councilors but he makes no specific connection with aristocracy. And he never gives a positive assessment to the liberty peculiar to democracy, as opposed to the freedom characteristic of any nondespotic regime.

telian sense—that is, in the actual offices of government. Tierney correctly observes that the difference in emphasis is due to the differing forms of political organization in the ancient and medieval worlds. In the Greek city-state the direct involvement of a large body of citizens was possible; the same was not true in a large medieval kingdom. As Tierney puts it: "Such an idea does begin to suggest modern constitutional theory where a complex central government derives its authority from the consent of the people."[40]

Thomas then sanctifies the mixed government by identifying it with the form established by God for the Jews:

> And this was instituted according to divine law. For Moses and his successors guided the people, ruling the people as it were by themselves, which is a certain species of kingdom. Moreover, they chose seventy-two elders according to virtue, for it is said in Deuteronomy 1: "I took from your tribes wise and noble men and established them as princes," and this was aristocracy. But it was democratic that those were chosen from all the people, for it is said in Exodus 18: "provide from all the people wise men, etc.," and even that the people chose them; whence it is said at Deuteronomy 1: "Give me from your wise men, etc." Whence it is clear that the ordering of princes that the law instituted was the best.[41]

It seems indisputable that Thomas is recommending this form of government as best absolutely, and not just as one suited only to the Jews. It is true that the starting point of this article is the question of whether God correctly ordained the government of His people, and that one conclusion is that God was wise in not at once setting up Jewish kings with full power. But the superiority of the mixed constitution is derived a priori from gen-

---

[40] Tierney, "Aristotle, Aquinas," p. 4. Tierney is not quite correct when he states that neither Aristotle nor other classical authors identified a democratic element with the right of election ("Aristotle, Aquinas," p. 4). Aristotle, in fact, does suggest this in several places (*Politics*, 2.6, 12; 3.11), although he makes little of it and in general sees election as an aristocratic device whose democratic analogue is selection by lot. Making office open to all is another idea that Aristotle describes once or twice as a democratic procedure, but again in general this is not his position. The very idea of selecting the best in an aristocracy implies the eligibility of a qualified person from any segment of society, however unlikely that such a one come from the lower orders.

[41] Thomas Aquinas, *Summa Theologiae*, 1–2.105.1. "Et hoc fuit institutum secundum legem divinam. Nam Moyses et eius successores gubernabant populum quasi singulariter omnibus principantes, quod est quaedam species regni. Eligebantur autem septuaginta duo seniores secundum virtutem: dicitur enim Deuteronomii 1: 'Tuli de vestris tribubus viros sapientes et nobiles, et constitui eos principes:' et hoc erat aristocraticum. Sed democraticum erat quod isti de omni populo eligebantur; dicitur enim Exodus 18, 'Provide de omni plebe viros sapientes, etc.:' et etiam quod populus eos eligebat; unde dicitur Deuteronomii 1, 'Date ex vobis viros sapientes, etc.' Unde patet quod optima fuit ordinatio principum quam lex instituit."

eral principles of what constitutes good government, and the Jews are brought in as an example to demonstrate that what he has deduced by reason is supported by the divine intention.

The other great example of a mixed constitution was, of course, the Roman Republic. Although Thomas was not aware of the Polybian tradition with respect to Rome, his comparison of Roman and Jewish history may be responsible for initiating the medieval rehabilitation of the Republic, and its identification as a mixed constitution. He writes that the Roman Republic, like the Jewish period of the Judges, was prosperous, and promoted the public good until an excess of freedom led to dissension which led to the establishment of the Empire in the one case and the Kings in the other.[42] Under the Empire the senate did not represent an independent element designed to temper the emperor, but was a public authority with the right to appoint an emperor and remove him if he failed to live up to his pact with the people, but with no control over his actual rule.

These passages are embarrassing to those who think Thomas was an absolute monarchist. Despite its central importance McIlwain mentions the Jewish mixed constitution only in one part of one paragraph in a footnote, and he fails to give any convincing arguments to make it conform to his position.[43] McIlwain might have directed our attention to Thomas's reply to objection 2 of the same article. He could have used it to make a strong argument for his position since it seems both to endorse regal monarchy and relate the mixed constitution specifically to the Jews. The objection itself castigates the Old Law for not instituting from the beginning the best form, that which imitates the divine government—kingship. Thomas replies:

> A kingdom is the best government of the people, if it is not corrupted. But on account of the great power which is conceded to the king, a kingdom easily degenerates into tyranny, unless he to whom such power is conceded possesses perfect virtue. . . . But perfect virtue is found in few; and especially were the Jews cruel and prone to avarice, through which vice above all men fall into tyranny. And therefore the Lord from the beginning did not institute a king for them with full power, but a judge and governor for their guardianship.[44]

[42] Thomas Aquinas, *De Regimine Principum* , 1.4.

[43] McIlwain, *Growth of Political Thought*, p. 331n. 1.

[44] Thomas Aquinas, *Summa Theologiae*, 1–2.105.1. "Regnum est optimum regimen populi, si non corrumpatur. Sed propter magnam potestatem quae regi conceditur, de facili regnum degenerat in tyrannidem, nisi sit perfecta virtus eius cui talis potestas conceditur: quia non est nisi virtuosi bene ferre bonas fortunas, ut Philosophus dicit, in IV Ethicis. Perfecta autem virtus in paucis invenitur: et praecipue Iudaei crudeles erant et ad avaritiam proni, per quae vitia maxime homines in tyrannidem decidunt. Et ideo Dominus a principio eis regem non instituit cum plena potestate, sed iudicem et gubernatorem in eorum custodiam."

Now, clearly, Thomas is speaking of a regal kingship here: he refers to "full power" and uses an analogy to universal kingship. If he were not thinking of regal kingship, he could have answered simply that, as he had just told us, the mixed constitution does have the equivalent of a king, regardless of his actual title. On the surface there seems to be an insurmountable contradiction: how can the *best* be both regal monarchy and the mixed constitution? First, Thomas makes an implicit distinction, which will become explicit in later writers, between simple forms of government, such as monarchy, aristocracy, and democracy, and compound forms. This is detectable in the already cited portions of this article: there are several species of rule (*species regiminis*) of which the best are monarchy and aristocracy. The best ordination of rulers (*ordinatio principum*) is the mixed constitution. The mixed constitution is not a species in the sense that monarchy and aristocracy are; rather it is a combination of species. Thus it is possible to use *best* here for two different forms—monarchy is the best of the simple forms, the mixed government the best form of government.[45]

This observation does not solve our difficulty. Thomas states both that regal monarchy is the best and that a mixed constitution is best, but a regal monarchy does not seem to be compatible with a mixed constitution. Hence, we must consider yet another distinction of the word *best*. Thomas admits that regal kingship is best abstractly, but denies that it is best considering the nature of humanity. When he points to the peculiar traits of the Jews he implies only that they especially are unsuited to regal government, not that others are suited to it. The king of perfect virtue is almost never found, and he might have added, as other medieval writers did, that even if there is such a one, what will happen after his death? Regal monarchy is best only in principle, in the abstract, in a realm of perfection such as the universe. Thomas's general principles of government also reflect his concern with human nature. The reason that all should have a share in power is ultimately that people are unsatisfied and will become rebellious if they cannot participate. This factor would be no less true in the rule of the one of perfect virtue than in any other form, and so he seems to say that regal monarchy is unsuitable even if the proper king could be found. Thus, in any meaningful sense the mixed constitution is the best government.

Those who have not grasped the distinction between regal and political power and Thomas's support for a political king in a mixed constitution are unable to make complete sense of his position without recourse to strained exegesis. Bound to the conception of regal monarchy as the normal and even definitive form of monarchy, Demongeot, for example, treats

---

[45] One could also argue that his meaning is that monarchy is the best form of government, mixed constitution the best type of monarchy.

the limited monarchy mentioned by Thomas as a concession by him to the actual facts of rule in particular places.[46] For the same reason Hanson perceives Thomas's king as essentially contradictory since, as he sees it, on the one hand Thomas wants an independently organized monarchical element, and on the other hand he seeks to strip the king of his regal attributes.[47] All of this misrepresents Thomas's thought. He is concerned chiefly with the difference between rule by law and will, and his rejection of absolute rule has to do with the inherent nature of people and not just the situation in this or that place. This is true not only for monarchy, but also for the other forms whether in isolation or within a mixed constitution: regal aristocracy or democracy is possible, but it should be rejected in favor of the political rule of law. Far from being a minor and somewhat conflicting classification of rule, it underlies Thomas's whole theory.

Only with a political king is the idea of tempering and balance in a mixed constitution possible. Otherwise the mixed constitution is, as McIlwain, Morrall, and Dunbabin think, little different from an absolute monarchy in which the monarchic element could be tempered only in the practical sense that the king could not ignore the united voice of the great men, and still less the combined demands of them and the people.[48] But there are always great men, the people always exist, and these two groups can always assert themselves against the king. The point would seem to be to give them some institutional machinery for doing this within the law rather than on their own. Thomas wants the three elements of his mixed government to be able to check the excesses of the others, and to do this on a regular basis, not just in extreme cases. Because of the political conditions of the time all the institutional answers were not clear to him, as they would be in a few centuries to the English theorists of the mixed constitution, and so he is not specific as to exact forms. There is simply no way to achieve Thomas's intent in a society governed by a regal king free from the laws and direct restraint of other agencies. This is why all of Thomas's effort was directed to deprive the king of his regal prerogatives, and to render him a political ruler bound to the laws. Looked at this way there is no problem integrating a king into the mixed constitution.

Thomas's choice of the mixed constitution as the best government is a result of his conclusion that, in general, it will best serve the common utility. The salient point, which above all recommends it, is that it denies sovereignty to any one element, and in this way avoids the tyranny of either the one, the few, or the many. Thomas may be vague about the institutions through which the power of the community could manifest itself, but he

---

[46] Demongeot, *Le Meilleur regime*, p. 33.

[47] Hanson, *From Kingdom to Commonwealth*, p. 243.

[48] As Demongeot, *Le Meilleur regime*, pp. 169–72, asserts.

is not at all vague about his purposes. He does not hesitate between alternate sources of authority since the question of government is not primarily a metaphysical question for him (even though he can demonstrate that his solution accords with the will of God). A political king ruling a people that is represented in government and that can restrain him will most effectively promote the common good, which for Thomas is the most important criterion for rule.[49]

To what degree are these ideas faithful to Aristotle's intent in the *Politics*? Certainly, Aristotle also put emphasis on advancing the common good. And, it is easy to understand how someone living among the thirteenth-century monarchies could have interpreted Aristotle's comments on regal and political rule as referring to monarchic authority in both modes, especially in light of William of Moerbeke's mistranslation, and the fact that Aristotle himself is not very clear in his exposition of monarchy. Aquinas always favors a king; Aristotle only if there exists one of transcendent virtue. This being said, if we equate Thomas's regal king with Aristotle's king, both authors agree with Aristotle's conditions for his rule, and although neither really expects that such a rule is possible, both agree that his superiority would give this king a right to rule, and that his rule would be abstractly the best. Failing this, both advocate a mixed constitution, and although it is only Thomas who insists on the inclusion of the three elements of monarchy, aristocracy, and democracy, both stress the importance of law.

Their views of the mixed constitution, however, are quite different. Aristotle's concern is the balancing of the various classes. His mixture itself can be seen as a mixture of classes rather than a formal one of the various constituents. He carries this to the extreme that one of his ideal forms is a mixed constitution in which in a sense the various elements disappear and the mixing consists of the assimilation of all citizens to a single class—this is his middle-class polity. All this is of no concern to Thomas, who ignores almost everything to do with class.[50] His concern is not balancing the

---

[49] Aquinas refers to kingdoms in which the people have the right to make laws and appoint the king and those in which they do not as if the two situations were equally valid and just. The only right anyone or any group has to rule is its superiority, and this is something to be decided in real situations. There can be no question of a general theory of sovereignty in Aquinas. It is useless to reproach him, as Hanson does, with a failure to choose an ultimate sovereign. The absence of a sovereign is typical of the mixed constitution in any of the classical, medieval, or early modern versions; it is one of the major criticisms that Bodin levels against the theory. Hanson, *From Kingdom to Commonwealth*, p. 243, misses this point and insists on distinguishing a true mixed constitutional theory from the theory of double majesty which he asserts Thomas is expressing.

[50] It is not that he is unaware of the existence of classes, just that he does not see their balance as the essense of the mixed constitution. In *Summa Theologiae* (1–2.108.2), he comments that "in cities a triple order of men is found: certain are highest (the optimates), certain

classes in society but balancing governmental forms to avoid the extremes of any of them. In this, as in his lack of confidence in the wisdom of the people, Thomas is rather closer to Polybius, whom he did not know directly or even indirectly through Cicero. Although the similarity is fortuitous, both stress the checks and balances of one form upon another. When Polybius was rediscovered in the sixteenth century, this affinity aided in the fusion of the Aristotelian and Polybian traditions.

In these ways and others Thomas created a truly original synthesis of Greek political theory and medieval thought. By distinguishing regal and political power and insisting on a political monarch, Thomas was able to preserve the participation characteristic of Greek society and the unity of rule found, at least in principle, in the medieval kingdom. There seems in principle, as Brian Tierney argues, no reason why Thomas should not have applied the same arguments to the Church that he had applied to secular rule, and have concluded that the mixed constitution is also the best government for it, especially since its institutions of pope, cardinals, and General Council could much more easily be fit into such a theory than the kings and incipient representative assemblies of the national monarchies. The fact is that he did not do this, and his exact ecclesiological views are still a matter of great controversy. As Tierney notes, the important point is that, "Thomas certainly developed, on a scriptural basis, a doctrine of the mixed constitution that was in principle applicable to the church."[51]

The generation of scholars that followed Aquinas would take his ideas and develop them in different and sometimes contradictory ways. Some would carry on the theory of the mixed constitution and alter it in subtle ways, apply it to the Church, or reject it altogether for some other favored form. But the idea of a mixed government had reentered the Western world after an absence of some one thousand years, and in one form or another it would survive and prosper throughout late medieval and early modern times. From the thirteenth to the sixteenth century the distinction between regal and political power, as this was interpreted by Thomas, remained an important part of this theory.

In the quarter of a century following the death of Thomas Aquinas, five men influenced by him developed and modified his political ideas. In their works we will see repeatedly the Thomist terminology and formulations of the basic problems, but often used for quite different purposes—although all endorse some sort of limited government similar to a mixed constitution, their conclusions are quite diverse, and it is sometimes astounding to

---

are lowest (the vile populace), and certain are middle (the honorable populace)." And certainly the mixed constitution reflects these three levels.

[51] Tierney, "Aristotle, Aquinas," p. 8.

think that they all started from the same source, and that most of them considered themselves legitimate continuers of Thomas's thought.

I wish to take up each of these five men—Giles of Rome, Peter of Auvergne, Ptolemy of Lucca, Engelbert of Admont, and John of Paris—in turn.

Chapter 4

GILES OF ROME

GILES OF ROME (c. 1243–1316), also known as Aegedius Romanus and Aegedius Colonna, was born in Rome of a rich family important in political and Church affairs. At the age of 14 he joined the Hermits of St. Augustine and subsequently studied at the University of Paris. Between 1269 and 1272 he evidently attended Thomas Aquinas's lectures in theology, where he picked up some ideas, such as the limited number of angels in any one species, that were condemned in Stephen Tempier's famous Paris Condemnations of 1277. As with that of Thomism in general, Giles's humiliation was short-lived; though he had temporarily to leave Paris, a few years later he became the vicar-general of his order and his teaching was made the standard for Augustinian education. For some time he served as tutor to the sons of Philip III of France, before that king's death in 1285, and in that same year he was reinstated in the University of Paris. Despite his connections to the secular monarchy of France, Giles was a high papalist, and his treatise *On Ecclesiastical Power* (1301) is generally believed to have been the inspiration for Boniface VIII's strident, hierocratic bull *Unam Sanctam* (1302), that ends, "It is altogether necessary for salvation for every human creature to be subject to the Roman Pontiff." He had several scholastic appellations: "Blessed Doctor," "Most Fundamental Doctor," and, more descriptively, "Verbose Doctor." He died at the papal court in Avignon.

Giles wrote his popular and influential treatise, *On the Government of Rulers*, in his role as the royal tutor and dedicated it to his former charge Philip IV in the first years of his reign.[1] His contemporaries greatly respected the work and circulated it widely; its French and Italian versions were the first translations into the vernacular of such a work. Written for a king, its monarchic leanings are not surprising, but it is one of only a few works, including also Engelbert of Admont's treatise of the same name, that combine an Aristotelian political orientation with the traditional "mirror of princes" literary form. This genre had the purpose of providing moral guidance to princes and exhorting them to observe the virtues proper to rulers, and, in general, it assumed monarchy as a given.

The thematic arrangement of the work betrays this tradition: the first book treats the ends of society and the proper virtues and passions of

---

[1] Giles of Rome, *De Regimine Principum Libri III*.

princes and kings, the second treats the family, and the third alone deals with political rule. By treating the virtues of princes before he determines acceptable or optimal political systems, Giles dismisses the Aristotelian idea that the virtue of the good citizen or ruler varies with the form of polity and relates virtue to an absolute end divorced from the particular conditions. Such restrictions almost guarantee the advocacy of monarchy.

Giles was very much involved in the political issues and struggles of his day, so that it is remarkable that he almost never mentions actual governments, historical or legendary. He justifies government on a priori metaphysical grounds, at once at odds with the contemporary Aristotelian consensus and with the political relativism that was to dominate in the fourteenth century.

Giles seizes upon those sections of Aristotle's *Politics* favorable to kingship and reworks or ignores those that are not. Giles has little to say about nonmonarchical or even nonregal forms. On almost every point about which Thomas Aquinas desired limitation of kingship—law, election, and "tempering," among others—Giles comes down on the side of uncontrolled rule. He gives the impression of being a supporter of absolute monarchy, unwilling to allot any function or power to other segments of society. The Carlyles interpret Giles in this way, as a repudiator of the medieval tradition of limited kingship, as an isolated thirteenth-century harbinger of the absolutism of the sixteenth and seventeenth centuries.[2]

It sounds as if Giles is an exception to my belief that mixed constitutional thought dominated in this period—but even this apparent exception strengthens my argument. Even one so committed to regal monarchy in this period was forced in a general political treatise to consider alternatives to it and to impose restrictions on it. Aristotelian political theory was exceptionally diverse, but no matter how much the various authors differed in aim, interests, motivation, or philosophical basis, all shared an underlying assumption of the desirability of limited government, of the necessity of participation or consent, of the normal supremacy of law. This is no less true of the "absolute monarchist" Giles of Rome than of the "republican" Ptolemy of Lucca. Whatever contradictions exist in Giles's theories reflect not oversights on his part,[3] but unresolved tensions in his thought, tensions which he later resolved only at the cost of abandoning much of his Aristotelianism. McIlwain sees *On the Government of Rulers* as a striking proof of the sudden and revolutionary change wrought by Aristotle in the development of political speculation during the thirteenth century.[4] But

---

[2] Carlyle and Carlyle, *Medieval Political Theory*, vol. 5, p. 75.

[3] In this I am in accord with Thomas J. Renna, *Royalist Political Thought in France, 1285–1303*, p. 79, although our explanations differ.

[4] McIlwain, *Growth of Political Thought*, p. 338.

by 1302 when he wrote his most famous work, *On Ecclesiastical Power*,[5] his Aristotelianism has become superficial; the contrast with *On the Government of Rulers* is so marked that Ullmann remarks that they almost seem to be written by two different people, while Sabine refers to his "mock Aristotelianism." With less justification, Ullmann also argues that his fundamental attitude has changed from superficial support for an ascending theory of authority, in which all power stems ultimately from the people, to endorsement of a descending one, in which all power flows from God or the king.[6]

There was little tension in Thomas Aquinas's thought. A devout Christian, he nonetheless believed implicitly that there could be no conflict between reason, represented by Aristotelian philosophy, and faith. His ingenuity produced a convincing synthesis in many areas; in others his belief enabled him to ignore the more intractible contradictions. Although it would not be correct to say that Thomas was more an Aristotelian than a Christian, it is certainly true that he was more an Aristotelian than an Augustinian.

The same cannot be said of Giles. As an Augustinian canon he must have been presented more directly than most with the possible conflicts between the views of Aristotle and those of the supposed founder of his order, especially on the origin and purpose of political authority. Giles wanted to believe both that government resulted from sin and that it was a natural outgrowth of human nature. He wanted a regal king who ruled by his own will, and yet he wanted law to prevail and the king to be bound by council. He wanted both a sovereign king and one basing his power on the consent of the people. He wanted to see the state as a natural outgrowth of the family, but he also wanted it to result from a social contract of its citizens.

All these conflicts are related to the basic conflict of Christian-Augustinian doctrine and Aristotelian philosophy, but they are also related to a conflict between the latter and Giles's perception of the French political situation. For the king to establish his hegemony throughout the nation, much of which was in the hands of his nominal vassal, the King of England, or under the control of other semi-independent lords, he needed greater per-

---

[5] Giles of Rome, *De ecclesiastica Potestate*. For the most part, modern commentary has been directed to this later work because of its relevance to the heated Church and state conflicts and because of its possible influence on the celebrated bull *Unam sanctam*. For its influence on *Unam sanctam*, see, e.g., Sabine, *History of Political Theory*, p. 274.

[6] Walter Ullmann, *Law and Politics in the Middle Ages: An Introduction to the Sources of Medieval Political Ideas*, pp. 274–75. Sabine, *History of Political Theory*, p. 280. Ullmann's division of all political theories into ascending and descending has been exceptionally influential, if controversial, among medieval historians for many years. His major thesis is that almost from its inception the papacy was determined to advance a hierarchical, descending power over all of Christiandom, a position never overcome until the victory of secular, descending forces in the late Middle Ages.

sonal authority. Giles does not write directly about this situation, but he wants his general treatment of politics to give theoretical support to the French monarchy.

In his attempts to come to terms with the contradictions, Giles places the family at the center, both physically as the subject of the second of three books and theoretically. This centrality forces me to comment extensively on Giles's theory of rule in the family, even though I have written on this topic elsewhere.[7] It seems clear to me that he hoped to find a model for government in the home that would resolve his contradictory political beliefs.

For Giles the question of the family assumes great importance since he, unlike Thomas, rejects Aristotle's separation of domestic and civil government, thus falling into what Aristotle had called Plato's error: he sees no qualitative difference between a large family and a small city. By establishing a hierarchical order from the universe to a kingdom to a city to a household to an individual person, and showing that a similar monarchic subordination and rule obtain at the endpoints (God over the universe, the soul over the body), Giles attempts to impose a similar necessary order on the intermediate city and home.[8]

Although Giles intends by this argument to defend monarchy at all levels, he does not, except incidentally and vaguely, advance a "moral patriarchal" outlook, to use Gordon Schochet's term. In other words he does not try to derive all government from the family and argue that since the patriarch rules absolutely in the family the king by right does the same in his kingdom.[9] Like Aquinas, he does not use the family as a model for rule, rather the reverse. Both authors normally define household government in terms borrowed from politics.

Unlike Thomas and Aristotle, however, Giles discusses the modes of rule (regal, political, and despotic) primarily in the context of the family, where for him, again opposing both Thomas and Aristotle, rule is purely monarchic, although the paterfamilias may exercise his power differently with respect to different family members: "In the community of male and female the male should be ruling and the female obeying, in the community of father and son the father should be commanding and the son complying, in the community of lord and servant the lord should be ordering and the servant ministering and serving."[10]

---

[7] Blythe, "Family, Government."

[8] Giles of Rome, *De Regimine Principum*, 2.1.14.154v.

[9] See Gordon Schochet, *Patriarchialism in Political Thought* and Blythe, "Family, Government."

[10] Giles of Rome, *De Regimine Principum*, 2.1.6.141r. "In communitate maris et foeminae, mas debet esse principans, et foemina obsequens: in communitate vero patris et filii, pater debet esse imperiens et filius obtemperens; in communitate quidem domini et servi, dominus

In order to specify the nature of these varieties of rule Giles refers to government in a city. There, he writes, a leader governs either by "sure laws and pacts" or according to his own will.[11] He identifies this difference with the Thomistic modes of regal and political rule, adding, however, that it is not law per se that distinguishes the modes, but whether the ruler or the citizens make the law: "Someone is said to have precedence by regal dominion when he has precedence according to his will and according to laws which he himself has instituted. But he has precedence in a political government when he does not have precedence according to his will, nor according to laws which he himself has instituted, but according to those which the citizens have instituted."[12]

By shifting attention to the legislator, Giles is able to solve a problem that Thomas had not addressed quite successfully. Thomas believed that all legitimate rule and rulers, whether in the family or in the state, were under law, in the first instance under natural law, which also served to underpin subsequent civil laws. Yet the definitions of regal and political rule as he understood them seemed to demand that legitimate human relationships could exist without law. Giles's distinction makes it evident that all valid governments are under law, and yet it preserves the regal and political modes as useful categories. Giles further subdivides rule by will: it is either for the good of the ruler, in which case it is despotic, or for the good of the subjects, in which case it is regal.

Returning to his original topic, he adds that these three modes of civic government are like the three modes found in the home.[13] His explication of this is much more specific than Thomas's. Conjugal rule, he writes, is political in essence because there are definite laws that are binding on the husband: laws of matrimony, as well as various conventions and pacts, including presumably the mutual consent that according to medieval canon law is the constitutive element of marriage. Although marriage itself is natural, Giles writes, the choice of a particular spouse is up to the contracting parties themselves. As one with a choice the wife can be said to be equal to

---

debet esse praecipiens et servus ministrans et serviens." Giles uses the words *principans, imperans*, and *praecipiens* interchangeably elsewhere, so probably no technical distinction is being made here.

[11] Giles of Rome, *De Regimine Principum*, 2.2.3.173v. "Nam omnes regens alios, vel reget eos secundum certas leges, et secundum certa pacta, et tale regimen . . . nominatur politicum vel civile. Vel regit eos secundum arbitrium."

[12] Giles of Rome, *De Regimine Principum*, 2.1.14.154v–155r. "Dicitur autem quis praeesse regali dominio, cum praeest secundum arbitrium et secundum leges, quas ipse instituit. Sed tunc praeest regimine politico, quando non praeest secundum arbitrium, nec secundum leges quas ipse instituit; sed secundum eas quas cives instituerunt."

[13] Giles of Rome, *De Regimine Principum*, 2.2.3.173v. "His autem tribus regiminibus, secundum quod videmus aliquos regnare in civitatibus et castris, assimilantur tria regimina reperta in una domo."

the man in certain respects. He writes of their relationship that "such a government is called political, because it is similar to that government by which the citizens, choosing their lord show him pacts and conventions which he must observe in his government."[14] It should be emphasized that Giles does not envision an ongoing process of lawmaking by husband and wife together, but rather a set of laws established once and for all at the time of marriage.

In contrast to the political rule of man over wife are those situations in which rule is according to the will of the ruler: the regal rule of a father over his children and the despotic rule of a lord over his servants. The father rules regally since according to his will he acts for what he sees to be expedient for his son, just as a king rules his people according to what is expedient for them in his eyes. "Children are not judged equal to their father," Giles writes, "nor do they choose their father, rather they are naturally produced by him."[15] In his section on the management of the household objects, that is, economics proper, Giles treats the servant as just another household fixture to be used by the lord, and justifies this relationship upon the supposed defect of reason found among natural servants. Like Aristotle, but unlike Thomas, Giles argues often and consistently that despotic rule promotes the common good of both, with the result that despotic rule in the state becomes easier to accept.[16]

This is only one way in which Giles, while ostensibly only pointing to features of the family similar to those of the polity, actually creates overtones that will carry over to civil government. His emphasis is only subtly different from that of Aristotle and Aquinas, but the implications are quite original. For Aquinas, the fundamental criterion of the modal classification was the freedom or lack of freedom of the subjects (children and wives are free, servants are not free), whereas for Giles it is the freedom or limitation of rulers (they rule children and servants by their will, their wives by law). In other words, Giles divides all rule into regal and political and the regal in turn into regal and despotic; Thomas divides rule into political and despotic, and the political in turn into regal and political. The double usage of the term *regal* is confusing (like Thomas's and Aristotle's multiple usage of *political*), but his implication is that despotic rule is a species of regal rule taken in its general sense, and, therefore, that it is good.[17]

[14] Giles of Rome, *De Regimine Principum*, 2.1.14.155r,v. "Dicitur ergo tale regimen politicum: quia assimilatur illi regimini, quo cives vocantes dominum, ostendunt ei pacta et conventiones quasdam in suo regimine observare."

[15] Giles of Rome, *De Regimine Principum*, 1.2.14.155v. "Filii autem non sic iudicantur ad paria cum patre, nec eligunt sibi patrem, sed naturaliter producuntur ab ipso."

[16] Giles of Rome, *De Regimine Principum*, 2.3.206r–238r, 2.1.5.137v.

[17] In this Giles differs only in emphasis from Ptolemy of Lucca who comes to opposite

Giles's treatment of conjugal rule further separates him from his predecessors, who were concerned by the difference between political rule, which according to Aristotle involved an alternation of office, and marriage, in which the husband always rules. Aristotle is content to note that the family is analogous to the polity in some ways only, but Thomas goes further in identifying the types of authority in the two different settings, but rejecting alternation as the normal concomitant of political rule. For Giles, there is nothing to explain: it is obvious to him that, whether there is law or not, one man, as in the family, will naturally rule the others, and he does not mention exchange or multiple rulers at all. For him political rule can only be the situation in which a king's rule is limited by the laws that the citizens themselves have instituted. With respect to matrimony all three thinkers would agree that man and wife may be equal in the contractual arrangement, but that the man must have precedence because of his superior ability to reason. Like Thomas, Giles uses the naturalness of the family to prove the naturalness of rule, if not to justify the varieties of rule. As usual, his emphasis is different—he gives as one of his proofs that servitude is natural the fact that man naturally is superior to woman in reason and therefore naturally rules her. If even the political conjugal rule is servitude, the inevitable conclusion is that all rule is a form of servitude. Although he putatively accepts the Aristotelian tenet that rule is natural to people and good, he cannot completely rid himself of the Augustinian idea that it is always servitude and exists only on account of sin.[18] In any case, Giles writes that a wife should be more a partner than a servant. By this he means that the husband should seek her counsel and that in some few cases (presumably to be determined by the superior judgment of the male) her ideas might actually be better.[19]

In the city or kingdom ruled politically these same characteristics apply. The king is bound by a largely customary law, of necessity seeks the counsel of the citizens who are to be seen as partners and allies instead of servants, and is legitimate only by the common consent and election of these citizens. But beyond this he, like the paterfamilias, rules absolutely. One point is unclear: If the essential characteristic of political rule is law, do counsel,

---

conclusions. Giles assimilates despotic to regal, Ptolemy of Lucca regal to despotic and, consequently, the one improves the image of despotism, the other tarnishes that of kingship.

[18] Giles of Rome, *De Regimine Principum*, 2.1.15.157v. "Vir debeat praeesse uxori, eo quod ratione praestantior." See also 2.2.23.168v–169r, 3.2.12.225v–226v. Thomas, on the other hand, argued that there was government in the Garden of Eden—but a government of direction only and not of servitude (*Summa Theologiae*, 1.96.4). Elsewhere, however, Giles also distinguishes conjugal rule from servitude (1.2.15.156v–157v).

[19] Giles of Rome, *De Regimine Principum*, 2.1.15.157v. "Nam licet vir debeat praeesse uxori . . . non tamen debet esse tanta imparitas inter virum et uxorem, quod ea uti debeat tanquam serva, sed magis tanquam socia." 1.1.23.169r. "In casu tamen potest esse muliebre consilium melius quam virile."

consent, and election apply only to a political government, or are they necessary for regal as well?

Election and consent certainly do not apply to paternal rule. In proving that the father rules regally, Giles implies that rule by law is possible only if the ruler is elected: "No pacts and conventions can interpose themselves between a subject and him who is preeminent unless it be in the power of the subject to choose a rector for himself—but it is not in the power of sons to choose their father."[20] Logically this does not demand that a regal king obtain his office by heredity or appointment by a higher authority. But the association of heredity with paternal rule and election with law binding on the ruler may be one of the underlying reasons Giles opts for heredity as preferable to election for regal rulers.

Neither Aristotle nor Thomas makes any attempt to elevate one type of rule within the family to a superior position—all three types are natural and appropriate in their place. But for Giles political rule, whether in the family or polity, is always bound to the particular circumstances and is dependent on the choice of those ruled. So even though the political relationship of man and wife, for example, is natural, it is not as natural as the regal relationship of father and son and, as such, is inferior to it.[21] Giles does not explicitly attempt to justify regal rule as best as a consequence of paternal rule, but he does come to that conclusion in the context of a discussion of family relationships. This may represent the first glimmerings of that "moral patriarchialism" not found by Schochet until the seventeenth century.

Despite his preoccupation with the various modes of monarchy, Giles does acknowledge Aristotle's sixfold schema of forms.[22] He actually refers at that point to existing governments to illustrate the rule of the few and the many, almost the only such references in his book. Perhaps, since he assumes monarchy, he thinks it necessary to show that the other theoretical kinds of rule actually exist. Elsewhere the rule of a plurality is brought up only to contrast it unfavorably with rule by one; it is never treated inde-

[20] Giles of Rome, *De Regimine Principum*, 2.2.3.173v. "Nam pacta et conventiones non interveniunt inter subditum et praeeminentem, nisi sit in potestate subiecti eligere rectorem: non est autem in potestate filiorum eligere patrem."

[21] Giles of Rome, *De Regimine Principum*, 2.14.155v. "Licet omne regimen (si sit rectum) sit naturale, attamen regimen politicum quantumcumque sit rectum, non est ideo naturale, sicut regale."

[22] Giles of Rome, *De Regimine Principum*, 3.2.2.268r. Giles implies that there is no proper name for polity because it is rare; Aristotle justified the common name for a number of reasons, but mostly because he saw it as the typical form of government. Giles (3.2.2.268r–269v, 3.2.12.285r) prefers to call polity and democracy the governance of the people (*gubernatio populi*) and perversion of the people (*perversio populi*) respectively, but I will use the usual names since he himself acknowledges them as equivalents.

pendently.[23] His model of rule of a few is obscure but refers to the medieval government of the city of Rome:

> For we often see in the city of Rome when the senate does not exist, in the intermediate time before another senator has been chosen, all the Roman people was governed by some few men: for, twelve men of good repute were chosen and the whole city was governed by their governance; whence, crimes committed are distinguished from the diversity of rules; some are said to be from the time of the senator, others from the time of the good men.[24]

Even here, he chooses to give as an example of aristocracy something exceptional: in the normal course of events Rome is ruled by one man, yet if there is an interregnum a few good men rule temporarily.

As might be expected, Giles chooses the communes of Northern Italy for his example of rule by the many:

> In the cities of Italy the many, that is, the whole people commonly dominate. There the consensus of the whole people is required in passing statutes, in choosing podestas (*potestatibus*), and in correcting them. For, although there is always some podesta or lord who governs the city, nevertheless, the whole people exercises dominion more than the lord noted, since the whole people has the right to elect him and correct him if he does badly, and to enact statutes which the lord may not transgress.[25]

[23] Likewise, Giles gives only cursory attention to the perversions of aristocracy and polity, and tends to assimilate them to tyranny. Whatever corruption is found in other perverse governments is found in tyranny as well, he writes. The evils of oligarchy—money, pleasure, personal protection—are found even more markedly in tyranny since without the love of his people depredation is the only method for acquiring the money the ruler needs. And, as in democracy, the tyrant endeavors to oppress the nobles (*De Regimine Principum*, 3.2.12.285v–286v). This part of his exposition is taken from Aristotle (*Politics*, 5.10.1310b–1311a), but with an opposite intention. Giles wishes to minimize the importance of oligarchy and democracy since both are in effect only dilute forms of tyranny. Aristotle, on the other hand, being much less interested in the rule of one, wants to assert that although tyranny is the worst it can be treated as a peculiar compound of the vices of the more familiar forms of oligarchy and democracy.

[24] Giles of Rome, *De Regimine Principum*, 3.2.268v. "Videmus enim pluries in civitate Romana, quod deficiente senatu, tempore illo intermedio, antequam alius senator eligeretur, regebatur totus Romanus populus quibusdam paucis viris: eligebantur enim duodecim viri approbati et boni testimonii, quos vocabant duodecim bonos homines; et horum gubernatione tota civitas regebatur: unde et maleficia facta distinguebantur ex diversitate principatuum. Dicebatur autem de aliquo maleficio fuisse factum tempore senatoris, de aliquo vero tempore bonorum hominum." In such an aristocracy, Giles adds, those of the people who are greater (*maiores in populo*) and who ought to rule the people are called optimates, since those who wish to have precedence over others should be the best. *Optimates* was the common term for the rich and powerful elements in the Northern Italian cities.

[25] Giles of Rome, *De Regimine Principum*, 3.2.269r. "Communiter enim in civitatibus Italiae dominantur multi, ut totus populus: ibi enim requiritur consensus totius populi in statutis condendis, in potestatibus eligendis, et etiam in potestatibus corrigendis. Licet enim

As in Giles's description of political rule, a single ruler is bound by laws made by the citizens and is subject to election and correction by them. Are the cities of Italy, then, polities or political monarchies? In other words, is the role of the many here different from that in a monarchy by law? Although Giles tends to see the other acceptable regimes in terms of the rule of one, which for him is the normal and rational way to order any human community, I think that there is a substantial difference. Any democratic government will usually find it necessary to choose an executive officer to carry out its day-to-day functions and business, and the distinction between polity and monarchy hinges on whether the many retain complete control or whether the officer has independent powers. In his description of political monarchy and conjugal rule, Giles talks about the citizens or wife binding the king or husband to an already established body of law. Except for this restriction the rulers are free to rule as they see fit (except for the necessity of taking counsel, as discussed later). In the Italian cities the citizens have a more active role; the actual practice there, the reference to statutes instead of law, and the whole tenor of the passage implies a citizenry involved continually in the process of government. The consent mentioned here is not the passive consent to the rule of a monarch but active consent to almost any measure taken by the city or its officers. The podesta has no authority beyond that granted directly by the people.

The other forms and modes of rule may be legitimate, but it is only regal monarchy that is perfect and ordained by God. The arguments that Thomas and others gave to show that monarchy (not necessarily regal) is an acceptable form, Giles takes as absolute justification for it: not only is the regal king most natural, he best preserves unity and the common good.[26] The polity is an entity hierarchically located between the universe and the individual, both of which are ruled regally, and each person is a microcosm (*minor mundus*):

> Just as all the universe is directed by one ruler, God, who is a separate and pure intellect, all things which are in a person, if they are properly to be governed, must be governed by intellect and reason. If, therefore, the government of the whole universe is assimilated to the government which ought to be in one person, since the city is part of the universe, much more should the government of the whole city be reserved to one house.[27]

---

semper ibi adnotetur potestas vel cominus aliquis, qui civitatem regat; magis tamen dominatur totus populus, quam dominus adnotatus, eo quod totius populi est eum eligere et corrigere, si male agat: etiam eius totius est statuta condenda, quae non licet dominum transgredi."

[26] Giles of Rome, *De Regimine Principum*, 3.2.3.269v–270r, 2.3.16.229v.

[27] Giles of Rome, *De Regimine Principum*, 2.1.14.154v. "Nam sicut universum dirigitur uno principe, ut uno deo, qui est intellectus separatus et purus: sic omnia, quae sunt in homine, si debite regi debent, regenda sunt intellectu et ratione. . . . Si ergo regimen totius

The soul and God rule regally in the full sense of the word, and this proves that regal rule is more rational.

Nonetheless, Giles frequently imposes restrictions and limitations on his regal king. Even a hypothetical medieval supporter of absolute kingship would maintain the supremacy of divine and natural law, but Giles also wants his "semidivine" ruler to obey even human law in most cases: "It is expedient that as much as possible all things be determined through the law, and that as few things as possible be committed to judgment by will."[28] The only normal exceptions are when particular circumstances make it desirable or necessary to suspend the law to protect equity or justice, but as the source of positive law the king cannot be bound to it absolutely. For this reason Giles argues that all of Aristotle's statements in support of the primacy of law refer only to natural law.[29]

Thomas also recognized the limitations of laws and allowed their suspension in particular cases and admitted that the king, though theoretically subject to law, was free from its coercive power and was above it in the sense that no one was competent to judge him.[30] Although their emphasis and underlying justification are entirely different, the two positions are not practically very different. Thomas strengthens the power of his political king; Giles weakens that of his regal monarch. Nevertheless, as the Carlyles insist, Giles's theoretical freeing of the king from positive law is a highly significant development in that it contradicts most medieval political theory to that time and paves the way for the genuine theories of absolute monarchy that reach their apex in early modern times.[31]

Giles, alone of Aristotle and the medieval Aristotelians, rejects any role for the multitude, either for expediency or their wisdom, but he does substantially dilute the king's unlimited power by requiring him to take coun-

---

universi assimilatur regimini quod debet esse in uno homine: cum civitas sit pars universi, regimen totius civitatis multo magis reservabitur in una domo."

[28] Giles of Rome, *De Regimine Principum*, 3.2.20.300r. "Expedit quantum possibile est per legem omnia determinari, et quam paucissima arbitrio iudicum committere." 3.2.30.317r. "Decet ergo reges et principes, ad quos competit esse quasi semideos . . . sic se habere ad legem divinam, naturalem, et humanam: ut sicut excedunt alios potentia et dignitate, sic eos superent bonitate et virtute."

[29] Giles of Rome, *De Regimine Principum*, 3.2.29.314v–315r. Of course, this is not what Aristotle meant at all. There is a primitive idea of natural law in Aristotle that is reflected in his ideas on natural rule, but this has nothing to do with the extensive medieval conception of natural law. The only law in a community that Aristotle recognizes is human law, made by those in the polity with authority to make law. This idea is not revived in medieval times until Marsilius of Padua, and even this is arguable. See *Defensor pacis*, 1.12.2–3, 1.13.8; and Alan Gewirth, *Marsilius of Padua. The Defender of Peace*, vol. 1, p. 170ff.

[30] Thomas Aquinas, *Summa Theologiae*, 1–2.96.5ad 3.

[31] Carlyle and Carlyle, *Medieval Political Theory*, vol. 5, p. 75. They, however, misinterpret Giles's categories of regal and political rule, and contrast monarchy per se with political rule.

sel with the wise few—who together can know more than the one.[32] Since Aristotle, in Giles's opinion, favored monarchy, he rationalizes the arguments in the *Politics* for the rule of the many as having been advanced relatively, or as the opinions of others—as straw dogs to be refuted—or as reasons for consulting the few:

> Aristotle, in the Third Book of the *Politics*, seems to touch on three reasons through which it seems to be proved that it would be better for a city or province to be governed by many than by one. Many eyes see more than one, many hands can do more, and many intellects rise above one in knowledge. Whence if many exercise dominion, there will be there more perspicacious reason, because the many will know more things than if one alone should rule. Whence Aristotle says in III *Politics* that when the many thus rule they constitute as it were one man with many eyes and hands. . . . A ruler has right intention if he does not intend his own good but the common good. . . . If the many exercise dominion, even if they intend only their own good . . . they do not wholly recede from the common good. . . . But the good of one is wholly a private good. . . . The one is more easily corrupted than the many. . . . [All these objections can be answered in the same way.] For, the ruler or the king . . . ought to associate to himself many wise ones that they might have many and good [qualities] and virtues, that he might have many feet and many hands, and in effect become as it were one man of many eyes, hands, and feet. It cannot then be said that the monarch does not know many things, for, insofar as it pertains to the rule of the kingdom, whatever all those wise ones know the king himself is said to know. . . . And if the king desires to exercise dominion rightly, he cannot possibly be perverted unless all the counsel and all the wise and just ones whom he associated to himself happen to be perverse. For such a one especially intends the common good.[33]

[32] Giles of Rome, *De Regimine Principum*, 3.2.17.294v. "Plura cognoscere possunt multi, quam unus."

[33] Giles of Rome, *De Regimine Principum*, 3.2.4.270v–272r. "Philosophus III Politicorum videtur tangere tres rationes, per quas probari videtur, quod melius sit civitatem aut provinciam regi pluribus, quam uno . . . plures oculi plus vident quam unus, et plures manus plus possunt quam una, et plures intellectus superant unum in cognoscendo: quare si dominentur plures, erit ibi perspicatior ratio, quia plura cognoscent, quam si principaretur unus tantum: unde Philosophus III Politicorum ait quod plures homines sic principantes quasi constituunt unum hominum multorum oculorum et multarum manuum . . . principans rectam habet intentionem, si non intendat bonum proprium sed commune . . . si dominentur multi dato quod intendunt bonum proprium . . . non omnino recedunt ab intentione communis boni . . . bonum unius est quasi bonum omnino privatum . . . facilius corrumpitur unus quam plures . . . ille princeps vel ille rex (secundum Philosophum III Politicorum) debet sibi associare multos sapientes, ut habeant [habeat?] multos oculos et multos bonos et virtuosos, ut habeat multos pedes et multas manus: et sic fiet unus homo multorum oculorum, multarum manuum, et multorum pedum. Non ergo dici poterit talem unum monarchiam non cognoscere multa; quia quantum spectat ad regimen regni, quicquid omnes illi sapientes cognoscunt,

The first part of this passage seems to mean only that a king will naturally want to get advice from experts. The last sentence seems stronger, as does a comment a few chapters earlier that, if the king spurns his council and follows his own whims, he would be a tyrant—something worse than the simple rule of many. All this implies that the king's council does have some sort of controlling power—the king seems bound to follow its advice.[34] In some ways it is more important than the ruler. Both Aristotle and Thomas Aquinas had insisted that a king must rule according to virtue, that his only claim to dominance was superiority. But Giles makes a startling innovation and denies this: "If there is some defect in the son and successor of a king, to whom the royal care ought to come, he can be completed through wise and good men to whom the king ought to join himself in society as if they were his hands and feet."[35]

Is the king nothing more, then, than a unifying figurehead? No, because the counselors have no independent existence, as do Thomas's few; the king appoints them, and although he must have advisors, their identity is his choice alone. In fact, he should choose his friends who will be most loyal and give the best counsel.[36] The model is not of king and parliament, but of king and privy council. Giles writes that Aristotle compared the king in his kingdom to the soul in the body, and Aristotle insisted that this rule is despotic.[37] The counselors are additional limbs for the king—and just like

---

totum ipse rex cognoscere dicitur . . . si rex recte dominari desiderat, non est possibile ipsum perverti, nisi totum consilium, et omnes sapientes, et bonos quos sibi associavit, contingeret esse perversos: talis enim maxime intendit commune bonum." See also 3.2.4.271v.

[34] Giles of Rome, *De Regimine Principum*, 3.2.4.272r. "Si autem aliter se haberet, ut spreto consilio, et dimissa societate sapientum et bonorum, vellet sequi caput proprium, et appetitum privatum, iam non esset rex sed tyrannus: tale ergo dominari non esset melius quam plures." On many other occasions Giles stresses the necessity and importance of counsel. See, e.g., 3.2.8.279v, 3.2.1.267r.

[35] Giles of Rome, *De Regimine Principum*, 3.2.5.274v. "Si aliquis defectus esset in filio regis, ad quem deberet regia cura pervenire, suppleri poterit per sapientes et bonos, quos tanquam manus et oculos debet sibi rex in societate coniungere." This is related to Giles's support for hereditary monarchy. Aristotle wrote that if there should happen to exist one man whose virtue exceeds that of all other citizens together, it seems only right that he should rule. This idea is barely mentioned by Giles. His only allusion to it is at the end of a long list of things a king should do to preserve himself in his dominion. He should be good and virtuous, and since greater virtue is required in the guardian of a city or kingdom than in any other leader, he should be as it were a semigod excelling others in dignity and power (3.2.15.291v). Kingship is right not because of the king's virtue, but because it reflects the divine order and brings peace to a community.

[36] Giles of Rome, *De Regimine Principum*, 3.2.18.297r. "Consiliarii debent esse non solum boni sed amici . . . quia amicorum est amicis vera et bona consulere."

[37] Giles of Rome, *De Regimine Principum*, 3.2.34.323v. "[Philosophus] comparat regem ad regnum sicut animam ad corpus." Aristotle, *Politics*, 1.5.1254.b.3. The king rules his counselors despotically, even though he rules the kingdom regally, since he uses them not for their own good but for his—which in this case is the common good of the kingdom. In a com-

other limbs they are to be used absolutely for the owner's purpose. The point is not that the king is bound to his council, but that his solicitude for his kingdom and fears for its safety will lead him to seek the advice of those who will be able to help him preserve it.[38] In no case is there to be any other basis for law than the will of the king. If he sincerely intends the common good he will naturally conform his actions to the wisest decision—in this sense he should not spurn his council, but there is no compulsion for him to assent to its will, and certainly not if its opinion is counter to the ends of the community. Thus, although the council might share in rule in that it fulfills many of the functions of the state, it lacks the independence necessary for an element of a mixed constitution.

Neither does the popular or aristocratic element participate by way of election of the monarch, as in Thomas's mixed constitution; Giles comes squarely down on the side of succession by heredity. His arguments, which essentially coincide with those of Peter of Auvergne, become the standard ones.[39] Speaking absolutely, he says, election is better: the effects of chance and fortune are minimized, and as a result there will be a better and more industrious king. But heredity is more expedient given the actual conditions in the world, and the corrupt desires of people. The king in this case will be more solicitous for the kingdom, those accustomed to power use it more wisely, and people will more willingly obey a long-familiar dynasty. Like all human arrangements, this procedure is not flawless, but it is less perilous than election.[40]

Giles's use of expediency as an argument for hereditary succession does not alter the observation that because of his infusion of divine and universal concerns into the achievement of the common good, questions of practicality and individual conditions have little hold on him. It is interesting to contrast the arguments that Giles uses to support monarchy in the first place with those used to defend heredity. In the first case he gives practical reasons to be sure, but his case rests on the harmony of monarchy with the natural order and its reflection of the divine hierarchy: kingship is better simply, and he is unwilling to make concessions to the particular conditions of different peoples. It is only with respect to election that he relies on expediency, or to be more precise, on experiential (*experimentaliter*)

---

pletely analogous way the paterfamilias rules his slaves despotically for the good of the household.

[38] Giles of Rome, *De Regimine Principum*, 3.2.15.291r. "Quicunque enim amat, soliciatur, et timet, ne aliquod inconveniens accidat circa amatum . . . adhibebit multa consilia qualiter possit bona regni promovere, et periculis imminentibus obviare."

[39] Thomas Aquinas gave arguments only in support of election. As usual, Demongeot, *Le Meilleur regime*, p. 59, attributes Peter of Auvergne's views to Thomas. Richard Scholz, *Aegidius von Rom*, p. 77, recognizes correctly that Giles's position represents a break with Aquinas.

[40] Giles of Rome, *De Regimine Principum*, 3.2.5.272v–275r.

data contrary to deductions from pure reason.[41] His rejection of election, which is better absolutely, because of the "corrupted desire of most men" still does not hinge on a pure criterion of expediency. Rather it refers to the effects of original sin, which is applicable in every, or almost every, situation.[42] That he does not try to base hereditary rule in nature reflects perhaps the influence of the practice of election of Church officials, including the ecclesiastical monarch, the pope, and his recognition that the arguments for election advanced by Aristotle and Aquinas were too powerful to be dismissed from first principles. In any case his initial deductions are based on reason alone. Only then, he implies, if experience teaches that our deductions are in error, should we alter our conclusions. Experience is neither the starting point nor the criterion of choice for determining the type of government and it can only contradict pure reason in exceptional circumstances—in this case because of the altered condition of fallen man.

This conclusion suggests why Giles gave scant attention to mixed constitutional theories: these were almost invariably approached from considerations of expediency.[43] How can certain ill effects of regimes be avoided? How can we unite the good features of different forms? How can everyone be satisfied? These are distant indeed from questions of the rule of the universe or the soul.

Although the metaphysical component of good government is absent in the thoughts of no medieval Aristotelian, it is only Giles who makes it the primary criterion. Polity, aristocracy, or political monarchy might be legitimate or even beneficial, but only regal monarchy is fully in harmony with the universe. This formulation brings down divine approbation upon the medieval kingdom and gives a theoretical justification for an extension of the monarch's authority, while stopping short of a Pauline justification of all government.

In *On the Government of Rulers* Giles is trying to impose an Aristotelian vision of politics on an underlying Augustinian outlook. The Aristotelian conception of humans as naturally social animals, which Giles picked up from Thomas Aquinas, forced him to see government as originating from the community, despite his Augustinian background. Giles responds by

[41] Lewis, "Natural Law," pp. 153–54, points out that in opposition to Thomas Aquinas, Giles and other papalists generally opposed the test of expediency as a criterion of good government, since such a criterion threatened any a priori structure on society. It is certainly true that the most insistent fourteenth-century proponents of expediency—Marsilius of Padua and William of Ockham—were strong opponents of the papacy.

[42] Giles temporizes with the word *most*; not wanting totally to reject the Aristotelian arguments, he raises at least the possibility that for some peoples election is better even now. Ptolemy of Lucca advances a similar argument—the nature of man is such that monarchy is usually best, but there can exist men virtuous enough for political rule.

[43] Lewis, "Natural Law," p. 159, also makes this point about mixed constitutional theories in general and expediency.

promoting the idea that Thomas Aquinas and Augustine shared a common view of the origin of political power. Thomas Aquinas had already taken some steps to make this assimilation possible and palatable. It was to become ubiquitous in late medieval political discourse, and can be found to the present day. In his commentary on the *Sentences*, Giles interprets the opening comments of Augustine's *City of God*, 19.15 (where Augustine denies that humans were to have dominion over any but irrational creatures) as referring only to servitude. That is, in any society there must be dominion, but before the Fall there was no despotic dominion.[44] As a natural product of the community, founded to serve the common good of the community (not from God as punishment for sin, as Augustine believed), the state could only exist by the consent of the community. This right is only implicit in *On the Government of Rulers*, but Giles states it explicitly in the later and generally less Aristotelian *On the Renunciation of the Pope*:

> But although the nature of the situation requires that those who know how to foresee dangers better be placed in authority over the others, so that the multitude is preserved under their governance, nevertheless it is necessary that they fulfill this through the consent of humans. And although it is perfected and fulfilled through the consent of humans that one is placed in authority over the others, it can happen in a contrary way by the consent of humans that the one in authority might fall or even be deposed.[45]

To this extent Ullmann is correct when he writes that *On the Government of Rulers* contains a superficial exposition of the ascending thesis of government.[46] And yet the idea of the regal king as the embodiment of a universal order is neither Aristotelian nor ascending. Giles could not resolve the tension between the two views, and in later works he opts for a divine source of power, what Ullmann would call a defense of the descending thesis of government. In essentials this argument is correct, but the strict contrast Ullmann draws between the two theses of government, however useful the concept has proved, is too simple, as many critics have already noted. The common formulation of authority as being "from God and the people" combines the two approaches, leaves room for a continuum of opinion, and makes a change of emphasis by the same writer easier to explain.

[44] Giles of Rome, *In Sententiarum*, 2.D.44q.1.a2–3. See R. L. Markus, "Two Conceptions of Political Authority," p. 97, n. 1.

[45] Giles of Rome, *De Renunciatione Papae*, chap. 16, 41b. "Sed quamvis sic requirit natura negotii, quod scientes melius pericula praevidere, aliis praeficiantur, ut sub eorum gubernaculo multitudo salvetur, oportet tamen quod hoc compleatur per consensum hominum. Et sicut per consensum hominum perficitur, et completur, ut quis aliis praeficiatur, sic per consensum hominum contrario modo factum fieri potest, quod Praefectus cedat, vel quod etiam deponatur."

[46] Ullmann, *Law and Politics*, p. 274.

Giles's analysis of sovereignty also reveals a conflict over the origin of power. He mentions four necessary factors in any government—the prince, council, judicial organs, and the people—and says that in a sense the state is a mixture of these elements.[47] But he does not envision any balance of these elements or any tempering effect of the one on the others. It is his position that sovereignty must reside in one of the elements. In this we see a real break in the medieval tradition, and once again Giles lays the groundwork for later monarchists. At one point he comes close to a critique of the mixed constitution:

> Even if many elements come together to the constitution of the same mixed body, it is necessary that there be some predominant element, according to which that mixed body reaches its proper motion or situation. Whence the earth dominates in all mixed things, since all such are heavy and naturally tend down. . . . Since human society is natural . . . never from many humans will one society or polity happen naturally, unless it be natural that some rule and others serve. Therefore, some are naturally lords, and some naturally servants.[48]

The problem is that a vesting of sovereignty in the king cannot comfortably coexist with a theory of consent by the people. If the king can only rule at the people's pleasure, it does not really matter whether he rules by his own will or by laws given by the people—sovereignty can logically in this case be ascribed only to the people. Giles tries unsuccessfully to have it both ways. He could have overcome this last contradiction through an explicit advocacy of a mixed constitution, giving both the people and the king a share of power. By so doing he could have nicely integrated his theory of a family united under a variety of regimes by one paterfamilias. By insisting on the necessity of the counsel of the wise, and by basing government on consent, and in the ideal case on the election of the people, Giles came close to doing just this. He does describe in this way the medieval reality in which government was a mixture of monarchy and aristocracy resting on the passive consent of the people. It was this reality that others interpreted as an Aristotelian mixed constitution.

[47] Giles of Rome, *De Regimine Principum*, 3.2. See also Scholz, *Aegidius*, pp. 77ff.

[48] Giles of Rome, *De Regimine Principum*, 2.2.13.225v. "Sic etiam si plura elementa concurrunt ad constitutionem eiusdem corporis mixti, oportet aliquod elementum praedominans, secundum quod illi mixto competat debitus motus aut debitus situs. Inde est ergo quod in omnibus mixtis dominatur terra: quia omnia talia sunt gravia et naturaliter deorsum tendunt . . . cum societas hominum sit naturalis . . . nunquam ex pluribus hominibus fieret naturaliter una societas vel una politia, nisi naturale esset aliquos principari et aliquos servire. Sunt ergo aliqui naturaliter domini, et aliqui naturaliter servi."

Chapter 5

PETER OF AUVERGNE

PETER OF AUVERGNE (1240s–1304), also known as Petrus de Alvernia and Peter de Cros (or Crocq), was born in the town of Crocq in Auvergne and ended his life in Clermont less than three years after Pope Boniface VIII appointed him bishop there. He studied at the University of Paris and probably attended Thomas Aquinas's lectures. Whether or not that is the case, he was dedicated to Thomas and his teaching, although he never joined the Dominican order. Instead, he became a secular master at the University and in 1275 the papal legate, Simon de Brie, named him rector in a temporarily successful attempt to conciliate between factions led by Siger of Brabant and Alberic of Reims. Afterwards, he again took up his theological studies, this time under Henry of Ghent and Godfrey of Fontaines, became a master of theology in 1296, and taught in Paris until 1302. During this period he became embroiled in a theological controversy with John of Paris over the nature of formal beatitude. After his episcopal appointment Peter traveled to Rome and then returned to Paris, where in 1303 he joined John and many others in supporting Phillip IV's appeal to a General Council against Boniface VIII.

Peter wrote a great number of commentaries and questions on Aristotle and Porphyry, as well as many theological works. He also completed several of Thomas Aquinas's unfinished works, including his *Exposition on Aristotle's Books of Politics* (henceforth, *Commentary*).[1] Today, there is some controversy over the extent of Thomas's influence on Peter's mature thought; scholars have detected the influence also of his various theology masters, Averroes, and Avicenna, and some have thought that his Aristotelianism goes beyond that acceptable to Thomas. But even in Peter's own lifetime, Ptolemy of Lucca, for example, called him Thomas Aquinas's "most faithful disciple."[2]

In the *Commentary* itself certain formal similarities have supported this opinion and have led most scholars to judge that Thomas's and Peter's methodology, approach, and conclusions are indistinguishable. In the ensuing seven hundred years there has been some controversy about which parts of the *Commentary* were written by Thomas Aquinas and which by

[1] Peter of Auvergne, *In Libros Politicorum Aristotelis Expositio.*

[2] Ptolemy of Lucca, *Historia Ecclesiastica*, 23.11. Much of what we know of Peter's life comes from Ptolemy's brief sketch.

Peter, but no one has yet suggested any significant differences. One modern scholar writes that there is "no change in emphasis from Thomas Aquinas."[3] Others, including Marcel Demongeot, go so far as consciously to use Peter's part of the *Commentary* in discussing Thomas Aquinas's political theory.[4] No matter how similar the two are, there is no way to justify this procedure unless, as many thought in the nineteenth and early twentieth century, Peter was simply transcribing or paraphrasing Thomas's lecture notes. This is not tenable. The two parts of the work differ stylistically: Peter is consistently more expansive than Thomas, and, significantly, the two commentaries actually overlap—both cover the first six lectures of book 3.[5] In my opinion one of the biggest stumbling blocks to understanding Thomas's beliefs—let alone Peter's—has been the tendency, even among those who should know better, to regard the whole *Commentary* as representing a single political outlook.

Because Peter has always been linked so closely to Thomas Aquinas, no one has written about him as an independent political thinker. The little that has been written is mostly concerned with problems of manuscript tradition and authenticity.[6] Fortunately, we need not rely on Peter's continuation of Thomas alone, for he was also the author of a *Questions on the "Politics"* (henceforth, *Questions*).[7] This work is largely abstract and philosophical and is completely without historical analysis and examples—Lagarde calls Peter's social ideas "superficial stammerings."[8] Its format, however, ensures a more or less clear-cut answer to certain fundamental problems in political theory.

When we reconstruct Peter's views from these two sources, a somewhat different picture emerges from the customary one. He is faithful to Thomas Aquinas in some matters and in his general approach. This formal agreement and the fact that Thomas Aquinas's distinction of regal and political power has generally been misunderstood perhaps account for the general consensus that their views are identical. But on the question of the best form of government, the contrast is striking. Peter shows little sympathy for Thomas's distinction between regal and political rule, and at first glance, seems to oscillate between support for a mixed constitution and

---

[3] Cranz, *Aristotelianism*, p. 161.

[4] Demongeot, *Le Meilleur regime*, p. 15.

[5] Peter of Auvergne, *In Libros Politicorum, the Inedited Part*. Gundissalvus Grech, the editor, discusses the controversy over Peter's debt to Aquinas on p. 51.

[6] See Grech, "Manuscript Tradition" and E. Hocedez, "La vie et les oeuvres de Pierre d'Auvergne," for biographical information and bibliography. Ullmann, *History of Political Thought*, p. 185, asserts promisingly, "Peter of Auvergne struck up quite radical materialist chords," but then relates this only to ideas on the limitation of family size.

[7] Peter of Auvergne, *Questiones super Politicum*.

[8] George de Lagarde, Review of Conor Martin's *The Commentaries on the Politics of Aristotle in the Late Thirteenth and Early Fourteenth Centuries*, p. 381.

support for a hereditary king ruling by his own will. In some cases his arguments seem closer to Giles of Rome than to Thomas Aquinas, although Giles more consciously rejected nonmonarchical rule. The contrast between Peter's two positions is particularly evident in the *Questions*.[9] I believe that Peter does hold a consistent position. Like Thomas Aquinas, Peter saw the mixed constitution as the best form of government, but envisioned it differently in its structure and in the function and nature of its component parts. In addition, he supports it for different reasons.

The key to Peter's position and one of his most striking differences with Thomas is his conception of the citizen body as a whole. Thomas insisted on a role for it for practical reasons only—to avoid strife and ensure contentment. It never crossed his mind that the many might actually be better rulers than the king or a few wise men. Aristotle, of course, realized that, quite aside from practical reasons, the many has a just claim to rule, and even at times praised its ability. Peter follows Aristotle and rehabilitates the people by seizing upon a distinction made casually in the *Politics*—that between a multitude that is "vile" or "bestial" and one that is not. Aristotle wrote: "If a multitude is not exceedingly vile, any member of it will be a worse judge than the knowledgeable men, but all gathered together will be better, or at least not worse."[10]

Peter takes this as his criterion for determining whether the many should rule:

> It is clear that it is more expedient for the whole multitude to exercise dominion than just a few. . . . But if the multitude is vile, in which no one is wise or prudent, it would not be expedient. . . . Two things are required for the government of a polity. One is right reason; this that [non-vile] multitude has through its wise men. The second is potency so that it can coerce and punish the evil; this however it [the multitude] has through the people.[11]

---

[9] If Cranz, *Aristotelianism*, p. 161, is correct that the *Questions* predate the *Commentary*, it may be that his views have become more consistent by the later work, but it must also be added that the views of the *Commentary* are more conservative and less divorced from the words of the *Politics*.

[10] Aristotle, *Politics*, 3.11.1282a.14f. "Si sit multitudo non nimis vilis: erit enim unusquisque quidem deterior iudex scientibus, omnes autem congregati meliores, aut non deteriores."

[11] Peter of Auvergne, *In Libros Politicorum*, 3.9.438. "Et manifestum est quod expedit magis dominari totam multitudinem quam aliquos. . . . Sed si esset talis multitudo vilis in qua nullus esset sapiens nec prudens, non expederet . . . duo exiguntur in regimine politiae. Unum est ratio recta; hoc autem habet ista multitudo per illos sapientes. Aliud est potentia, ut possit coercere et punire malos: hoc autem habet per populum." The point about the multitude possessing wisdom and power is one he makes frequently. See, e.g., *In Libros Politicorum*, 4.4.581, 4.5.594. In 3.11.459 Peter essentially repeats the argument here (substituting "right ruling" for "right reason") that a nonvile multitude should rule. See also 3.8.426 for the bestial multitude.

In a way this rehabilitates the many, and certainly leaves the way open for active and substantial participation. On the other hand it takes away the absolute right to have at least some share in government—if it is bestial it has no right to anything. Peter expects every or almost every person to make a contribution, if only of agreement to the ideas of the wise. If the majority is without reason it will not be able to understand the common good and, therefore, should not rule. Even if most are reasonable, the wise should still propose actions for the multitude to ratify. So when Peter refers to the rule of the reasonable multitude, he really is talking about a mixed constitution: it is aristocratic in that the few virtuous rule according to their reason and prudence, it is democratic in that the many rules by reason of its power.

Peter himself refers to a nonbestial multitude as being mixed from wise men and the common people in a passage that takes up the whole question of the best government:

> Therefore, the ruling [person] ought to be prudent and virtuous in himself. Besides, since it is necessary that the citizens should obey him as a lord, it is necessary that he have power consequently of coercing rebellious subjects and repulsing adversaries, and, therefore, that he should have firstly and in himself prudence and virtue, but potency he has accidentally and consequentially. Therefore, what is meant is that a non-persuasible multitude of erring people is one thing—this is a bestial multitude and it is born to be under despotic rule. A well-persuasible multitude mixed from the wise and the common is another thing. If, therefore, one asks about the first multitude, I say that it is certainly not worthy to rule. Now, it is expedient by right that the first be ruled by despotic [rule] since it does not have virtue and prudence, since although it has potency it is hot-headed and non-persuasible. But if the question is understood about the second multitude, it must be said that that ought more to rule than the few virtuous. The reason is that . . . it is more expedient that that rule which attains simultaneously to those three things which are necessary to rule than that which only attains to two. But this is that multitude, for in so far as there are prudent men in it it has prudence and virtue, and in so far as there are many it has potency. But the few attain to two, and, therefore, it is more expedient that such a multitude dominate than the few virtuous.[12]

[12] Peter of Auvergne, *Questiones*, 3.q.15.295rb–295va. See also *Questiones*, 3.q.16.295vb and *In Libros Politicorum*, 3.9.435. "Ideo principans per se debet esse prudens et virtuosus. Ulterius quia oportet ut cives ei sicut domino obediant. Oportet autem ut potestatem ex consequenti habeat subditos rebelles fierunt cohercendi et adversarios expugnandi et ideo eum per se et primo habere prudentiam et virtutem potentiam autem per accidens et ex consequenti. Intendum ergo quod quidam est multitudo erronum ut[sc. in]persuasibilis et hoc est multitudo bestialis et nata subesse principatu dispotico. Altera autem multitudo bene persuasibilis mixta ex sapientibus et ex vulgatibus bene persuasibilis. Si ergo queritur de prima multitudine dico quod omnino non est dignum principari. Nunc hoc expedit primo secun-

Although the multitude comprises the whole mass of the people—the common people, the rich, the virtuous, and the nobles—its virtue is not, as it was for Aristotle, the summation of all the individual virtues, which necessarily yielded a greater wisdom than that of any smaller group. In this Peter stands between Aristotle and Thomas—he denies the collective wisdom of the multitude and ascribes its superiority to the submultitude of the wise and virtuous. The multitude itself provides the power naturally present in its size.[13] This explains, incidentally, why a bestial multitude requires a despotic government: although the many are devoid of virtue, power still resides in their number. They cannot be ruled as free men against their wishes, and they are incapable of choosing wisely; therefore, they must be subdued by force.

The most important idea in this passage is that if the multitude is not bestial it should itself rule. This may sound tame enough, but it has a revolutionary consequence far surpassing anything dreamed of by any previous (or most future) mixed constitutionalists: all good, legitimate government is mixed government. In particular, pure monarchy or aristocracy—the rule of one or a few for the common good—is impossible, for in both the many must also rule. Otherwise, if the multitude were bestial, only despotism would be suitable. So, calling a government "monarchic" or "aristocratic" simply identifies the dominant element of a mixed constitution. But what of the simple form of polity? The same conclusion is valid. Since the many properly rules in collaboration with the wise, simple polity must itself be a mixture of polity and aristocracy. Elsewhere, with Aristotle, Peter depicts polity as a mixture of oligarchy and democracy, which in this

dum iure debet despotico principatu [principari] cum quia non habet virtutem at prudenciam. Cum licet habeat potentiam habet cum hoc impetum ferventius et est inpersuasibilis. Si autem intelligatur questio de secunda multitudine, dicendum quod expedit illam magis principari quam paucos virtuosos. Cuius ratio est quia . . . illud magis expedit principari quod attingit simul ad illa tali [sc. tres] qui exiguntur ad principatem quam illud quod solum attingit ad duo. Sed hoc est ista multitudo in quantum enim in ea sunt prudentes, habet prudentiam et virtutem. In quantum autem multi habet potentiam. Pauci autem ad prima duo tamen attingunt et ideo magis expedit multitudinem talem dominari quam paucos etiam virtuosos."

[13] In part, this difference rests on yet another mistranslation of Aristotle, who speculated that the combined virtue of all the individual people might not produce a superior result in every community (*Politics*, 3.11.1281b.15). Moerbecke's translation makes Aristotle wonder whether the "whole multitude," which is better than the few virtuous, refers to the whole people or only to the multitude of the virtuous. See *In Libros Politicorum*, 3.8.287. "Siquidem igitur circa totum populum et circa totam multitudinem, contigit hanc esse differentiam multorum ad paucos studiosos, immanifestum." Peter goes on to deny the superiority of the whole multitude if the multitude is bestial, and thereby demonstrates that he also questions its applicability to every people, but he also takes the hint provided by the mistranslation (*In Libros Politicorum*, 3.8.426). "Immanifestum est utrum huiusmodi differentiam contingat esse circa multitudinem, et circa populum totum ad paucos virtuosos, quod scilicet tota multitudo melior sit quam illi pauci virtuosi."

context means the same thing.[14] The mixture of polity, this time a threefold one, is also what he has in mind when he writes that wherever the people rule they appropriate aspects of the other polities since they choose captains and one man over those.[15] Of course, Peter does not come right out and say that all good government is mixed, but the implication is unavoidable. What I have talked about so far concerns mostly the many or few, but there is no doubt that Peter favors monarchy above all other forms, at least given the best conditions. We would expect this monarchy to be mixed. He writes that it is best because it is according to right reason, and as such it will last the longest. Also because simply speaking it alone provides unity and as such is most similar to natural government. So much so that any other rule is good and valid only insofar as it imitates monarchy.[16] In the *Questions* Peter describes the mixture of forms in his perfect monarchy when he defends it against the charge that the many is more suited for rule than one:

> Or it may be argued by saying that that reasoning does not prove simply that it is better for many to rule than one. But if there is one, under him many can rule who might see and judge. For, one cannot occupy himself with all things. Therefore, this line of reasoning seems to ask whether under such a one there should be many who judge, for since he cannot do and intend all things it is necessary that under him there should be some as counselors who might judge, and this is a kingdom with the virtue of aristocracy. Likewise, it is necessary that a polity under a kingdom remain an oligarchy. For, if there are some notable and noble men they would desire some dignity from the king, and similarly it is necessary that the people attain some dignity, and thus it happens that a regal-oligarchy-monarchy as it were in virtue contains all other polities—I do not say this according to excellence and excess of them, but according to something else.[17]

[14] See, for example, Peter of Auvergne, *Questiones*, 4.q.9.

[15] Peter of Auvergne, *In Libros Politicorum*, 3.14.503. "Verumtamen ubi populus dominatur, aliquid accipitur ab aliis politiis. Faciunt enim aliquos capitaneos et unum supra illos."

[16] Peter of Auvergne, *In Libros Politicorum*, 4.1, 3.13, 5.11, and 5.12; *Questiones*, 3.q.26.

[17] Peter of Auvergne, *Questiones*, III.q.26ad rat., 300ra. "Vel arguitur dicendum quod ista ratio non probat simpliciter quod melius sit principari plures quam unum. Sed si sit unus sub illo possunt plures principari qui videant et iudicent. Unus enim non potest vacare omnibus. Et ideo hec ratio querere videtur utrum sub tali uno sint plures qui iudicent. Oportet enim cum ad omnia non possit vacare et intendere quod sub ipso sint aliqui ut consiliarii qui iudicent et hoc est regnum in virtute aristocracie. Item oportet quod policia sub regno maneat oligarchia si enim sint aliqui insignes et nobiles a rege optineant alicam dignitatem et similiter oportet quod populus ad aliquam dignitaciam attingat et sic contigit quod oligarchia monarchia regalis quasi virtute contineat omnes alias policias non dico secundum excelentiam et excessum eorum sed secundum aliquid aliud." Notice that the word *plures* is used here (and sometimes elsewhere) to denote the few wise and virtuous men who are many but still not the whole multitude. The concluding phrase means that the mixed constitution does not

Peter is arguing that one ruler may be best absolutely, but for theoretical and practical reasons he must share his power with the wise, the nobles, and the whole people. Theoretically, the many and the wise can contribute effectively to the common good, and all these groups have a claim based on their power and significance to society that cannot be ignored. This last is especially relevant with respect to the oligarchs—who may have no particular virtue to contribute to government—but nobles exist and want to be recognized, so they cannot be ignored. Peter's idea of counselors differs from that of Giles of Rome, for whom these officials are tools of the ruler and do not represent the rule of any social group. In contrast, "under the king" for Peter means that the king is the first power in the state since it is a monarchy, but that the other groups have a right to exist and to have a share of government independent of the king. The monarchy, as he says, contains all other polities.[18]

The question then arises: What is to be the exact role of the multitude and of the few wise in a state in which a king is the dominant force? In his discussion of this point Peter sometimes seems to take away in practice much of what he has granted theoretically. At first Peter's statements may seem contradictory and confused, but it turns out that he simply has a different understanding of the mixed constitution than did Thomas Aquinas. Neither the few nor the many, he writes, is suited to the highest office in a state: "[Neither the many] nor the few can rule except insofar as they can reach consensus as one. Therefore, it is more expedient that one rule in the highest rule, and not many."[19]

An obvious objection to this argument is Peter's own often-repeated opinion that only the multitude has the requisites for rule: prudence, virtue, and power. His response?

> One unanimously elected to the highest rule has all those things in himself, for he has those things which are necessary in themselves for rule, namely, unity and prudence. Moreover, he has consequentially that which is required consequentially for rule, namely, potency. For, it follows that to be a ruler subjects

---

properly contain the simple polities, each somehow dominating, but is similar to each in some respects.

[18] This last comment suggests that at this point Peter is using a fourfold classification of government such as the one used by Thomas Aquinas and later by Engelbert of Admont. The similarity to the latter is most striking at this point—Engelbert will also refer to the mixture of monarchy, aristocracy, democracy, and polity as the mixture of all forms, and will also argue that all good government is mixed and write of the regrettable necessity of including the nobles. Engelbert, and possibly Peter, got this fourfold classification from Aristotle, *Rhetoric*, 1.8.1365b–1366a.

[19] Peter of Auvergne, *Questiones*, 3.q.16.295vb. "Item nec pauci possunt principari nisi inquantum consenciunt in unum. Ergo magis expedit principari unum principatu maximo et non multitudinem." Aristotle denied the highest rule to the many, but for a different reason—because they have no claim to goodness or excellence.

and electors obey him and thus consequentially he has potency through them, and therefore he has thus potency rightly, just as it is required for rule, that is, consequentially.[20]

Although power remains an accidental quality of the monarch, it seems that it can come from the passive consent of the multitude alone—for the few who serve as electors may have wisdom, but not power—unless Peter means that the whole multitude should serve to elect the king. What is most likely, and what accords with all that Peter writes about the nonbestial multitude, is that the few wise should propose the ruler for approval by the multitude—either explicitly or, in most cases, implicitly. In this sense the whole multitude should elect the prince:

> It is expedient that . . . a mixed and justly ordered multitude attain to that . . . because the election of a ruler requires two things, namely, counsel about investigating a good ruler and potency to compel that the elected one be accepted . . . therefore, it is especially expedient that [that which is to elect] have in itself counsel and power—but this is the multitude because it has prudence through its wise parts and power in itself . . . humans love their own works as sons, as is stated in the *Ethics* Book IX, and the multitude . . . will obey a ruler more insofar as it chooses. Likewise, with respect to correction since when a ruler has sinned it is required that a punishment be decided on and inflicted on him. But this is suitable for the multitude to do because the wise can discern the punishment, and it can be inflicted through the people.[21]

Peter poses some possible objections to election and correction and refutes them. At first his objections are limited to arguments for restricting these functions to the few wise men. His answer is just what we would expect: the few by themselves lack sufficient potency. His next argument is

---

[20] Peter of Auvergne, *Questiones*, 3.q.16.295vb. arg. 1 (posed), ad rat. 296ra (answered). "Item principatum maximum oportet habere potestatem et prudentiam. Sed hic duo habet sola multitudo, ergo, etc. . . . Unus unanimitus electus ad summum principatus omnia ista habet per se. Enim habet ea que per se ad principatus exiguntur, scilicet, unitatem et prudentiam, ex consequenti autem habet quod ex consequenti ad principatus requiritur, scilicet, potentiam. Nam ad esse principem sequitur ut subditi ei obediant et electores et sic ex consequenti habet per illos potentiam et ideo recte sic ipse habet potentiam sicut ipsa ad principatus requiritur hoc est ex consequenti."

[21] Peter of Auvergne, *Questiones*, 3.q.17.296ra–296rb. "Expedit . . . multitudinem tum mixtam et orditam iustam est attingere ad ista . . . quia electio princeps duo requirit, scilicit, consilium de principe bono investigando et potentiam ad cogendum electum ut recipiat . . . ergo maxime expedit quod in se habet consilium et potestatem. Sed hoc est multitudo quia per sapientes partes sui habet prudentiam, per se autem potentiam . . . homines diligere sua opera ut filios ut IX Ethicorum, et multitudo . . . principi quantum eligit magis obediat. Item ad correctos dum princeps peccavit exigitur . . . penam inveniendi et penam eam infligendi. Hoc autem convenit multitudinem quia sapientes penam discernent per populum autem eam infligere potest."

also familiar—he repeats Aristotle's statement that it is dangerous to allow the multitude to participate in the highest rule, interprets this as meaning having anything to do with the highest rule, even election and correction, and replies that this argument can apply only to the bestial multitude.[22] The exact role of the multitude is still unclear, but his contrast of the situation in which the few alone participate with that in which the many also participate with the few suggests something a bit stronger than passive consent, and certainly requires the active role of the few in any case.

But elsewhere Peter argues the opposite; namely, that hereditary rule is better than electoral in any case. His position is actually quite close to that of Giles of Rome: although election is better *per se*, succession is better *per accidens*.[23] He even advances some of the same justifications for this as did Giles: a king will be more solicitous for the kingdom if his son is to inherit his position, and custom renders hereditary rule more acceptable.[24] In addition, he provides some new arguments: "In election it can happen that there be dissension among the electors. Likewise, sometimes the electors are evil, and, therefore, it happens that they may choose a bad [ruler]. Both of these produce evil in the city. . . . Likewise, it is hard and strange that he who is today equal to another should tomorrow exercise dominion over him and be a ruler to him."[25] The last argument is really just another version of the argument from custom. While he did not do so, Peter could have easily overturned the first two by appealing to his favorite concept— the bestial multitude—for, as he says frequently, if it were not bestial neither objection would apply, and it would be deserving of rule. Probably Peter is trying to justify the de facto hereditary succession in the national monarchies of his day, such as the one in his native France. But in this case, what is left for the many, since it must properly have a share of rule?

First of all, correction. Peter never argues against this, and except for the force of custom, none of his criticisms of election could apply to correction

---

[22] Peter of Auvergne, *Questiones*, 3.q.17.296ra. "Sapiens est eligere et corrigere . . . cuius est eligere cuius est consiliari et conferre. Sed hoc est sapientes"; Aristotle, *Politics*, 3.11.1281b.16.

[23] Peter of Auvergne, *In Libros Politicorum*, 3.14.504. "Et est intelligendum quod per se semper melius est assumi regem per electionem quam per successionem: sed per successionem melius per accidens." See also *Questiones*, 3.q.25.299rb–299va. There is no way to tell if Peter got this argument from Giles. At least he was not using the same corrupt text since, unlike Giles, Peter understands correctly Aristotle's comment about it being difficult to believe that a father could refuse to hand power over to an unfit son, which Giles read as saying just the opposite.

[24] Peter of Auvergne, *Questiones*, 2.25.299va.

[25] Peter of Auvergne, *In Libros Politicorum*, 3.14.504. "In electione contingit esse dissentionem inter eligentes. Iterum quandoque eligentes mali sunt; et ideo contingit quod eligant malum. Utrumque autem istorum malum est in civitate . . . Iterum durum et extraneum est, quod ille qui est hodie aequalis alicui cras dominetur et sit princeps illi."

by a nonvile multitude. Second, the offices of counsel and judgment, which, as Peter repeatedly states, are not only within the competence of the many, but can actually be performed better by it.[26] Peter never goes into the details of these offices, either in their function or in their relationship to the king and the people, but certain aspects are clear. Since counsel is an aspect of the rule of the many, it is likely that Peter saw it as being constituted independently of the king. Since the few who serve as counselors derive their power from the people, Peter's arguments would make them subject to correction and, possibly, to election by the people. So even a hereditary monarchy could be a mixed government in a real sense. This is indeed how, for example, sixteenth- and seventeenth-century English theorists treated their own government and what was implied by Fortescue in the fifteenth century.

Unlike them, however, Peter equivocates about the place and proper source of law. Unlike Thomas Aquinas, Peter uses the terms *regal* and *political* loosely and thus cannot ground his mixed constitutional theory on it. Since his *Commentary* does not treat the sections of the *Politics* dealing with the family, in which the concepts are introduced, he never actually defines the terms, and although he does often associate regal rule with full power of the ruler and political rule with law, he also often identifies them with monarchy and rule of the many respectively. Like everyone else he also uses *political* to refer to any nondespotic government. In one description of the three good forms of polity Peter brings together all his meanings of political and thoroughly conflates the modes and forms of rule:

> He says that the royal status (*regius status*) is that to which a multitude is subject which is born to be subject by natural inclination to someone superexcelling in the virtue necessary for political or regal rule. The status of the best (*status optimatum*) is that to which a multitude is subject which is born to sustain the dominion of the multitude of studious, which multitude is born to be ruled by the rule of the best and of free men by those who rule according to the virtue ordered to political rule. The political status (*politicus* [*status*]) is a multitude which is born sometimes to be subject and sometimes to rule according to law, according to which rule or dignities are distributed.[27]

[26] Peter of Auvergne, *Questiones*, 3.q.26, 3.q.15; *In Libros Politicorum*, 3.14.495, 3.9.438. See also *Questiones*, 3.14.503.

[27] Peter of Auvergne, *In Libros Politicorum*, 3.1.16.524. "Dicit quod regius status est cui subiicitur multitudo quae nata est subiici secundum inclinationem naturalem alicui superexcellenti in virtute ad principatum politicum vel regalem. Status optimatum vero est cui subiicitur multitudo quae nata est sustinere dominium multitudinis studiosorum nata est regi principatu optimatum et liberorum ab his qui principantur secundum virtutem in ordine ad politicum principatum: politicus autem est multitudo quae nata est subiici et principari quandoque secundum legem, secundum quam distribuuntur principatus vel dignitates."

Although Peter does not insist on distinguishing regal and political rule, he does make what can be interpreted as the strongest statement in defense of law before Nicole Oresme in the late fourteenth century. Paradoxically, this comes in the midst of an argument for the ruler's ability to annul law, an argument made by Thomas Aquinas and virtually every other medieval Aristotelian:

> If something be discovered according to reason better than the positive law determines, it is relegated to the ruler so that he might ordain on behalf of law. So that two things are relegated to the ruler: one is to judge and dispense particulars rightly through the law, where it is possible that this be done by law; the second is that where the written law fails in some particular case he might direct, and this by his own virtue. But if the positive law is not well-ordained according to reason, it is relegated to the ruler, that with it relegated he might find a better, either by himself or from the consensus of the multitude, and that he might ordain by the law.[28]

Now everyone, including Aristotle, argues that the law might have to be put aside if it does not work in particular cases. What distinguishes Peter is that he assumes that new law is the remedy for this situation, and that the prince's will is not a valid basis for rule—except perhaps for a temporary emergency. This is clear from the change in prepositions from the beginning to the end of this passage: if the law fails the prince must act on his own on behalf of law (*pro lege*), but he should change the law so that he might act by law (*per legem*). In fact, Peter goes considerably further than Thomas Aquinas in insisting on a change of law when something is found which is better. Thomas had cautioned against change in any but an intolerable situation and after much consideration, but Peter favors a change for any good reason.

Surprisingly he argues, however, that this supremacy of law rather than will is not best theoretically, but only practically:

[28] Peter of Auvergne, *In Libros Politicorum*, 3.15.512. "Si aliquid inveniatur secundum rationem melius quam lex posita determinet, istud dimittendum est principi ut ipse ordinet pro lege. Ita quod duo dimittuntur principi: unum est iudicare et disponere recte particularia per legem, ubi possibile est hoc fieri per legem: secundum est quod ubi lex scripta deficit in aliquo casu particulari, dirigat, et hoc est per virtutem ipsius propriam: vel si lex posita non sit bene ordinata secundum rationem, dimittitur principi, ut illa dimissa inveniat meliorem, vel per se, vel de consensu multitudinis; et ordinet per legem." The same message is given at 3.9.439: The law should be master, but the ruler should rule in uncertain cases. See also 3.14.493: The ruler should know and lay down the law, but he should rule according to law except where the law cannot determine simply or well. Even in the *Questiones*, two questions after he defends the will of the ruler over the laws, he demonstrates his usual support for law by asking whether in those things which the law does not determine it is better that one or many rule (3.q.24).

I say that if we speak of those things about which the law determines, about these it is better per se that the city be governed by the best man than by the laws, and I say this per se. The reason is that the city is governed better per se and it is according to reason per se, etc. . . . but the best man attains to prudence per se and essentially, but the law only by accident. . . . By accident, therefore, it is better to be governed by laws. The reason is that it is better by accident that the city be governed by that which wholly lacks passion, than that which has it, at least by accident. . . . But if we speak of those things which the law does not determine, namely the ends, about these certainly it is necessary to be governed by the best man and not by the law.[29]

At first this seems to be a defense of absolutism in the best circumstances (as both Thomas Aquinas and Aristotle also argued), but, in fact, I believe it to be a refutation of arguments for rule by will. Will is superior, Peter says, but only in the abstract: will, like election, is better in principle, but in practice it is better to rely on law and heredity. Nevertheless, like Giles of Rome, Peter is willing to accept law made by the prince alone, so long as the many gives its consent. To this extent he agrees with Giles. This is brought out clearly in a passage responding to Aristotle's comment that if there is no law there is no polity. Perhaps Aristotle is not speaking of monarchy, he writes, or perhaps "it might be said more correctly that in all right polities the ruling [part] exercises dominion according to laws, since in every polity someone governs according to some regulation, which we call law. But in some that rule is interior, existing in will and reason, in some exterior in writing. In a regal monarchy the monarch has that regulation which is in his will and reason."[30]

Because Peter, unlike Thomas, cannot ground his mixed constitution on the distinction between regal and political power, he is compelled to assign more importance than did Thomas Aquinas to the various specific forms of polity: monarchy, aristocracy, democracy, and so forth.[31] In so doing,

---

[29] Peter of Auvergne, *Questiones*, 3.q.22.299va. "Dico quod si loquimur de eis de quibus lex determinat circa melius per se est regi civitatem viro optimo quam legibus et hic dico per se. Cuius ratio est quia per se melius est regi civitatem et quod per se ad rationem, etc. . . . sed vir optimus per se et essentialiter ad prudenciam attingit, lex autem non nisi per accidens. Ergo, etc. Per accidens tamen melius est eam regi legibus. Cuius ratio est quia melius est per accidens eo regi civitatem quod omnino caret passione quem quod saltem per accidens habet. . . . Si vero loquimur de eis qui lex non determinat, scilicet, de finibus circa omnino necessitate est regi eam viro bono et non lege." See also *In Libros Politicorum*, 3.16.25 and 3.13.486, for other statements supporting rule by will.

[30] Peter of Auvergne, *In Libros Politicorum*, 4.4.583. "Aliter dicendum est et melius, quod in omni politia recta principans doninatur secundum leges, quia in omni politia principatur aliquis secundum aliquam regulam, quam dicimus legem. Sed in quibusdam illa regula est interior existens in voluntate et ratione, in quibusdam est extra in scripto. In monarchia regali, monarcha habet istam regulam quae est in voluntate et ratione eius."

[31] Peter uses the sixfold classification in most instances, as opposed to the fourfold scheme

he constructs a mixed constitutional theory differing from that of Thomas Aquinas; it is at once more Aristotelian in its assessment of the many, and less Aristotelian in its virtual abandonment of the idea of balance, either of classes or of forms. It is this last that fully explains what I have been treating as an equivocation. Balance or "tempering" is of no consequence to Peter, and neither is the source of law or the mechanism of election or correction. Rather he is concerned with what virtues the various groups can bring to the mixed constitution and in how these virtues can be blended to form the best regime. This is the view that Demongeot, using Peter's portions of the *Commentary*, ascribed mistakenly to Thomas Aquinas. In this, Peter develops an idea at best implicit in Thomas Aquinas, and initiates an important strain in medieval mixed constitutional theory.

Almost every one of Demongeot's references to the virtues and advantages of the several polities is in fact to Peter's portion of the *Commentary*. A few examples: monarchy is best because it is according to right reason. Virtue is the guiding principle of both monarchy and aristocracy, but only in an aristocracy do public and private virtue coincide. The many are more competent and understand more than one, less susceptible to passions, and more incorruptible.[32]

This concern for the virtues of each form reflects the fact that for Peter, more than for those who came before, the form of rule to be chosen is contingent upon the particular circumstances. Giles of Rome, for example, asserted that any king not totally depraved who could collect decent advisors was better than no king at all, but Peter insists on a king surpassing the other citizens in virtue.[33] In some situations another form might be better: "If we speak of better and best *ex suppositione*, nothing prevents

---

favored by Thomas Aquinas. He also has a greater tendency to use the Aristotelian terminology; thus, for example, we find *politia* and *democratia* in many cases instead of Thomas's *status popularis* or *plebius status, aristocracia* instead of *status optimatum*, and *oligarchia* instead of *status paucorum*, although all of these forms do occur. It is confusion about the differing usage of Peter and Thomas Aquinas that leads Demongeot (*Le Meilleur regime*, p. 37) to his strained explanation that Thomas does not use the term *polity* for the good rule of the many since he recognizes a polity as itself being a mixed form. It is true that Peter believes that a polity is a mixture of oligarchy and democracy (*Questiones*, 4.q.9).

[32] Peter of Auvergne, *In Libros Politicorum*, 4.1, 3.13, and 5.11–12; 3.12, 5.2, 3.1, 4.18, 4.7, 5.8, 4.6, and 5.1; 3.4. See Demongeot, *Le Meilleur regime*, pp. 80, 88; 99, 92, 101. For the last set of qualities Demongeot actually says that the argument is that a virtuous elite is better than one. But in all cases Peter speaks of the "many," and although he occasionally uses this word to refer to the few, there is no reason to assume that he is being restrictive here. He is probably referring either to the situation in which all citizens have some virtue or to the idea that the whole has wisdom through its enlightened part.

[33] Peter of Auvergne, *Questiones*, 3.q.26. "Declaratio est, scilicet, quod non est melius semper unum principari cuicumque multitudinem. Non enim melius enim principari multitudinem compositum ex similibus et equalibus. . . . In multitudinem autem que non equaliter attingit ad virtutem expediat principari unum optimum."

something which is not better simply from being better than some others, as in a city if some citizens are equal in liberty, it is better for them to be governed democratically than by a republic of the middle class."[34]

In most, and the optimal, cases the mixed constitution is best, but it is superior to its components not because they temper or restrain each other, but because each element has something to offer that the others cannot in themselves provide: the king, unity; the few, wisdom; the many, power. This is a large step toward the Renaissance theory of the union of unity, wisdom, and liberty. Thomas Aquinas had really written only of virtue and liberty in this respect, and he did not at all stress the union of these qualities in the mixed constitution. Peter also relates virtue to monarchy and aristocracy, and liberty to democracy,[35] but never seems to consider the benefits of adding liberty to a mixed constitution.

Just as Demongeot describes Peter more accurately than Thomas with respect to the mixed constitution, so did he when he failed to find a coherent theory of regal and political power in Thomas. Peter does toy with this notion, but he never attaches much importance to it; indeed, the king in his mixed constitution seems to possess characteristics of both political and regal rule, exactly as Demongeot asserts about Thomas's king. And Demongeot's point that there is no contradiction between the one ruling by will and the many sharing in rule since the role of the many is in deliberation, which requires competence, whereas the role of the one is in deciding, does fit well with Peter's ideas.[36] The many have the right to give counsel and judgment and correct the ruler; the ruler decides on law and executes it. If it is inappropriate, he puts it aside. Since election of the king is better simply, there may be some places with a good enough populace to justify it. Likewise, since rule by will is better simply, it may be expedient if there is a good enough king. Even this case would not negate the mixed constitution in Peter's formulation of it—a king ruling by will instead of laws would still be obliged to share rule with the other elements of society in the ways already discussed. For Thomas the political character of the ideal monarch was of first importance; for Peter it was not.

Once Peter is removed from the shadow of his master it becomes apparent that he is the originator of a number of important ideas that many medieval and early modern writers subsequently took up and developed. In most cases these ideas were at variance with those of Thomas: the idea

---

[34] Peter of Auvergne, *In Libros Politicorum*, 4.10.643. "Si loquamur de meliori et optima ex suppositione, nihil prohibet aliquam, quae non est melior simpliciter, esse meliorem aliquibus: sicut si in civitate aliqua cives sint aequales in libertate, melius est eis regi populari, quam republica media."

[35] Peter of Auvergne, *In Libros Politicorum*, 3.16.525 and 4.4.574.

[36] Demongeot, *Le Meilleur regime*, p. 101. His examples are from Peter's part of the *In Libros Politicorum*, 3.15.14, 3.11.6.

that all good government is mixed, the distinction of the bestial and nonbestial multitude, the idea that the few should propose actions or rulers for the assent of the whole people, the concept of blending the virtues of the simple forms, the emphasis on relativism. Finally, and of greatest importance, Peter is the first of the medieval Aristotelians to assign a positive role to the multitude. It is given a role not to pacify it and thereby provide stability to the state, but because if it is not utterly degenerate, it has something to offer. From Peter of Auvergne to Ptolemy of Lucca this idea will gather force and eventually become a platitude of modern society. For all these reasons Peter seems to me to be one of the most influential of medieval political theorists, one whose influence rivals that of Thomas himself.

Chapter 6

PTOLEMY OF LUCCA

PTOLEMY OF LUCCA (c. 1236–1327), also known as Tolomeo da Lucca or Bartholomew of Lucca, grew up in a middle-class family. He joined the Dominican order and studied at the University of Paris under Thomas Aquinas in 1261–68 and subsequently traveled with him in Italy. They were together when Thomas died in 1274, and much of what we know of Thomas's life comes to us by way of Ptolemy's *Ecclesiastical History*. In the 1280s and 1290s Ptolemy served as prior in several Tuscan houses, and he spent much of the first two decades of the thirteenth century at the papal court in Avignon writing, doing research, and possibly serving as papal librarian. John XXII appointed him Bishop of Torcello, near Venice, in 1318 and protected him in a dispute with the Patriarch of Grado, who actually imprisoned him for a time. In 1323 Ptolemy was tried and acquitted of the patriarch's charges in Avignon, where he probably attended canonization ceremonies for his teacher in July of that year. He died in Torcello at the age of about ninety.

Ptolemy is one of the half dozen most remarkable medieval political theorists and, with the possible exception of Marsilius of Padua, the most revolutionary. Unlike other medieval writers, he dismisses kingship as a form of despotism unworthy of a virtuous people and presents a paean to republican rule, in the process rehabilitating the Roman Republic, which for over a millennium had been subordinated to the Empire. Ptolemy identifies Julius Caesar, and by implication the endless line of his Eastern and Western successors, as a tyrant and usurper. He looks forward to a republic founded by humans, not God, that by the very harmony of its inner workings, with all citizens participating, could expect to endure forever. His vision inspired generations of political thinkers from Savonarola in his eschatological and millennial expectations for the city of Florence to John Fortescue in his influential, if more mundane, analysis of the English constitution.

His authority was great, for Ptolemy was chiefly read as the continuer of Thomas Aquinas's *On the Government of Rulers*, under whose name the entire work circulated until the twentieth century. To modern eyes this attribution is obviously false; the second and larger part of the work differs from the earlier sections in style, content, emphasis, organization, and choice of materials. Ptolemy also wrote under his own name the well-known *A Short Determination of the Rights of the Empire*, a treatise defending papal power against imperial claims.[1]

Most modern authorities also believe that Ptolemy's ideas represent a radical departure from the thought of Thomas Aquinas.[2] Only Carl Friedrich argues that Ptolemy followed Thomas's intent. He asserts that the ideas in the last part of the treatise accord with Thomas's views in his other works; he explains the contradictions between the two parts of *On the Government of Rulers* as a result of Thomas's dedication of the treatise to the king of Cyprus and consequent emphasis on monarchy.[3]

Of course, because I believe that the first part of *On the Government of Rulers* does fit in well with the rest of Thomas's writing, I partially disagree with Friedrich. But I do agree that in many respects Ptolemy of Lucca followed and legitimately developed Thomas's ideas; more so, at least, than did Peter of Auvergne, whom most regard as indistinguishable from Thomas. Like Thomas, and unlike Peter, Ptolemy places great emphasis on the distinction between political and regal power. Although they construe it somewhat differently, it is at the center of both their theories. Again, like

---

[1] Ptolemy of Lucca, *De Regimine Principum* and *Determinatio Compendiosa*. Few modern scholars doubt the attribution of *On the Government of Rulers* 2.4 (part)–4.28 to Ptolemy. A few older ones, such as E. Flori, "Il trattato 'De Regimine Principum' e le dottrine politiche di S. Tommaso," attempted a few unconvincing arguments against it, but these were definitively refuted, e.g., by A. O'Rahilly, "Notes on St. Thomas. IV. 'De Regimine Principum,' V. Tholomeo of Lucca, The Continuator of the 'De Regimine Principum,' " who also adduced evidence that the treatise was recognized by some as Ptolemy's work as early as the fourteenth century. See Charles T. Davis, "Roman Patriotism and Republican Propaganda: Ptolemy of Lucca and Pope Nicholas III," p. 411, n. 2.

[2] Demongeot, *Le Meilleur regime*, p. 15, wrote that Ptolemy "departs so visibly from the thought of St. Thomas." Others concur: both Charles Davis, who in two articles, "Ptolemy of Lucca and the Roman Republic" and "Roman Patriotism," has provided the most complete and intelligent examination of Ptolemy's political theory to date, and McIlwain, *Growth of Political Thought*, p. 337, contrast Thomas's monarchism with Ptolemy's republicanism; both stress Ptolemy's view that a king is by nature above the law, and that therefore all limited government must be nonmonarchic; both see Ptolemy's support for political rule as a new and important development. Dunbabin, "Aristotle in the Schools," p. 73, and Carlyle and Carlyle, *Medieval Political Theory*, vol. 5, p. 74, emphasize Ptolemy's relativism: they point out that Ptolemy has something good to say about every form in the proper circumstances; the Carlyles, in particular, contrast this approach with Thomas's mixed constitutionalism. Ullmann, *Law and Politics*, p. 274, encountering his bugbear—papal monarchy—condemns Ptolemy's whole political theory as "stale hierocratic and descending," and unfavorably contrasts it with Thomas Aquinas's ascending view of society.

[3] Carl Friedrich, *Transcendent Justice: The Religious Dimension of Constitutionalism*, p. 26. Other treatments of Ptolemy's political theory can be found in Wilks, *Problem of Sovereignty*, p. 120f., who explains Ptolemy's use of the utility principle as an attempt to bring theory in line with contemporary practice, that is, to unify feudalism and Aristotelianism; Markus, "Two Conceptions of Political Authority," p. 96; Tilman Struve, *Die Entwicklung der Organologischen Staatsauffassung im Mittelalter*, p. 165; and C. T. Davis, *Dante and the Idea of Rome*, p. 72; all of whom stress Ptolemy's attempt to transform Augustine into an Aristotelian.

Thomas and unlike Peter, Ptolemy studies the implications for political
theory of the history of the Roman Empire and Republic and the mythol-
ogy of the Old Testament, in the former case expanding and developing
Thomas's ideas, and in the latter case applying the categories of regal and
political power to situations not mentioned by Thomas. He also develops
Thomas's ideas (and in this case Giles of Rome's also) on the subject of the
accommodation of traditional Augustinian and Pauline political doctrine
with Aristotelianism, another subject of little interest to Peter. Finally, and
most significantly, although neither Ptolemy nor Peter mentions the mixed
constitution directly, both support one in essence. Ptolemy's arguments
for it, however, are much closer to those of Thomas than are Peter's: both
Ptolemy and Thomas stress the value of balance rather than the uniting of
qualities.

No medieval writers used the terms *regal* and *political* rigorously; no
matter how strict a definition they give, they all go on to apply the words
loosely to kingship and republican government respectively. This is not to
say that the conception behind the strict definition was not central, as with
Thomas. Ptolemy identifies four kinds of dominion: sacerdotal and regal,
regal alone, political, and economic.[4] This formulation, strictly his own, is
provocatively similar to, and no doubt derived from, Aristotle's four
modes of rule—political, regal, economic, and despotic—mentioned in the
very first chapter of the *Politics*.[5] There Aristotle reproved Plato for distinguishing the four types by number of subjects rather than by mode of rule,
thereby treating political and regal rule as forms only for large groups,
economic rule for the smaller family, and despotic for a few slaves. Aristotle
sharply distinguished the various communities but showed that political
and regal rule exist within the family and despotic rule in large groups.
Consequently, for him, economic rule is not really a mode of rule, and we
are left with the regal, political, and despotic modes. Ptolemy follows Plato's views and thereby creates a hierarchy of usual modes of rule based on
size: sacerdotal and regal rule for the world, regal rule (in general) for the
kingdom or province, political rule for the city, and economic rule for the
home.[6] (I say "in general" because Ptolemy allows and often advocates po-

----

[4] Ptolemy of Lucca, *De Regimine Principum*, 3.10.128. "Recepit igitur divisionem dominium quadrimembrem ex eadem causa et ratione, quia quoddam est sacerdotale et regale simul;
aliud autem est regale solum . . . tertium vero politicum; quartum autem oeconomicum."

[5] Aristotle, *Politics*, 1.1.1252a.7f.

[6] Ptolemy of Lucca, *De Regimine Principum*, 4.2.178, 3.10.128. "Regimen politicum maxime consistit in civitatibus . . . provinciae enim magis ad regale pertinere videntur." This anticipates Bartolus of Sassaferrato's more complete relation of size to monarchy, aristocracy,
and democracy. In the same place Aristotle also reproved Plato for failing to find a qualitative
difference between the home and the polity. Thomas Aquinas followed Aristotle on both
points. Giles of Rome followed Plato on the first point and attempted thereby to prove that
monarchy is suitable for all communities.

litical rule even in a large polity.) Over the entire universe is the divine and universal dominion of God.

Ptolemy quickly treats the first and last of these modes and then abandons them for the remainder of his treatise. In *On the Government of Rulers* he is interested in the organization of actual political communities, to which pertains directly only the regal and political modes. As a high papalist Ptolemy has no doubts about who properly exercises the highest human dominion. Like Christ, the pope is both supreme priest and king: sacerdotal and regal dominion was prefigured by the Old Testament prophets, first fully realized in Christ, and passed on by him to his vicar. Because of its divine origin it surpasses all other modes. At the other extreme is economic rule in the smallest political unit, the family, in which he shows little interest, except to specify completely his hierarchy of rule.[7]

In his formulation Ptolemy apparently ignores Aristotle's despotic rule, since for him despotic rule is more or less the same as regal rule. He writes that regal is included in the term *despotic*, and that "despotic" rule can be reduced to regal rule, as is clear from the Bible."[8] This startling conclusion, the more startling since he thinks that regal rule is the usual mode for a large polity, Ptolemy supports with yet another misinterpretation of the *Politics*. In several passages Aristotle contrasted political and despotic rule, in each case using *political* in its general sense of rule over free people, which includes both political and regal rule in their more limited modal senses. But here and elsewhere Ptolemy uses the words *despotic* and *regal* almost interchangeably. Aristotle distinguishes two types of rule, he writes, political and *despotic*. "Rule is political when a region, or province, or city, or camp is ruled by one or many according to its statutes . . . in *regal* dominion . . . since one is not obligated by law, one may judge by that which is in the breast of the ruler."[9] (Italics mine.)

---

[7] Ptolemy of Lucca, *De Regimine Principum*, 3.10.128. "Primum autem caeteris antefertur multiplici via, sed praecipua sumitur ex institutione divina, videlicet Christi. Cum enim eidem secundum suam humanitatem omnis sit collata potestas . . . dictam potestatem suo communicavit vicario . . . merito summus Pontifex Romanus Episcopus dici potest rex et sacerdos." *Determinatio Compendiosa* treats this mode more fully. For a discussion of analogies between polities and the family in Ptolemy (only treated significantly in one passage of his *Hexameron*) and others, see Blythe, "Family, Government."

[8] Ptolemy of Lucca, *De Regimine Principum*, 4.8.200. "Quaedam autem provinciae sunt servilis naturae, et tales gubernari debent principatu despotico, includendo in despotico etiam regale." 2.9.73. "Est autem hic advertendum, quod principatus despoticus dicitur, qui est domini ad servum . . . quem principatum ad regalem possumus reducere, ut ex sacra liquet Scriptura."

[9] Ptolemy of Lucca, *De Regimine Principum*, 2.8.69, 72. "Duplex enim principatus ab Aristotele ponitur in sua *Politica* . . . politicus videlicet et despoticus. . . . Politicus quidem quando regio sive provincia sive civitas sive castrum per unum vel plures regitur secundum ipsorum statuta . . . per regale dominium . . . dum, non legibus obligatus, per eam censeat, quae est in pectore principis." Cf. Aristotle, *Politics*, 1.7.1256b, 3.4.1277b, and

This, except for the substitution of despotic for regal rule, is precisely Thomas Aquinas's distinction. There is no a priori reason why there cannot be a political king. Ptolemy denies this possibility and fuses the sixfold schema of polity types with the regal and political modes of rule, a distinction carefully maintained by Thomas. Polity and aristocracy share the characteristic of plurality, Ptolemy writes, and for this reason both are properly called political and can be distinguished from regal or despotic rule. At the same time, Ptolemy does not abandon the criterion of law; in the very next paragraph he returns to this theme:

> Political rectors are bound by laws, nor can they proceed beyond them in the pursuit of justice; which does not happen with kings and other monarchs, because laws are hidden in their breasts according as cases occur; and that which pleases the ruler is held for law, as the laws of nations hand down, but this is not found concerning political rectors, because they do not dare to do anything new beyond the written laws.[10]

This same conception is found in Giles of Rome: both political and regal rulers rule by law, but for the king the law is internal and by his own will; for the political ruler it is written. But whereas Giles made this point to argue for a king, Ptolemy, by identifying regal and despotic, seeks to discredit kingship.

Still, in one passage Ptolemy does admit the political rule of one. There was no contradiction in Ptolemy's mind, as he associated a whole complex of characteristics with political rule: plurality and law, yes, but also alternation of rulers, election, judgment of past rulers, mildness of rule, and salaries for rulers as well. Likewise, regal rule not only is without written law and plurality, it also is characterized by permanence, heredity, immunity of the ruler, harsh rule, and no salary.[11] It is by a combination of alter-

---

3.17.1287b.37f. The fact that Ptolemy misinterprets Aristotle in this way somewhat diminishes the effect of a mistranscription by William of Moerbeke, pointed out by Rubinstein and, following him, Davis. In this case Aristotle did mean to distinguish political and regal as modes and wrote: "There is by nature justly and advantageously despotic, regal, and political rule." In the Latin version, only two forms, "despotic and political" appear. Aristotle, *Politics*, 3.17.1287b.37f. See Rubinstein, "Marsilius of Padua," p. 52; Davis, "Ptolemy of Lucca," p. 48.

[10] Ptolemy of Lucca, *De Regimine Principum*, 4.1.175–6. "Et quoniam utrumque pluralitatem includit, ista duo genera [aristocratia et politia] ad politicam se extendunt, prout dividitur contra regale seu despoticum . . . legibus astringuntur rectores politici, nec ultra possunt procedere in prosecutione iustitiae, quod de regibus et aliis monarchis principibus non contingit, quia in ipsorum pectore sunt leges reconditae, prout casus occurrunt et pro lege habetur quod principi placet, sicut jura gentium tradunt: sed de rectoribus politicis non sic reperitur, quia non audebant aliquam facere novitatem, praeter leges conscriptas." Nicole Oresme, *Le Livre de Politiques*, 3.24, p. 157, makes a similar but stronger statement—that a king, unlike other rectors, can rule in those areas not covered by law, whereas the others must always act by law.

[11] See, e.g., Ptolemy of Lucca, *De Regimine Principum*, 2.8, and 4.1, 7. For Aristotle alter-

nation with his idea of plurality that he is able sometimes to consider the rule of one as political. If there is alternation of office or rule only for a limited period, plurality exists even if only one rules at a time. This is how Ptolemy, in distinction from Thomas, can call the rule of the Roman dictator aristocracy.[12] In this way he can define political rule as the rule of one or many under law, and still maintain his criterion of plurality and his fusion of mode and species of rule.

Naturally, Ptolemy must realize that some regimes might share in only some of the various criteria, but then they would not be purely political or regal. In his view the characteristics that he associates with each mode seem to him to go together naturally; in general, they will be found in the same government. He is quite willing to recognize, however, that there will be many concrete instances that cannot easily be fit into either category, that may share some traits of each form. Thomas's definition was crisper and all-comprehensive, but it was also somewhat less empirical in that it forced existing constitutions into an a priori framework. Ptolemy sets up two theoretical poles but recognizes that not all governments will exactly correspond to them. This reflects Ptolemy's greater concern with historical development and concrete examples.

Imperial rule stands midway in the continuum: it is political in that office is elective and open to all; it is regal in that emperors have the jurisdiction of kings, take tributes and taxes, are crowned, institute the laws, and have arbitrary power over their subjects.[13] The crux of the matter is that the power of the emperor depends on the many and so is political, but he rules by will and so is regal. If it were just a matter of rule by will or law, as it was for Thomas, and as Davis interprets Ptolemy, there would be no question but that imperial rule (as Ptolemy understood it) would be purely regal. But generalizing Thomas Aquinas's and Giles of Rome's theory, Ptolemy includes as partially a political rule the case in which the many participate in some other way than making law. Thus, I cannot unequivocally endorse Davis's conclusion that "for Ptolemy the crucial political distinction was between arbitrary rule and rule regulated by statute,"[14] although I do agree it was of great and central concern to him.

---

nation was the decisive criterion of political rule; Thomas relegated it to a secondary characteristic often but not always associated with political rule. Significantly Ptolemy does not cite in *On the Government of Rulers* any of the examples of political rule given by Thomas Aquinas or Giles of Rome in which there is one unchanging ruler, such as the relationship of husband and wife. The idea of salary associated with political rule seems to be original with Ptolemy and no doubt stems from Northern Italian practices.

[12] Ptolemy of Lucca, *De Regimine Principum*, 4.1.175.

[13] Ptolemy of Lucca, *De Regimine Principum*, 3.20.162, 164. See also *Determinatio Compendiosa*, chap. 30, p. 61.

[14] Davis, "Ptolemy of Lucca," p. 48. At one point Ptolemy does say without qualification that imperial rule is regal (*De Regimine Principum*, 3.10.128). "Aliud autem est regale solum sub quo imperiale sumitur." But here he means only that the emperor has no sacerdotal func-

The importance of law is nowhere more apparent than in Ptolemy's identification of despotic rule with regal rule. Davis argues fairly convincingly that Ptolemy at times understood Aristotle's distinction between regal and despotic, but tended to lump them together since both depend on the will of the ruler and not on law. But if the emphasis is not on the end of rule but on whether or not it is by the will of the ruler or the power of the many, as it is for both Ptolemy and Giles of Rome, it is difficult conceptually to separate regal and despotic rule, especially since in contradistinction to tyrannical rule both of these at least incidentally benefit those subject to them.

What does Ptolemy mean when he writes that despotic rule "can be reduced to regal rule"? An answer to this question will explain why Ptolemy rejected regal government as best and will lead to his rationale for another, better, form of rule. To answer it we must look at the Bible, as he himself suggests, and at his perception of historical political experience. He perceives a conflict between two types of kingship, that which Moses described and practiced, which has the beneficial characteristics Ptolemy in some places identifies as regal,[15] and that which Samuel predicted would characterize the Jewish kings to come, which appears despotic, even tyrannical. Why would God, the source of all power, establish such a regime for his chosen people? Ptolemy tries to justify the existence and difference of the two forms by recourse to two not completely compatible notions of sin: the original sin of Adam and Eve, and the particular sins of certain peoples. "Despotic government," he writes, "is reduced to regal . . . especially by reason of the sin on account of which servitude was introduced, as Augustine says." But a few lines later, he writes: "In such bad-tempered regions despotic rule is necessary for kings, not indeed on account of the nature of regal dominion but according to the merits and stubbornness of the subjects . . . Aristotle . . . shows that among certain barbarous nations regal dominion is certainly despotic because otherwise they cannot be governed."[16] The first passage implies that although regal and despotic rule have different natures in themselves, in postlapsarian times the rule of a king is despotic. This is what is meant by the one form being "reduced" to

---

tion (Ptolemy has just mentioned regal and sacerdotal rule), and does not mean to deny a political character to the rule.

[15] E.g., Ptolemy of Lucca, *De Regimine Principum*, 3.11.135. "He is a legitimate king who principally intends the good of his subjects . . . who has the care of his subjects that he might act as if a pastor of sheep."

[16] Ptolemy of Lucca, *De Regimine Principum*, 3.11.138. "Principatus despoticus ad regale reducitur . . . praecipue ratione delicti propter quod servitus est introductua, ut Augustinus dicit. . . . In talibus ergo regionibus sic dyscolis necessarius est regibus principatus despoticus, non quidem juxta naturam regalis dominii sed secundum merita et pertinacias subditorum. . . . Philosophus . . . ostendit apud quasdam barbaras nationes regale dominium esse omnino despoticum, quia aliter regi non possent."

the other. The second qualifies this conclusion: even now some peoples may be sufficiently virtuous to escape servitude. Actual examples of non-despotic government in the Bible, in Aristotle, and in later history, to which I will return, force Ptolemy to this conclusion.

Clearly, the second contradicts standard Christian-Augustinian thought, and, indeed, many of the tensions in Ptolemy's political theory, as in that of Giles of Rome, result from his rationalization of conflicts between Aristotle and Augustine. In many respects *On the Government of Rulers* can be seen as an extended, often inconsistent, struggle to reconcile them. Ptolemy never fully succeeds, but comes closer to success than did Giles of Rome. R. A. Marcus strongly disagrees:

> The transition from Augustine's words to Aristotle's *Politics*, effected . . . without the slightest misgiving, is part of his inheritance from St. Thomas and was only made possible for him by his master's work. There is no trace here of any sense of tensions of thought, no trace of an inward struggle to reconcile a cherished tradition with new insight. Without scrutiny all roads can now be assumed to lead in the same direction. Ptolemy of Lucca was the herald of a comfortable obliviousness to a profound cleavage in the tradition of Christian political thought.[17]

Ptolemy never openly admits any conflict between Augustine and Aristotle, but "comfortable obliviousness" is hardly the way to describe Ptolemy's wriggling. It is true that Ptolemy's argument builds on that of Thomas, but it goes much further and sometimes conflicts with it. Flawed as it is, it is one of Ptolemy's most original contributions. Ultimately he replaces original sin with local and contingent sin, and in so doing rejects the Augustinian theory of government by misrepresenting it. Much more it is Thomas who seems little concerned with the obvious contradictions involved and who never even brings up the key passages.

If he wants to make Augustine into an Aristotelian, one of his greatest challenges lies in explaining the society of Eden—if humans are naturally political animals, government must have existed even then; if government came about only as a result of sin and for the purpose of repressing that sin, it should not. Ptolemy tries to have it both ways. He begins by arguing that Aristotle, the Bible, and Augustine all agree that humans naturally possessed dominion over the lower species, and thus that some rule existed from the beginning.[18]

---

[17] Marcus, "Two Conceptions of Political Authority," pp. 96–97.

[18] Ptolemy of Lucca, *De Regimine Principum*, 3.9.125–27. Ptolemy gives these references: God, in Genesis 1:28 gives humans power over fish, birds, and animals; Augustine refers to this in book 18 of the *City of God*; Aristotle, in the first book of the *Politics* proves hunting and fishing to be natural. In proving his assertion he conflates Aristotle and Augustine: "First, from the process of nature itself . . . matter exists on account of form, and more imperfect

What about the rule of human over human? Deliberating and directing, he writes, are natural and existed even in the state of innocence. Since Ptolemy cannot assume a natural superiority of some human or humans, he needs a stronger argument to justify this than to justify rule over animals. This he finds in the nature of humans as social and political animals and in Thomas Aquinas's interpretation of Aristotle that any society must be ordered and that any ordered society must have something directing it. Such an order implies inequality and dominion, if not natural superiority, as, Ptolemy adds, Augustine's definition of order as "the disposition of equal and unequal things, giving each its due" demonstrates. Thus, "the dominion of human over human is natural, it exists even among the angels, and it existed in [humanity's] original condition."[19]

Thomas Aquinas or Giles of Rome had already made most of these same points, but only Ptolemy deduces the necessary structure of paradisial government, though logically Thomas would have preferred a political government (although he said only that it was not servile) and Giles a regal monarchy. For Ptolemy it must be political:

> Political government is preferable to regal . . . if we refer dominion to the integral state of human nature which is called the state of innocence, in which there was not regal government, but political, because there was not then the dominion which implies servitude, but preeminence and subjection in disposing and guiding the multitude according to the merits of each one, that thus either in influencing or receiving influence each was disposed according to the harmony of its nature.[20]

---

form exists on account of more perfect . . . so also in the use of natural things: for the more imperfect things are for the sake of the more perfect. . . . Second, this is clear from the order of divine providence, which governs inferiors by superiors. . . . Third, this is clear from the peculiar nature of humans and other animals. For in other animals a certain participation of prudence in some particulars . . . is found; but in humans is found a certain universal prudence, which is reason. . . . But all which is through participation is subject to that which is through essence universally."

[19] Ptolemy of Lucca, *De Regimine Principum*, 3.10.127. "In his autem quae sunt ad invicem ordinata, oportet semper aliquid esse principale et dirigens primum, ut tradit Philosophus in I Politica. Hoc etiam ostendit ipsa ratio ordinis sive natura quia, ut per Augustinum scribitur in praedicto libro [*City of God*, 19], 'ordo est parium disparriumque rerum sua cuique tribuens dispositio.' Unde manifestum est quod nomen ordinis inaequalitatem importat, et hoc est de ratione dominii; et ideo secundum hanc considerationem dominium hominis super hominum est naturale, et est in Angelis, et fuisset in primo statu."

[20] Ptolemy of Lucca, *De Regimine Principum*, 2.9.74. "Regimen politicum regali praeponitur . . . si referamus dominium ad statum integrum humanae naturae, qui status innocentiae appellatur, in quo non fuisset regale regimine sed politicum, eo quod tunc non fuisset dominium quod servitutem haberet, sed praeeminentiam et subiectionem in disponendo et gubernando multitudinem secundum merita cujuscumque, ut sic vel in influendo vel in recipiendo influentiam quilibet esset dispositus secundum congruentiam suae naturae." Cf. *Determinatio Compendiosa*, chap. 17, p. 36.

Despite his disclaimer that it is sin that converts regal rule to despotic, it is clear that Ptolemy thinks of regal rule even in the state of innocence as implying servitude—it is in the nature of the rule itself, not in the character of either the ruler or the ruled.

One argument that everyone including Ptolemy had advanced for regal rule was that laws are universal statements that do not fit all particulars, and that therefore political rule by these laws is inadequate. A regal king, bound only by reason, can best handle changing circumstances.[21] Before the Fall this problem did not exist. In its natural state everything acts according to natural law, and therefore the law cannot fail in particulars. This is what Ptolemy means when he writes that at that time "each is disposed according to the harmony of its nature." So not only would a regal ruler, if such could have arisen there, have imposed servitude in Paradise, but there would not even have been any compensatory benefits.

How was the character of government changed by sin? Augustine insisted that political authority came about only because of sin, and even in the interpretation favored by Thomas Aquinas and Giles of Rome it is the cause of servitude. One obvious conflict is between Augustine's view that corrupted humanity needs to be restrained by a repressive state and the Aristotelian view that servitude is the destiny only of humanity's most primitive elements. If servitude was made necessary by sin, how can it be dispensed with by sinful humanity? And if not, how *does* the Fall affect human government? Giles can partially escape this dilemma since he favors a regal regime that, although it is not despotic, can strongly correct its citizens; Thomas, in favoring a political regime, has no easy way out and simply ignores the problem. Ptolemy does not satisfactorily address it either, but he is quite explicit in his assumption that fallen humanity *may* aspire to the virtue necessary for a paradisial type of government, and he does attempt to resolve some of the conflicting ideas.

Several times he paraphrases Augustine's definition, taken from Cicero, of a city as a multitude of men bound in one chain of society.[22] Augustine also argues that without true virtue, that is, without justice, which can come only from concord with God's will, kingdoms are nothing but gangs of criminals on a large scale.[23] Only in the metaphysical City of God can

[21] Ptolemy of Lucca, *De Regimine Principum*, 2.8.74.

[22] Ptolemy of Lucca, *De Regimine Principum*, 4.2, the same with "which is rendered blessed by true virtue" added, 4.23; with "which is the love of its citizens" added, 4.4. Augustine gives two definitions of *commonwealth*. He shows that the one related by Scipio in Cicero's *On the Commonwealth*, which includes the phrase about "true justice," is untenable since true justice cannot exist except in the City of God (*City of God*, 19.21. See also 2.21). The other, "the association of a multitude of rational beings united by the objects of their love" (*City of God*, 19.24), Augustine finds more applicable to actually existing governments. Ptolemy conflates the two, most often insisting on virtue.

[23] Augustine, *City of God*, 4.4.

such concord be found; since any earthly government will necessarily include the ungodly, no true republic can exist on earth. Nevertheless, Ptolemy confidently asserts that there is no conflict between Augustine and Aristotle. Both, he writes, place political happiness in the perfect rule of a polity:

> The virtue by which a political rector guides the city is the architect with respect to which are all other virtues which are in the citizens, because other civil virtues are ordered to that one. . . . And therefore since it is the supreme virtue, political felicity consists in its operation. . . . It happens thus in the true and perfect polity. . . . And if the supreme virtue, which is reason, directs the other inferior powers, and they are moved according to its command, then a certain suavity and perfect delight of strengths arises in both, which we call harmony. Whence Augustine says . . . that a well-disposed republic or city is comparable to a melody of voices. . . . And for this reason the philosopher Plutarch was moved to assimilate the republic or polity to a natural and organic body, in which movements are dependent on one or two movers, as are the heart and brain; and nevertheless there is an appropriate operation in any part of the body . . . which also the Apostle confirms in I Corinthians. . . . Order is "the perfect disposition of equal and unequal, giving to each its due." . . . By this definition there exist various grades in a polity with respect to the execution of offices and the subjection or obedience of the subjects: whence there is then the perfect social congregation when each person has their proper disposition and operation in their own state. Just as a building is stable when its parts are well-placed, thus it happens with a polity. . . . Because there is no contradiction there, consequentially there will be perpetual firmness of state and the highest sweetness—according to Aristotle this is appropriate to political felicity.[24]

[24] Ptolemy of Lucca, *De Regimine Principum*, 4.23.242–44. "Virtus enim qua rector politicus civitatem gubernat architecta est respectu cujuslibet aliarum virtutum quae sunt in civibus, quia caeterae virtutes civiles ordinantur ad istam. . . . Et ideo in operatione ejus, cum sit virtus suprema, consistit felicitas politica. . . . Sic enim de vera et perfecta politia contingit. . . . Et si virtus suprema quae est ratio caeteras dirigat inferiores potentias et ad suum moveantur imperium, tunc insurgit quaedam suavitas et perfecta delectatio virium in alterutrum, quam harmoniam vocamus. Unde Augustinus dicit . . . quod respublica sive civitas bene disposita melodiae vocum comparatur. . . . Et ex hac quidem ratione motus fuit Plutarchus philosophus assimilare rempublicam seu politiam naturali et organico corpori, in quo sunt motus dependentes ex uno movente sive ex duobus, ut sunt cor et cerebrum, et tamen in qualibet parte corporis est operatio propria . . . quod et Apostolus confirmat in I ad Corinthianos. . . . Ordo est 'parium dispariumque sua cuique tribuens dispositio'. . . . Per quam definitionem habemus diversum gradum in politia, tam in executione officiorum quam in subiectione sive obedientia subditorum; unde tunc est perfecta socialis congregatio, quando quilibet in suo statu debitam habet dispositionem et operationem. Sicut enim aedificium est stabile quando partes ejus sunt bene sitae, sic de politia contingit. . . . Et quia ibi nulla est

Augustine treated his perfect City of God as a mystical community that could never be realized on earth or by human agency, but Ptolemy selects snippets of Augustine, Aristotle, and the Bible to suggest that secular virtue alone provides the potential for an Aristotelian polity comparable to Eden. "Whence among wise and virtuous humans as were the ancient Romans," he writes, "political government in imitation of that nature [of sinless humanity] was better."[25] Original sin has become a sin like any other that people of sufficiently good character, even pagans, can overcome. Ptolemy attempts to equate true virtue, which for Augustine can be nothing less than harmony with God, with the political virtue of people living in the best community. Aristotle realized that in general the virtue of a good person was not the same as that of the good citizen, but did equate them in the perfect polity which would lead people to virtue.

This perfect polity is a real possibility in Ptolemy's mind, corresponding to the City of God in its harmony, virtue, felicity, and permanence. Though the product of time-bound and imperfect man, this polity cannot decay because of its internal harmony: "It has firmness and perpetuity when everyone works properly in their own rank, whether rector, or officials, or subjects, as the action of their condition requires."[26] There are, as Ptolemy says, no contradictions to cause its collapse.

The problem of the possibility of permanence for time-bound republics is one which has provided the inspiration for Pocock's influential *The Machiavellian Moment*.[27] He argues that it was only in the Renaissance that these ideas were taken up seriously. As in the case of the rehabilitation of the Roman Republic, the roots are to be found much earlier, to a slight extent in Thomas Aquinas and more fully in Ptolemy of Lucca. The influence is direct: many of the Renaissance authors considered by Pocock used Ptolemy's *On the Government of Rulers*. For example, Girolamo Savonarola used Ptolemy's ideas as the basis for his theory of millennial republicanism and the perfection of virtue in the postlapsarian world.[28]

After much equivocation, Ptolemy in practice discounts the role of original sin in the transformation of regal into despotic government. Original sin was a necessary but not sufficient condition for servitude and coercion. The most that can be said is that original sin predisposes people to sin and

---

repugnantia, consequenter ibi erit summa suavitas et perpetua firmitas status, et hoc est proprium felicitatis politicae, ut Philosophus tradit."

[25] Ptolemy of Lucca, *De Regimine Principum*, 2.9.74. "Unde apud sapientes et homines virtuosos, ut fuerunt antiqui Romani, secundum imitationem talis naturae regimen politicum melius fuit."

[26] Ptolemy of Lucca, *De Regimine Principum*, 4.23.244. "Firmitatem habet et perpetuitatem quando quilibet in suo gradu, sive rector sive officialis sive subditus, debite operatur ut suae conditionis requirit actio."

[27] Pocock, *Machiavellian Moment*.

[28] See Donald Weinstein, *Savonarola and Florence*, pp. 290, 293, 304, 309.

to regal rule—which they can transcend through virtue. Regal rule did not exist before the Fall, which, far from changing the nature of regal rule, created the rationale for its existence and its justification for most peoples: "But because 'the perverse are corrected with difficulty, and the number of idiots is infinite,' as is said in Ecclesiastes [1:15], in corrupt nature a regal government is more fruitful [than a political one], because it is necessary that human nature, thus disposed as it were to flux, be checked with limits. But this the regal type does."[29] Since political rule is possible and desirable for some, if only the virtuous few, that sin which transforms regal rule to despotic rule must be that of kings who oppress their peoples or peoples whose corruption only the harshest rulers can restrain. That this is true is demonstrated by Ptolemy's analysis of the two forms of monarchy described in the Old Testament.

In Deuteronomy 17:14–20, Moses prescribes the form that Israelite kingship will take in the Promised Land. The king will not enrich himself or oppress his people; he will carefully study the Law that he might obey and fear God. In I Kings 8:11–18 Samuel describes the future king in radically different terms: he will impress the people to his service and he will seize land and money for his own use until the people cry out for relief. Thomas Aquinas passed over the Mosaic precepts—quite likely he thought them to be describing a continuation of the political kingship begun by Moses in his interpretation. He also entirely rejected the legitimacy of Samuel's king: "That right was not given to the king by divine institution, rather it was foretold that kings would usurp that right by framing unjust laws and by degenerating into tyrants who preyed on their subjects."[30]

Ptolemy cannot easily accept this interpretation. Both sections of the Bible ostensibly describe "regal laws,"[31] and the kings were established and anointed by God in the person of his prophet. Even if God took this step reluctantly, how can the kings not be true kings? Ptolemy's answer follows the same circular path seen previously. He begins in an Aristotelian spirit with a distinction between regal and despotic rule, but Augustinian ideas then bring him back to the conclusion that the two cannot be separated.

Deuteronomy and I Kings, according to Ptolemy, establish kingship differently, "but both nevertheless in the person of God. For in Deuteronomy he ordains the king for the utility of his subjects, which is the proper func-

---

[29] Ptolemy of Lucca, *De Regimine Principum*, 2.9.74. "Sed quia 'perversi difficile corriguntur et stultorum infinitus est numerus,' ut dicitur in Ecclesiasticis, in natura corrupta regimen regale est fructuosius; quia oportet ipsam naturam humanam sic dispositam quasi ad sui fluxum limitibus refrenare. Hoc autem facit regale fastigium."

[30] Thomas Aquinas, *Summa Theologiae*, 1–2.105.1.ad 5.

[31] Ptolemy of Lucca, *De Regimine Principum*, 2.9.73, "leges regales"; 3.11.133, "leges regalis."

tion of kings, as Aristotle relates." The difference, Ptolemy writes, corresponds to Aristotle's distinction of regal and despotic rule:

> Samuel says that the laws which he hands down are regal, although they are utterly despotic. Aristotle in VIII *Ethics* agrees more with the first set of laws. . . . From of which [Aristotle's comments on kingship] it is sufficiently manifest that according to that the despotic [mode] is much different from the regal, as the same Philosopher seems to say in I *Politics*. . . . A kingdom does not exist on account of the king, but the king on account of the kingdom, since for this God has provided for kings that they should guide and govern their kingdom and preserve everyone in their own rights, and this is the end of rule. But if they do otherwise, by turning everything to their convenience, they are not kings but tyrants. . . . The common good is said by Aristotle in I Ethics to be a divine good, so that just as God who is the "King of Kings and Lord of Lords," by whose virtue rulers command . . . guides and governs us not for himself but for our well-being, so should kings and other dominators in the world do. . . . A legitimate king ought to guide and govern thus, according to the form handed down in Deuteronomy.[32]

Ptolemy's position is quite different from Thomas's. For Thomas the defects of the Jews made political rule the only workable form; when it was abandoned tyranny resulted. For Ptolemy the same defects made tyranny inevitable and desirable:

> The laws of regal dominion handed down to the Israelite people through the prophet Samuel were given by this consideration, that the said people on account of its ingratitude and because it was stiff-necked deserved to hear such laws. For sometimes when a people does not know the benefit of good government, it is expedient to have tyrannies, since even these are instruments of divine justice. Whence certain islands and provinces according to what the

---

[32] Ptolemy of Lucca, *De Regimine Principum*, 3.11.133. "Et primo quidem in sacra Scriptura aliter leges regalis dominii traduntur in Deuteronomium per Moysen aliter in I Regibus per Samuelem prophetam, uterque tamen in persona Dei. In Deuteronomium enim ordinat regem ad utilitatem subditorum quod est proprium regum, ut Philosophus tradit. . . . Samuel leges quas tradit, cum sint penitus despoticae, dicit esse regales. Philosophus autem in VIII Ethicorum magis concordat cum primis legibus. . . . Ex quibus omnibus satis est manifestum, quod juxta istum modum despoticum multum differat a regali, ut idem Philosophus videtur dicere in I Politica . . . regnum non est propter regem, sed rex propter regnum, quia ad hoc Deus providit de eis ut regnum regant et gubernent et unumquemque in suo jure conservent, et hic est finis regiminis; quod si aliud faciunt in se ipsos commodium retorquendo, non sunt reges sed tyranni . . . bonum commune dicitur a Philosopho in I Ethicorum esse bonum divinum, ut sicut Deus qui est 'Rex regum et Dominus Dominantium,' cujus virtute principes imperant . . . nos regit et gubernat non propter se ipsum sed propter nostram salutem, ita ut reges faciant et alii dominantes in orbe . . . legitimum regem secundum formam in Deuteronomio traditam sic debere regere et gubernare."

histories relate, always had tyrants on account of the evil of the people, because otherwise, without an iron rod, they could not be governed.[33]

Ptolemy goes on to say that both Aristotle and Augustine approve this view. Once again the problem is in reconciling the two. Aristotle supported some despots, not for punishment but for necessity over natural slaves who could not govern themselves. On the other hand neither he nor Thomas or Giles could support a tyrant under any circumstances. For Augustine (and I Kings, by Ptolemy's interpretation) all rule is from God, who often supports a tyrannical rule for the forcible repression of naturally sinful humanity. It is because he cannot quite bring these two conceptions together, even though he substitutes the sins of individual peoples for original sin, that he uses *tyrant* and *despot* synonymously in these two passages.

For these reasons Ptolemy accepts Samuel's king as a legitimate king, and his "regal laws" as God's will. The result is that he has difficulty in finding a place in the real world for the beneficent king of Aristotle and Deuteronomy. If a people is virtuous it deserves and is best served by a political government. If it lacks virtue it can only be restrained by the rigors of regal rule, but because of that people's sinful nature, regal rule is inevitably despotic. That this is so is confirmed by Ptolemy's discussion of the political rule of the Judges:

> Whence Samuel, who judged the said people in certain times, said to them, wanting to show that his government was political and not regal, which [latter] they desired [in I Kings 12:3] said: "Tell me . . . whether I have taken anyone's ox or ass; if I have wronged anyone; if I have oppressed anyone; if I have taken a bribe at anyone's hand . . . ," which indeed those who have regal dominion would do, as will be clear below, and as the said prophet shows in I Kings.[34]

---

[33] Ptolemy of Lucca, *De Regimine Principum*, 3.11.138. "Leges vero traditae de regali dominio Israelitico populo per Samuelem prophetam hac consideratione sunt datae, quia dictus populus propter suam ingratitudinem et quia durae cervicis erat merebatur tales leges audire. Interdum enim dum populus non cognoscit beneficium boni regiminis expedit exercere tyrannides, quia etiam hae sunt instrumentum divinae iustitiae; unde et quaedam insulae et provinciae, secundum quod historiae narrant, semper habuerunt tyrannos propter malitiam populi, quia aliter nisi in virga ferrea regi non poterant."

[34] Ptolemy of Lucca, *De Regimine Principum*, 2.8.27. "Unde Samuel qui dictum populum certis judicavit temporibus sic ait ad ipsos, volens ostendere suum regimen fuisse politicum et non regale quod eligerant [I Regibus 12:3]: 'Loquimini,' inquit '. . . utrum bovem cujusquam tulerim aut asinum, si quempiam calumniatus sum, si oppressi aliquem, si de manu alicujus munus accepi'; quod quidem qui regale dominium habent non faciunt, ut infra patebit et in I Libro Regum dictus Propheta ostendit." I have translated *non faciunt* as "would do," which seems to reverse the meaning. But in context Ptolemy must mean what I have written. There is either a misprint or mistranscription, or it may be that he means "a regal ruler would not do this," i.e., would not refrain from such oppression.

Servitude is of the nature of kingship; the regal laws introduced servitude to the Israelites, who had been better served by the political government of the Judges.[35]

That Ptolemy is not simply using the term *regal* loosely, sometimes in the technical sense of one ruling without laws, which he condemns, sometimes as a synonym for king, who could be good, is proved by his failure to attach the "regal laws" of Deuteronomy to any actual or hypothetical kings. In particular, he does not, as did Thomas, identify Moses as a king. None of the Aristotelian distinctions can save Ptolemy from his underlying belief that regal and despotic rule are essentially the same in the real world. He cannot accommodate the virtuous king working for the common good either to the Augustinian insistence on corrupt man or to his own belief that at least some peoples can overcome their corruption. This is why he says that regal and despotic governments can be reduced to each other.

Thus is demonstrated Ptolemy's preference for political rule and his distaste for regal, two categories that have for him largely replaced the sixfold and fourfold schemata of Aristotle, Thomas, and the rest. He reduces all forms dependent on multiplicity—including the rule of one who is dependent on others (which neither Ptolemy nor Giles of Rome calls monarchy), aristocracy, polity, and presumably oligarchy and democracy—to political rule, and all forms dependent on one alone—monarchy, despotism, and tyranny—to regal rule.

But although Ptolemy clearly thinks that political rule is best, contingent factors often make other forms more suitable. Among these factors are the nature and character of the people (determined greatly by astrological influences) and the region, the size of the community, and the availability of good leadership. Although all arguments against alternation evaporate if good rectors can be found, he writes, in a situation where this cannot happen a king would be better.[36] Various modern scholars have seized either on Ptolemy's relativism or emphasis on political rule to present an unbalanced picture of his thought. Dunbabin and the Carlyles, for example, point out that Ptolemy has something good to say about every form of government, while Davis sees him as the first great defender of republicanism and attacks the Carlyles for "glossing over Ptolemy's republicanism by saying that he showed indifference in choosing between regal and political rule."[37] The truth lies somewhere between these two positions.

Ptolemy does acknowledge that each form of government has its place,

---

[35] Ptolemy of Lucca, *De Regimine Principum*, 2.9.73. "Traduntur enim leges regales per Samuelem prophetam Israelitico populo, quae servitutem important . . . regimen politicum, quod erat Judicum et suum fuerat, fructuosius erat populo."

[36] Ptolemy of Lucca, *De Regimine Principum*, 4.8 (see also 2.8, 9); 4.2.178; 4.8.201.

[37] Dunbabin, "Aristotle in the Schools," p. 73; Carlyle and Carlyle, *History of Medieval Political Theory*, vol. 5, p. 72; Davis, "Roman Patriotism," p. 413.

but it is also clear that he thinks that political rule is best whenever possible and more natural for humanity. When it comes to his native Italy, or to cities anywhere, Ptolemy is indeed a champion of republicanism. But in most places for most peoples and for large kingdoms, he favors regal rule. This is not a mere afterthought to justify what actually exists; it is basic to his theory of the effects of sin. It is only the exceptional community blessed with a favorable climate, a fortunate configuration of stars, and great virtue that can profit from political rule. Others need the rigor of rule which only regal rule can provide.

Thus, Davis is wrong in imputing a thoroughgoing republicanism to Ptolemy. His comparison of Ptolemy and Aquinas is even more misguided when he asserts that only Ptolemy defends political rule as the best form, and that only Ptolemy comes out unequivocally in favor of the rule of law.[38] Though both do support political rule and law, Thomas endorses them more strongly than does Ptolemy: except for a hypothetical and unlikely situation, Thomas insists on political rule and law in every human community, Ptolemy only in some instances. Ptolemy goes beyond Thomas in two significant areas, but ones not germane to Davis's conclusion: his development of a natural basis for political rule and his rejection of regal rule in the Aristotelian sense of the rule of one over a free people. It is Ptolemy's recognition of the inseparability of servitude from regal rule that Davis mistakes for a rejection of nonpolitical rule, whereas Ptolemy actually believes that servitude is best for most people. Only later will others take the further step and argue that since a king is incompatible with freedom, kingship is unacceptable.

Davis also errs when he imputes a more authentic Aristotelianism to Ptolemy than to Aquinas. It is true, as he notes, that Ptolemy, as might be expected from a native of a North Italian city-republic, emphasizes the city more than Thomas, but in most other respects Thomas follows Aristotle more closely. Thomas's accommodations to Augustine and Christian political theory were slight; he wanted to defend a naturalistic foundation of government, which he did easily by ignoring Augustinian political theology. Given that Thomas misunderstood Aristotle at certain crucial points, and given that his medieval background forced him to interpret many of Aristotle's ideas in peculiar ways not intended by Aristotle, his ideas accord well with the *Politics* in the classification and the best forms of government. Ptolemy, as Davis himself shows, attempted a radical transformation of Augustine, and he was determined to work the idea of the earthly monarchy of Christ and the pope into his scheme.[39] His synthesis of what are ultimately unreconcilable systems is never quite consistent, but it represents a bold, if not completely successful, attempt toward an Augustinian

---

[38] Davis, "Ptolemy of Lucca," pp. 47, 50.
[39] See Davis, "Roman Patriotism," pp. 416, 423; *Dante*, p. 72.

Aristotelianism. His ideas can be put in the service of a radical republicanism more easily than can Thomas's, but in themselves they are neither more
Aristotelian nor more republican.

Bearing all this in mind, it must still be asked how Ptolemy envisioned
political government among the favored few who deserved it. It turns out
to be in all respects a mixed constitution (although he never uses these
words), as can be seen from his analysis of the Roman Republic, his prime
example of such a government. Surprisingly, for a papalist, his analysis of
the Church also suggests a mixed constitution.

In his *Crisis of the Early Italian Renaissance* Hans Baron maintains that it
was the crisis in foreign affairs in Florence around the year 1400 that stimulated the development of what he calls "civic humanism." As part of this
process there was a shift in emphasis from the typical medieval praise of
the Roman Empire as exemplified by Dante's *On Monarchy* to praise of the
Roman Republic and denigration of the Empire. It is true that the decisive
rehabilitation of the Republic occurred in Florence at that time. But even
Baron admits that there were at least a few isolated instances of advocacy
of the Republic before Leonardo Bruni's *Laudation* and *Dialogues*: he cites
Petrarch's *Africa* and Ptolemy of Lucca who, he wrote, "showed an aston-
ishing openness of mind toward the role played by free city-republics in
the ancient world. . . . [He] had formed the clear-cut judgment that the
power of Rome had been built up under the consuls and free councils of
the Republic." In spite of this, Baron feels that neither Petrarch nor Ptolemy had ventured any kind of coherent historical critique of the Empire;
the former expressing merely a form of racial nationalism, the latter simply
reflecting the republican ideals of the existing Northern Italian communes.[40]

I cannot completely agree with Baron. Others do applaud the Roman
Republic, and the description of the Roman government in I Machabees
as an example of a virtuous regime is widespread among the medieval Aristotelians. Davis effectively refutes this part of Baron's thesis in his series
of articles on Ptolemy of Lucca. Further, Ptolemy criticizes the Empire in
the very terms demanded by Baron—the destruction of virtue.

Ptolemy writes that Rome (and Athens as well) was more suited to political than to regal rule by reason of its astrological position and the virtues
of its citizens. Being under the sign of Mars, Romans resisted subjection,
could not abide superiors, and found kingship intolerable. Further, he is
fulsome in his praise of the ancient Romans. As Davis demonstrates in
detail, Ptolemy draws heavily on the *City of God*, changing what was there
backhanded or ambivalent approval into unbounded admiration. Ironi-
cally, considering that Augustine was a bitter enemy of astrology, Ptolemy
attributes even the moral superiority of the Romans in part to the influence

[40] Baron, *Crisis of the Renaissance*, pp. 55–57.

of the stars. They were humble and moderate, they did not exhibit hate or jealousy, and they cared for the Republic with their own wealth and thus were more solicitous for its well-being.[41] Because of these and other virtues—the zeal of their patriotism, the sanctity of their laws, and their civil benevolence—God granted them good government and dominion over others.[42] After the expulsion of the kings, Ptolemy writes, Rome flourished under the political rule of consuls, dictators, and tribunes for 444 years until the time of Julius Caesar.[43]

Drawing on both biblical and classical sources, Ptolemy argues that Roman government developed gradually, that its various institutions were added when the need became evident. Romulus instituted the senate, which persisted from the period of kings to the Empire. After the expulsion of the last king, Brutus established two annual, equal consuls to ensure moderation and preclude insolent rulers. Later, because of the Sabine threat, the senate added the office of dictator who was to rank above the consuls, but who was also limited in the length of his rule. Still later the people, who felt themselves to be oppressed by the consuls and the senate, instituted the tribunate.[44]

The Book of Machabees portrays the Roman government in action through the eyes of one of the conquered people: "[The Romans] commit its magistracy to dominate all its lands to one person for each year . . . no one wears a diadem, or wears the purple . . . there is no hate or jealousy among them . . . they daily consult the council of 320, deliberating always about the multitude that they might do that which is worthy."[45]

---

[41] Ptolemy of Lucca, *De Regimine Principum*, 2.8. Ptolemy refers to 1 Machabees 8.16 and to Cicero's statement that a prince should be fortified with charity and benevolence, not arms. Ptolemy's idea about wealth, lifted from the *City of God*, raises a problem for him. Not all of the Roman rectors were wealthy; he mentions Fabricius as a poor yet distinguished consul. Yet Aristotle, he points out, felt that it was a mistake to allow paupers to rule. Ptolemy solves this conflict by christianizing Roman rule in a way suggested by his own times and condition as a Dominican friar: he distinguishes between voluntary and involuntary poverty. The end of the former, he writes, is virtue, and therefore is best suited for any rule which has the same end, that is, political rule; the end of necessary poverty is material gain, in that these poor covet wealth, and, therefore, it cannot be the basis of good rule. Christ and his disciples chose voluntary poverty, and so too, he concludes, did Fabricius and the other Roman consuls who showed contempt for wealth so that they might faithfully govern the Republic (4.15).

[42] Ptolemy of Lucca, *De Regimine Principum*, 3.4–6. See also *Determinatio Compendiosa*, chap. 21, pp. 42–45. All power is from God, Ptolemy writes there, but especially the Roman. Augustine's *City of God*, he continues, gives reasons for this: the Romans' virtue, their tradition of just laws, and their civil benevolence.

[43] Ptolemy of Lucca, *De Regimine Principum*, 2.9. Ptolemy's chronology of Roman history is neither accurate nor internally consistent.

[44] Ptolemy of Lucca, *De Regimine Principum*, 4.26, 2.10. Ptolemy has the idea that the dictator ruled for five years.

[45] Ptolemy of Lucca, *De Regimine Principum*, 2.8.69, 71. " 'Per singulos annos committunt uni homini magistratum suum dominari universae terrae suae . . . nemo portabat diadema nec induebatur purpura . . . non est invidia nec zelus inter eos.' " 4.1.176. " 'Quotidie con-

This is presumably a description of Rome at its best, but Ptolemy characterizes the entire course of Republican history as political. He asserts that Roman rule was always relatively mild and possessed a "certain civility." The consuls depended for their power on the many, who could judge even the greatest consuls, such as Scipio Africanus.[46] Fearing citizens' wrath, most consuls ruled moderately. Nevertheless, the consuls, and even more so the dictators, enjoyed dominion over all, and Ptolemy wonders whether their rule might not be regal. He rejects this possibility because there is no way in which any of these officials can be called single rulers. They were elected, their power, however great, depended on the many, and they were not always nobles, so that their rule was political.[47]

The way the various governmental organs were added suggests the Polybian model of the naturally-developing mixed constitution. The tempering effect of each organ on the others also suggests the Thomist model. This is something completely missed by Davis, who is intent only on proving Ptolemy's republicanism, and by the Carlyles, who contrast Ptolemy's indifference to forms of rule to Thomas's mixed constitutionalism. I believe that Ptolemy followed up the hint provided by Thomas Aquinas when he compared the Jewish and Roman governments, describing the Jewish polity as a mixed constitution, but not further characterizing the Roman at all.[48]

Ptolemy describes the expansion of the Roman government as follows:

> If such a government is guided by a few virtuous men it is called aristocracy, as it was by the two consuls, or even by the dictator in the Roman City in the beginning after the expulsion of the kings. But if [it is guided] by many, as by the consuls, dictators, and tribunes as happened in the same city in the course of time and afterwards by the senators, as the histories relate, such a government they call a polity.[49]

Since Ptolemy had already said that the rule of the consuls alone depended on the many, he is saying something new here. Any political rule depends on the many, but not every political rule is the rule of the many. Since the consuls still existed, it seems as though what happened was not that rule was turned over completely to the many, but that a democratic

---

sulebant trecentos viginti, consilium agentes semper de multitudine, ut quae digna sunt gerant.' " [1 Machabees 8.14]. See also 3.20 and *Determinatio Compendiosa*, chap. 21, p. 46.

[46] Ptolemy of Lucca, *De Regimine Principum*, 2.8.69; 4.1.177.

[47] Ptolemy of Lucca, *De Regimine Principum*, 3.20, 2.8, 4.1. Those few instances in which a son succeeded are accidental—he too was elected and had no a priori right to rule.

[48] Thomas Aquinas, *De Regimine Principum*, 1.4.

[49] Ptolemy of Lucca, *De Regimine Principum*, 4.1.175. "Si tale regimine gubernatur per paucos et virtuosos vocatur aristocratia, ut per duos consoles vel etiam dictatorem in urbe Romana in principio expulsis regibus; si autem per multos, veluti per consules, dictatores et tribunos, sicut in processu temporis in eadem contigit Urbe, postea vero senatores, ut historiae narrant, tale regimen politiam appellant."

element (the tribunes) was added to the aristocratic government, producing a mixed government of the type most common in Aristotle's *Politics*: the mixture of the few and the many. Ptolemy is reluctant to consider the dictator or consul as a monarchic element since he depends on the many, but he certainly represents the power of one. It would be a small step then to see this government as a mixture of the one, the few, and the many. That this conclusion is not out of line with Ptolemy's thought is shown by his comments on the "Chalcedonian" (Aristotle's Carthaginian) government. He compares the situation in which their king governed with the counsel and consent of the few virtuous to that described in 1 Machabees in which the yearly ruler consulted daily with the 320 wise men.[50] The Carthaginian government was, of course, one of Aristotle's examples of a mixed constitution, and there seems little doubt that Ptolemy saw the Roman Republic in the same terms.

Another recital of the same events shows even more strongly Rome's mixed constitutional nature. After the kings' expulsion,

> At first, the two consuls were established; later . . . the dictator and the Master of Horsemen. The whole civil government was in the hands of these officials, and thus the city was governed by an aristocratic rule. Later the tribunes were devised to favor the plebians and the people, without whom the consuls and other officials I mentioned were not able to exercise their government—and, in this way, democratic rule was added on. But in the course of time the senators assumed the power of governing, although they were not newly created but rather had been created by Romulus right from the beginning. For he divided the whole city into three parts: senators, soldiers, and plebians, and then, when there were kings in Rome, the senators held a place corresponding to the Elders, who were called Ephors in Sparta, Kosmoi in Crete, and Gerusia in Chalcedonia, as was made clear above.[51]

The word *adjoined* definitely suggests a Polybian mixed constitution. The officials Ptolemy mentions were from the very polities which Aristotle used as examples of mixed constitutions. Besides confirming that Rome under the Republic was a mixed constitution, we have the even more remarkable

---

[50] Ptolemy of Lucca, *De Regimine Principum*, 4.19.233.

[51] Ptolemy of Lucca, *De Regimine Principum*, 4.19.234. "Creati fuerunt consules qui erant duo, postea dictator et magister equitum . . . ad quos pertinebat totum civile regimen; et sic principatu aristocratico regebatur. Ulterius inventi sunt tribuni in favorem plebis et populi sine quibus consules et alii praedicti regimen exercere non poterant; et sic adjunctus est democraticus principatus. . . . Processu vero temporis senatores assumpserunt regendi potestatem, licet senatores primo a Romulo sint inventi. Divisit enim totam civitatem in tres partes: in senatores, milites, et plebem; et tunc existentibus regibus in Urbe tenebant locum senum qui erant in Lacedaemonia qui Ephori dicebantur, sive in Creta quos Kosmos appellabant, sive in Chalcedonia quos nominabant Gerusios, ut supra est manifestum."

suggestion here that Rome even under the kings was to some degree a mixed government, a mixture of monarchy and aristocracy.

Ptolemy tries to show a sequence of types of rule in Rome, which seems to go through four of Aristotle's six forms. After the kings came aristocracy. Then, he writes, when the senators' power grew under the Republic, "since they were chiefly from the multitude, the rule of the Romans was political," here using the term *political* in Aristotle's sense of "polity," that is, good democracy. Finally, the corruption of a few during the civil wars brought oligarchy.[52] In each instance the change that occurred left in place the earlier offices, so that the labels here should be seen as descriptive of the most powerful element of the mixed constitution. This again is a Polybian idea: as the mixed constitution attempts to temper one group with another there is a perpetual struggle for balance; only when there is perfect balance (in the case of Rome this was never achieved) will there be stability.

Ptolemy closes with the cryptic comment that "these things are said in order to show that the rule of the Greeks at the time of Aristotle is very similar to that of our own time and place," that is, I suppose, at the time of ancient Rome.[53] Presumably what he means is that all the forms of government described by Aristotle were experienced by Rome. If we interpret the decline of the senators' rule as a transformation of polity to democracy, the only form missing is tyranny. It would seem reasonable to assume that this could be represented by the Empire. For some reason Ptolemy does not make this connection here—but he does just that elsewhere: "In the Roman government dominion was political from the expulsion of the kings until the usurpation of command, which was when Julius Caesar with his enemies prostrate . . . and with the world subjugated, assumed singular dominion to himself as a monarch and converted the polity into a despotic or tyrannical rule."[54]

In summary, the Roman Republic developed by gradually elevating more and more segments of the community to an active role in govern-

---

[52] Ptolemy of Lucca, *De Regimine Principum*, 4.19.234. "Quia senatores cum primis erant in multitudine, ideo tunc principatus Romanorum politicus dicebatur. Quando vero corrumpebatur politia per potentiam aliquorum, puta tempore quo exorta sunt bella civilia, tunc regebatur oligarchico principatu."

[53] Ptolemy of Lucca, *De Regimine Principum*, 4.19.234. "Haec pro tanto sint dicta ad ostendendum regimen Graecorum multum concordare cum nostra etiam tempore Aristotelis."

[54] Ptolemy of Lucca, *De Regimine Principum*, 4.1.176. "In regimine Romano a regum expulsione dominium fuerit politicum usque ad usurpationem imperii, quod fuit quando Julius Caesar prostratis hostibus . . . subjugatoque orbe, singulare sibi assumpsit dominium ut monarchiam convertitque politiam in despoticum principatum sive tyrannicum." Note that Ptolemy, as he often does, equates tyranny and despotism. It is interesting to compare this cycle of polities with that suggested by Aristotle—kingdom, polity, oligarchy, tyranny, and democracy (Aristotle, *Politics*, 3.15.1286b).

ment. Afterwards, as virtue declined, authority became concentrated in fewer and fewer hands until one man finally assumed tyrannical power, and the Republic came to an end. The Republic was greatest and most praiseworthy when the greatest number of citizens had a share in their own government; that is, when the Republic most resembled a mixed constitution.

I wish now to turn to another traditional aspect of the mixed constitution: counsel. Both those writers who favor regal kings and those who do not insist on the obligation of a king to seek advice. For Thomas Aquinas and Peter of Auvergne the counselors were an independent element in a mixed constitution; for Giles of Rome they were strictly subordinate to a sovereign king. Ptolemy, who like Giles (although for a different reason) takes care to depict the king as an absolute monarch, would presumably not give an independent role to the council under a king. Indeed in *On the Government of Rulers* counselors are treated as one more resource to be managed by the prudent ruler.[55] This assigns them a role inferior even to that given them by Giles of Rome, who at least thought they could act to make up for the defects of an unwise king. When the council is given an independent role, as in the case of the Machabean account of the Roman government or in Carthage, Ptolemy tends to deny the character of kingship to the one ruler, no matter how powerful. If the independence of the king from his advisors and his complete dominance over them is an essential of regal rule, which, after all, is only an expedient and not an absolutely best form of rule, all the more should it characterize the divinely appointed regal and sacerdotal rule of the pope. Most of Ptolemy's comments on the papacy can be so construed, but several passages in *A Short Determination* cast doubt upon this interpretation of counsel with respect to a king, and, more surprisingly, with respect to the pope. This shows the deep influence on Ptolemy of mixed constitutional ideas.

Attempting to refute the Donation of Constantine, which traced the pope's secular power to the will of the Emperor Constantine, but maintaining the pope's inherent supremacy, Ptolemy refers to those who argued that Constantine needed the counsel and consent of his subordinate rulers [princes] to make such a grant. Constantine, he replies, was simply recognizing that Christ was the true lord of the world; his grant gave nothing to the pope but that which was his already as Christ's vicar. Further, Constantine did do this, "together with all his satraps and the whole senate and optimates and the whole people."[56] Nowhere in his refutation does Ptol-

---

[55] Ptolemy of Lucca, *De Regimine Principum*, 1.10, 3.21–22.

[56] Ptolemy of Lucca, *Determinatio Compendiosa*, chap. 26, pp. 50–51. "Quod autem obiciebatur postea de Constantino, quod non potuit conferre imperium sine consilio et assensu suorum principum, ad hoc est duplex responsio . . . verus et proprius dominus orbis ac per se Christus. . . . Quod ergo imperium Constantinus Silvestro dimisset, non fuit per viam collationis, sed potius per viam cessionis tamquam vicario veri et proprii domini. . . . Secunda vero

emy deny the claim that the emperor does need the consent of the great men to take certain substantive actions, at least those involving the alienation of imperial power. True, Ptolemy will later argue that imperial power partakes of both regal and political rule. But even then he will see the actual power of an emperor and his relationship to law as regal. In *A Short Determination* the king and emperor are treated as even more similar, the only substantive difference being the pope's role in the anointing of the emperor. Naturally, in a defense of the pope against imperial ambitions Ptolemy was concerned more than he would be in *On the Government of Rulers* with minimizing the emperor's prerogatives. But he does imply that a king is restricted in some ways by the great men, and possibly by the people as a whole.

A biblical example strengthens this conclusion and extends it to the papacy itself. Speaking of Moses and his "coadjutors" Aaron and Hur, Ptolemy writes:

He [Moses] said to the elders of Israel, according to Exodus 24 [:14]: "You have Aaron and Hur with you, and if any question should arise, refer it to them." By this we are shown that those assigned to the salutary councils that I have mentioned ought to help and support the leaders of the faithful. On the one hand, the Aaronites, that is, the cardinals and other major prelates of the churches, ought to support the ecclesiastical leader, for which reason they were long ago instituted. On the other hand, the Hurites, that is, the rulers [princes] and barons, ought to strengthen the civil leader, whether he be a king, or emperor. For this reason they established parliaments, which ought to set themselves to the end of taking counsel to profit the leader's government, otherwise, if by chance something should be decided incautiously with hasty counsel, what comes from the throne of buffoons may easily be revoked by their successors, as in fact we see. Hence Solomon writes in Proverbs 13 [:10], "They who do all things with counsel are ruled by wisdom," whose duty it is to ordain all things according to wisdom. Likewise, Proverbs 33 [actually 24:6] says, "Where there is much counsel there will be safety." The ancient Romans, as is clear from what I said above, are especially commended for this in the period in which the Republic flourished. For he to whom they had committed its magistracy or consulate for a year, as the Book of Machabees relates, took counsel daily with the senate concerning the multitude, so that they might do those things that are worthy. The Roman Church acts in the same way today, for the highest pontiff takes counsel with the cardinals, who hold the position of the senators.[57]

---

responsio . . . ut ex Gestis Constantini habetur et capitulum est *Decreti* D.96, c. Constantinus, ibi expresse dicit se hoc fecisse una cum omnibus satraphis et universo senatu et optimatibus ac universo populo." The argument to be refuted was originally stated at chap. 2, p. 7.

[57] Ptolemy of Lucca, *Determinatio Compendiosa*, chap. 31, pp. 63–64. "Dixit senioribus

A Short Determination was written twenty years before *On the Govern-ment of Rulers*, and I think that a significant change occurred in Ptolemy's thinking during that period. In the earlier work he was more immediately influenced by Thomas Aquinas's conception of moderate or tempered monarchy. He had not yet come to the conclusion that a king in the true sense of the word is almost invariably despotic, and cannot be bound by others or the law. His threefold comparison—the Church, the Roman Re-public, secular kingdoms—is an extension of Thomas's treatment of the Mosaic kingship. Just as there were councils of the Jews that ruled jointly with Moses, so too do the Roman Senate, the College of Cardinals, and national parliaments share in the rule of their respective polities. The head is the most important element—this is why most of these are called mon-archies—but the other elements rightfully have a share of the rule and must be consulted by the head. The identification of the senate with the College of Cardinals is extremely important. Current canonistic thought supported the idea that the pope must consult the cardinals, and the cardinals were called senators as early as the eleventh century by Peter Damian.[58] But in bringing these elements together and in making a comparison with Mosaic kingship and the Roman Republic in an Aristotelian treatment of political power, Ptolemy prepares the way for the consideration of the Church as a mixed constitution, something which would happen in a very few years, first in an isolated remark of Peter John Olivi, and more fully a little later by John of Paris.

Ptolemy himself retreats from this direction; in *On the Government of Rulers* he never asserts that a king, let alone a pope, must share his power, although there are remnants of that idea, and Ptolemy never wholly dis-poses of it. On the other hand, Ptolemy's identification of monarchy with

---

Israel, Exodo XXIIII, 'Habetis Aaron et Hur vobiscum, si quid questionis natum fuerit, re-ferte ad eos.' Per quod nobis ostenditur, quod duces fidelium eo modo assignatis in predictis salutaribus consiliis ferri debent ac substentari, dux quidem ecclesiasticus Aaronitis, id est cardinalibus et aliis ecclesiarum prelatis maioribus, propter quod fuerunt ab antiquo consilia instituta, dux vero civilis sive rex sive imperator fulciri debet Huritis, id est principibus et baronibus, et ideo ab eisdem instituta sunt parlamenta, que ad hunc finem disponi debent, ut profectibus sui regiminis consulatur, ne, se forte consilio festinato aliquid diffiniatur incaute, per eorum successores, ut de facto videmus, quod cedit in sedis ridiculum, faciliter revocetur. Hinc per Salomonem scribitur, Proverbis XIII: 'Qui cuncta agunt cum consilio, reguntur sapientia,' cuius est omnia secundum sapientem ordinare. Item Proverbis XXXIII: 'Salus erit ubi multa consilia.' De quo specialiter veteres commendantur Romani, ut supra patuit, quando floruit res publica. Ille enim, cui magistratum seu consulatum pro suo anno commi-serant, ut in libro Machabeorum continetur, cottidie agebant cum senatu consilium de multi-tudine, ut, que digna sunt, gerant, quemadmodum adhuc hodie Romana observat ecclesia, summus pontifex cum cardinalibus, qui locum possident senatorum."

[58] See Brian Tierney, "A Conciliar Theory of the Thirteenth Century"; Davis, "Roman Patriotism," p. 423; Stefan Kuttner, *"Cardinalis*: The History of a Canonical Concept," p. 174.

regal rule is perhaps responsible for an important feature of future mixed constitutional theories. It may have been this aspect of Ptolemy's thought, together with his view of imperial rule as both regal and political that influenced Fortescue and thereby the whole later tradition of the mixed constitution to consider the English constitution as a mixture of regal and political rule. Further, in his insistence on matching the polity to the particular people, Ptolemy anticipates the widespread relativism of the fourteenth century.

In *A Short Determination* church and state are seen as completely analogous with respect to their organization (although, of course, the pope is given ultimate power over any state). The canonists and Thomas Aquinas had begun this process of assimilation; it would be continued by many others—John of Paris, for example, and especially William of Ockham. In *On the Government of Rulers* Ptolemy destroys this symmetry. Ptolemy's championship of political rule without kings cannot fruitfully be extended to the Church without the destruction of papal monarchy. This was the last thing that Ptolemy intended. That is not to say that there was a tension or inherent contradiction in Ptolemy's thought on this subject. It is quite consistent, as many of the imperialists of the period such as Dante and Marsilius of Padua argued with respect to the emperor, to insist that God has ordained one man for the general direction of the world, but that within this framework each city, region, or nation is responsible for its own organization, and that this government ultimately rests with the people.[59] Ptolemy is the most interesting political theorist of his generation because of the latent revolutionary content of his work; from his ideas could come the abolition of kingship and the overthrow of papal hegemony, once his uneasy synthesis of Aristotle and Augustine was discarded. If monarchs are by nature despots, why should they be tolerated in either the secular or spiritual spheres? Ptolemy replies that most people need such rule, but the doubts that he raises and the hostility he shows toward monarchy show the way toward a more radical resolution.

[59] Ullmann, *Law and Politics*, p. 274, fails to understand this. For him every person must select either a descending or ascending basis for his political theory. For this reason, given the prominence of papal hierocratic sentiment in Ptolemy's work, Ullmann gives Ptolemy (with Giles of Rome and Remigio di Girolami) as an example of one on whom Aristotelian doctrine had little effect. He was, Ullmann writes, unable to detach himself from traditional [i.e., descending] ideas of government; despite his background, Ptolemy's theory was "stale hierocratic and descending." Certainly papal monarchy is alien to Aristotelian thought, and certainly as the new ideas are more thoroughly applied, the theory of papal power will be revised, but Ptolemy's theory of the best secular state is both Aristotelian and descending.

Chapter 7

ENGELBERT OF ADMONT

ENGELBERT OF ADMONT (c. 1250–1331), also occasionally known as Englebert of Volkersdorf (because of his birthplace), had some of the widest interests of anyone of the time; he composed poetry and history, made translations, and wrote about science, ethics, philosophy, politics, and theology. The son of a noble and important Austrian family, he joined the Benedictine order at Admont at the age of about seventeen and studied at the Universities of Prague and Padua, where he came under the influence of Thomism. Forced to leave Prague in 1274 because of a war between Bohemia and the Empire, Engelbert wrote a patriotic poem in honor of Emperor Rudolph I. In 1288 he became Abbot of an abbey in Salzburg and, ten years later, of his first monastic home at Admont. Because of advancing age, he retired to Gallenstein Schloss in 1327 and died there a few years later.

Engelbert's *On the Government of Rulers*, composed sometime in the last decade of the thirteenth century, differs considerably in scope and development from the works of the same name by Thomas Aquinas/Ptolemy of Lucca and Giles of Rome, though in different ways.[1] The first tract and parts of the second deal with the varieties of rule and the conditions that make government necessary for humanity; in this it is similar to Thomas's and Ptolemy's approach and assumes that the best form of government is something to be deduced from general principles or local conditions and customs. The remaining, and larger, part of the treatise, however, is more related to the "Mirror of Princes" genre,[2] more concerned with abstract ethical considerations and practical methods for maintaining power, and tends to assume monarchy as a given. In this it is similar to Giles of Rome's *On the Government of Rulers*, but it lacks the same insistence on monarchy as the only proper, or even the only acceptable, form. Indeed, Engelbert, going beyond his medieval predecessors, shows an openness to every variety of government.

Most modern historians have paid little attention to Engelbert, perhaps

---

[1] Engelbert of Admont, *De Regimine Principum*, Heinrich Schmidinger, *Romana Regia Potestas: Staats- und Reichsdenken bei Engelbert von Admont und Enea Silvio Piccolomini*, p. 8, thinks that there is a great similarity in the themes of varieties of states, their degeneration, and emphasis on kingly virtues. Some similarity is of course inevitable since all three are discussions of Aristotle's *Politics*, but Engelbert's treatment is quite distinctive.

[2] Engelbert himself was the author of one of these, *Speculum virtutum moralium*.

because *On the Government of Rulers* is not available in a modern edition. This is unfortunate; his approach is unique and fascinating. Basing himself more on Aristotle's *Rhetoric* and *Ethics* than the *Politics*, Engelbert's classification of government differs from that of any other medieval writer. More significantly, he is the only writer, ancient or medieval, who presents a systematic analysis of mixed governments—he lists and discusses all of the mathematically possible permutations of the simple forms. What is more, he gives actual historical examples of most of them.

Engelbert's *Treatise on the Rise, Progress, and End of the Roman Empire*, written about twenty years after *On the Government of Rulers*, has received somewhat more attention.[3] The result has been a rather one-sided picture of Engelbert as a defender of the Empire, despite the fact that his tepid and conditional acceptance of the permanence of Rome lacks the enthusiasm of more zealous imperialists such as Dante. Engelbert does state plainly that monarchy is best, yet he also insists that local conditions determine the best government, and he also strongly approves the mixed constitution. I interpret his words to mean that he regards pure monarchy as a perfect but unrealizable abstraction (as did Thomas Aquinas), that only local conditions can justify any government, but that a mixed constitution is best in most cases.

Engelbert derives his classificatory schema, essentially a sevenfold one, from Aristotle, but it is not exactly the same as Aristotle's or anyone else's. He begins by declaring that there are three types of rule: monastic rule for the singular life (for which Engelbert, characteristically, cites no Christian source, but rather Aristotle's *Ethics*), economic rule for domestic life, and political rule for civil life. In stating his intention to concentrate on the third type, Engelbert makes clear his overriding interest in monarchy. He wishes to focus on political rule, he says, so that "we might come in that way to the doctrine and art of royal government, since the government of kings is a species of political government."[4]

Any community, Engelbert writes, must concern itself primarily with the difficult task of advancing the common good, whether it submits itself

---

[3] Engelbert of Admont, *Tractatus de ortu, et progressu statu et fine Romani Imperii*. Even the best of the more recent studies of Engelbert's political thought, Marlis Hamm's "Engelbert von Admont als Staatstheoretiker," while certainly not ignoring *On the Government of Rulers*, puts most of its emphasis on the ideas of *Treatise on the Rise of the Roman Empire*. Many older studies such as Ottokar Menzel's "Bemerkungen zur Staatslehre Engelberts von Admont," deal exclusively with this treatise.

[4] Engelbert of Admont, *De Regimine Principum*, 1.4.13–14. "Omissis igitur primis duabus speciebus regiminis vitae humanae, scilicit regimine Monastico et Iconomico, de Politico et speciebus ipsius aliquid breviter est dicendum, ut hoc ordine ad doctrinam et artem regalis regiminis veniamus: quoniam regimen regum est species regiminis Politici, ut patebit." Again, when he comes to talk of mixed constitutions (1.7.20), Engelbert reiterates that regal rule is his primary concern, but wants to talk about composite forms first.

to one, a few, or many rulers.[5] In the choice of the best ruler Engelbert subscribes to what Hamm calls the "aristocratic principle," meaning that the governing element should always be better in some sense than that which is governed.[6] "Better" is a relative term, depending on what a particular community values and interprets as the civil good: virtue, wealth and honors, or freedom. Combining these three criteria appropriately with the numerical possibilities for rule leads to four simple types of polity: monarchy, aristocracy, democracy, and oligarchy.

In a monarchy one best person, more virtuous than all others, "either in truth or according to the opinion of the multitude," rules. In aristocracy the few virtuous govern. In oligarchy the rich and powerful have precedence, those who, "are presumed to be wiser than others since wealth and power are acquired and preserved through some wisdom or industry." Finally, in democracy "the middle class or common people" rule and serve freedom. In such a polity "opinions and decisions in doubtful cases are resolved according to the consensus of the greater part of the people, and the people choose rectors" from among themselves.[7]

Engelbert states that rulers who seek their own interests can undermine each of the four simple forms. In this way monarchy becomes tyranny and aristocracy oligarchy. Oligarchy itself "passes over to a hereditary rule" and becomes what Engelbert calls *cleros*. Finally, democracy becomes barbarism if the people abandon their traditional and rational laws and establish uncustomary and useless institutions. Since oligarchy is at once one of the good simple forms and one of the corrupted ones, there are a total of seven distinct polities.[8] Notice that not only do the end of the society and the

---

[5] Engelbert of Admont, *De Regimine Principum*, 1.5.14–15.

[6] Engelbert of Admont, *De Regimine Principum*, 1.5.15; Hamm, "Engelbert," p. 373. "Regens semper est melius et potius eo, quod regitur."

[7] Engelbert of Admont, *De Regimine Principum*, 1.5.15–17. "Si multi, tale regimen vocatur Democratia, id est, principatus mediocrum seu popularibus . . . ubi feruntur in dubiis sententiae et diffinitiones et consensum majoris partis populi: et populus eligit, et de populo eliguntur rectores. . . . Si ergo aliqui assumuntur ad regimen propter suam prudentiam seu virtutem, tale regimen vocatur Aristocratica. . . . Si vero contigat aliquos assumi ad regimen propter divitias seu potentiam, tale regimen vocatur Olicratia, in Divitiores et potentiores praesumuntur sapientiores aliis esse, eo quod divitiae et potentia per aliquam sapientiam seu industriam acquiruntur et conservantur. . . . Et quia ad regem non assumuntur nisi optimi vel secundum veritatem vel secundum opinionem multitudinis. . . . Regem oportet optimum omnium esse: et qui talis est, ut solus virtute excellat omnes." Engelbert actually uses the word *olicratia* for oligarchy and *kingdom* for monarchy, but I will generally use the more common term. There are actually five more possibilities that Engelbert ignores, for if one ruled toward the end of wealth or freedom, if the few ruled toward freedom, or if the many ruled in pursuit of virtue or wealth, there would be a violation of the aristocratic principle: the best rulers would not have been chosen for the desired goal.

[8] Engelbert of Admont, *De Regimine Principum*, 1.18.40–42. "*Cleros*" is a curious term. It comes from the Greek κλῆρος, which has nothing to do with a hereditary caste, but rather

objective suitability of the rulers determine the appropriateness of rulers, but also the *perceived* quality of the rulers. Because Engelbert associates the best government with the end chosen by the society itself rather than with some objectively best end, this principle suggests a relativistic approach to government and begins to hint at the idea that the people as a whole should determine appropriate ends, and consequently that it possesses the right to institute the government it thinks most suited to that purpose. One caveat imposed is that saying that the community chooses an end or perceives certain things is not the same as saying that the people actively chooses or perceives it.

This sevenfold classification, as such, is unique to Engelbert. Perhaps attempting to combine Aristotle's usual two schemata (the sixfold one and the one comprising only oligarchy and democracy), Engelbert takes as his source for the good polities the classification used by Aristotle in his *Rhetoric*.[9] Here Engelbert found the four basic forms of his classification and also a version of the ends to which a state entrusts the common good. Like Engelbert, Aristotle stated that the end of democracy is freedom, of oligarchy wealth. However, Aristotle gave the maintenance of education and institutions as the end of aristocracy instead of virtue, and instead of stating an end for kingship mentioned the end of tyranny—preservation of the tyrant. Of course, in many other places, especially in the *Politics*, Aristotle did relate virtue to both kingship and aristocracy. Aristotle clearly meant these four forms to include both the good and bad polities; for example, he stated that there are two forms of monarchy: kingship and tyranny. But in order to bring his classification in line with the *Politics*, Engelbert was forced to invent degenerate forms of oligarchy and democracy. His idea of a hereditary caste of the rich and powerful was undoubtedly drawn from observation of the success of certain powerful, contemporary families in a number of Northern Italian cities, and of barbarism from the common Greek and medieval image of the utter chaos of mob rule inevitably leading to the despotism of a demagogue. It is this situation of a people incapable of ruling themselves or others that Aristotle saw as barbarism. Engelbert adds that barbarism properly is the situation of a community without ra-

---

with the selection of officials by lot. Κλῆρος and the adjective κληρωτὸς appear in both the *Politics* and the *Rhetoric* (e.g., *Politics*, 1300.a.19, 1330.a.15; and *Rhetoric*, 1356.b.34, 1393.b.4), but were translated correctly with words such as *sors, sorte,* and *sortiales* in both Moerbeke's translation of the *Politics* and the old Latin translation of the *Rhetoric*. Perhaps Engelbert's copy was defective at some point.

[9] Aristotle, *Rhetoric*, 1.8.1365b–1366a. Thomas Aquinas also used the *Rhetoric* and the four types of rule described there. He, however, did not attempt to blend the two sources, and therefore goes back and forth between a fourfold and a sixfold schema. Peter of Auvergne also at times uses this classification.

tional laws. The Greeks and Romans first discovered such laws, he says, and called almost all other peoples barbarians.[10]

Engelbert justifies the existence of each of the four good, simple forms of government as being naturally established in the family: "For they are natural, that is, as it were discovered and instituted by nature itself, which is clear from the similarity which they have to the modes [that is, forms] of government in the first community, which is certainly from nature and not from [human] institution. For the first community is the home, which according to Aristotle in I *Politics* is from nature."[11] In this, Engelbert differs in two significant ways from his predecessors—Thomas Aquinas, Giles of Rome, and Ptolemy of Lucca. First, none of these used the family as justification for rule. Rather they treated it only as analogous in some ways and with few implications for it. Engelbert's style of argument did not become common until the seventeenth century, and then usually only in defense of monarchy.[12] Second, Engelbert does not generally use the modal classification for rule that the others did, and so he finds analogues to the forms and not the modes of rule in the family. A paterfamilias, Engelbert writes, dominates his wife aristocratically, his children regally, and his servants tyrannically. The elder brother by virtue of his wealth and power dominates his siblings oligarchically, but otherwise, Engelbert suggests (but does not say directly), the relationship of brothers is democratic: "In other things they are equal in so far as they are brothers."[13]

Thus, Engelbert believes that nature instituted all four good forms and, apparently, even the bad form of tyranny. I say *apparently* because Engelbert is reluctant to make bad rule natural, even though he thinks the lord-servant relationship is. Since he does not distinguish modes of rule, he cannot call the rule of servants despotic, as all others had done; rather he

[10] Engelbert of Admont, *De Regimine Principum*, 1.8.42.

[11] Engelbert of Admont, *De Regimine Principum*, 1.6.18. "Sunt etiam naturales, id est, a natura ipsa quasi inventae et institutae: quod patet ex similitudine, quam habent ad modos regiminis primae communitatis, quae utique est a natura, et non ab institutione. Nam prima communitates est domus, quod secundum Philisophum in Primo Politicorum est a natura."

[12] See Schochet, *Patriarchialism* and Blythe, "Family, Government."

[13] Engelbert of Admont, *De Regimine Principum*, 1.6.18–19. "In ista autem communitate semper unum est praedominans et regens, et in isto regimine seu principatu naturali secundum quod dicit Philosophus in IX Ethicorum: vir dominatur mulieri principatu Aristicratio, id est, secundum virtutem. . . . Item vir dominatur liberis principatu regali. . . . Frater vero dominatur fratri Olicratico principatu, qui aestimatione vulgi propter aetatem, et per consequens propter divitias et potentias reputantur meliores, quod contigit in fratre seniore respectu juniores: quia frater fratri praeponitur propter aetatem. . . . In alii enim sunt aequales, in quantum fratres." Engelbert relies more on Aristotle's *Ethics* and *Rhetoric* than on the *Politics*, and in the *Ethics* Aristotle did relate particular forms to the family. In the later *Treatise on the Rise of the Roman Empire*, chap. 16, p. 765, Engelbert alludes to the modal distinction, but he makes no use of it. Political rule, which he equates with polity, is strictly by written law, whereas regal rule is by both written and unwritten law.

must call it tyrannical since it does not exist primarily for the benefit of the servant. Yet, he also writes that tyranny, "is not a species of some natural rule but a corruption and transgression of regal rule." Realizing the contradiction, Engelbert continues: "There is a great difference, as will be seen, between the tyrannical rule of a lord over a servant and of a bad king over his subjects."[14] Although he promises to, Engelbert never expands upon this statement. Clearly, he intends to distinguish, as had Thomas Aquinas, between public and private authority, with the result that the family is only partially an analogue of the state, but without resorting to a distinction of modes it is impossible for him effectively to defend the lord-servant relationship and yet attack a tyrannical king.

Lacking the concept of modes, Engelbert also cannot follow the usual distinction between the rule of a wife and of children, which is that the former is regulated by law and the latter is not. Nor does he suggest that the wife shares in rule. The rule of a wife is aristocratic, he writes, because it is according to virtue, since the man excels in body and mind. This statement, together with his assertion that the one-man rule of his brothers by the eldest son is oligarchy since it is based on wealth and power, suggests that for him the forms of rule may not always be determined by the size of the ruling group so much as by the qualities of the rule.[15] In other words, Engelbert includes a modal concept in his application of forms of rule. This is exactly what Aristotle did in the *Ethics*, before he developed an independent concept of modes.

Engelbert gives two slightly different accounts of the principles that animate the various polities and direct them to the same goal—the common good or liberty—by different means. In both, reason guides monarchy and virtue aristocracy. Law or choice (which he equates with will) directs democracy, and will or wealth impels oligarchy.[16] Again the terms are com-

---

[14] Engelbert of Admont, *De Regimine Principum*, 1.6.19. "Iterum etiam vir in domo dominatur servis principatu tyrannico, qui non est species principatus naturalis alicuius, sed corruptio et transgresso principatus regalis. Nam paterfamilias dominatur servis ad utilitatem suam propriam, et non ad utilitatem servorum . . . tamen differentia magna sit inter principatum tyrannicum, qui est domini ad servum, et qui est mali Regis ad subditos, sicut postmodum patebit."

[15] Engelbert of Admont, *De Regimine Principum*, 1.6.18. "Vir enim in virtute corporis et animi mulierem excellit. Unde mulier naturaliter viro est subjecta propter virtutem viri." Unlike Engelbert, Aristotle, when he writes of forms of rule and the family in the *Ethics*, did say that the rule of a wife is aristocratic because the husband gives up part of his rule to her in areas in which she is more competent. Should he assume full command, his rule would become oligarchic. Aristotle's example of timocracy (equivalent to Engelbert's democracy) is the relationship of brothers (*Ethics*, 8.10.1160b.27–1161a.9). For the Middle Ages, with its practice of primogeniture, Engelbert's association of brothers with oligarchy is more reasonable.

[16] Engelbert of Admont, *De Regimine Principum*, 1.10.25–26, 28. "Quatuor sunt principia, secundum quae et ex quibus procedit regimen vitae civilis, videlicet ratio, virtus, lex, et electio

pressed: law, associated by Thomas Aquinas and Aristotle with the political mode of rule, Engelbert ascribes to democracy, which corresponds to Aristotle's polity. Will, a characteristic for most medieval writers of regal rule, is displaced to oligarchy, since by regal rule Engelbert means only monarchy, a specific form and not a mode of rule. Engelbert does not mention unity, the characteristic most frequently associated with monarchy in the Middle Ages.

Engelbert recognizes that, in fact, every form of rule uses all of these principles to varying degrees, but argues that one dominates in each and describes the intentions of the ruling group. Ferdinand Cranz disputes this interpretation and asserts that in two cases the overlap is so great that Englebert identifies aristocracy and monarchy on the one hand and democracy and oligarchy on the other.[17] Indeed, Engelbert writes, "aristocracy in this is assimilated to regal rule since," according to the *Ethics*, "virtue always works with right reason" and, "democracy and oligarchy are opposed more directly to regal government since they are not according to virtue or reason but according to written or unwritten law and according to the consensus and will of humans." But in context he is really just trying to explain why in a certain passage of the *Ethics* Aristotle mentions only monarchy, democracy, and oligarchy and answers that Aristotle assimilated the two pairs for the reason given. His own opinion is that any form can approach any other by using the other's principle, and he consistently emphasizes the interpenetration of species of rule. Insofar as aristocracy, or democracy, or even oligarchy uses reason it approaches regal rule, insofar as it retreats from reason it is opposed to regal rule (only tyranny is completely opposed). Insofar as a king uses written law, or will beyond reason, he approaches democracy or oligarchy. And so forth. Species of government differ, "in the intention and mode alone by which the governing [part] holds itself to the government, according to reason, virtue, law, or will, although those governing can use diverse species of government."[18]

---

seu voluntas: et secundum illorum quatuor principiorem differentiam et comparatiam et differentia et comparatio quatuor simplicium politiarum ad invicem. Nam regimen regni . . . procedit secundum rationem: regimen Aristocratiae secundum virtutem: regimen Democratiae secundum electionem et legem: regimen Olicratiae secundum voluntatem." In the second version (1.10.27) he quotes Aristotle and says that, "all intend toward liberty." "Sicut dicit Philosophus Quarto Politicorum, 'omnes intendunt ad libertatem,' quam Monarchia quaerit ex ratione, Aristocratia ex virtute, Olicratia ex divitiis, Democratia ex lege." The difference between goal and principle corresponds to Aristotle's distinction between final and efficient cause, since each community tends toward its goal but is impelled by its principle.

[17] Cranz, *Aristotelianism*, p. 266.

[18] Engelbert of Admont, *De Regimine Principum*, 1.10.26–27. "In quibis verbis Philosophi notabile est, quod mentionem Aristocratiae non facit, sed regni et Democratiae et Olicratiae: quia regimen Aristocratiae in hoc assimilatur principatui regali, quod regimen eius procedit secundum virtutem, ac per hoc secundum rationem: quia virtus semper operatur cum ratione

A corollary is that in Engelbert's opinion the simple forms can never exist in their pure form, that the simple polities are abstractions derived from observation of the varieties of mixed constitutions, which are all that exist in reality. It is just that, for convenience, when one principle dominates, the simple name can be used.

Insofar as we can speak of simple forms, Engelbert writes, one based upon a superior principle may be inherently better than another. He says that monarchy is best, for reason imitates nature and is the greatest of the principles, than which nothing is greater save God; it is greater than law and will because it is infallible and can take particular circumstances into account.[19] Monarchy is also the way of the animal and insect world and of all well ordered bodies, such as armies.[20] Aristocracy is better than all except monarchy because its principle, virtue, is more reliable than the wills of individuals upon which both democracy and oligarchy depend. Finally, democracy is better than oligarchy since law and the consensus of most people is better than rule by the will of a few.[21]

Engelbert argues that any true, nondegenerate polity must either be one of these four good, simple forms or a combination of them. Combining

recta, secundum quod dicitur Tertio Ethicorum Democratia vero et Olicratia directius opponuntur regali regimini: quia regunt non secundum virtutem vel rationem, sed secundum legem scriptam vel non scriptam et secundum hominum consensum et voluntatem. . . . In quantum Aristocraticus principatus et Democraticus aut Olicraticus in suo regimine utuntur ratione propter legem vel virtutem seu voluntatem, in quantum accedunt ad assimilationem principatus regalis, et in quantum utuntur leges aut virtute aut voluntate propter rationem, in tantum opponuntur principatui regali. Sicut e converso principatus regalis declinat ad naturam illorum, si quando utitur in suo regimine lege scripta aut voluntate praeter ratione. . . . Sed differentia regiminum ad invicem secundum speciem consistit in sola intentione et modo, quo se habet regens ad regimen, secundum rationem vel virtutem, vel secundum legem, vel secundum voluntatem, licet Regentes possint diversis speciebus regiminum uti."

[19] Engelbert of Admont, *De Regimine Principum*, 1.11.28–29. "Nam virtus non est operatrix boni, nisi in quantum cum ratione recta operatur. Et sicut ratio praecellit vel simpliciter, et voluntatem dependentem ad legem . . . ratio, quando arte vera fuerit informata, est certa et infallibilis regula. Sed voluntas seu consensus aut electio absque arte fallit in multis. . . . Ergo regimen, quod est secundum rationem, melius est regimine, quod est secundum consensum hominum et voluntatem." 1.13.32. "Unde sicut regalis principatur melior est omnibus aliis ex eo, quod habet se ad regimen secundum rationem, quae imitatur naturam, ratione autem nihil est melius nisi θεὸς."

[20] Engelbert of Admont, *De ortu*, chap. 1, p. 754, c.15.763–64, *De Regimine Principum*, 1.10.26.

[21] Engelbert of Admont, *De Regimine Principum*, 1.13.32. "Nam inter simplices politias meliores sunt, quae ex melioribus principiis procedunt, et secundum meliora principia, motiva et inductiva ad regimen se habent, et ad fines meliores respiciunt. Unde sicut regales principatus melior est omnibus aliis ex eo, quod habet se ad regimen secundum rationem . . . principatus Aristocraticus melius est aliis ex eo, quod regit secundum virtutem: virtus autem certior est et firmior voluntatibus singulorum. Ideo etiam principatus Democraticus melior et firmior est principatu Olicratico. Nam Democraticus habet se ad regimen secundum observationem legis et secundum consensum maioris partis populi."

them by twos, threes, and fours, eleven possible mixed constitutions are possible. Engelbert wants to enumerate all possible arrangements, but at the outset he warns that he is speaking only of mathematical possibility and not necessarily of situations that actually exist.[22] Nevertheless, with two exceptions (kingdom and oligarchy, kingdom and democracy) he gives examples, and, in all but two further cases, specific examples of existing regimes with the given structure.

These examples are most interesting, since his descriptions of the mixtures themselves are formulaic. If there is a monarchic element he says, "one rules according to reason"; if there is an aristocratic element he says, "some [or some few] rule according to virtue." About a democratic component he comments, "the people rule according to the consent of the greater part concerning judgments and statutes in great things or new things"; about an oligarchic element he writes, "those greater by nobility or wealth rule, not according to the virtue of the one chosen but through succession, or descent, or grade of nobility, or of power, or of wealth."[23]

The mixture of kingdom and aristocracy and the mixture of all four types are two Engelbert clearly thinks actually exist, but for which he provides no contemporary example. About the first he writes:

> Such seems to be the government of those kingdoms in which consuls and rectors are taken up for the government of the Republic, not by right of heredity, or from title of descent, but from choice of virtue and probity—those who are worthy to be called "friends of the king." Whence Aristotle in III *Politics* says, "those chosen to be rulers with the king should be friends who love the good of the king.[24]

The citation of Aristotle is interesting since in the *Politics* Aristotle is not referring to a mixed constitution at all but is considering what kind of advisors a king should have. Would Engelbert call any kingdom in which the king chooses good counselors a mixed constitution? I will return to this question later.

---

[22] Engelbert of Admont, *De Regimine Principum*, 1.6.18. "Nam cum multae sunt species politiae, unaquaeque tamen componitur ex aliquibus praemissarum quatuor," 1.7.20. "Secundum igitur, quod politiarum compositarum ex duabus, quaedam ex tribus, quaedam ex omnibus quatuor politiis. Et loquimur hic de compositione politiarum non secundum realem usum, sed secundum possibilitatem combinationis simplicium: quia, sicut dicit Philosophus quarto Politicorum, 'non solum existentes sed etiam possibiles existere politias oportet considerare.' "

[23] Engelbert of Admont, *De Regimine Principum*, 1.7–9.20–25.

[24] Engelbert of Admont, *De Regimine Principum*, 1.7.21. "Quale videtur esse regimen illorum regnorum, in quibus consules et rectores assumuntur ad regimen Reipublicae, non ex iure haereditatis seu ex titulo generis, sed ex electione virtutis et probitatis, qui sunt digni vocare amici regis. Unde dicit Philosophus Tertio Politicorum [3.16.1287b], quod, 'dignum est, illos esse principantes Regi ut amicos, qui diligunt bonum Regis.' "

Engelbert postpones final judgment of the mixture of all four polities until later, and so will I, but his initial comments sound negative: "Although it is a rather difficult and laborious government, nevertheless it is in common enough use on account of the idleness and negligence of rulers and kings about the observation of the best and most suitable government . . . whether such a government is useful or not, will afterwards more fully become clear in the proper place."[25]

Engelbert is more specific about all the other mixed constitutions, and especially about the mixture of aristocracy and democracy. His enthusiasm for this form—he says that the best-governed cities in Italy use it—is really quite out of character. The aristocratic element comprises a podesta and a group of greater consuls, Ancients, chosen from the common people. Engelbert praises the method of their selection and the way in which the common people participate

[so that] the choice of podestas and consuls and the establishment of statutes permitting or forbidding something proceed without fear and danger according to virtue and truth; individuals express their consent for this side or that not through words but through certain lots which they call ballots. This seems very reasonable and considered since according to Aristotle in I *Rhetoric*, "there exist two things which especially impede right counsel: fear and error." In ballots fear is guarded against through lot because it is not known who consents to a proposition or is against it. But error is guarded against by art, because everyone is free to counsel, which seems rather useful. But since nobles for the greater part aspire more to power and its excellence and to their own good than to the common good, for this reason the cities under a better government are accustomed rarely to choose or admit nobles to the consulate and to governments, but they choose good men according to virtue and love from the common people.[26]

[25] Engelbert of Admont, *De Regimine Principum*, 1.9.24–25. "Quae licet sit magis difficilis et laborosi regiminis, est tamen in usu satis communis propter desidiam et negligentiam Principum et Regum circa observationem optimi et convenientissimi regimen. . . . Tale regimen utrum utile vel inutile sit, postmodum plenius in suo loco patebit."

[26] Engelbert of Admont, *De Regimine Principum*, 1.7.22. "Et in electione Potestatum et Consulum, et conditione statutorum et faciendorum vel non faciendorum sine timore et periculo procedat secundum virtutem et veritatem, consensum exprimunt singuli pro hac parte vel illa, non per verba sed per sortes quasdam, quas ballotas vocant. Quod valde videtur rationabile et consultum: quia secundum Philosophum in Primo Rhetoricae, 'duo sunt, quae praecipue impediunt rectum consilium, scilicet timor et error.' In ballotis igitur timori praecavetur per sortem: quia nescitur, quis consenserit in propositum vel in oppositum. Errori vero praecavetur per artem: quia nihilominus liberum est unicuique consulere, quod utilius videatur. Sed quia nobiles pro majori parte aspirant magis ad potentiam et excellentiam suam et suorum, quam ad bonum commune, propter hoc civitates, meliori regimine utentes, raro consueverunt nobiles eligere vel admittere ad consulatus et regimina: sed de popularibus eli-

Engelbert's remarks apply to a number of Northern Italian city-states during the period of the *popolo* (that is, the period in which the guilds dominated), when the right to hold office and to participate in government was extended to its widest extent in any stable regime during the Middle Ages—to the *popolo*, which meant not the people as a whole but the guildsmen. The office of Ancients originated in Bologna in 1231 and spread rapidly, not always under the same name. In Florence, for example, the priors were in a similar position. Many of these cities instituted so-called "antimagnate" legislation defining and then restricting the hereditary nobility in the late thirteenth century, but by 1300, many of these same cities had succumbed to the forces they had been trying to control and had become subject to despots (*signorie*), and most of the rest were in danger of following suit.[27] So Engelbert is writing in defense of a system currently endangered by the rich and powerful.

That he recognizes this danger is shown by his comments on the mixture of aristocracy, democracy, and oligarchy—the situation in some of the cities that formerly had enjoyed a mixture of aristocracy and democracy, but that were forced to allow the participation of the optimates. The cities of Italy under this "less good government" are "often jeopardized by many discords and some are destroyed inwardly. For, although the first and chief rectors . . . intend the common good, nevertheless the powerful and wealthy, who minister under them in part of the government, always strive to draw a part of the people to them and their friends, and thus parties form and seditions occur in the cities."[28]

The mixture of aristocracy and oligarchy shares some of the same problems. It is "common enough in many cities of Italy in which podestas are chosen from foreigners according to virtue and probity, but consuls and rectors are raised to office from the city as they excel in wealth or power."[29]

For all the other mixed constitutions Engelbert simply mentions a specific, if somewhat elusive, example with no elaboration: a mixture of democracy and oligarchy prevails in "many cities and provinces of Germany [*Teutoniae*]," "many kingdoms, and duchies, and provinces, and cities es-

---

gunt bonos viros secundum virtutem et amorem, quo se habent multi de talibus ad bonum commune."

[27] See Hyde, *Society and Politics*, pp. 112–15, 146.

[28] Engelbert of Admont, *De Regimine Principum*, 1.7.24. "Sicut in aliquibus civitatibus Italiae, minus bono regimine utentibus invenitur, quae propter hoc etiam saepe multis discordiis periclitatae sunt, et aliquae penitus sunt destructae. Nam rectores primi et praecipui, qui sunt boni, quamvis intendant bonum commune, tamen potentes et divites, qui subministrant eisdem in parte regiminis, semper nituntur partem populi ad se et suos amicos retrahere, et sic fiunt partes et seditiones in civitatibus."

[29] Engelbert of Admont, *De Regimine Principum*, 1.7.21. "Quod regimen taliter permixtum satis commune est in multis civitatibus Italiae, in quibus Potestates eliguntur de extraneis secundum virtutem et probitatem; consules vero et rectores de ipsa civitate assumuntur, secundum quod excellunt in potentia vel divitiis."

pecially in the principate of Germany [*Alemanniae*]" have a mixture of kingdom, aristocracy, and oligarchy; the kingdom of Hungary once had a combination of kingdom, aristocracy, and democracy; and most of the duchies and principates of the Slavs are characterized by a mixture of kingdom, democracy, and oligarchy.[30]

Engelbert evaluates these mixed constitutions using the same criteria as for the simple polities; within each group, determined by the number of simple components, he ranks them lexigraphically according to this already established order: monarchy, aristocracy, democracy, oligarchy.[31] His position seems to be that a mixed constitution too is better the closer it approaches to pure monarchy. Here he does not directly compare mixed constitutions with varying numbers of elements.

Of all these forms, which is best? Engelbert's evaluations seem to leave room for only one answer: monarchy. In an absolute sense this is true. Human society guided by pure and perfect reason could not be improved. But this answer is misleading. I believe that in most cases Engelbert favors a mixed monarchy, but that his ultimate criterion for good government is expediency; that is, that which is best is determined by particular conditions and not a priori arguments. Aristotle's frequent recourse to expediency forced a certain recognition of it upon all medieval Aristotelians, but the idea of an absolutely best polity—or at least, taking into account human nature, one that was best for all communities—dominated. Engelbert shares this prejudice to some degree, but starting with him the emphasis begins to shift in the other direction, toward relativity of political forms. In my conclusion about Engelbert's preference, I am in substantial agreement with Marlis Hamm, despite a number of other disagreements.[32]

Engelbert begins to undermine the absolutist position immediately following his evaluation of the simple and mixed constitutions. "In the preceding comparisons," he writes:

> We do not intend to say that this or that polity is the best or worst of all; because, just as Aristotle says in III *Ethics*: "Perhaps the best polity has not yet been discovered." But we do intend to say that of those which are in use ac-

---

[30] Engelbert of Admont, *De Regimine Principum*, 1.8.22–24. "Ex Democratia autem et Olicratia est illud regimen . . . quam in pluribus Teutoniae civitatibus et provinciis est in usu. . . . Ex regno igitur et Aristocratia et Olicratia . . . quale regimen iam quasi communiter in multis regnis et ducatibus et provinciis et civitatibus, maxime in principatu Alemanniae [obtinet]. . . . Ex regno vero et Aristocratia et Democratia est illud regimen . . . quale regimen dicitur aliquando fuisse in regno Hungariae." Presumably, the reference to Hungary is to the brief period between the imposition of the Golden Bull on King Andrew II by the Hungarian nobles in 1222 and the Mongol devastation of 1242. Under this charter, a Mass Diet of all nobles had great authority, powerful counts became removable and nonhereditary, and local assemblies were set up.

[31] Engelbert of Admont, *De Regimine Principum*, 1.14–15.33–37.

[32] Hamm, "Engelbert," pp. 404–5.

cording to the possibility of combination or mixing of the simple [forms], or even among the simple [forms] themselves, one is better than another and one is worse than another. Nevertheless, any one has something of danger and fear. As Aristotle says in I *Rhetoric*: "The best excepted, all are excessive, just as in tones beyond the consonate all others above and below exceed right consonance." Whence "not yet discovered" is according to use not understanding: because to find such a king who does nothing beyond reason, or a good and virtuous consul who in nothing exceeds the median of virtue, or such a rich and powerful one who intends nothing according to reason and virtue but all according to his will, this happens rather according to imagination and intellect than according to the thing and act. We can form such men more mentally than discover them really.[33]

This goes considerably beyond Thomas Aquinas's (or, slightly later, John of Paris's) statement that although a regal king would be best absolutely, almost no one is virtuous enough for the role. Engelbert is saying that the whole structure of the classification of polities is intellectual and artificial; as such it does not correspond exactly to reality. There is never a pure simple polity, and even in a mixed constitution the monarchical, aristocratic, democratic, or oligarchic elements never truly represent these forms. Abstractly we can say that this or that form is better, but in practice we must consult the particular conditions and the particular government.

According to Engelbert, many factors, including climate and custom, determine how many should participate in a polity. In this regard he cites Aristotle's contention that those living in hot climates are easily ruled, those in cold climates are incapable of political organization at all, and those in the middle (namely Greece and Italy) are best suited for civil rule. In order to live well, which is the end of the city, he writes, different cities

[33] Engelbert of Admont, *De Regimine Principum*, 1.17.38. "Ad praedictarum autem comparationum et differentiarum maiorem intellectum sciendum est, quod ex praedictis comparationibus non intendimus dicere, quod ista vel illa politia sit optima omnium vel pessima: quia sicut dicit Philosophus Tertio Ethicorum, 'nondum forsitan inventa est optima politia.' Sed intendimus dicere, quod earum, quae sunt in usu, secundum possibilitatem combinationis seu commixtionis simplicium vel etiam inter ipsas simplices una est melior quam alia, et una deterior quam alia. Unaquaeque tamen habet aliquid periculi et timoris. Quia, sicut dicit Philosophus in Primo Rhetoricae, excepta optima politia omnes alienae excedunt, sicut in tonis praeter illos, qui sunt consonantes, omnes alii supra et infra excedunt rectam consonantiam. Unde, quod dicit Philosophus, quod, 'nondum inventa est optima politia,' hoc intelligendum est secundum usum potius quam secundum intellectum: quia invenire talem Regem, qui in nullo faciat aliquid praeter rationem, vel Consulem bonum et virtuosum, qui in nullo excedat medium virtutis, vel talem divitem seu potentem, qui nihil intendit secundum ratiionem et virtutem, sed omnia secundum suum voluntatem, hoc contingit potius secundum imaginationem et intellectum, quam secundum rem et actum. Tales enim homines plus mentaliter fingere possumus, quam realiter invenire."

must establish different governments according to their climate and location.[34]

Unity of country, language, customs, and rites is necessary for concord, which is in turn a requisite of a good polity. Engelbert insists that no particular written or unwritten law can apply to diverse peoples since they have different customs, languages, and the like.[35] Therefore, each place should have its own law, and by inference a government most suited to it. In order to find useful laws, he writes, you need to know all about a locality.[36]

Size and time in history also partially determine the appropriate type of government. Engelbert approaches the problem of justifying the large kingdom or the Empire by Aristotelian arguments more directly than any previous author. He recognizes the difference in scale, and also observes a difference in kinds of rule:

> The community of the city gathered and established from many joined nearby villages is called "the people." And in these communities in our time there are aristocratic, democratic, and oligarchic governments, and another government composed from them. In antiquity, there were singular kings of singular cities in many parts of the world who are properly called kings of peoples; just as is read concerning Romulus, first king of the Romans, who was king of the city of Rome alone.[37]

The situation is different in Engelbert's time:

> A nation differs from a city or a people . . . kings of villages or cities distant in latitude and longitude of the lands are properly called kings of nations. Such kings are great kings as of Germany, France, Spain, Greece, and other like places. Whence it is clear that the government of a king as is now in use differs

[34] Engelbert of Admont, *De Regimine Principum*, 3.19.70; 2.2.45. See also 6.8.178–79.

[35] Engelbert of Admont, *De ortu*, chap. 16, p. 765. "Lex sive scripta, sive non scripta, non potest esse una diversis gentibus secundum diversas linguas et patrias, et patrios mores et ritus." See also chap. 14, p. 763. Engelbert gives this as an argument against the empire, which argument he later rejects. The part that I cite is still valid, however, since his conclusion is that there must be local government and law to take into account local conditions, but nothing prevents there from being universal government and law with respect to those things held in common, i.e., natural law and the law of nations (*De ortu*, 1.18.768).

[36] Engelbert of Admont, *De Regimine Principum*, 3.9.63. "Ad inventionem autem tam legum utilium, quam institutionum municipalium prodest praecipue praecognoscere et praescire descriptus situs et qualitatis et naturalis rerarum et hominum in singulis terris habitantium vicinorum ipsorum."

[37] Engelbert of Admont, *De Regimine Principum*, 1.12.31. "Et ita communitas civitatis collecta et constituta ex vicis pluribus conjunctis vocatur populus. Et in istis communitatibus, ut nunc temporis, sunt regimina Aristocraticae, Democratiae, et Olicraticae, et alia regimine ex suis composita. Et antiquitus etiam erant Reges singuli singulorum civitatum in multis partibus Mundi, qui vocabantur proprie Reges populorum: Sicut legitur de Romulo Rege primo Romanorum, qui erat rex solius civitatis Romanae."

from other species of civil government or of small kingdoms by the multitude of humans and by the distance of longitude and latitude of provinces and cities, and not only according to species.[38]

Elsewhere Engelbert reiterates that in his day aristocracy, democracy, and oligarchy are the suitable form for cities, and that large kingdoms are best.[39] In one way this is a more primitive form of the argument that Bartolus of Sassoferrato will use a quarter of a century later when he gives a hierarchical scheme for the different species of polity based on the size of a community. In another way, however, it is more advanced in that Engelbert shows a concern not only with different types of community but with historical development as well.[40]

The idea of expediency goes along with the prevalent idea that the common good is the criterion for the evaluation of governments. By this theory no one has the right to rule unless it can be shown that they would promote the common good. The difference between Engelbert and those who advocate one particular form as universally best, as does Giles of Rome, for example, is that the latter authors regard their favored form as the best for promoting the common good in all times and places. As the idea of sovereignty developed, this theory of the common good gave way to the doctrine that a certain group, usually the people, possessed an inherent right to rule itself or subject itself to any desired government regardless of whether its choice most effectively promoted the common good. Writing in a transitional period, Engelbert, John of Paris, and Ptolemy of Lucca all to varying degrees managed to express both of these ideas. To this Engelbert adds the idea that the common good itself is relative—that it partially depends upon the citizens' conception of it.

In Engelbert the idea of sovereignty is rather rudimentary. Gierke declares that he is, "the first to declare in a general way that all *regna et principatus* originated in a *pactum subiectionis* which satisfied a natural want and instinct."[41] The actual statement of the social contract is, in fact, somewhat weaker than Gierke would have it—Engelbert says only that the people

[38] Engelbert of Admont, *De Regimine Principum*, 1.12.31. "Gens vero differt a civitate, seu a populo. . . . Et proinde Reges vicorum seu civitatum distantium per latitudinem et longitudinem terrarum appellantur proprie Reges gentium, quales Reges sunt Reges magni sicut Alemanniae, Franciae, Hispaniae, et Graeciae et consimiles. Unde patet, quod regimen Regni, ut nunc est in usu, differt a caeteris speciebus regiminum civilium vel regnorum parvorum multitudine hominum et distantiae longitudinis et latitudinis provinciarum et civitatum, et non solum secundum speciem." See also 2.2–3.44–46 and *De ortu*, chap. 12, p. 761.

[39] Engelbert of Admont, *De ortu*, chap. 13, pp. 761–62. See also *De Regimine Principum*, 1.6.19.

[40] Bartolus of Sassoferrato, "Tractatus de regimine civitatis."

[41] Gierke, *Political Theories*, p. 146, n. 138. See also J. W. Gough, *The Social Contract*, pp. 39–40.

chose the first kings for the sake of protection; nonetheless, there is the implication throughout Engelbert's writings that government is based on the consent and voluntary subjugation of the people, even though, as Hamm notes, it is not clear whether once having submitted itself to a ruler the people retains the right to rule directly.[42]

It does, however, have the right to depose a king, but perhaps only if he violates the social contract. Emperors can, Engelbert asserts, be deposed for disobedience to the Church, and, he adds, "a deposition of them [kings and emperors] can occur on account of pride and avarice, worthlessness and evil with regard to pursuing justly the governance of the republic."[43] The context suggests that the Church might be the deposing agency, but the examples Engelbert gives of the valid removal of kings—Saul, Roboam, and Ahab from the Old Testament and Tarquin and Julius Caesar from Roman history—show that the people itself has this right. Saul alone of these four was deposed by God; the others suffered their punishment at the hands of the people. Caesar and Tarquin forfeited their right to rule because they were tyrants and refused to let others participate in government. Engelbert writes that Caesar wanted to be all things; from this desire he converted the common good to his own personal good.[44] It was for his crimes that "the senate with the Roman people" expelled Tarquin.[45] These examples could support Schmidinger's and Hamm's contention that the people's deposition of kings is purely declarative—as tyrants these rulers cannot be true kings, and the people's actions merely recognize this fact.[46] Roboam's case is different. He was justly deprived of his office by the peo-

---

[42] Hamm, "Engelbert," p. 382.

[43] Engelbert of Admont, De ortu, chap. 23, p. 772. "Imperatorum at Regum Romanorum quidam reprobati sint propter suam inobedientiam, eo quod fuerint inobedientes et rebelles Ecclesiae, cum tamen extra Ecclesiam non sit, nec possit esse imperium: Quorundam vero temporibus, propter Imperatorum et regum superbiam et invidiam est detrunctum regnum Romanorum . . . propter ipsorum superbiam et avaritiam, ignaviam et malitiam (quoad gubernationem republiciae iuste gerendam) poterit fieri ipsorum depositio." See Hamm, "Engelbert," p. 389.

[44] Engelbert of Admont, De Regimine Principum, 7.35.253. "Seditiones faciunt . . . quando Princeps seu Dominus nullum dignum honore vel lucro permittet eis participare, sed vult omnia solus esse. Haec enim fuit causa seditionis Senatus contra Julium Caesarem, quod, ut dicit Lucanus de ipso, 'Omnia Caesar erat.' " De ortu, chap. 23, p. 772. "Legimus tres reges iniquos et reprobos in veteri Testamento: unum a Deo reprobatum propter inobedientiam, videlicet Saulem. . . . Item alium, cuius regnum fuit detruncatum propter superbiam, videlicet Roboam. . . . Item tertium, cuius regnum fuit ab eo, et a sua successione in totum ablatum propter suam avaritiam et violentiam, scilicet Achab."

[45] Engelbert of Admont, De ortu, chap. 5, pp. 756–57. "Qui ideo Superbius vocatus est . . . cuius filius Lucretiam, nobilissimam pudicissimamque matronam, Collatini senatoris uxorem, violenter oppressit propter quod senatus cum populo Romano patrem et filium simul de regno et urbe expulit, et annuos deinceps sibi consules."

[46] Schmidinger, Romana, p. 9; Hamm, "Engelbert," pp. 387–89.

ple for his pride, which manifested itself in his contempt for the council of elders and his favor for the council of juniors.[47] In this case it was not so much that Roboam was a tyrant as it was that he violated the constitutional arrangements of the Jewish state. A similar regard for the social contract is shown by Engelbert's favorable reference to Cicero's story of a senator's remark to the emperor, specifically referring to the obligation to honor contracts and agreements: "If you will not have me as Senator, I will not have you as emperor."[48] In neither of these examples is there any implication that the removal of a ruler is simply a declarative judgment.

It is perhaps significant that many of Engelbert's references to the people's sovereignty are found in his later work, *Treatise on the Rise of the Roman Empire*. To what extent he may have been affected in the interim by the writings of John of Paris or Ptolemy of Lucca is not known, and the similarities are too vague for us to be able to trace their influence, although demonstrably he knew John's work and most probably Ptolemy's as well. All three share a negative view of Julius Caesar (Ptolemy and Engelbert's views are rather close on this point), and all three insist that the people can dethrone a monarch. In itself this is not significant since most medieval writers approve the deposition of tyrants; the difference is in the hint that the people can do this by right if the king does not honor the established political forms, even if he is not a tyrant.

The absolute right of the people to enforce the constitution is not a right to political participation in the normal course of events. As I have shown, the question of who is to enjoy such participation has no answer valid for all times or all peoples. Nevertheless, I believe that Engelbert in most cases supports a constitution mixed from all the good polities, although he would prefer if possible to eliminate oligarchy.[49] This is not obvious; he

[47] Engelbert of Admont, *De ortu*, chap. 23, p. 772. "Item alium, cuius regnum fuit detruncatum propter superbiam, videlicet Roboam, de quo dicitur 3 Regum 12 quod per superbiam contempto consilio seniorum, et usus consilio iuniorum populo dure et superbe respondit, et populus provocatus dixit: 'Non est nobis pars in David, neque haereditas in filio Isai: Revertere Israel in tabernacula tua, etc.' "

[48] Engelbert of Admont, *De Regimine Principum*, 3.21.74. "Et secundum Articulum adhuc addit Tullius in Primo Officiorum, videlicet quod distincta iura et honores contractionibus et collocutionibus singulis a singulis exhibeantur et serventur pro debito et decenti. Sicut legitur quidam Senator Romae dixisse ad Imperatorem: 'Si tu non habebis me in Senatorem, neque ego te habebo ut Imperatorem.' "

[49] Hamm agrees that Engelbert would be happiest with a mixture of monarchy, aristocracy, and democracy, but bases this conclusion on a distortion of Engelbert's statement that in such a polity "reason, virtue, and law or consensus of the multitude are not greatly mutually opposed." ("Engelbert," p. 403; Engelbert of Admont, *De Regimine Principum*, 1.15.35.) He takes this quotation out of context. All that Engelbert actually says is that for the reason Hamm cites the mixture of monarchy, aristocracy, and democracy is the best of the mixed constitutions with three elements.

often seems ambivalent about mixed constitutions. Writing of the combination of all four good polities Engelbert writes:

> About this polity Aristotle in III *Politics* says that certain people judge the best polity to be mixed from all. Nevertheless, he himself does not much praise or censure such a polity. It seems to be less odious than other polities since all have some part in such a government. It even seems to be less dangerous because it is difficult for the rich and powerful there to rise up against the king, or to oppress, or to draw the populace to them so long as the king provide lest the rich and powerful be or become such that with their strengths they can resist him and the good men who love justice and the common good. He may provide lest those who now begin to be rich and powerful remain long in government and potency, especially if they begin to oppress others and draw others to them. As Aristotle writes in III *Politics*, "it is terrible that the same men should always be rulers and remain long in their government."[50]

Engelbert's purpose in this chapter is to compare the polity mixed from all the simple forms with those mixed from fewer elements; the previous two chapters dealt with comparisons of polities mixed from two and three elements respectively. His tepid praise—"it seems to be less odious than other polities"—may simply be meant in comparison to the other mixed constitutions, and thus reflect only a relative goodness.

I do not think that this is the case. At this point Engelbert does not take a definite stand; he feels that Aristotle did not argue for or against the mixed constitution, but he wants to give some reasons why it might be the best form of all. The reasons he gives—giving all a part and balancing the elements—would be valid in any discussion of polities. These are the same reasons given by Thomas Aquinas to justify the mixed constitution (some of the words are even the same), even though Engelbert defines his mixed constitutions as a union of principles, in the manner of Peter of Auvergne. He, like Peter, seems even to give a positive role to the people—it is not only to give it a part to prevent discontent that its presence is tolerated, as it was for Thomas. Law and consensus, though not as pure qualities as reason and virtue, are good.

---

[50] Engelbert of Admont, *De Regimine Principum*, 1.16.37. "De hac politia dicit Philosophus Tertio Politicorum, quod quidam aestimaverunt optimam politiam ex omnibus esse mixtam. Tamen ipse Philosophus talem politiam non multum laudat nec vituperat. Videtur enim minus odiosa esse aliis politiis, eo quod omnes habent partem aliquam in tali regimine. Videtur etiam minus periculosa esse, eo quod difficile est potentes et divites ibi insurgere contra Regem vel opprimere aut ad se trahere populares, dummodo Rex provideat, ne sint vel fiant adeo divites vel potentes, quod suis viribus (possint) resistere sibi et viris bonis, diligentibus justitiam et bonum commune. Provideat etiam, ne illi, qui incipiunt iam ditari et potentes esse, diu permaneant in suo regimine et potentatu, maxime si incipiunt alios opprimere et alios ad se trahere, quia sicut dicit Philosophus Tertio Politicorum, 'formidabile est valde, semper eosdem esse principantes et diu in suis regiminibus permanere.' "

If Engelbert were engaged only in comparing the mixed constitutions and held that pure monarchy was indisputedly better than any of them, he would have to conclude with respect to mixed constitutions, as he did for simple polities, that the one which most closely approaches kingship would be best. This would necessarily be the mixture of the two forms, monarchy and aristocracy. But he does not; on the contrary, he implies here that if one mixed constitution were best it would have to be the mixture of all four forms, since it alone provides participation of all and balance of the elements. Against his positive evaluation of this form must be weighed his comment that its very existence is a consequence of kings' and rulers' negligent attitude toward the best government.[51]

In his *Mirror of Moral Virtue* Engelbert provides another example of a mixed constitution—Sparta. He begins with an analysis of the causes of discord since, as he puts it, "the greatest cause of concord is the opposition to the causes of discord." These are three: inequality of honors, inequality of money, and inequality of status and liberty. Engelbert continues:

> Because unequal participation in honors, and monies, and freedoms is the whole cause of discord and ruin of cities, the first and most ancient lawgivers provided in their laws and edicts against all things which would induce inequality, as is clear from the Laws of the Twelve Tablets which Lycurgus first brought forth to the Spartans. . . . It was established by law that the administration of the Republic was through divided and mutually subalternating orders by conceding to the kings power of soldiers and wars, to the magistrates judgments and annual constitutions, to the senate guardianship and defense of judgment and laws, and to the people the right of choosing podestas and magistrates, providing in this for the discord of citizens on account of contention for honors. . . . It was established by law that the land was divided equally among all. . . . It was established by law that the greatest honors were not given to the rich and powerful but to the elder and the wise, lest there be contention among the rich and powerful for honors.[52]

[51] Engelbert of Admont, *De Regimine Principum*, 1.9.24–25.

[52] Engelbert of Admont, *Speculum virtutum moralium*, chaps. 15–16.409–12. "Maxime autem causae concordiae in civitate vel quacunque communitate sumuntur ex opposito illarum causarum, quae maxime solent generare discordiam Civium. Tres autem sunt praecipuae causae inter cives, videlicet primo inaequalitas honorum. . . . Secundo inaequalitas lucrorum. . . . Tertio inaequalitas statuum et libertatum. . . . Et quoniam, ut dictum est, tota causa discordiae Civium et exidii civitatum est inaequalis participatio honorum et lucrorum et libertatum, propter hoc primi et antiquissimi latores legum providerunt suis legibus et edictis contra omnia, quae inaequalitatem participationis honorum et lucrorum et libertatum inducebant: sicut patet ex legibus XII tabularum, quas primus edidit Lycurgus Lacedaemoniis . . . lege statuit administrationem Reipublicae per ordines dividi, et ad invicem subalternari, concedendo Regibus potestatem militum et bellorum, Magistratibus iudicia et annuas constitutiones, Senatui custodiam et defensionem iudicii et legum, populo ius elegendi et potestates et magistratus, providens in hoc discordiae civium propter contentionem honorum. Sexta

This does not exactly correspond to Aristotle's description of the Spartan state. In particular, having the democratic element consist of election of officials and the whole basic structure of the constitution comes instead from Thomas Aquinas's description of the Jewish mixed constitution. As in Thomas the emphasis is on balance and the participation of all.

Engelbert's Sparta includes only three of the four good polities: kingship, aristocracy (as represented by the senate and the magistrates), and democracy. The rich and powerful have been forcibly suppressed, the land has been evenly divided, and it seems likely given Engelbert's second cause of discord that wealth must also have been more or less equalized.[53] With regard to this state Hamm alleges that Engelbert considers both the virtue of a single ruler and the cooperation of classes necessary for harmony and concludes that the combination is best.[54] This is not quite correct. The state succeeds because of a suppression of one class, the class that normally dominates.[55]

I think that this passage explains the seemingly contradictory remarks Engelbert makes about the mixture of four elements, namely that it is, "less odious . . . [and] less dangerous," on the one hand, and that it is a consequence of the rulers' negligent practices on the other. He means that in the abstract, if the oligarchs could be eliminated, the mixture of three elements would be best, but since rulers are often lax, and since it is difficult to control the rich and powerful, in most cases they must be taken into account. In most places and times it is less dangerous to give them a role, as restricted as possible, in government. He is not happy about this necessity, and therefore he is lukewarm in his praise of this practice; for the same reason he puts most of his emphasis here on the measures that must be taken to ensure that the king can balance the power of the oligarchs.

Given the specific examples Engelbert uses it is also apparent that he developed his theories under the influence of Italian politics. Surely the German free cities that flourished at this time must also have had their

---

lege terram inter omnes aequaliter divisit . . . lege statuit maximos honores in civitate, non divitibus vel potentibus, sed Senioribus et sapientibus deferri, in hoc providens, ne inter divites et potentes fieret contentio propter honores."

[53] It is one of Aristotle's criticisms of the Spartan constitution (at least as it developed after the death of Lycurgus) that there was great inequality in land (Aristotle, *Politics*, 2.9).

[54] Hamm, "Engelbert," p. 401.

[55] Engelbert no doubt is thinking of the Italian antimagnate laws of the late thirteenth century. The equalization of wealth is a frequent theme in *On the Government of Rulers*. At one point Engelbert cites Aristotle to the effect that a well-ordered polity is long-lasting and free of sedition and tyranny. These conditions can best obtain in a polity in which the middle class is numerous and rules. Engelbert continues: "Where the city is constituted mostly of the wealthy, there it will perish from discord. Where it is mostly of paupers, there it is deficient from need. But where it is of the middle class and equals, there it is saved on account of concord and common sufficiency" (*De Regimine Principum*, 1.17.39–40).

effect, but his mention of them is vague, and he saves most of his praise of contemporary politics for Italy and Hungary. As a Northerner, he is more inclined to monarchy than the Italians were, and so he seeks to adapt Italian republicanism to a Thomistic theory of monarchy. But it is the Italian polities that most impress him and demonstrate to him the urgency of controlling the optimates. This is yet another reason for defending monarchy—the aristocratic and popular parties by themselves have proven incapable of keeping the optimates under control.

For Engelbert any pure form of government is an abstraction, especially monarchy, which, as for Thomas Aquinas, exists only in the imagination. Monarchy as it actually exists, and as it must exist, is mixed monarchy. He does not often write about contemporary monarchies except for the Church and Empire, but he comes close to describing France as a mixed constitution: "France has princes and leading men of the kingdom called *regales* who are twelve in number and are deputed to counsel the king and to the ordination of the kingdom." Eighty years later Nicole Oresme described the French monarchy in similar terms.[56]

Engelbert used a pragmatic criterion for good government: a state was good insofar as it supported the common good of the people and reflected its will, its individual traditions, and its particular conditions. Different peoples might require different forms of government, but in most cases, and in those places where the best government was possible the mixed constitution of monarchy, aristocracy, democracy, and, if unavoidable, oligarchy would best provide for the common good. The mixed constitution also provides most directly for the consent of the people which Engelbert required for a legitimate government. In justifying the mixed constitution Engelbert combined the reasons given by his predecessors: it gave everyone a part and therefore led to contentment, it combined the virtues of its constituent parts, and by effecting a balance of the forms it prevented the disintegration to which each simple form was prone.

[56] Engelbert of Admont, *De Regimine Principum*, 3.21.75–76. "In regno Franciae quod principes et proceres regni, qui apellantur regales et sunt duodecim numero, deputati ad consilium Regis et ordinationem Regni. Nicole Oresme, *Le Livre de Politiques*, chap. 13, p. 145.

Chapter 8

JOHN OF PARIS

OTHER THAN that he was born in Paris, studied at the University of Paris (but not under Thomas Aquinas), and joined the Dominican order, we know almost nothing about the early life of John of Paris (c. 1250–1304), also known as Jean Quidort before the 1280s when he wrote a controversial *Commentary on the Sentences*. His views on the Eucharist in that work came under attack, but he defended himself successfully in an *Apology* of 1287, and in the same year he wrote his *Correction of the Correction of Brother Thomas*, in which he defended 118 theses of Thomas Aquinas that had been attacked by the Franciscan Walter de la Mare. In the next decade John became one of the most famous teachers and preachers in Paris. He wrote works on theology, natural philosophy, and politics, of which twenty-two survive. "With these works," John Watt writes, "John emerges as one of those whose common range of intellectual interests, brotherhood in religion and philosophical allegiances united to form the first school of Thomism."[1] In 1304 he again got in trouble for his ideas on the Eucharist, specifically for his argument that consubstantiation was as likely as transubstantiation, which at this time was coming to be accepted as dogma. (Later, Reformation thinkers cited him for this belief.) This time, however, a special commission condemned his opinion, forbade him to teach or preach, and sentenced him to perpetual silence. He appealed to Pope Clement V, then in Bordeaux, but died before the pope decided his case.

Certainly a factor in his later relations with the Church must have been his outspoken writing against papal authority in secular affairs. In the years of the second great struggle of Church and state between Pope Boniface VIII and Phillip IV the Fair of France (1301–3), John became one of many royal propagandists. In many ways this conflict was decisive for the emergence of the modern state. Boniface, the most assertive of a long line of hierocratic popes, watched the papal authority erode in an era of secular centralization and nascent nation-states. Still smarting from his humiliating defeat at Phillip's hands four years before when he had been forced to concede the king's right to tax the clergy, he felt it necessary to put the whole prestige of Roman Catholicism behind the Bishop of Pamiers, whom Philip had arrested for blasphemy, heresy, and treason. For his part

---

[1] John Watt in the introduction to his translation of John of Paris, *On Royal and Papal Power*, p. 9.

Phillip sought to unite the entire French nation and settle once and for all the issue of secular independence from the papacy and the supremacy of the king in all matters concerning the welfare of the French people. As part of this aim, Philip in 1303 called the first Estates General, a body representing the clergy, nobles, and people of France, to stir up support for his policies.

This crisis stimulated a great outporing of propaganda, of polemics and counterpolemics, of attacks and defenses on both sides, including Giles of Rome's *On Ecclesiastical Power* (1301), and the anonymous *Dialogue Between a Soldier and a Cleric* and *The Pacific King* (which John may also have written). John wrote his polemic, *Treatise on Royal and Papal Power* (1302) for an immediate purpose: the defense of Phillip IV's side in the conflict with the papacy. He accomplished this by sharply delineating the areas of authority and influence of the two powers and by insisting on the supremacy of the monarch in temporal affairs. His title gives equal weight to kingship and papacy, and the treatise itself develops these two in a way that suggests that each in its own sphere is completely analogous to the other. "God and the people" institute both king and pope. "The people" or its representative can depose either of them. Each has the unrestricted use of his own "sword." The pope is superior in dignity to the king, but since their areas of responsibility are disjoint, one can have power over the other only "conditionally and contingently." On only two points does the analogy fail. First, God ordained both papal monarchy and the plenitude of power inherent in it, whereas the exact form of secular rule is contingent, the responsibility of each people. Second, papal jurisdiction is universal, whereas that of secular princes is restricted to individual nations.[2]

Most modern historians have followed this interpretation, praising John for one of the earliest systematic defenses of dualism and the national state, for a thoroughgoing refutation of all the prevalant hierocratic arguments, and for his location of ultimate authority in the people. By distinguishing between office and person, and by applying a corporate analysis to both powers, they argue, he was able to overcome the seeming conflict of the origin of power from below and above and to achieve a dualistic synthesis in which divine origin and unitary leadership could coexist with an ultimate regulatory function vested in the entire community.[3]

[2] John of Paris, *De Potestate Regia et Papali*, chap. 13, p. 138, with respect to papal power. As a partisan of the king of France, John rejects the universal dominion of the emperor (chap. 21, pp. 190–91). He insists that secular rule is better when divided and attacks the ancient Roman Empire as a time of misery and war. John Watt's translation is useful but deficient in a number of respects, particularly because it is not careful to translate terms such as *regalis*, *regnum*, or *monarchia* literally or consistently.

[3] See, for example, Wilks, *Problem of Sovereignty*; Ullmann, *History of Political Thought*; Brian Tierney, *Foundations of the Conciliar Theory*; McIlwain, *Constitutionalism* and *Growth of*

More recently, in two books and a series of articles written in the 1970s, Thomas J. Renna has attacked this traditional approach. He feels that John's dualism is superficial, that it is a clever and appealing cover for an underlying Erastianism. Although John always treats Church and state as parallel, the type of authority given to each ensures that in fact the secular power must always prevail. As Pierre Flotte allegedly said to the pope, "Your power is verbal, ours is real." Renna argues that this outcome was precisely John's intention.[4]

This argument about Church and state affects an analysis of ideal government because Renna extends the idea of royal absolutism to the internal government of states. John's "synthesis of the dualist and statemonist traditions," Renna writes, served his "one aim": a "natural law kingship unfettered by constitutional restraints." The people, he argues, is brought in as the constitutive element of government only to complete the parallel with the Church and as an answer to the pope's claim to have instituted the secular power. John never intended the people to have any active role in government, according to Renna; at most it is passively to legitimize the king by tolerating him.[5]

For this analysis the central question is this: John advocates the mixed constitution as best for the Church. Does this imply that he also favored it for the state? If we accept that he perceives church and state as parallel institutions we must answer yes. This has been the traditional view. Watt, for example, explains John's reluctance to say this directly as the natural consequence of the purpose of his treatise: the defense of the French king. In such a work he could hardly be expected to undermine the power of his patron. Renna opposes this view. He argues that John intended the mixed constitution only for the Church—for the state he favored pure monarchy.[6]

Renna's charges must be considered seriously. Although at times his attacks obviously misrepresent John's thought, Renna does often succeed in undermining the traditional position. For this reason, I will make many of my points about John in the form of a polemic against Renna. There is no doubt in my mind that John stands foursquare in the tradition of Aristotelian mixed constitutionalism.

Political Thought; John Watt, introduction to *On Royal and Papal Power*; Gordon Leff, *William of Ockham*; M. F. Griesbach, "John of Paris as a Representative of Thomistic Political Philosophy."

[4] Thomas J. Renna, "Aristotle and the French Monarchy," *Church and State in Medieval Europe: 1050–1314*, "Kingship in the *Disputatio inter clericum et militem*," "The *Populus* in John of Paris' Theory of Monarchy," *Royalist Political Thought*. Ullmann, *History of Political Thought*, p. 202, cites Flotte's words without reference.

[5] Renna, *Royalist Political Thought*, pp. 9, 246; "*Populus*," p. 245.

[6] Watt, *On Royal and Papal Power*, p. 53; Renna, "*Populus*," pp. 260–61, *Royalist Political Thought*, p. 228.

Renna states repeatedly that John supports a regal, as opposed to a political, monarchy. This being the case, the argument goes, there simply is no room for a mixed constitution in any meaningful sense. If the king be granted all power, neither the aristocrats nor still less the people can have more than an advisory role. I agree that John was a monarchist; I can easily show that he makes no clear choice for regal monarchy (this is one area in which Renna misuses the text in rather obvious ways). In addition, I argue that, in any case, even a regal king fits most comfortably and suitably into a mixed constitution as John describes it.

It is not even obvious that John is a monarchist at all. He bases all government on the consent of the people and at times appears to argue that the best form of government is altogether dependent on the particular circumstances of each people.[7]

According to John, the people has an absolute right to choose the form of rule to which it is to be subject, and this right can be exercised at any time—even when there is a government: "It pertains to [the people]," he writes, "to subject itself to whom it desires without prejudice of another."[8] The people can change the government for good reason—for example, if there is an external threat and the leadership is weak or if it did not consent in the first place to a government imposed by force. The first reason justifies the translation of the Roman Empire to the Germans, the second the rebellion of peoples subjected to the Roman Empire, such as the Gauls and Franks.[9] But a good reason is not absolutely necessary. All that he requires is the will of the people: "Just as jurisdiction is given by the consent of humans, so it is taken away by a contrary consent."[10]

The people can exercise its right to depose a ruler itself, or its representatives can do it. John explains this most clearly with respect to the pope: "Although his is the highest virtue in a person, nevertheless there is an equal or greater in the College, or in the whole Church. . . . He can be

---

[7] Lewis, "Natural Law and Expediency," p. 158, for one, believes that John justifies government solely by the criterion of expediency.

[8] John of Paris, *De Potestate Regia et Papali*, chap. 15, p. 151. "Cuius est se subicere cui vult, sine alterius praeiudicio."

[9] John of Paris, *De Potestate Regia et Papali*, chap. 15, pp. 150–51. "Amplius non fuit factum per solum papam, sed populo acclamante et faciente"; chap. 21, p. 191. "Si ergo Romani per violentiam dominium acceperunt, numquid iuste per violentiam etiam abici potuit dominium eorundem vel etiam contra eos prescribi?"

[10] John of Paris, *De Potestate Regia et Papali*, chap. 25, p. 209. "Et ideo sicut per consensum hominum iurisdictio datur, ita per contrarium consensum tollitur." The same holds true for the Church; the pope, if he be unwilling to resign, "can be deposed in such a case by the consent of the people, because the pope himself and any other prelate rules not for himself but for the people. . . . The consent of the people in such a case to depose him although he is unwilling if he seems totally useless, and to choose another, is more efficacious than his will to renounce voluntarily . . . when the people are unwilling" (chap. 24, p. 201).

deposed by the College, or even more by the General Council."[11] In so doing, the cardinals act in the place of the whole Church:

> To resign his office it suffices that [the pope] give cause to the College of Cardinals . . . which is there in the place of the whole church. . . . Deposition should be done by a General Council. . . . But nevertheless I believe that the College of Cardinals suffices simply for a deposition of this kind: since their consent in place of the Church makes the pope, it seems that similarly it can depose him.[12]

Writing about the state, John sometimes argues that the people can depose a king and sometimes that the "barons and peers" can.[13] For political reasons he may not want to state unequivocally that the barons stand in the place of the whole people who has the primary right, but he surely cannot expect readers to form any other conclusion given the close parallels drawn between the situation in church and state. Renna denies this. There is a good reason, he says, why John does not say straight out that the barons represent the people or even that the people are the citizens, namely that John adopts contemporary ideas that identify the people with the barons.[14]

This is not tenable. The people, as John presents it, possesses all the characteristics of Aristotelian citizens: it chooses the form of government and the specific rulers, and it removes rulers. John stresses the right of the people to submit itself to any desired government, and the obligation of the government to rule on behalf of the people. These principles cannot, in any Aristotelian theory of government, apply to the barons alone; they must refer to the whole population. This is not to say that John gives active power to the assembly of all humans in France—he may well restrict this role to the feudal nobility. Just as the cardinals represent the whole Church, but the General Council or the congregation of the faithful in some sense is the whole Church, so in France the barons may represent the kingdom but the whole body of people is the kingdom. All societies basing themselves on the whole people deny participation to those not judged

---

[11] John of Paris, *De Potestate Regia et Papali*, chap. 25, p. 207. "Licet sit summa virtus in persona, tamen est ei equalis vel maior in collegio sive in tota ecclesia . . . potest deponi a collegio vel magis a generali concilio."

[12] John of Paris, *De Potestate Regia et Papali*, chap. 24, pp. 201–2. "Ad renunciationem sufficit quod causam alleget coram collegio cardinalium quod est ibi loco totius ecclesie. Sed ad depositionem decet quod fiat per concilium generale. . . . Credo autem quod simpliciter sufficeret ad deopsitionem collegium cardinalium, quia ex quo consensus eorum facit papam loco ecclesie, videtur similiter quod possit eum deponere."

[13] John of Paris, *De Potestate Regia et Papali*, chap. 13, p. 139. "Ubi vero peccaret rex in temporalibus quorum cognitio ad ecclesiasticum non pertinet, tunc non habet ipsum corrigere primo, sed barones et pares."

[14] Renna, *"Populus,"* pp. 246–49.

competent or worthy to play a part, yet do not thereby feel they are any the less based on the whole people.

No more credible is Renna's insistence that for John the king's power is immediately from God and that the people is given no actual role. John may well be motivated, as Renna argues, primarily by the desire to discredit the pope as the human agency for choosing rulers when he writes, "Therefore, the royal power neither in principle nor in actuality is from the pope, but from God and from the people choosing a king as a person or as a family."[15] It is true that John is vague on the institutional machinery through which the people may act, but it is clear that it has a continuing right to do so—it is God who has no real part. God has endowed humanity with a political nature, and to fulfill it humans should choose appropriate rulers. In this choice God may inspire the people, but it is the people which makes the actual choice, and God will support the choice so long as it accords with reason.[16] What John has done is to construct a supernatural defense of the people's right to institute a government of its choice and to change it if it so desires for any reasonable cause. This right is guaranteed in any legitimate government, not just in a "political" government, as Renna claims.[17]

It may be true, as Renna asserts, that John describes the parallel structures of Church and state for the sole purpose of undermining papal power by vesting sovereignty over the Church in the whole body of Christians. Nonetheless, the logic of this attempt forces him to give the people sovereignty over the secular state as well, and John, whatever his intentions, has been justly perceived as a disciple of dualism and as a prophet of popular sovereignty with respect to both Church and state. In fact, this sovereignty applies with greater force to the state: the form of the Church is immutable, having been established by Christ himself, but the form of civil government is completely at the discretion of the people.

In itself this does not say anything about whether there is one best form for everyone, but John seems to argue that different forms of government may be better for different societies. He writes that although all people's spiritual needs are the same, their temporal needs are not:

[15] John of Paris, *De Potestate Regia et Papali*, chap. 10, p. 113. "Ergo potestas regia nec secundum se nec quantum ad executionem est a papa, sed a Deo et a populo regem eligente in persona vel in domo."

[16] See, for example, John of Paris, *De Potestate Regia et Papali*, chap. 3, p. 82; chap. 19, p. 173, where John says that the emperor is created by the people or army with God's inspiration and adds that in the *Ethics* Aristotle wrote that a king is made by the will of the people; and chap. 20, p. 180, where John quotes Plato in this regard: "That which once has been rationally instituted, it is not the divine will that it should be changed."

[17] Renna, *Royalist Political Thought*, p. 227.

From natural instinct, which is from God, they know to live civilly and in a community; and in consequence, for living well they should choose in their community diverse rectors according to the diversities of their communities . . . secular power has more diversity because of its secular nature and because of the diversity of climates and complexions. . . . Thus, it is not necessary that all the faithful be united in some common polity, but there can be diverse modes of living and diverse polities depending on the diversity of climates, languages, and conditions of humans, and that which is virtuous in one nation is not virtuous in another.[18]

Since Aristotle and Ptolemy of Lucca, in particular, associate such ideas of varying climates, languages, and so forth with the concept of relative goodness, it is easy to read this passage as a defense of expediency.

A closer reading shows that this is not what John is saying. He is arguing only against one universal monarch. His point is that since peoples' customs and characters differ, one monarch cannot effectively rule them all. But, refuting another argument for Empire, he implies that a monarch is preferable for any given people:

Nevertheless, what is said in the *Decretum*, C.7, q.1, c.7 does not obviate this, where it says that one ought to have precedence and not many, because there it speaks about one thing, where it is not expedient that many should exercise dominion in undistinguished areas, as is shown by Romulus and Remus, who exercised dominion at the same time and in undistinguished areas, and therefore one committed fratricide against the other.[19]

Since each people is united in temperament and custom, John would conclude that it is best served by a king. He barely touches on any form of government but monarchy. Virtually his only mention of the sixfold schema, for example, comes as he explains his definition of *kingdom*: the words "for the good of the multitude" are included, he writes, "to differentiate it from tyranny, oligarchy, and democracy, where the rectors intend only their own good"; the words "[rule] by one" are included, "to differentiate it from aristocracy, that is, rule of the best or of the optimates,

[18] John of Paris, *De Potestate Regia et Papali*, chap. 3, pp. 82–83. "Ex naturali instinctu qui ex Deo est habent ut civiliter et in communitate vivant et per consequens ut ad bene vivendum in communi rectores eligant, diversos quidem secundum diversitatem communitatum . . . secularis potestas plus habet diversitatis secundum climatum et complexionum diversitatem. . . . Non sic autem fideles omnes necesse est convenire in aliqua politia communi, sed possunt secundum diversitatem climatum et linguarum et condicionum hominum esse diversi modi vivendi et diverse politiae, et quod virtuosum est in una gente non est virtuosum in alia."

[19] John of Paris, *De Potestate Regia et Papali*, chap. 3, p. 84. "Nec tamen huic obiat quod dicitur VII, q.1, 'In apibus,' ubi dicitur quod unus debet praeesse et non plures, quia ibi loquitur in re una ubi non expedit plures ex indistincto dominari sicut ostendit de Remo et Romulo qui simul ex indistincto dominabantur et ideo unus in alium fratricidium commisit."

namely where a few exercise dominion according to virtue, which some call government according to the *Responsa Prudentium* or *Senatus Consulta*, and to differentiate it from *polycratia* [polity], where the people exercises dominion by plebiscite."[20] He does not define tyranny, oligarchy, or democracy, or even state that aristocracy and polity are for the common good. And immediately after this distinction of forms, John declares his preference for monarchy: "Every multitude with each seeking their own good will dissipate and be dispersed into diverse parts unless it be ordered to the comon good through some one, who has care of the common good. . . . It is more useful for the government of a multitude [that it be ruled] by one who has precedence according to virtue than by many or a few virtuous."[21]

Nowhere does he have a single word of praise for aristocracy or polity or a single argument supporting them—not even as an argument to refute. On the other hand he reels off the usual reasons why monarchy is best and the others worse: if many rule there will be disagreement, united virtue is stronger than divided virtue, monarchy assures unity and concord, mixed natural bodies contain one element which dominates, the soul rules the body, social animals are ruled by one, and so forth. Further, it was the primitive form both of the ancient Israelites and the earliest human government under Belus and Ninus.[22] Thus, in no way is John a relativist.

What is the nature of the best king? Renna says that he is regal.[23] He assumes that John clearly distinguishes regal and political rule on the basis

---

[20] John of Paris, *De Potestate Regia et Papali*, chap. 1, p. 75. "Ad bonum multitudinis ordinatum ponitur ad differentiam tyrannides, oligarchiae, et democratiae, ubi rector solum intendit bonum suum et praecipue in tyrannide. Ab uno ad differentiam aristocratiae id est principatus optimorum seu optimatum, ubi pauci dominantur secundum virtutem, quod regimen vocant aliqui secundum responsum prudentum vel senatus consulta, et ad differentiam polycratiae ubi populus dominatur secundum plebiscita." With respect to both aristocracy and polity, John makes a connection with the ancient Roman government, but he never follows through with a more detailed analysis.

[21] John of Paris, *De Potestate Regia et Papali*, chap. 1, p. 76. "Omnis autem multitudo quolibet quaerente quod suum est dissipatur et in diversa dispergitur nisi ad bonum commune ordinetur per aliquam unum cui sit cura de bono communi. . . . Est autem utilius regimen multitudinis per unum qui preest secundum virtutem quam per plures vel paucos virtuosos."

[22] John of Paris, *De Potestate Regia et Papali*, chap. 21, p. 190; chap. 1, p. 77; chap. 19, p. 175. John also curiously twists an argument of Aristotle in favor of the rule of many into an argument for monarchy. Aristotle wrote that the more rulers there are the more the self-interest of the ruling class represents the common good of the people. John implicitly recognizes this when he states that tyranny is the worst form because the tyrant least represents what is common. But just before this comment John writes, "One prince intending the common good has an eye more to the common than if many rule, even according to virtue. And the more the many are chosen [to rule], the more the residue is less common; and the fewer the more the residue is common." (chap. 1, pp. 76–77).

[23] See, for example, Renna, *Royalist Political Thought*, p. 228, and nn. 82–84.

of the origin of law and opts for a royal source. In fact, the whole notion of regal and political power plays an extremely minor role in John's thought and would hardly be worth mentioning except to refute this argument.

His only mention of the distinction comes in a section devoted to a refutation of the proposition that the pope is the primary source of and authority for secular law:

> To say, as those masters say, that the pope hands down laws to the rulers and that the ruler cannot take laws from another source unless they should be approved by the pope, is to destroy regal and political government . . . because according to the Philosopher in I *Politics*, rule is called regal only when someone has precedence according to the laws that he himself institutes. But when he has precedence not according to his own will, nor according to laws which he himself institutes, but according to laws which the citizens institute, it is called civil or political rule, and not regal. If, therefore, no ruler should govern except according to laws handed down by the pope, or according to those first approved by him, no one would rule by regal or political rule, but only by papal rule, which is to destroy the kingdom and to make void all ancient rules.[24]

Renna is undoubtedly correct when, as he himself admits, he asserts that the only purpose of mentioning regal and political rule at all was to show that the pope is not the source of law.[25]

Only in this one passage can we say with certainty that John is using *regal* in distinction to *political*—usually he uses *regal* to mean the rule of any king. This is true in the very passages cited by Renna. In chapter 1

[24] John of Paris, *De Potestate Regia et Papali*, chap. 17, p. 161. "Dicere autem ut isti magistri dicunt, quod papa tradit leges principibus et quod princeps non potest aliunde leges sumere nisi per papam fuerint approbate, est omnino destruere regimen regale et politicum . . . quia secundum Philosophum I Politicorum principatus tunc solum dicitur regalis quando aliquis praeest secundum leges quas ipsemet instituit; cum vero praeest non secundum arbitrium suum nec secundum leges quas ipse instituit sed secundum leges quas cives instituerunt dicitur principatus civilis vel politicus et non regalis. Si ergo nullus princeps regeret nisi secundum leges a papa traditas vel ab eo primo approbatas, nullus principaretur principatu regali vel politico sed solum papali, quod est regnum destruere et omnem principatum antiquum evacuare."

[25] Renna, *"Populus,"* p. 257. Like Thomas, John implies that there will be a single ruler in any case, but he follows more closely Giles of Rome's definition in his *On the Government of Rulers* rather than Thomas's. See Thomas Aquinas, *In Libros Politicorum*, 1.1.3,4; Giles of Rome, *De Regimine Principum*, 2.1.14.154v–155r. Giles is often portrayed as the person against whom John of Paris composed his treatise. Watt, *On Royal and Papal Power*, p. 43, argues that there is not enough textual evidence to prove that John used Giles's *On Ecclesiastical Power*, and, in fact, that the two were composed about the same time. The closeness of these two passages seems to show that John did in fact use Giles's *On the Government of Rulers*, which was written some twenty years earlier.

John sets out to discover, "What is a regal rule, and whence does it come?" Here, John specifically distinguishes regal rule as one of the six simple forms of government, not as regal rule in its strict sense, as Renna would have it. In the same chapter it is the rule of one, as such, which is compared favorably with the rule of many, not regal rule which is called the best kind of monarchy, as Renna also asserts. Again, when John states that "government of kings is better than aristocratic rule" he means simply that the rule of one is better than the rule of many, not that regal rule strictly speaking is better, another claim of Renna's.[26] There are many similar examples.

John writes that Moses and his successors did not enjoy the "full power" characteristic of those with the "pure government of kings," but his reason is that it is compounded with other simple forms, not because it is political.[27] An unmixed king will have full power in some sense, whether he is regal in the restrictive sense or not. For John, the distinction between regal and political has to do only with the making of the law; beyond this the king has complete discretion within the conditions demanded of all legitimate government: consent of the people and obedience to law. John quotes Averroës to this effect: "The king exists by the will of the people, but when he is king it is natural that he should exercise dominion."[28]

John requires the king to obey the law,[29] but he never describes the lawmaking process clearly enough for us to decide whether he favors regal or political rule. The absence of any clear statement suggests that he wished to leave the decision up to each particular community. Renna's assertion seems to be based purely on the use of the word *regal*. Most of John's references to the king's power are to his right to use the material sword—yet this has no direct bearing on lawmaking, but only on the king's jurisdiction. John mentions the distinction only to show that the pope is not the source of civil law.

Renna insists that John's formal support of a mixed constitution is simply one more weapon to be used against the pope, and has no implications for a king, whose power is unrestricted. Whatever his motives, John's theory as it stands leads unavoidably to the conclusion that the mixed constitution is the absolutely best constitution for a secular state.

[26] Renna, *Royalist Political Thought*, p. 251, nn. 83, 85, p. 228; John of Paris, *De Potestate Regia et Papali*, chap. 1, p. 75. "Quid sit regimen regale et unde habeat ortum?" (chapter title); chap. 1, p. 76. "Est autem utilius regimen multitudinis per unum qui praeest secundum virtutem quam per plures vel paucos virtuosos"; chap. 21, p. 190. "Melius est regimen regium quam aristocraticum." Watt's translation is especially misleading on this usage. It uses the words "regal," "kingdom," and "monarchy" indiscriminately with little reference to John's actual words.

[27] John of Paris, *De Potestate Regia et Papali*, chap. 19, p. 174.

[28] John of Paris, *De Potestate Regia et Papali*, chap. 19, p. 173. "Rex est a populi voluntate, sed, cum est rex, quod dominetur est naturale."

[29] See, for example, John of Paris, *De Potestate Regia et Papali*, chap. 13, pp. 139, 136.

John introduces the mixed constitution in reply to one of forty-two arguments used to justify the pope's authority in temporalities: "The Lord instituted priests for his people Israel from the start, but he did not institute a king for them, but only allowed it by their will. . . . From which it is clear that God did not approve regal government, but, indignant, he only permitted it, and it was more approved by God, that the world should be governed in all things by a pontiff alone."[30] John replies to these two objections by insisting that God had indeed established a king, in the person of Moses, before or simultaneously with the priesthood, and that God's later displeasure was not directed against kingship per se, but only against a change from the original kingship. John brings in the mixed constitution in order to defend his relatively weak argument, taken from Thomas Aquinas, that Moses and his successors, the judges, were kings:

> They were kings in a way in so far as they singly had precedence over that whole people, which is a species of kingdom; only they did not represent a pure government of kings because it was mixed with aristocracy in which many exercise dominion according to virtue and democracy, that is, rule of the people, as will be seen. . . . This was better than pure regal rule, at least for that people.[31]

In order to account for God's displeasure at the Israelites' request for a king with full power, John had to defend the mixed constitution as a better form. He explains why:

> Because he chose that people as peculiar to him, as Deuteronomy 7 [in fact, Deuteronomy 6] states, he instituted for them at first a government better than a purely regal one, namely a mixed government, which indeed was better than a pure regal one, at least for that people. There are two reasons. One is that although a government of kings in which one rules singly according to virtue is better than any other simple government, as the Philosopher shows in III *Politics*; nevertheless, if it is mixed with aristocracy and democracy, it is better than the pure one, in as much as in a mixed government all have some part in rule. Through this the peace of the people is served and all love and guard such a dominance . . . and thus it was mixed best, in that all had some

---

[30] John of Paris, *De Potestate Regia et Papali*, chap. 11, p. 125. "Dominus populo suo Israel a principio instituit sacerdotum sed non instituit eis regem sed solum permisit eorum arbitrio. . . . Ex quo patet non esse Deo acceptum regimen regale, sed solum ipsum permisit indignatus, et magis esset Deo acceptum quod per solum pontificem mundus in omnibus regeretur."

[31] John of Paris, *De Potestate Regia et Papali*, chap. 19, p. 174. "Erant aliquo modo reges in quantum toti illi populo praeeerant singulariter, quod est species regni. Non erat tamen regimen regium purum, eo quod commiscebatur aristocratiae, in qua plures dominantur secundum virtutem, et democratiae id est principatui populi, ut videbitur . . . erat melius puro regali saltem illi populo."

part in that government. . . . Another reason . . . although regal government would be best in itself, if it is not corrupt . . . on account of the great power, which is conceded to a king, a kingdom easily degenerates to tyranny, unless he to whom such power is conceded has perfect virtue. But this perfect virtue is found in few and especially in that people, since the Jews were cruel and prone to avarice, through which vices especially they fall into tyranny. And therefore the Lord from the beginning did not institute a king for them with such great plenitude of power, but a judge and governor to protect them in the way described, because this was more suited for them. And therefore afterwards he instituted a king in answer to their petition, he was as it were indignant, namely because they rejected another government more useful to them.[32]

It is in the course of his argument in the middle of this passage for a mixed constitution on the grounds of everyone having a part that John introduces in a rather offhand way his contention that the mixed constitution would be good for the Church: "And thus certainly it would be the best government for the Church if under one pope many were chosen by and from each province, that thus all might have their part in the government of the Church."[33]

For centuries one current of canonistic thought had presented the cardinals and the congregation of the faithful as groups limiting the power of the pope. But the idea that the Church is or should be an Aristotelian mixed constitution was relatively new. John is the first to introduce this opinion directly in the context of a general discussion of political power, but several years earlier in a treatise on the resignation of Pope Celestine

---

[32] John of Paris, *De Potestate Regia et Papali*, chap. 19, pp. 174–76. "Quia illum populum sibi eligerat ut peculiarem Deut. VII, et instituerat eis prius regimen melius puro regali, scilicet regimen mixtum, quod quidem erat melius puro regali, saltem illi populo, propter duo: unum est quia licet regimen regium in quo unus singulariter principatur multitudini secundum virtutem, sit melius quolibet alio regimine simplici, ut ostendit Philosophus in III Politicorum, tamen si fiat mixtum cum aristocratia et democratia melius est puro in quantum in regimine mixto omnes aliquam partem habent in principatu. Per hoc enim servatur pax populi et omnes talem dominationem amant et custodiunt . . . et sic erat optime mixtum in quantum omnes in regimine illo aliquam habebant partem. . . . Aliud . . . licet regimine regale sit optimum in se si non corrumpatur, tamen propter magnam potestatem quae regi conceditur de facili regnum degenerat in tyrannidem, nisi sit perfecta virtus eius cui talis potestas conceditur. . . . Haec autem perfecta virtus in paucis reperitur et praecipue in populo illo, eo quod Judaei crudeles erant ad avaritiam proni, per quae vitia maxima in tyrannidem incidunt. Et ideo Dominus a principio non instituit eis regem cum tanta plenitudine potestatis, sed iudicem et gubernatorem in eorum custodia modo predicto, quia sic eis magis competebat. Et ideo postea ad petitionem eorum constituit quasi indignatus, quod scilicet regimen aliud utilius abiciebant."

[33] John of Paris, *De Potestate Regia et Papali*, chap. 19, p. 175. "Sic certe esset optimum regimen ecclesiae si sub una papa eligerentur plures ab omni provincia et de omni provincia, ut sic in regimine ecclesiae omnes aliquo modo haberent partem suam."

V, Peter John Olivi associated the mixed constitution with the existing government of the Church. He discussed the corporate nature of the Church and the areas in which the cardinals were superior to the pope. Then, he continued:

> Besides, even among the pagan philosophers, namely Aristotle in the *Politics*, right reason dictated that that civil government is best which was mixed from monarchy, and from that in which in part the greater and better of the common people [*plebs*], in part the whole common people [*plebs*] participate together. For just as unity of the head prevails against schisms and divisions, and even because it is easier to find one perfectly wise and good man than many, on account of which monarchic government is more useful; thus, [only?] minor deceptions can be committed by the monarch, when in important matters he must use the counsel of the many and the better. By that which the subjects participate together in certain elections and councils is the government more acceptable to them and through this it becomes more responsible, more honorable, and more authoritative; because it would be more difficult and incredible for one together with many to err than for one alone.[34]

Clearly, Olivi associates the pope with monarchy, the cardinals with aristocracy, and the congregation of the faithful with democracy. He attempts to ground this interpretation in the Bible, and so refers to the situation of the Jews under Moses and Joshua. Apparently, however, he was not familiar with Thomas Aquinas's presentation of the subject, which would have fit in well, although he does use the Thomist idea of participation to ensure contentment with the regime. In the passage previously cited Olivi associates aristocracy and democracy both with participation in election and in councils, but with respect to Moses only with the election of the leader. Even though God chose Moses and Joshua, they were chosen from and in the presence of all the people, so that presumably they were installed with the people's consent.[35]

In the absence of divine intervention Olivi believes that the people or its representatives has the right to elect the monarch. In the case of the pope,

---

[34] Peter John Olivi, *De renuntiatione papae*, pp. 354–55. "Preterea etiam philosophis paganis, puta Aristoteli in libro Politicorum, recta ratio dictavit, quod illud civile regimine est optimum, quod erat commixtum ex monarchico et ex eo, in quo partim maiores et meliores plebis, partim tota plebs conparticipant. Nam sicut unitas capitis valet contra scismata et scissuras et etiam quia facilius est invenire unum perfecte sapientem et bonum quam plures, propter quod monarchicum regimen est utilius: sic minores fraudes possunt a monarcha committi, quando in quibusdam precipuis oportet eum uti consilio plurium et meliorum. Eo vel ipso quo subditi comparticipant in quibusdam electionibus et consiliis, est ipsum regimen eis acceptius et vel per hoc fit consultius et honorabilius et auctoritabilius: quia difficilius et incredibilius est unum cum pluribus simul errare, quam ipsum unum solum." See also Tierney, *Religion, Law*, p. 91.

[35] Olivi, *De renuntiatione papae*, p. 355.

its assent is necessary, but because of the inconvenience and possible dangers of a popular election, the cardinals stand in the place of the whole people.[36] From his brief comments it is difficult to determine what powers Olivi allots to the nonmonarchical elements in the Church. Certainly he allows election and approval of resignation, but he also envisions an ongoing role, as evidenced by his talk of necessary councils in a mixed constitution and about the corporate relationship of head and members. Finally, he suggests that the cardinals can act in any matter at all if utility or necessity demands it.[37]

Returning to John of Paris, it can be concluded that his words establish a prima facie case for the contention that he favored a mixed constitution as the best form for both Church and state. The burden of disproof is on Renna.

Renna argues that John introduces the mixed constitution, in a place where it seems irrelevant, where his one aim is to defend royal rule, in order to appeal once again to a conciliar theory of the Church.[38] For some reason Renna fails to see the importance of the mixed constitution in this argument. John's concern is not simply to defend the divine origin of royal rule but also to show that it existed by divine will before the priesthood, and that it was not God's wish that it be subordinated to the priesthood. John's source, Thomas Aquinas, brings up the mixed constitution to answer the objection that God established an inferior, that is, nonregal government for his chosen people. Both Thomas and John for different reasons are compelled to prove that Moses and the Judges were kings. But they clearly were not kings in the same way as Saul and his successors. The mixed constitution provided them with a way around this difficulty: the mixed constitution was a monarchy, one better for several reasons than a pure monarchy.

Renna undermines his own position that John uses the ecclesiastical mixed constitution to limit the pope when he argues that even should a mixed constitution exist, it would not restrict a king's powers, that the aristocrats merely carry out his orders and the people or their ancestors merely passively consent to his rule.[39]

Renna argues, without explaining himself, that John's mixed constitution is a distortion of Aristotle's.[40] This seems irrelevant to John's support or nonsupport of the form, unless he means that what John calls a mixed constitution is simply a disguised royal rule, a possibility I will consider presently. In another place he says that the identification of the seventy-

---

[36] Olivi, *De renuntiatione papae*, pp. 356–57.

[37] Olivi, *De renuntiatione papae*, p. 357.

[38] Renna, *Royalist Political Thought*, pp. 230–31.

[39] Renna, *Royalist Political Thought*, pp. 233–34; *"Populus,"* p. 261.

[40] Renna, *"Populus,"* p. 261.

two elders with Aristotle's aristocracy is a distortion of the *Politics*.[41] He does not explain his statement, but if anything the distortion seems to be of Deuteronomy, since John says in perfect harmony with Aristotle that the seventy-two are a few who rule according to virtue, but it may well be argued that this is not their biblical role.

Renna argues that although the mixed constitution may be better for the Jews or the Church, royal government is best in itself. But John explicitly states that when he says royal rule is best, he means that it is the best of the simple forms and refers to the Third Book of the *Politics*, where Aristotle distinguished between simple and mixed polities.[42]

Renna argues that John thought that the mixed constitution was suited only to the ancient Jews and for the Church, for which the Jews were a type. He distorts John's clear statement that a mixed constitution is better than pure royal rule: "First, although the best type of monarchy *per se*, John continues, is one in which a single man rules according to virtue, mixed monarchy can be better (*melius*) than a purely royal rule."[43] By paraphrasing, Renna can obscure John's identification of regal rule as the best simple form, but this is venial compared to his deliberate substitution of "can be" for "is" (*est*). His curious decision to provide us with the Latin for "better"—surely neither an unusual nor significant usage—can only be explained as a cover for his suppression of the word *est*. Anyone arguing against John's support of the mixed constitution must explain what John can mean when he says that the mixed constitution *is* better than a pure regal government. Renna has not done this.

Renna argues that John thought that the mixed constitution was suited only to the Jews because the Jews were immoral and corrupt, and therefore that a regal governnment in this case would lead to tyranny.[44] John, following Thomas Aquinas, does give this argument as one of several in favor of the Jewish mixed constitution. His statement, however, could easily apply to any people. It is not just that the Israelites were immoral; the perfect virtue needed for pure regal rule is "found in few." The Israelites are just one example of a people that is especially unlikely to produce the perfect king. Since without perfection regal rule is disastrous, John implies that it would be a rare nation that should embark on it.

A more telling refutation of Renna on this point is that the argument from corruption is only John's second defense of the mixed constitution. He first maintains, like Thomas Aquinas, without any particular reference

---

[41] Renna, *Royalist Political Thought*, p. 233.

[42] Renna, *Royalist Political Thought*, pp. 231–32. John is the first explicitly to contrast simple and mixed forms in this context; in the corresponding passage of the *Summa Theologiae*, (1–2.105.1), Thomas Aquinas only hints at the distinction.

[43] Renna, *Royalist Political Thought*, pp. 228–32; "*Populus*," pp. 260–61.

[44] Renna, *Royalist Political Thought*, pp. 230–31.

to the Jews, that it is better than pure monarchy because in it everyone has a share in government. Although John then illustrates his idea with an exposition of the supposed actual constitution of the ancient Jews (taken from Thomas Aquinas), his theoretical statements are perfectly general: if a share in rule promotes peace and contentment, it would logically be wise for every government to be mixed.

Renna argues that John treats the Old Testament polity as a type for the Church, but does not really explain this except to say that John applies principles from the Jews to the Church. He implies that since John does not say that the Church is corrupt he must be making the extension from the Jews by typology.[45] This is nonsense. Again Renna ignores the fact that there are two arguments for the mixed constitution—and John mentions the mixed constitution for the Church right after the first argument (that everyone should have a share), before he says anything about the Jews' defects. Actually, Renna's point strengthens my argument: if the Church is not corrupt yet still would be better served by a mixed constitution corruption is not necessary for its justification.

It certainly was traditional to play on the kind of typology Renna mentions, but it is not obviously present in John of Paris. His source, Thomas Aquinas, proved that the mixed constitution was the best government for the Jews and by extension for the secular state, but he did not apply it to the Church. John was drawn in that direction because of his desire to reduce the power of the pope; surely if he had intended a typological argument he would have said so, both to strengthen his position and avoid the possibility that others, against his intentions, would apply his argument to the secular state. Also, he would have brought up the mixed constitution within a discussion of God's plan or at least when he was directly discussing the Jews. Instead he inserts it when he is defending the mixed constitution as a government in which everyone has a share. Thus, he seems more concerned with bringing a better government to a troubled Church and promoting peace within it than anything else.

Further, it is more difficult to apply the mixed constitution to the Church than to the state. In secular affairs, according to John, the people has the right to choose any form it pleases; in the Church, however, it is bound to papal monarchy and even to the plenitude of power, since these were established by God's own words. John obviously thinks that these can coexist with a mixed constitution, but he never says that God intended a mixed constitution for the Church. All of his arguments for it are from the point of view of utility. Surely, to give himself more credibility, he would have said that Christ instituted a mixed constitution if he believed it to be true.

---

[45] Renna, *Royalist Political Thought*, p. 232.

Finally, Renna argues that the mixed constitution (and then only that of the Jews), "is good not because it 'limits' the king's power, but because it serves the 'peace.'" I do not deny that this is an important, even the primary justification for a mixed constitution as John sees it. But John does say that the king's power is and should be limited in any mixed constitution. First, he states that Mosaic kingship lacked full power. This was true, John continues, because of the mixture; thus, the lack of full power is an essential not an accidental concomitant of a mixed constitution. Second, John's second argument for a mixed constitution is that the less than perfect king cannot be trusted with full power because he will become a tyrant. Therefore, the mixed constitution must limit his authority. Renna tries to find a way around this by arguing that the part the few and the many play in the mixed constitution is to advise the king, carry out his orders, and depose him if he becomes intolerable.[46] But this cannot be what John intends: the first two duties cannot prevent the corruption of the king, and the third is the right of any people under any form of government, including the regal form. Renna could, but does not, argue that the institutionalization of the right to depose the king in parliamentary bodies would obviate this last objection, that it would represent something sufficiently different from the vague right of any society to justify the term *mixed constitution* for it. On the contrary, Renna insists that John never intended any institutional power for the nonregal element, even in a mixed constitution.

Renna neglects to mention one related point that I think would be his strongest argument against the limitation of the king's power in a mixed constitution. John accepts that the pope has and must have, by God's precept, a plenitude of power in the Church. Yet he clearly thinks that this can coexist with a mixed constitution. Does this not imply that even in a mixed constitution the king's power is unlimited? I do not think so. John rarely uses the phrase "plenitude of power," and then only in the traditional formula: the pope has greater needs than inferior bishops, "who are called to a part of the care, not to the plenitude of power." This comment appears in the midst of a denial that the pope has lordship over Church property, a denial justified by a corporate analysis of the Church. In this context plenitude of power seems to mean only that the pope has universal jurisdiction as corporate head or steward of the Church, not that he has unrestricted power. John would seem, then, to distinguish between the phrases "plenitude of power," which refers to jurisdictional extent, and "full power," which refers to the actual possession of complete power. Watt suggests that in the ecclesiastical mixed constitution John is trying to combine the traditional plenitude of power of the pope with communal sover-

---

[46] Renna, *Royalist Political Thought*, pp. 232, 171; *"Populus,"* p. 261. John of Paris, *De Potestate Regia et Papali*, chap. 19, p. 174.

eignty.[47] This, I think, is largely correct; John wants to describe a constitution for the Church which preserves the regal dignity of the pope and yet gives ultimate authority to the congregation of the faithful.

All in all, Renna's arguments have proved ineffective. John can be presumed to mean exactly what he says: the mixed constitution is the best form of government for both Church and state.

On most points John and Thomas Aquinas, his source, agree. Both support the mixed constitution, and for the same reasons: it will lead to peace and contentment among the people, and it will prevent tyranny by balancing the governmental forms, thus avoiding the excesses possible with monarchy. Both admit that pure monarchy is absolutely best and is desirable if one of perfect virtue be found. Both think this unlikely, and both might opt for a mixed constitution even in that case since it is important that everyone should have a share in government. Both allow democracy in their mixed constitution, not because of any positive contribution that the many can make, but because the many will only be content if it has a share.

On this last point, however, Thomas is more explicit. John, although he does not ascribe virtue or wisdom to the many, does vest them with sovereignty: the people can subject itself to any person or government it desires, and the people retains the ultimate right to change its government or ruler, at least if it has a good reason for doing so. This is a step beyond Thomas, who based government on the common good but never gave to the people ultimate power or an inherent right to choose its government. This factor changes the nature of the mixed constitution: no longer is it, as in Aristotle, the inclusion of all powers that have a right to govern, nor, as in Thomas Aquinas, the formal balancing of governmental forms. Instead it is the best way the people can exercise its authority: the monarch and aristocrats provide the virtue and ability that the multitude lacks, but it takes part and retains the ability to remove these if necessary, and so is content. John's treatise is a step toward a strict theory of popular sovereignty.

Aristocracy occupies an odd position in John's scheme. For Thomas aristocracy and monarchy are the best simple forms, and so their combination is best. John says nothing about aristocracy being good and includes

[47] Watt, *On Royal and Papal Power*, p. 56. John of Paris, *De Potestate Regia et Papali*, chap. 6, pp. 92–93. "Papa . . . amplius facit sibi fructus suos de bonis communibus pinguiores, secundum exigentiam sui status, quam prelati inferiores qui vocati sunt in partem sollicitudinis [non in plenitudinem potestatis]." The words in brackets are found only in some manuscripts, but they are a traditional part of the formula, and John would have implied them even without explicit quotation. See Tierney, *Foundations*, p. 164ff., for an analysis of the corporate aspect of John's treatise. See also John of Paris, *De Potestate Regia et Papali*, chap. 12, p. 131, where John gives the "opinion of some" that Peter is distinguished from the other apostles only in his authority to distribute ecclesiastical jurisdiction.

it, as he does democracy, on the grounds that it will promote peace. Renna's argument that "the people" is to be completely identified with the barons cannot be taken seriously.[48] Although, as Renna points out, John does not state explicitly that the barons can depose a king because they represent the whole people, he does say that the cardinals can depose a pope for this reason. In the description of the Jewish constitution this is precisely the relationship between the seventy-two and the Israelite people, and these two groups are clearly separated. John emphasizes that everyone is to have a share; if "the people" were to refer to barons alone, what sense would there be in saying the constitution included both aristocracy and democracy? I admit that John never intended the lower classes of society actually to participate in government; however, he did feel that the power of the king and barons rested on the whole people, even though he might have interpreted this word to exclude the majority of the population: women, children, serfs, and slaves. But, then, all medieval writers excluded these, and even modern "democratic" societies have only recently and partially enfranchised some of them. John recognizes the actual power of the barons in feudal society, and includes them as the aristocratic element, the actual institutional check on the king.

Finally, John's emphasis on law is less pronounced than Thomas's. To be sure, the king and everyone else in the society are bound to the law, but the law is not central to John's theory, as it was to Thomas's. In Thomas's misunderstanding of Aristotle, political and regal rule were distinguished by whether the king had full power or was subservient to the law—in this sense John's king is political, but so even is Giles of Rome's. On the more complicated question of who is to make the law (John's and Giles's criterion for political and regal rule), John is silent. It is significant that John follows the tradition of Giles of Rome rather than that of Thomas and Ptolemy of Lucca in his distinction of regal and political rule. In Thomas's version a mixed constitution can exist only with a political king, but Giles and John hold open the possibility of a regal king in a mixed constitution. Nicole Oresme and John Fortescue will combine this possibility with Ptolemy of Lucca's modification of Thomas's approach in the later mixed constitutional theories.

[48] Renna, "*Populus*," pp. 246–49.

PART 3

The Fourteenth Century

Chapter 9

ARISTOTELIAN POLITICAL THOUGHT IN THE FOURTEENTH CENTURY

THE EARLY TO mid-fourteenth century is one of the most important periods for the development of Western political thought as a whole. William of Ockham and Marsilius of Padua were two of the most significant political philosophers of the Middle Ages and Bartolus of Sassoferrato, perhaps the greatest jurist of the later Middle Ages. The Englishman Walter Burley and the Frenchman Jean Buridan were widely read in their own day. Yet this period—except for the turn-of-the-century writers Engelbert of Admont, Ptolemy of Lucca, and John of Paris—is of somewhat lesser import for the particular theme of this study. Most writers of this period shied away from championing any one form of political organization; they repeated and developed the arguments for and against the various polities, but for the most part judged them not by a priori qualities but by their suitability to the particular community. The mixed constitution, in all but a few very important exceptions, was simply one of several arrangements. While writers often assumed that one form was best absolutely, they also often recognized that it was not always the best practically. In many ways this political relativism developed ideas already present to some extent in the earlier Thomists, and the secularization of political thought that generally went along with relativism prepared the way for the modern concepts of the state and the origin of political authority.

In 1324 Marsilius of Padua insisted on a definite concept of sovereignty, and, in my opinion, favored a mixed constitution but left the particular organization of government open. William of Ockham argued for suitability as the criterion of good government. Walter Burley elaborated the many arguments on the virtues of the several forms and took the first tentative steps toward identifying the English monarchy as a mixed constitution. Bartolus of Sassoferrato presented legal justification for various forms and concluded that communities of different sizes require different forms of government. Jean Buridan favored monarchy but gave arguments for participation.

More peripheral to my concerns is the great poet Dante Alighieri (1265–1321). His influential treatise, *Monarchy*, written sometime between 1310 and his death, sets out a defense of the universal monarchy of the Roman Empire.[1] Although he bases himself on the *Politics* and adopts a syllogistic approach to argument, Dante's political thought is in many respects not Aristotelian in spirit.

In order to justify a world monarchy he rejects the idea that governments are formed to advance purely individual ends freely chosen by different peoples. "It is foolish," he writes, "to think that there is an end to this or that society, and not that there is one end of all of them." The one overriding goal of all humanity—intellectual growth—is a transcendental goal for Dante, as both Reeves and Peterman demonstrate, and as such is best incorporated in a divinely mandated government. Dante says that Aristotle associated intellectual superiority with natural rule, which idea accords with the stated goal. Of course, Aristotle said no such thing, except in regard to despotism, and then, as Peterman points out, he was concerned with a qualitative not a quantitative difference. For Aristotle it was only necessary that a ruler excel in some quality relevant to rule.[2]

Dante's emperor is a regal ruler in the two senses that he is the source of law and that he rules by his own will:

> Whence the opinion of Aristotle is that those things which can be determined by law should in no way be left to a judge. And this must happen because of fear of cupidity, which easily twists the minds of men. Where, therefore, there is nothing which can be desired, there cannot possibly be cupidity. . . . But the [universal] monarch has nothing which he can desire.[3]

The world government rules the world so that by a common rule it might lead all to peace.[4]

In all these ways Dante goes against not only Aristotle but the trend of medieval political thought, which increasingly insisted on limited government adapted to particular conditions. As an active participant in Florentine republican politics, Dante supported monarchy only at the highest level and adopted a more typical position toward smaller communities.

[1] Dante, *Monarchia*. Dante was disillusioned about the ability of republican government to survive in the Italian city-states after his own faction of White Guelphs was defeated and exiled by the Black Guelphs in 1302. He concluded that only a world monarchy could control factionalism and permit local city government to flourish.

[2] Dante, *Monarchia*, 1.2, p. 139. "Esse autem finem huius civilitatis et illius, et non esse unum omnium finem arbitrari stultum est." 1.3, p. 143. "Innotescit illud Politice: intellectu, scilicet, vigentes aliis naturaliter principari." Larry Peterman, "Dante's Monarchia and Aristotle's Political Thought," pp. 14–15; Marjorie Reeves, "Marsiglio of Padua and Dante Alighieri," p. 94; Aristotle, *Politics*, 1.5

[3] Dante, *Monarchia*, 1.11, p. 155. "Unde sententia Phylosophi est ut que lege determinari possunt nullo modo iudici relinquantur. Et hoc metu cupiditatis fieri oportet, de facili mentes hominum detorquentis. Ubi ergo non est quod possit optari, inpossibile est ibi cupiditatem. . . . Sed Monarcha non habet quod possit optare."

[4] Dante, *Monarchia*, 1.14, p. 165.

The Empire allows such smaller units; Dante points out that not every municipal regulation could come directly from the world government. On the contrary, laws must vary according to climate and other conditions; the world government deals with what is common. As an example, Dante mentions Moses, who chose the chiefs of the tribes but left to them all lesser judgments.[5] Compare this with Thomas Aquinas's and John of Paris's portrayal of Mosaic government as a mixed constitution and with Ptolemy of Lucca's, Engelbert of Admont's, and others' use of local conditions to justify a variety of local regimes.

Only a few comments in the *Monarchy* show that Dante accepted nonmonarchical government at any level, perhaps because the arguments he gives for world monarchy for the most part could easily be used to prove that monarchy is best in each particular case. But he does mention the sixfold schema of government and suggest that monarchy, aristocracy, and polity are all good:

> Only with a [universal] monarch commanding does the race of humans exist for its own sake and not another's, for then only are perverted polities controlled—namely democracies, oligarchies, and tyrannies—which compel the race of humans into servitude, as is clear by considering them all. Kings, aristocrats, whom they call optimates, and champions of the people's liberty act politically [*politizant* here refers to rule in any nonperverted form]. . . . Whence Aristotle in his *Politics* says that in perverted polities a good person is a bad citizen, but in a right polity a good person and a good citizen are the same.[6]

Although Dante accepts the three good forms at the local level, he feels that it is only the world monarch, not any mixed constitution, that can prevent their degeneration. Note that he also distorts Aristotle's comment that in the *best* government the good man and the good citizen are identical.

Of all the early fourteenth-century writers, only Marsilius of Padua (and much more feebly Walter Burley) attempted what I interpret, in opposition to all modern scholarship, as a comprehensive defense of the mixed constitution as the necessarily best and proper form of government for most or all peoples. He submerges this belief because his most pressing task is to defend all government against the incursions of papal monarchy.

---

[5] Dante, *Monarchia*, 1.14, p. 164.

[6] Dante, *Monarchia*, 1.12, pp. 159–60. "Genus humanum solum imperante Monarcha sui et non alterius gratia est: tunc enim solum politie diriguntur oblique—democratie scilicet, oligarchie atque tyrampnides—que in servitutem cogunt genus humanum, ut patet discurrenti per omnes, et politizant reges, aristocratici quos optimates vocant, et populi libertatis zelatores. . . . Unde Phylosophus in suis Politicis ait quod in politia obliqua bonus homo est malus civis, in recta vero bonus homo et civis bonus convertuntur."

I do not want to ignore the early and mid-fourteenth century writers, for their ideas were influential; neither do I want to examine their works comprehensively. So I have chosen to abandon my previous pattern of examining one thinker after another and instead focus on the themes of early and mid-fourteenth century political thought: first, the growing influence of relativism (centering my argument on William of Ockham) and, second, ideas of limited kingship, popular sovereignty, and the mixed constitution. Because of my purpose this second part will be by far the longer. In this I will focus especially on Marsilius of Padua.

The end of the century, in contrast, provided a thinker of the utmost importance to the theory of the mixed constitution. Nicole Oresme was a polymath who contributed not only to political theory and philosophy, but also to physics, economics, astronomy, and mathematics. Writing around 1375, he produced a synthesis of the views of all his predecessors in which he set out a powerful defense of the mixed constitution, limited government, and law. The analysis of his work provides a fitting close to the major portion of this study and points the way to the concluding sections that take up the later medieval developments of mixed constitutionalism among the conciliarists, the apologists for the French and English monarchies, and the humanists.

Chapter 10

RELATIVISM AND THE BEST POLITY

IN THE fourteenth century political relativism became commonplace. It was not new; indeed Aristotle's approach forced honest readers to confront the possibility that contingencies such as climate, temperament, local custom, the nature and quality of a given people, and even astrological influences might determine or limit what government was best or possible. Every author that I have so far discussed accepts these factors to some extent, although many would still insist on one form or another in all or most situations. Ewart Lewis, to whom I have frequently referred, makes the case that relativism was a primary characteristic of Aristotelian political thought from the time of William of Moerbeke's translation of the *Politics* and Thomas Aquinas's interpretation of it.[1] I agree to some extent but still find a new direction appearing around the turn of the fourteenth century: instead of simply making a gesture of respect toward Aristotle's relativistic statements, some authors now embrace them wholeheartedly and insist on the absolute contingency of political organization. I have previously argued that this shift began with Engelbert of Admont, who wrote just before 1300. Although I do not want to get into philosophical issues, it cannot be a coincidence that it is precisely at this same time that radical nominalism with its insistence on the absolute contingency of the created universe is emerging, finding its most articulate champion in the English Franciscan William of Ockham (c. 1285–1347), whose political theories form the core of this chapter.

From the start Ockham aroused controversy. By 1321 he had completed the requirements for a master of theology at Oxford and even gave his inaugural lecture but never became regent master (hence his nickname "Venerable Inceptor") because the Chancellor, John Lutterell, opposed him and in 1323 denounced him as a heretic to Pope John XXII. Summoned to Avignon and examined by a special commission that recommended censure, Ockham was not formally condemned until his escape in 1328 with Michael of Cesena, the leader of the Franciscans, and flight to the pope's enemy Ludwig of Bavaria, first to Pisa and then in 1330 to Munich, where he remained for the rest of his life. During this period Ockham produced a large number of works attacking the pope as a heretic and

---

[1] Lewis, "Natural Law and Expediency." She also argues that Ockham, Aquinas, and others relate the common good and expediency to a fundamental pattern of natural law.

defending the Franciscan position. His philosophical thought was the basis of the "modern way," the leading scholastic school in opposition to Thomism for the next two centuries.

I am not saying that Ockham was a political relativist pure and simple. No medieval writer is more complex or more controversial than he is, and his voluminous political writings have given rise to many and divergent interpretations. Some question whether it is even possible to extract a coherent theory from his writings. The task is made especially difficult by William's habit, especially in his most important work, the *Dialogue* (1343), of spewing forth every opinion he can think of on an issue, without clearly indicating his own preference.[2] Sometimes it seems easy to decide which preference is his, but it is usually arguable.

What I am saying is that Ockham most frequently and in most cases relates the best government to the particular time, place, and culture. Most modern writers concur. Those who dissent feel that he does not really care about governmental structure, only about theological controversies or the struggle between Empire and papacy.[3] Arthur McGrade, whose analysis in some other areas is deficient, points out many of the same passages I cite to demonstrate Ockham's pragmatism. He argues that since William judges government by its ends and not for metaphysical values, he feels that different circumstances demand different kinds of regime and that there is no necessary connection between the goal of the common good and the means to that goal. Morrall also stresses William's pragmatism and his realization that the ideal form is not always ideal and may even be harmful for some. On the other hand, he puts too much emphasis on the passages that suggest the necessity for consent and popular sovereignty, which for William are purely contingent and secondary to the practical question. Leff denies any effective theory of popular sovereignty, but does stress at least initial consent to rule as well as pursuit of the common good as requisites for rule.[4]

Ockham characteristically treats the Church and state as analogous political entities. When he writes about the government of the Church he applies Aristotelian arguments about the structure and efficacy of each polity; when he writes of the state he refers to ecclesiastical principles. In fact,

---

[2] William of Ockham, *Dialogus*. Other relevant arguments occur in *Eight Questions*.

[3] Richard Scholz's *Wilhelm von Ockham als Politischer Denker und sein Breviloquium de Principatu Tyranico* and *Unbekannte kirschenpolitische Streitschriften aus der Zeit Ludwigs des Bayern (1327–1354)* are now rather dated and his idea that Ockham based the structure of both Church and state on divine revelation alone is untenable. See Arthur McGrade, *The Political Thought of William of Ockham*, p. 29ff. Georges de Lagarde, in "Marsile de Padoue et Guillaume d'Ockham" and *La Naissance de l'esprit laïque*, vol. 5, p. 271; vol. 4, p. 230, is more adept at presenting Ockham as indifferent to political form.

[4] McGrade, *Political Thought*, pp. 112, 122–24; J. B. Morrall, "Some Notes on a Recent Interpretation of William of Ockham's Political Philosophy," pp. 354–56; Leff, *William of Ockham*, pp. 624–25.

most of his interesting comments on the best secular polity occur in the book of the *Dialogue* in which he poses the question: "Is it expedient for all the community of the faithful to be subject to one faithful head?," and to a lesser extent in the seemingly more relevant question of the *Eight Questions* that inquires "whether the pope and the Roman Church institute temporal jurisdiction."[5] John of Paris and Marsilius of Padua also tended to treat the two spheres as analogous, and clearly William had some of the same motivations as these men in opposing the pope's power and defending a king or emperor. Marsilius and he were even involved in the same struggle and undoubtedly knew each other since both were living at Ludwig's court. What is striking about William's approach is that he uses arguments from the two spheres freely and casually and apparently sees no need to justify this procedure—it is obvious to him that Aristotelian political precepts apply equally to the order of the Roman Catholic Church. Although he occasionally mentions the divine institution of the papacy, the thrust of his argument implies that regardless of its origin its form, like that of a secular polity, can be changed for any good reason.

Ockham gives arguments in support of all the good simple forms. In fact, the first nineteen chapters of *Dialogue* 3.1.2 consist of a back-and-forth debate over which form of government is best for the Church. The general impression is that he does, for the ideal case at least, favor monarchy as the best of the simple forms, and not just for the Church, since the arguments he gives apply equally to the state. Ockham provides both pragmatic and metaphysical support for monarchy; for the other forms, only pragmatic. He says, for example, that kingship is more natural since it is more similar to the rule of the paterfamilias. Characteristic of his arguments is expediency. William writes that the question of whether a king should be chosen is to some degree a practical question:

> If, however, there is some part so potent that it could stir up a dangerous sedition in the whole community which could not be checked, and it is unwilling to accept the rule of one, then someone should not be preferred over all similar ones and others, but the institution of such a rule must be deferred to another time . . . minor evils are often permitted to avoid greater. . . . Aristotle understood that it is unjust that someone should rule some similar in virtue [to that person], unless from some utility or necessity. . . . Aristotle seems to prove absolutely and without distinction that it is unjust that someone should rule those similar [to that person], since there should be equal honor and dignity to those equal in virtue . . . nevertheless, when it is not possible or useful, or less useful, especially for the common good . . . someone . . . can be preferred to others who are equal and similar. And if some rise up

[5] William of Ockham, *Dialogus*, 3.1.2; *Octo Questiones*, 3.1.

for this and are provoked to make sedition . . . [they are] ambitious and jealous preferring their honor to the common good.[6]

Even the papal monarchy, William argues, results from the primacy of the common utility—it was for this reason alone that Christ instituted it,[7] and for the common utility the form of church government can be changed. In the secular state sometimes aristocracy is best, sometimes monarchy—the ancients, the Romans in particular, changed back and forth as necessity demanded, and the congregation of the faithful no less than any civil community has power with respect to all expedient things.[8] There is no essential difference in this regard between New Testament kingship, which derives from purely human law, and the papacy or Old Testament kingship, which derives from divine law—in either case necessity justifies a change in governmental form.[9] Christ did not mean to exclude utility in

[6] William of Ockham, *Dialogus*, 3.1.2.9, p. 796; 3.1.2.15, p. 800. "Si autem est aliqua pars tam potens, quod possit seditionem periculosam toti communitate suscitare: quae compesci non posset; et principatum unius vellet nullatenus sustinere: tunc non esset aliquis omnibus sibi similibus et alliis praeferendus: sed esset talis principantis institutio ad tempus aliud differenda . . . saepe permittuntur minora mala, ut maiora vitentur. . . . Aristoteles intelligit, quod iniustum est, quod aliquis aliquibus similibus in virtute et aequalibus principetur, nisi ex aliqua utilitate vel necessitate. . . . Ad rationem vero Aristotelis, qua absolute et sine distinctione vel modificatione videtur probare, quod iniustum est, quod aliquis sibi similibus principetur: quia aequalibus secundum virtutem debetur aequalis honor et dignitas . . . tamen quando non est possibile, aut non est utile, vel est minus utile, praesertim communi bono . . . aliquis . . . potest similibus et aequalibus praeferri. Et si alii in hoc turbarentur, et ad seditionem faciendam provocarentur . . . tanquam ambitiosi et invidi praeferentes honorem proprium bono communi."

[7] William of Ockham, *Octo Questiones*, 3, chap. 4, p. 103. "Dicitur itaque quod ad optimum principatum primo exigitur quod sit propter bonum commune subditorum, non propter bonum principantis proprium institutus. . . . Talis autem principatus est papalis et episcopalis, quantum est ex ordinatione Christi; quod Christus insinuasse videtur quando beatum Petrum ordinavit in papam dicendo ei: 'Pasci oves meas' " See also *Dialogus*, 3.1.2.20, p. 807. "Sed communis utilitas est causa, quare unus summus pontifex debet praeesse cunctis fidelibus."

[8] William of Ockham, *Dialogus*, 3.1.2.20, p. 806. "Amplius, communitate fidelium quantum ad omnia, quae necessaria sunt pro his quae sunt propria Christianis, optime est provisum: et non minus bene, quam cuicunque communitate vel genti, ut in omnibus talibus quantum ad omnia quae expediunt et ut expediunt habeat potestatem."

[9] William of Ockham, *Octo Questiones*, 5, chap. 3, p. 156. "Unctio enim sacerdotalis et etiam episcopalis est ex institutione divina; unctio vero regalis, licet in Veteri Testamento fuerit ex praecepto Dei, tamen in Nova Lege est solummodo ex institutione humana." Cf. *Dialogus*, 3.1.2.20, p. 808. " 'Necessitas legem non habet.' . . . Et consimiles non tantum de legibus humanis positivis, sed etiam de legibus divinis positivis, nisi in eisdem legibus divinis contrarium caveatur, debet intelligi, ut necessitas legi Divinae positivae non subiaceat. . . . Nam non minorem potestatem super principatum sacerdotum mutandum habent Christiani in lege novo, quam habuerunt illi qui erant sub legi veteri constituti. . . . Ergo et Christiani habent potestatem constituendi plures summos pontifices, non obstante quod Christus ordinaverit aliquem unum esse in summum pontificem sublimandum." See also 3.1.2.21–24, pp. 808–11.

his ordination, but in any case "for necessity it is licit to go against the divine precept expressed about those things which are not evil in themselves, but are evil only because they are forbidden. Therefore, given that Christ ordained one highest pontiff to preside over all the faithful, it is licit for the faithful for common utility to institute another rule, at least for a time."[10]

The fact remains that monarchy—for Church and state—is abstractly better for Ockham, even if there is not one person better than all others. Alternating rule might be more expedient to prevent sedition, but one should rule if the many good are willing to accept a king.[11] On the other hand, he writes, the rule that is best simply may not be best for all—all may not be good enough for the best.[12] Echoing Engelbert of Admont, William comments that true regal government, unbound by law or custom, may not even exist in his day.[13]

In all of William's arguments there is a significant lack of concern with the source of power and with law. The universal and particular necessity of rule coexists with the contingency of the singular manifestation.[14] All postbiblical secular rule is purely from human ordination, but although tacit consent may be required for government, it is not the criterion for it.[15] Nor ultimately is there a metaphysical criterion. Regal rule, he says, cannot in the last analysis be assimilated to any form of natural principate.[16] The

[10] William of Ockham, *Dialogus*, 3.1.2.20, p. 808. "Sed pro necessitate licet facere contra praeceptum Divinum expressum in his, quae non sunt de se mala, sed solum sunt mala, quia sunt prohibita. Ergo esto, quod Christus ordinasset unum summum pontificem esse praeciendum cunctis fidelibus: liceret fidelibus pro communi utilitate alium instituere principatum, saltem ad tempus." See also 3.1.2.22, p. 809. For a weaker argument that although states can be changed the Church cannot, see 3.1.2.27, p. 815.

[11] William of Ockham, *Dialogus*, 3.1.2.17, p. 802. "Vult Aristoteles, quod expedit omnes participare principatum secundum partem, id est quandoque principari, quandoque subiici: quando probabiliter timetur, quod aliter periculosae seditiones orientur, nisi quilibet qui est aeque dignus aliquando principetur. Si autem de huiusmodi seditione minime formidatur, expedit si aliquis invenitur idoneus, ut unus tanquam rex omnibus principetur, etiam secundum totam vitam suam."

[12] William of Ockham, *Octo Questiones*, 3, chap. 11, p. 112. "Ita optimus principatus simpliciter non est omnibus optimus, immo aliquibus est nocivus et nonnunquam inductivus corruptionis et periclitationis boni communis. Quod accidere potest tam ex malitia subiectorum quam ex malitia vel insufficientia ad principatum huiusmodi assumendi."

[13] William of Ockham, *Dialogus*, 3.1.2.6, p. 795. "Ideo forte his diebus non est in universo orbe talis principatus scilicet primus regalis."

[14] William of Ockham, *Dialogus*, 3.1.2.17, p. 802. "Sicut tam universalis quam particularis est necessaria, cuius tamen quaelibet singularis est contingens."

[15] William of Ockham, *Octo Questiones*, 5, chap. 3, p. 156. William gives the example of Abimilech (Judges 9:6), who persuaded the men of Sichen to have him as king, as an example of consent. See also Morrall, "Some Notes," p. 359.

[16] William of Ockham, *Octo Questiones*, 5., chap. 6, p. 158. "Nullus tamen principatus regalis est naturalis, quamvis principatus regalis assimuletur in multis principatui naturali: sed omnis principatus regalis est ex institutione positiva, divina vel humana."

sole criterion is the common good; given this, the question of who institutes government and whether this institution is licit or illicit according to
positive law and whether it proceeds according to established law and custom is secondary. If a government rules for the common good, he says, it
does not matter how it comes about.[17]

Basing himself solely on expediency, William makes no concession to the
idea that everyone has a right to play a part in government or has a natural
desire to participate. Nor does he feel that universal participation is necessarily expedient, as did Thomas Aquinas—he gives no indication that the
many counselors are any but the wise few. Even if everyone is good, he
writes, it may be expedient for a few of them to rule aristocratically.[18] This
is a complete departure from Peter of Auvergne's and others' theory that if
the multitude is nonbestial it deserves to rule. In this respect William is the
least Aristotelian political theorist that I have considered, since he is not
influenced by the idea of humans as political animals who naturally desire
a share in government. His only concern is expediency. In the next chapter,
I will show that Ockham feels that the mixed constitution is usually most
expedient.

Marsilius, also called Marsilio or Marsiglio, of Padua (c. 1275–after
1342) was a younger contemporary of Ockham and for centuries was
treated as the other great radical of the early fourteenth century. Most
probably he attended the University of Padua, the city of his birth, and
then studied medicine and philosophy at the University of Paris. He was
teaching there when he wrote his most famous work, *The Defender of Peace*,
in 1324. Forced to flee because of the Church's hostility, he took refuge
with the Emperor Ludwig in Bavaria and took part in the latter's expedi-
tion against Italy in 1327. After Rome fell, the emperor, possibly under
Marsilius's influence, held a series of popular assemblies of the Roman people and got them to declare him emperor, depose Pope John XXII, and
appoint the antipope Nicholas V. Marsilius himself played a leading part
in the persecution of the clergy that remained loyal to John. Eventually the
people themselves turned the imperial forces out of Rome, and Marsilius
spent the rest of his life in Germany.

Possibly more than most medieval political thinkers, Marsilius was influenced by his experience of the Northern Italian situation. His native Padua
remained free if unstable with government in the hands of a broadly based

---

[17] William of Ockham, *Octo Questiones*, 3, chap. 9, p. 111. "Nam cum talis iurisdictio vel
potestas bono communi debeat expedire, non refert a quo instituatur."
[18] William of Ockham, *Dialogus*, 3.1.2.17, pp. 802–3. "Si autem non inveniuntur aliqui
pauci, qui sunt caeteris meliores: sed sunt multi in sapientia et virtute aequales; et tot, quod
non esset expediens omnes principari: tunc non potest fieri, ut principantes aristocratice sint
caeteris meliores: et tamen principatus aristocraticus est toti commmunitati expediens, si principatum regalem noluit sustinere."

Great Council that elected a podesta. But everywhere in Italy there was continual factionalism and strife, and in many city-states republican governments were giving way to despots. Padua itself struggled to keep its own clergy under control. It is no wonder that Marsilius was so concerned with the problems of peace and unity and with the harm that can come from a church with great secular power.

Though I argue that he strongly preferred a mixed constitution, there are relativist aspects to his thinking. He has been open to one of the same charges as Ockham: that he really did not care about the type of government and was concerned only with the struggle against the pope. This is Conal Condren's position; he argues that Marsilius formulated his central concept—the legislator—solely as an ad hoc theoretical obstacle to the secular claims of the pope and purposely made the concept vague so that it could apply to any reasonably well- or long-established government. To support his argument Condren quotes Marsilius's statement that the "weightier part" of the citizenry, which Marsilius equates with the legislator, can be determined "in accordance with the honorable custom of politics."[19]

In the next chapter I will refute most of this argument; for now I note that there is some degree of truth to it. Marsilius is certainly most concerned with defending all secular power against the papacy and therefore is not clear about his optimal political principles. He does indeed leave the particular form of government open and subject to local conditions, customs, and needs, but behind the particular officials and governmental organs he demands the consent and participation of a much wider "legislator" if the government is to be legitimate. But whether this legislator expresses itself through a monarchy, aristocracy, or democracy is up to it and relative to the local situation and traditions.

Bartolus of Sassoferrato (1313–57) was the greatest of the fourteenth-century authorities on Roman Law and, in Skinner's view, with Marsilius of Padua, Ptolemy of Lucca, and Remigio de Girolami one of the most important proponents of republicanism and medieval sources of Italian civic humanism.[20] He studied at the universities of Perugia and Bologna and later was a professor of law at Pisa and Perugia. In his vast and influential commentaries on the corpus of Roman Law and in several short treatises he sought to resolve the problem of the relationship of the Roman Empire to other political entities. How could the theoretical universal hegemony of the Empire be reconciled with the de facto existence of independent national states and the smaller but still independent city-states of

[19] Conal Condren, "Democracy and the *Defensor pacis*: On the English Language Tradition of Marsilian Interpretation."

[20] Skinner, *Modern Political Theory*, vol. 1, pp. 51–52.

Northern Italy? Bartolus chose a practical solution that recognized the rights of separate political entities and justified them by prescription, but at the same time preserved the Empire as a universal authority theoretically superior to any other. In practice, however, Bartolus accepted and supported the existing division of nations and city-states. This approach of adapting Roman Law to contemporary conditions, which Bartolus followed in all areas, distinguished those of his school, called the post-Glossators, from those, the Glossators, who came before and tried simply to understand the literal meaning and intent of the Law.

For the most part Bartolus pursued his objectives using Roman Law as his sole authority and avoiding the more theoretical questions of best government and sources of political power. Only in one work did he explicitly try to bring Roman Law together with Aristotelian political philosophy—the *Treatise on the Government of the City*.[21] Here he adapts Aristotle's six-fold classification of polities to contemporary reality and asks what form is the best according to law.

Cecil Woolf, in the only full-length biography and analysis of Bartolus to date, insists on the overriding importance of Roman Law even in this treatise. Aristotle's influence was minimal, according to Woolf, and Bartolus was no admirer of Aristotle despite some dependence on Giles of Rome. "Where Bartolus went beyond the Glossators," Woolf continues, "he did so not because he was influenced by new Aristotelian political theories but because his object, unlike that of the Glossators, was to evolve from his texts a law rather practically acceptable than scientifically correct." Walter Ullmann, though his ultimate conclusions are far different, admits that Bartolus aimed to produce a practical justification for existing political arrangements and also plays down the importance of Aristotle. Skinner argues that Ullmann and others seriously underestimate Aristotle's influence.[22]

That Bartolus was interested in empirical data derived from existing governmental practice is shown by his addition of a seventh form to those normally found in Aristotle's sixfold classification and the fact that he refers each of the other forms to a stage in the history of Rome. At first, he says, the people governed, which, Bartolus writes, Aristotle called "political" or "polity," but he himself prefers to call it "government to the people." This form is opposed to democracy or "perversion of the people." The rise of the Senate saw the transformation of government to the rule of a few good, prudent, and wealthy men, a form he calls "rule of the greater" or "rule of the senators." The evil form of this he calls *obligratia*, that is, oligarchy.

²¹ Bartolus of Sassoferrato, *De Regimine Civitatis*.

²² Cecil N. Sidney Woolf, *Bartolus of Sassoferrato: His Position in the History of Medieval Political Thought*, p. 387; Ullmann, *History of Political Thought*, pp. 215–17; Skinner, *Modern Political Theory*, vol. 1, p. 51.

Under the Empire, monarchy, which form properly includes various forms of the rule of one—not only empires but kingdoms, duchies, and counties—was reestablished. The perverted form of monarchy, tyranny, serves commonly as a term for all the bad forms. Finally, observing the disorder of medieval Rome, Bartolus feels called upon to describe a form unknown in Aristotle's day and worst of all—the government of many tyrants.[23]

In form this presentation is like that of most of the thirteenth- and fourteenth-century Aristotelian political commentators. There are, however, a few significant differences. The use of Roman history for examples of the Aristotelian forms is common, but Bartolus's interpretation is novel. It was usual, for example in the work of Ptolemy of Lucca, to regard Rome after the kings as aristocratic and to see the tribunes as responsible for the incorporation of a democratic element. Ptolemy himself saw the Empire as the victory of tyranny. The Polybian and Renaissance view regarded the consuls as monarchical. Bartolus's arrangement is precisely the one suited to his theory of the relationship of size to optimal political form. Missing is any suggestion that as the forms developed the earlier ones remained to become elements of a more complex mixed constitution.

That Bartolus felt the necessity of defining a seventh form shows that there must be some unity of action or sovereignty among the ruling class of a polity for it to qualify as a true ruling class. Otherwise, this final form would be simply a particularly pernicious oligarchy. It also demonstrates Bartolus's openness to empirical data beyond or contradictory to Aristotle

[23] Bartolus of Sassoferrato, *De Regimine Civitatis*, 127rb–va. "In primo quot modis regitur civitatis ex legibus nostris colliguntur tres modi regendi boni et tres eis contrarii. Aliquos modus apertius declarat Aristotelis tertio politicorum et ibi eos modos suis nominibus nominat: nos vero et de illis nominibus mentionem facimus et nomina sccundum presens tempens congruentius inseremus: in urbe quedam romana expulsis regibus tres modi fuerunt regendi. Primus per populum . . . istud regimen vocat Aristoteles politia seu politicum. Nos autem vocamur regimen ad populum et hic quando regimen tale bonum est cum pro regentes consideratur bonum commune principaliter omnium secundum statum suum; sed si illa multitudo regentium intenderat ad suum commodum et ad oppositionem divitium vel alicuius gentis tunc est regimen malum et greco nomine vocat Aristoteles democratia. Nos autem appellamus populum perversum. . . . Secundus regendi modus in urbe romana fuit per senatores et sic per paucos divites bonos et prudentes . . . et tunc si illi pauci tendunt ad commune bonum principatus est bonus et per Aristotelem appellatur regimen maiorentium. Nomen autem magis commune . . . principatus vel regimen bonorum. Et si illi pauci non tendunt ad bonum commune sed alique divites vel potentiores opprimentes alios intendentes ad proprium lucrum . . . vocat per Aristotelem obligratia. . . . Tertius regendi modus est per unum et istud secundum Aristotelem appellatur regnum. Nos vero si iste est dominus universalis appellamus imperium. . . . Si vero particularis aliqui appellatur regnum aliqui ducatus marchia vel comitatus. . . . Si vero tendat in malem finem . . . appellatur tyrannides . . . omne regnum malum potest communi nomine appellatur tyrannides, scilicet tyrannides populi, tyrannides aliquorum, et tyrannides unius. Est septimus modus regiminis que est in civitate romana nunc pessimus ibi sunt multi tyranni per diversos regiones adeo fortes quod unus contra alium non prevalet." I will generally use the more common names for the six forms.

and, more importantly, Roman Law. For every other form Bartolus is able, with some distortion, to find a precedent from Roman Law. But this one is meant to describe the new situation in fourteenth-century Rome.

Quite often Bartolus follows Giles of Rome's arguments for kingship, the role of counsel, and the like. From this one might take him to be a monarchist—which of course he is at the highest level of the Empire. But then Bartolus produces his own theory that is quite different from Giles's. Everyone agrees that monarchy is best if the king is good, he says, but there are other factors to consider. The most expedient form depends upon the size of the political community. He divides all relatively large cities and peoples into three "grades of magnitude" of increasing size.

The smallest, the "cities of the first grade of magnitude," are suited to political government. They are too small to provide the wealth necessary to support a king, and the multitude would resent it if the few governed alone. This was the situation in Rome immediately after the expulsion of Tarquin and with the ancient Jews—it was because of the latter's size that God was unhappy when they wished to replace their political rule with a monarchy. Perugia, his own home, Bartolus tells us, is a modern example of a small political community, and the Emperor Charles IV, Bartolus's patron, commended this form for such cities.[24]

Bartolus seems to see the political state as he describes it here as a middle class polity, not in the Aristotelian sense that the population is largely of the middle class, but in the sense that the middle class dominates. The multitude he refers to is not the whole citizen body—rather the "most vile" and some magnates are explicitly excluded from the alternation of rule. He seems to be referring specifically to the practices in Perugia in this description, but it is clear that such restrictions are generally acceptable and that workers and presumably even lower guildsmen should be excluded from participation. By eliminating the *vulgus* as well as the magnates from the government, Bartolus distinguishes between this form and democracy, which in the usual understanding is depraved because it considers the interests of the lower classes to the exclusion of others.[25]

---

[24] Bartolus of Sassoferrato, *De Regimine Civitatis*, 128ra–b. "Si loquimur de gente seu populo magno in primo gradu tunc dico quod non expedit illi regi per regem . . . qua cum civitas romana erat in primo gradu magnirudinis expulit reges qui conversi erat in tyrannidem . . . de natura regum est esse magnificos. . . . Sed redditus regales unius popupi magni in primo gradu magnitudinis non sufficerent ad expensum. . . . Status ergo . . . tendit ad tyrannidem. . . . Et hic est ratio quare deo displicuit quod populus regem petiit . . . nec expedit tali populo per paucos . . . multitudo populi de illorum paucorum regimine indignabitur quantumcumque bene regat . . . expedit . . . regi per multitudinem . . . hic etiam experimur in civitate perusina que isto iure regitur in pace et unitate crescat et floret . . . hunc regendi modum dictus illustrissimus imperator [Carolus IV] cum apud eum esset maxime commendavit."

[25] John N. Figgis, "Bartolus and European Political Ideas," p. 160, says that Bartous un-

The medium-sized cities, those of the "second grade of magnitude," are suited to aristocracy. Monarchy is inexpedient for the same reason as it was for smaller cities; on the other hand it is not expedient for the many to govern since it would be difficult to assemble them all. Actually, many govern here too since there are a large number of rich and good people. Rome in the time of the senatorial supremacy and Venice and Florence in Bartolus's day are examples of this kind of city.[26]

Finally, the largest peoples, those who exercise dominion over many cities and provinces, are best suited to the government of one. Here the many good will have a role as counselors to the king and in the election of the particular king. The Roman Empire is this type of community. When, in Deuteronomy, God promises the Jews a good king in the future he is looking forward to the time when they would have grown larger.[27]

This schema leaves out of account the smallest cities and people; Bartolus calls even those cities of the first magnitude "great cities." He feels that smaller places cannot fruitfully maintain their independence and must by needs submit to a larger political entity as a "tutor and curator." As an example he cites the cities and villages under the "protection" of Perugia.[28]

Bartolus does not hold rigidly to his classification. Figgis undoubtedly is correct when he insists that although he had his ideals regarding best and proper government, "he definitely recognized the actual assemblies of ter-

derstood by "political rule" delegation of the power of the many. Bartolus, he writes, "knows nothing of a representative assembly." But Bartolus refers directly to alternation of power and to the difficulty of assembling in a larger city—both of which suggest widespread participation, and the latter of which suggests not simply a representative assembly but actually a general assembly of a very large group.

[26] Bartolus of Sassoferrato, *De Regimine Civitatis*, 128rb. "Tunc istis non expedit regi per unum regem pro rationes super aductas nec expedit regi per multitudinem. Esset enim valde difficile et periculosum tantam multitudinem congregari. Sed istis expedit regi per paucos hic est per divites et bonos homines illius civitatis . . . ubi aucta civitate romana facti sunt senatores eisque data est omnis potestas. Sic enim regitur civitas venetiarum. Sic civitas florentie . . . licet regi per paucos dico quod pauci sunt respectu multitudinis civitatum sed sunt multi respectu ad aliam civitatem."

[27] Bartolus of Sassoferrato, *De Regimine Civitatis*, 128rb. "Populo maximo. . . . Hic autem fere posset contigere in civitate una per se. Sed si esset civitas que multum aliis civitatibus et provinciis dominarent huic genti bonum est regi per unum . . . ubi aucto multum imperio romano et captis multis provinciis deventum fuit ad unum scilicet ad principem . . . in tanta enim multitudine de necessitate sunt multi boni per quos oportebit se regem consulere et in iusticie via se ponere. . . . Innuit [deus] quod parva gens habitura est regem. Sed magna que est in magno statu et multis dominatur sicut dictus est super ex eo quod dicit deus eligerit."

[28] Bartolus of Sassoferrato, *De Regimine Civitatis*, 128va. "De populis autem parvis non dico. Illi enim non vel alteri civitati subsistunt . . . vel alteri civitate vel regi confederantur aliquo federe ita quod alterius maiestatem venerantur. . . . Et videmus in civitatibus et castris qui sub protectione civitatis huius perusine sunt. Sicut enim corpus humanum stabile et parvum non potest per se rege sine ex auxilio tutoris et curatoris ita ista populi parva per se nullo modo regi possunt nisi alteri submittantur vel alteri adhereant."

ritorial sovereignty wherever they existed as a fact."[29] This extended not only to prescription against the Empire, but also to local variety in rule violating his ideas on what would be the best city government. He recommends those forms, "unless it appears otherwise concerning the ancient way of governing. For it can be that one nation or people is so accustomed to a certain mode of governing that to them as it were it is converted into nature and they do not know how to live in such a way [the best]. Then the antique mode of governing must serve."[30] Unlike his Aristotelian source, Giles of Rome, Bartolus accepts any government that works for the common good even if it is not the best possible: government in its particulars is a human institution for human benefit not subject to a priori metaphysical, or even theoretical, restraints.

Both Figgis and Woolf refer to Salvemini's contention that Bartolus's relativism is ahead of its time, and is not again recognized or developed until Montesquieu picks it up in the eighteenth century.[31] Both also object that Savonarola certainly shared these ideas, and Woolf mentions John of Paris and Althusius as well. They are at once right about Bartolus's relativism and misguided about its historical position. Certainly, as this study has shown, medieval relativism is not unique to Bartolus of Sassoferrato. Indeed, all authors at least refer to Aristotle's comments that climate, region, and so on, are related to appropriate forms of government. All, in relating good government to the common good, leave open the possibility that certain peoples might be more suited to one form than another. I have also shown that various authors, Thomas Aquinas most prominently, have held up monarchy as the ideally most perfect form, but one not suited to the actual nature of fallen man, and that early and mid-fourteenth century political thought was dominated by such relativism. For these reasons Figgis is wrong when he asserts that Bartolus, "differed from most writers (like

---

[29] Figgis, "Bartolus," p. 160.

[30] Bartolus of Sassoferrato, *De Regimine Civitatis*, 128rb. "Predicta vero nisi de antiquo regendi modo civitatis aliud appareat. Potest enim esse quod una gens vel populus ita assuefacti sunt certo modo regendi quod eis quasi in naturam conversum est taliter vivere nescirent tunc antiquus modus regiminis servandus est." Ullmann, *History of Political Thought*, pp. 215–18, manipulates the facts to argue that Bartolus, like Marsilius of Padua, developed a theory of popular sovereignty to justify the de facto popular sovereignty in the Northern Italian city-states. A free people, he writes, was its own prince and should rule through a general assembly that would elect a council that, "represents the mind of the people" and rules by numerical majority. Even he is forced to admit, almost as an afterthought, that Bartolus excludes clerks from rule and only supports this regime for small states. But this last is an essential difference. For Marsilius the source and justification of power could only come from the people. All Bartolus says is that there can be valid popular sovereignty, and that in some circumstances this will be best. Nowhere does he express the right of the people always to take control of their own government.

[31] Figgis, "Bartolus," p. 161; Woolf, *Bartolus*, p. 394, n. 1; Gaetano Salvemini, *La Teoria del Bartolo da Sassoferrato sulle Constituzione Politiche*.

St. Thomas) of his own or succeeding days in regarding circumstance, history, and size as of more importance in fixing the form of government than abstract reasoning and ideal perfection."[32] Only Giles of Rome, perhaps, would fit Figgis's statement. And Bartolus's schema of the best forms, though practical, is in fact based on abstract reasoning about what form is theoretically best for particular types of community. In this way he differs but little from his contemporaries. Neither does his willingness to recognize traditional deviations from his schema represent a divergence from the views of the others.

But his particular schema is original, and it is in regard to this that Figgis, Woolf, and Salvemini all make another error. For while John of Paris, Savonarola, Althusius, and Montesquieu all advance relativist arguments, none reproduces this schema. Although there may possibly be an earlier author who does this, the first one that I know of is Rousseau. In his work *The Social Contract* he writes: "Generally, democratic government suits small states, aristocratic government those of middle size, and monarchy great ones." Girolamo Savonarola, in particular, bases his relativism on the Aristotelian distinctions of geography and race, and especially on the nature of each individual people. Thus, according to Savonarola, Florence is particularly suited for a civil government, that is, Aristotle's simple form of polity, because the intelligence and audacious spirit of its people renders it unable to tolerate a monarchical government, which is abstractly best. Johannes Althusius talks about different existing forms of government and about what he thinks best, but he never makes Bartolus's size distinction. Baron de Montesquieu does write about government in relationship to size, but about types of laws needed and not about forms of government. Although he gives no specifics, he also says that the form of government that is best for a particular community must be based in part, along with many other factors, on the number of inhabitants.[33] Salvemini, Figgis, and Woolf, apparently, did not realize that relativistic thinking was common in the fourteenth century—it could only be in this sense that they could say that Bartolus anticipated the later authors they mention.

Jean Buridan (late 1200s–c. 1370) was one of a distinguished line of French Aristotelian masters and their students who made important contributions to medieval political theory; he was followed sequentially by Nicole Oresme, Pierre d'Ailly, and Jean Gerson. Born in Bethune in Northern France, he spent almost all his life, aside from a trip or two to the papal court at Avignon, in Paris, teaching at the university for about

---

[32] Figgis, "Bartolus," p. 161.

[33] Jean Jacques Rousseau, *The Social Contract*, chap. 3, p. 410; Girolamo Savonarola, *Treatise on the Constitution and Government of Florence*, p. 236; Johannes Althusius, *The Politics of Johannes Althusius*; Baron de Montesquieu, *The Spirit of the Laws*, vol. 2, pp. 1–27; vol. 1, chap. 3, p. 6.

fifty years, where he also served as rector on two occasions. He is famous
for the problem of "Buridan's ass," which he probably did not formulate,
but which asks the question whether a starving ass equidistant from two
piles of hay would starve from indecision or exercise free will and choose
one. Apparently no one thought to try an experiment. Although he was
one of the leading moderate nominalists of his day, he is principally remembered for his theory of impetus, which replaced the previously accepted Aristotelian theory that required the continual presence of a force
for motion. He applied this theory to heavenly bodies, which he regarded
as made of ordinary matter, not, as Aristotle assumed of the perfect element, ether, which by its very nature was believed to move with an unvary-
ing spherical motion. Among his many other works Buridan produced
Questions on the *Ethics* and the *Politics*, both of which are characterized by
an extreme logical formalism unsurpassed by any in an age characterized
by logical formalism.[34]

In most cases Buridan supports a strong monarch, but his underlying
theory of sovereignty suggests that at least in some circumstances another
form might be better. He who is best abstractly, he writes, is not always
the most useful.[35] The question of presiding in temporal matters is not laid
down by divine law; rather, it is a function of human and positive law.[36]
This is not immutable; we can change human law to improve it according
to the dictates of reason or to reflect changing customs and dispositions.[37]
Different peoples with different customs require different laws.[38] It is
futile and wrong simply to emulate biblical examples; God instituted different regimes for different times, and so should rulers now.[39] He even

[34] Jean Buridan, *Questiones super Decem Libros Ethicorum*; *Questiones super Libros Politicorum*.

[35] Buridan, *Questiones super Libros Politicorum*, 6, q.6, f.90vb. "Ad principandum non est
assumendus melior probatur quia non est utilior ad principandum."

[36] Buridan, *Questiones super Libros Politicorum*, 8, q.5, f.113rb. "Presidentia spiritualis immediate ex divina ordinatione constituitur ergo nullus homo potest illam mutare. Sed prese-
dentia in temporalibus non est ex iure divino nec immediate ex iure naturali sed ex iure hu-
mano et positivo et ideo secundum exigentias temporum et diversitates eorum et necessitates
tale ius potest imutari immo deseri ab homine puro."

[37] Buridan, *Questiones super Libros Politicorum*, 5, q.9, f.73ra. "Lex humana licite potest mu-
tari et variari quantum est ex parte rationis . . . [et] ex parte humanum. . . . Probatur quia
continue consuetudines et dispositiones variantur."

[38] Buridan, *Questiones super Libros Politicorum*, 5, q.9, f.73va. "Lex humana uno tempore
est iusta et recta; sed tamen propter varias consuerudines [sc. consuetudines] lex non semper
manet recta; et etiam propter varias personas que secundum hoc requirunt diversas leges quibus actus eorum regulantur etc."

[39] Buridan, *Questiones super Libros Politicorum*, 8, q.5, f.113va. "Secundum diversitatem et
qualitatem et temporis necessitatem expedit principibus moralium regimine variare . . . secundum quod deus disposuit sed deus quandoque disponit quod sit unus solus princeps secula-
rium suo populo fideli; ut patet de david et helyseo super populum israel. Quandoque vere
statuit et ordinat quod essent plures ut patet de roboham et multis aliis."

goes so far as to undercut his support of regal rule by stating that in modern times when goodness has decreased law is a better basis for rule than the judgment of a ruler.[40]

There are, then, two aspects to Buridan's theory of the best government. First, as much as any writer of this period he is a relativist; he recognizes the varieties of peoples and conditions requiring different laws and different regimes. He does not recognize the absolute right of any group to rule, but believes that the type and agency of rule should be related to expediency and necessity. He even admits that not only the best form but also the best individuals might not always be the most expedient choice. Second, when the best form is possible there should be pure regal monarchy, but he denies that this is possible at all in the modern world. For now, a quasiregal monarch is best who will rule in collaboration with the wise men and, if it be rational, the multitude. As did Peter of Auvergne, Buridan defends the participation of the nonbestial multitude on the basis of expediency and not of right. I will discuss this arrangement in more detail in the next chapter.

In this way Buridan combines the relativism of the fourteenth century with the absolutism of Marsilius of Padua—in contrast to Marsilius and like the relativists Buridan admits all the good forms of government as valid and possibly best in some circumstances. The whole people is not the only rightful and only real sovereign as Marsilius thought; rather the sovereign is determined in each particular case. On the other hand, like Marsilius and unlike most of the relativists, Buridan tends to argue that the sovereign, whatever it may be, is absolute and above the law. Law, although it is the necessary basis of government, is what the sovereign decrees and that to which it gives coercive power. Though subject to divine and natural law it is entirely free of prior human and positive law, and since divine law does not dictate concerning government (at least in the modern period or with respect to general principles) the sovereign is free to impose whatever measures it feels best serve the common good.[41]

---

[40] Buridan, *Questiones super Libros Politicorum*, 3, q.4, f.34vb. "Temporibus modernis simpliciter melius est civitatem regi bona lege sine principe quam quocumque principe sine lege."
[41] Buridan, *Questiones super Libros Politicorum*, 8, q.5, f.114ra.

Chapter 11

KINGSHIP, POPULAR SOVEREIGNTY, AND THE MIXED CONSTITUTION

THE RELATIVISTIC VIEWS that I have been outlining are typical of those expressed by many authors at this time. But it is also true that most favored, at least in some cases, a limited monarchy with some or all of the characteristics of a mixed constitution. And usually they find this form to be ideally best or best in most circumstances. This is the subject of this chapter. I begin by giving each author's arguments for monarchy, then for popular participation and the mixed constitution.

Like most medieval writers William of Ockham finds paternal and regal rule and nuptial and political rule to be analogous. The former pair, he writes, are similar in that in both there is unity of rule and full power.[1] But Ockham does far more than simply notice similarities; he uses this analogy to argue for the inherent superiority of regal rule. "Regal rule is more similar to natural rule than aristocracy or polity taken strictly since it is more similar to the community of the home, in which one paterfamilias rules."[2] At first this conclusion seems completely unjustified in Aristotelian terms. Previous authors had argued at most only that regal (and political and despotic) rule were natural in that they found a model in the home. How can Ockham maintain that the analogy supports regal rule in the sense in which he has just defined it? At most, one would think, he could defend monarchy in this way, since by most traditions the paterfamilias does rule in each of the household relationships. But for Ockham the rule over children is more perfect than the other relationships because male children are better than the female spouse, because marriage is principally established for the sake of such children, and because a father naturally loves his sons more than his wife.[3]

At one point Ockham states flatly that the kingdom is the best secular

---

[1] William of Ockham, *Dialogus*, 3.1.2.9, p. 797.

[2] William of Ockham, *Dialogus*, 3.1.2.9, p. 796. "Principatus autem regalis magis assimilatur principatui naturali, quam principatus aristocraticus vel politicus stricte sumptus, quia magis assimilantur comunitate, quae est domus, in qua principatur unus paterfamilias."

[3] William of Ockham, *Dialogus*, 3.1.2.8, p. 797. I show in "Family, Government" that Ockham's argument represents the first fairly straightforward defense of "moral patriarchalism," a term that Schochet, *Patriarchalism* uses to describe the justification of monarchy by extension of natural family government, which he finds to be nonexistent in the Middle Ages.

polity,[4] and clarifies this in the midst of his exposition of the sixfold schema: "According to Aristotle in VIII *Ethics*, a polity of this kind is best in its best mode . . . when someone reigns and rules in a kingdom not according to law but according to his will . . . he is bound by no purely human positive laws or customs . . . although he is bound by natural laws."[5] God himself expressed a preference for monarchy by favoring the Old Testament kings and Peter as sole pope.[6] Ockham never attempts to refute any of the metaphysical or analogical arguments for monarchy, and so we may take them as his own; that is, if it is possible and can be instituted optimally, monarchy, and from the previous it seems absolute monarchy, is best.

His other arguments for monarchy are less privileged—they are put forward but the contraries are also discussed and occasionally, I think, more forcefully. Most of these arguments assume that if there is one best person, that person should be king—the question is whether monarchy is still best if no one person is outstanding. Unity, he writes, is best served in any case by monarchy,[7] and there are other advantages: there is easier access to the ruler and judgments are made more easily.[8] For the same reasons, any one people is best ruled by a king—even if there should not be one universal monarch secular or spiritual.[9] The corruption of any one of the multitude will spoil its rule, and so the rule of many carries with it great risks—why, says Ockham, using his famous razor, should many serve when one suffices?[10] Finally, the Bible teaches us, he avers, that Peter was not better than

---

[4] William of Ockham, *Dialogus*, 3.1.2.1, p. 790. "Politia autem optima secularis est regnum, teste Aristotelis."

[5] William of Ockham, *Dialogus*, 3.1.2.6, p. 794. "Et huiusmodi politia secundum Aristotelem octo Ethicorum est optima secundum optimum modum ipsius . . . quando aliquis regnat et principatur in regno, non secundum legem, sed secundum voluntatem suam . . . nullis legibus humanis pure positivis vel consuetudinibus alligatur . . . licet legibus naturalibus astringatur."

[6] William of Ockham, *Dialogus*, 3.1.2.14, p. 799. "Talis regimen maxime expedit toti congregationi fidelium, quo Deus tam in Veteri Testamento, quam in Novo voluit populum suum gubernari, cum ipse omnis regiminis virtuosi et utilis sit optimus et sapientissimus instructor. Sed Deus tam in Veteri Testamento, quam in Novo voluit totum populum suum gubernari ab uno, qui per totam vitam suum esset omnium gubernator."

[7] William of Ockham, *Octo Questiones*, 3, chap. 5, p. 107. See also *Dialogus*, 3.1.2.21, pp. 808–9.

[8] William of Ockham, *Dialogus*, 3.1.2.18, pp. 803–4. "Facilius habetur accesus ad unum, quam ad plures . . . unus principans facilius potest regulariter (quando occutit necessitas) facere iudicium et iustitiam, et periculum vitare, quam plures."

[9] William of Ockham, *Octo Questiones*, 3.1, p. 97. "Nam unus populus, si est optime ordinatus, uni gubernatori et non pluribus debet esse subiectus; quoad Salomon insinuare videtur, dicens Proverbiorum XI: 'Ubi non est gubernator, populus corruet.' "

[10] William of Ockham, *Dialogus*, 3.1.2.19, p. 805. "Frustra sit per plures, quod aeque bene potest fieri per unum." This goes against the usual argument that the corruption of a small part of the multitude will have less effect than if one or some of the few are corrupt.

the other apostles, nor were the Old Testament kings and judges better than others living at that time, and yet God made them monarchs. Clearly, this must be his will.[11]

Even some of Ockham's arguments in favor of multiple rule prove, on closer inspection, to be monarchist. When he speaks of the possibility that many rulers (or even in one case many popes!) might be necessary, he usually means, as did John of Paris, that each of many groups is best served by its own monarch:

> One alone can best take care of all the business of a partial people, but no one can take care of even all the most important business of all Christians. Although Aristotle says that a kingdom is the best polity in a city, he is speaking only of polities in cities; nevertheless, a kingdom is not the best polity in the whole world, nor in every part of the world. . . . Regularly it is expedient that the whole world should be governed by many [kings], of which no one is superior to another, but in some cases which could happen, it would be expedient that the whole world be governed by one than by many [kings].[12]

Ockham also applies two arguments usually used to support the claims of the many to support the idea of many kings: one can be more easily corrupted than many, and no one person can take cognizance of all matters.[13]

Ockham gives some indication that his preferred monarchy is best realized as a mixed constitution. Several of his arguments for monarchy, in fact, are concerned with the necessary participation of the many. "Without the council of the many," Ockham writes, "no great community can be well-ruled." For support he cites Proverbs and the oft-quoted passage from Machabees that describes the Roman government of one ruler who daily consults the Council of 320. One ruler, he writes, is best in that he can establish the time and place for the council's meetings and can regulate

---

[11] William of Ockham, *Dialogus*, 3.1.2.14, p. 799. "Sed Deus tam in Veteri Testamento, quam in Novo voluit totum populum suum gubernari ab uno, qui per totam vitam suam esset omnium gubernator, quamvis non esset omnes alios in sapientia et virtute praecellens. Nec enim invenitur, quod aliquis iudex et rex in Veteri Testamento omnes alios excelleret sapientia et virtute. Sanctus etiam Petrus non videtur fuisse sanctior universis Apostolis et aliis orthodoxis." William argues, for instance, that when God said that he chose Saul, who was the greatest, he did not mean in virtue, but in height (*Dialogus*, 3.1.2.17, p. 803).

[12] William of Ockham, *Dialogus*, 3.1.2.30, pp. 818–19. "Omnia negotia unius populi partialis potest sustinere unus solus: nullus autem unus potest sustinere omnia negotia etiam maiora omnium Christianorum . . . quamvis regnum sit optima politia in una civitate secundum Aristotelem, qui solummodo loquitur de politiis, quae in civitatibus custodiuntur . . . tamen regnum non est optima politia in toto orbe, nec in omni parte orbis . . . regulariter expedit ut regitur a pluribus, quorum nullus sit superior alio, quamvis in aliquo casu, qui possit accidere, magis expediret quod totus orbis regeretur ab uno, quam a pluribus." See 3.1.2.25, pp. 812–14 for his comments on many popes.

[13] William of Ockham, *Dialogus*, 3.1.2.30, p. 818. "Nemo mortalis possit omnia huiusmodi negotia sustinere . . . facilius per malitiam inficiatur unus quam plures."

those to be admitted and expelled from it.[14] The many are better judges than the one, but for all the reasons above, they better serve as counselors than as direct rulers.[15] Ockham also refers to the Law of Moses. God gave the Jews one supreme judge (Moses), but allowed recourse in certain cases to the Levitical priests. Therefore, there should be one head and many counselors in the best government.[16]

The council's purpose is not purely advisory. The ruler must follow its advice and it can punish a disobedient ruler.[17] In fact, Ockham argues that the rule of one is better precisely because the council can more easily correct an erring ruler or one refusing their counsel than they could several rulers who could find more defenders.[18] It seems that the monarch and council each has independent powers and an independent right to exist. The monarch provides unity and the council wisdom. This arrangement is a mixed constitution of aristocracy and monarchy after the model of Peter of Auvergne, in which each of the elements contributes a particular virtue to the mixture. On the other hand the element of balance is present in that the council exists in part to check the excesses of the king.

Unlike Ockham and most of the other fourteenth-century writers, the Englishman Walter Burley (1275–after 1344) gives few arguments for expediency. He admits only that if the best form is not possible another will have to do. Around 1340 he produced what was to prove one of the most

[14] William of Ockham, *Dialogus*, 3.1.2.18, p. 803. "Sine consilio multorum nulla possit bene regi magis communitas, iuxta illud Salomonis Proverbium 24, 'erit salus, ubi multa consilia.' Unde in laude dicitur Romanorum 1 Machabees 8 quod quotidie consulebant trecenti viginti, consilium agentes semper de multitudine, ut quae digna sunt gerant: melius regetur eorundem communitas, si unus ab aliis princepetur, qui de tempore et loco consilii, et omnibus (puta de consiliariis admittendis, vel repellendis, et consimilibus) valeat ordinare . . . magis expedit sibi regi ab uno et sapiente, qui de consilio velit agere sapientum, qui aliter non est bonus, quam a pluribus bonis et sapientibus."

[15] William of Ockham, *Dialogus*, 3.1.2.19, p. 804. "Plures melius et certius saepe iudicant quam unus: et turba melius, quam unus, et ideo bene requiritur disceptatio, consilatio et iudicium plurium: non tamen tanquam principantium necessario, sed saepe sufficit ut adsint tanquam consiliarii solummodo."

[16] William of Ockham, *Dialogus*, 3.1.2.1, p. 789. "Colligitur, quod in tali casu non est recurrendum ad unum caput vel iudicem, sed ad plures, cum dicat expresse, 'veniesque ad sacerdotes Levitici generis ad iudicem,' igitur in veteri lege fuit recurrendum ad plures in huiusmodi casu. . . . Respondetur tibi, quod de praecepto Dei unus debet esse in populo Iudaico iudex supremus, caput omnium atque rector sive sacerdos sive alius: qui tamen de consilio sacerdotum decidere debuit causas maiores: et ita recurrendum fuit tunc ad unum tanquam ad caput et iudicem supremum, et ad plures tanquam ad consiliarios capitis et iudicis."

[17] William of Ockham, *Dialogus*, 3.1.2.18, chap. 19, p. 805. "Quod si principans nollet sequi eorum consilium, et immineat periculum notabile, haberent corrigere ipsum."

[18] William of Ockham, *Dialogus*, 3.1.2.18, p. 803. "Facilius potest corrigi unus, si orbitaverit, quam plures, quia plures haberent plures defensores quam unus."

popular commentaries on Aristotle's *Politics*,[19] a copy of which he presented to Pope Clement VI in 1343 on a visit to Avignon. Burley, the "Intelligible" or "Perspicacious Doctor," as he was called, studied at Oxford and Paris, where he became master of theology in 1322. Throughout his career he was associated with the English royal family, serving as Edward III's envoy on several occasions, as clerk in his household, as almoner to Philippa of Hainalt at her marriage to Edward, and as tutor to Edward's son, Edward the Black Prince. Undoubtedly this association and his loyalty to the English monarchy affected his political theory. Burley wrote a number of commentaries and treatises on logic and philosophy (in the course of which he attacked William of Ockham from a moderate realist perspective), some works on natural philosophy, and a very popular book of biographies of and stories about famous philosophers.

The popularity of Burley's commentary on the *Politics* did not stem from any originality of thought—apart from two or three short but provocative passages it is largely, as Ferdinand Cranz calls it a "free adaptation of Thomas Aquinas and Peter of Auvergne's commentary."[20] Rather, his contemporaries found his thematic organization, similar to that of the earlier *Questions*, convenient. Most passages are either direct quotation or paraphrase of Thomas Aquinas, Peter of Auvergne, or Moerbeke's translation of the *Politics*. He reserves most of his favorable comments for monarchy, though he tends to repeat all the arguments of his authorities. Conor Martin finds his treatment contradictory. On the one hand, he says, Burley is alone of the commentators in "explicitly applying Aristotle's ideal 'absolute' kingship to his own country"; on the other hand he often gives a role to the barons, wise men, and people.[21] The contradiction disappears when we realize that Burley does not support an absolute king at all but rather a limited king in a mixed constitution.

Martin's misapprehension probably comes from the fact that Burley treats his ideal monarch, personified in his own king and patron Edward III, as the supremely virtuous person that Aristotle and Aquinas felt would be deserving of regal rule if such a one could ever be found. Aquinas, at least, doubted it. Burley does dutifully repeat Aquinas's distinction of regal and political rule, but then uses *regal*, in those few cases in which he uses the word at all, as a synonym for *monarchy*. In this, as in much else, Burley follows Peter of Auvergne. Burley does favor law in his best polity. He concludes, for instance, after a lengthy discussion on whether the best law or the best person ought to rule that: "Law ought to rule principally," and

[19] Burley, *Expositio*.
[20] Cranz, *Aristotelianism*, p. 181.
[21] Martin, "Some Medieval Commentaries," p. 39.

that the king and law should share in ruling.[22] In the course of this discussion Burley relates all of the Aristotelian and Thomist arguments why law or the king is best. In particular, he repeats the common belief that the law can only judge universals, whereas the king can better take account of particulars. In concluding as he does, Walter puts himself firmly in the camp of those who favor political rule in the Thomist sense.

Although he also presents the usual arguments for the rule of the many and for all the various good, simple forms of government, Burley favors monarchy in general. This is clear from the very beginning when, like Thomas, he assumes that both political and regal rule refer to monarchies. He does not grant Edward, or any king, absolute power, even under law; he, and every other king, is simply the first element of a mixed constitution. His two comments on the governance of England illustrate this and are his most important contributions to political theory. In the first he argues that the multitude does have a role in a monarchy, and thus that the advantages of the rule of the many can be combined with those of monarchy. In this he goes further than any medieval writer in insisting that the elements of the community be concretely and institutionally reflected in a mixed central government:

> It must be understood that in right rules other than a kingdom the multitude, that is, the many rules, and moreover in a kingdom the multitude constituted from the king, nobles, and wise men of the kingdom rules in a certain way. So a multitude of this kind rules as much or more than the king alone, and on this account the king convokes Parliament for conducting difficult affairs.[23]

This description of a kingdom is quite close to a commonly accepted theory of church government. The king in Parliament is stronger and more authoritative than the king alone, just as canonists wrote about the pope in a General Council. The king and pope are both true monarchs whose authority is necessary for the convocation of the respective assemblies. On the other hand the king must of necessity convoke Parliament since his authority alone does not suffice for more serious matters, just as the pope must call General Councils since only they can make the most authoritative declarations of dogma and Church organization.

Burley promises that his meaning will become more apparent in the "Treatise on the Kingdom," which is his title for his analysis of chapters

[22] Burley, *Expositio*, 1, tr.1, c.1, f.1va; 3, tr.3, c.2, f.24vb. "Lex debet principaliter dominari."

[23] Burley, *Expositio*, 3, tr.2, c.3, f.21vb. "Intelligendum quod in rectis principatibus aliis a regno principatur multitudo et hoc est plures et adhuc in regno multitudo constituta ex rege et proceribus et sapientibus regni quodammodo principatur. Itaque tantum vel magiis principatur huiusmodi multitudo quam rex solus, et propter hoc rex convocat parliamentum pro arduis negociis expediendis."

14–17 of book 3, which deal with the several varieties of kingship.[24] He
never fulfills this promise. Although he reprises the types of kingship put
forward by Aristotle, he has nothing to say about necessary or desirable
limitations on the king. However, immediately before this section Burley
returns to his analysis of England as the perfect polity:

> One superexcelling in virtue ought to rule. . . . For in the best polity on ac-
> count of such a ruler superexcelling others in the good of virtue, all consider
> themselves to be much honored, and all love their own rank and are content,
> and all desire the singular honor of the king, and it seems to all that they co-
> govern in the king and with the king, and on account of the deepest love of
> the citizens for the king there is the deepest concord among the citizens, and
> it is a most powerful kingdom, just as today is clear concerning the king of
> England, on account of whose exceeding virtue there is the greatest concord
> among the English people because all are content in their own rank under the
> king.[25]

The importance of these descriptions is that for the first time a medieval
political writer describes England in terms that strongly suggest the mixed
constitution. They are also the first references to the English Parliament in
a work of political theory. As in Engelbert of Admont's Hungary, only the
nobles and wise men have a direct role, although Burley does require at
least the passive consent of the whole people. There are, however, some
differences between Burley's view and some contemporary descriptions of
mixed constitutions.

As with Ockham, the role of the many is questionable. In the first passage I cited the multitude of rulers is still only a very few: the king, the
nobles, and the wise. There is no suggestion even that the wise are to be
chosen by the whole people. The second passage does say that each person
in some way is a co-governor with the king, but this seems really only a
statement of consent and contentment: because the king is so virtuous and
so loved the people feel that he truly represents them in his rule.[26] Burley

---

[24] Burley, *Expositio*, 3, tr.2, chap. 3, f.21vb. "Ista magis patebunt in tractatu de regno."
S. Harrison Thomson, "Walter Burley's Commentary on the Politics of Aristotle," p. 577,
thinks that "Treatise on the Kingdom" must refer to some work that Walter planned to write
but never executed. But Walter clearly labels his analysis of this section of book 3 (tr.2, chap.
4, f.23vaf) with this title.

[25] Burley, *Expositio*, 23rb–23va. "Superexcellentem in virtute deberi principari. . . . In optima enim policia quilibet propter talem principem superexcellentem alios in bono virtutis
reputat se multum honoratum, et quilibet diligit gradum suum et contentus est, et quilibet
vult singularem honorem regis et videtur sibi quod in rege est [sc. et] cum rege conregnat, et
propter intimam dileccionem civium ad regem est intima concordia inter cives, et est regnum
fortissimum sicut hodie patet de rege anglorum propter cuius excedentem virtutem est maxima concordia in populo anglicano, quia quilibet est contentus de gradu suo sub rege."

[26] This idea of passive consent is what he has in mind when he repeats Aristotle's comment

does adopt Peter of Auvergne's principle that a multitude ought to rule so long as it is not vile, but again this multitude may not nearly represent the whole people.[27] Burley's mixed constitution can be seen as the rule of the one, the few, and the many, but the many is more restricted than it was for Thomas Aquinas, John of Paris, or Marsilius of Padua.

The role of the nonmonarchic elements is in the tradition of Peter of Auvergne and not of Thomas Aquinas. There is no indication of balance or separation of elements; on the contrary in the description of Parliament Burley talks of king in Parliament as the ruling body. The few and the many have a role only because and insofar as they can make a positive contribution; those who are not capable are to be excluded. Concord exists not, as in Thomas Aquinas, because each person shares in rule, but because the prince is virtuous.

Burley's description of his perfect mixed constitution coincides, as he intended, with the actual situation in fourteenth-century England. The Parliament was only beginning to formulate its rights, and was still seen as dependent upon the king and as existing primarily to help the king and approve his requests. Commons had not yet separated itself out as a distinctive and necessary part of English government. And although the towns were represented, there was as yet no right of townspeople to elect representatives, and in practice the aristocrats and wealthy dominated. It was only later with election, the House of Commons, and the perceived right to oppose the king that the classical mixed constitution of monarchy, aristocracy, and democracy would be applied to England. But Burley represents an important step in this direction and a perfect example of the adaptation of Aristotle to contemporary political reality.

Although Bartolus of Sassoferrato is a relativist in that for him the most suitable government depends upon a contingent factor, that is, the size of a polity, his sympathies too are with monarchy. He chooses to use as his authority on medieval Aristotelian political thought, and in particular on theories of the best government, that most monarchist of thinkers, Giles of Rome, whom he prefers to Aristotle for his clarity and whom he calls "a great philosopher and master of theology." His concept of a king includes what Giles of Rome described as regal rule (although Bartolus does not so name it): a king makes law according to his will and has cognizance of all matters.[28]

(5.10.1311a) that monarchy is over a willing people but that tyranny shares the vices of oligarchy and democracy. See Thompson, "Walter Burley's Commentary," pp. 575–76.

[27] Burley, *Expositio*, 3, tr.2, chap. 3, f.22vb–23ra. See also 3, tr.2, chap. 3, f.21vb.

[28] Bartolus of Sassoferrato, *De Regimine Civitatis*, 127va–vb. "Videndum est quis sit melior modus regendi . . . quod tractat Aristoteles tertio politicorum sed clarius tractat Egidius romanus de ordine fratrum sancti augustini . . . fuit magnus philosophus et in theologia ma-

Immediately after defining the seven forms of government Bartolus moves on to ask the question of which form is best. He distinguishes his approach to this question from that of the Aristotelian commentators and justifies his contribution to an already crowded field by announcing that he will not be concerned with philosophy, as was Giles, but rather with the legal justifications for rule.[29] It appears, then, that Bartolus intends to justify Giles's conclusions by legal means. To a point this is true; Bartolus repeats Giles's arguments proving that monarchy is best: it most preserves unity, it most strengthens the city, it is more natural, and it is proven better by experience.[30] He then takes up Giles's arguments for the rule of many, and concludes like Giles that these arguments are obviated by the observation that the king does not rule alone, that he needs counsel and will be transformed into a tyrant if he follows only his own advice. For each of these points Bartolus provides legal references supporting it. It is at this point that Bartolus introduces his theory of the best form for each rank of polity, a theory quite different from Giles's.

Although Bartolus has nothing to say about the mixed constitution, his conception of monarchy does contain some of those restrictions commonly associated with a mixed constitution. The many have a role in a kingdom as counselors and as electors. In this last he is somewhat at odds, as he realized, with Giles of Rome. Giles wrote that election is better in principle, but that heredity is better in practice. Bartolus says that election is more divine and universal than succession; for this reason the heads of the universal Church and Empire are elected. But particular kings are more from humans than from God directly, and therefore succession is acceptable, if not best, for them.[31] Bartolus asserts that this is what Giles of Rome meant, but in reality there is an important difference. Giles felt that heredity is always better for humanity given its nature; Bartolus accepts heredity as valid, only in the same way that he accepts any other government that serves the common good as valid.

As I showed in the last chapter, Jean Buridan is not nearly so much a monarchist as he seems on the surface, though the surface dominates. In his *Questions* on the *Ethics*, even those sections of the eighth book that mention the varieties of government do so only in passing; Buridan's in-

---

gister. . . . Quandoque unus regit civitatem vel provinciam qui facit leges prout vult et omnia ad eum pertinet, et istud dicitur regimen regis."

[29] Bartolus of Sassoferrato, *De Regimine Civitatis*, 127va.

[30] Bartolus of Sassoferrato, *De Regimine Civitatis*, 127va–b. "Regimen plurium est bonum propter unitatem ergo multo magis est melius regimen ipsius unitatis quam quidem sit propter unum . . . ipsa civitas et respublica redditur potentior . . . in hominem naturali videmus unum caput et multa membra ergo civitas si sic regatur melius regitur quia magis imitatur naturam . . . ex experimento quam dicit se videre provincias non existentes sub uno rege esse in penuria non gaudere pace et molestari dissensionibus et guerris."

[31] Bartolus of Sassoferrato, *De Regimine Civitatis*, 128rb–va.

terest is the proper degree of affection and responsibility owed by subjects to their king and the king to his subjects. In the *Questiones* on the *Politics* he clearly states his preference for monarchy and insists that the prince be above the law and the sole source of law.[32]

Mario Grignaschi, the only modern scholar to comment extensively on Buridan's political theory, disputes this picture by pointing to Buridan's weak arguments for monarchy and stressing his insistence on limitation of monarchy by collaboration with the prudent, by consultation with the subjects, and by election and correction of the king. He adds, however, that like all other fourteenth-century commentators except Marsilius of Padua, Buridan denied the absolute right of anyone to have a part in government, and that he put forward no theory of consent. At most, Grignaschi says, Buridan agrees that a regime cannot persist in the face of the subjects' opposition.[33] I believe that each of these points, with the possible exception of the last, is valid, but I interpret them rather differently than does Grignaschi.

In his definition of the three good, simple forms Buridan identifies monarchy with regal rule in that the king rules by his own will and is not bound by law. There are three forms of rule for the common good, he writes; in the first, "there is one alone ruling and that rule is called regal not existing under laws."[34] When he comes to distinguish regal and political rule Buridan implies the same distinction, but does not explicitly refer to law, instead stressing the independence of the ruler: "Rule is multiplex, namely political by which a ruler rules a polity. A second is regal rule, namely by which a king governs a polity. And there is a difference between them. For a ruler in political rule is not free, being dependent upon a superior; but a king is free."[35] I think that Buridan means the same thing in all of his statements about regal rule, but that in the latter statement he wishes to stress that not only is the king free from restraining law but from any other superior power.

---

[32] Buridan, *Questiones super Libros Ethicorum*, 8, q.14–15, 180v–182v. See also 8, q.11, 178r–179r; *Questiones super Libros Politicorum*, 3, q.3, f.34vb; 3, q.13, f.40vb; 4, q.13, f.58rb.

[33] Mario Grignaschi, "Un commentaire nominaliste de la Politique d'Aristote: Jean Buridan," pp. 128–31, 134, 137, 142.

[34] Buridan, *Questiones super Libros Politicorum*, 1, q.2, 3rb. "Unus solum principans et ille principatus dicitur regalis non sub existens legibus."

[35] Buridan, *Questiones super Libros Politicorum*, q.3, f.33vb. "Multiplex est principatus: scilicet politicus quo princeps policie principatur. Secundus est principatus regalis quo scilicet rex regit policiam. Et est differentia inter istos. Nam princeps in principatu politico non est liber, sed eius potestas dependet a superiore; sed rex est liber." Conversely, a ruler, no matter how powerful, who holds his authority from another, as, say, some rulers from the emperor or a podesta from a commune, is not regal but political. An interesting corollary is that no single ruler subject to law can be considered a king—that rule would have to be called aristocracy or oligarchy.

Buridan's phraseology might suggest that like Thomas Aquinas Buridan assumes a single ruler in any case. His explication of the word *ruler* shows that this is not necessarily the case, although he does tend to think in these terms. He wishes to argue that the king or ruler alone has the force of law. One objection to this view, he notes, could be that in a timocracy the people, not a king or rulers [princes], have the force of law. He responds: "In that polity the whole people is reckoned as one king or as one ruler [prince]."[36] I will return to this extremely significant comment later in a discussion of Buridan's theory of sovereignty.

Buridan repeatedly states that regal rule is best, but as Grignaschi asserts he gives minimal justification for this view: "Regal rule is better than political rule," he writes. Why? "Because regal rule is assimilated to the most principal rule, namely to the monarchy of the whole universe, and therefore Aristotle says that a plurality of rulers is evil." He repeats this reasoning elsewhere, saying that regal rule is best, but the only other argument he presents is that in some unspecified sense it is more voluntary than any other form.[37]

Buridan's comments on regal rule lead to the conclusion (which I discussed in the last chapter) that, like Thomas Aquinas, Buridan felt that regal rule was best in the abstract but not suitable for the world as it is. The difference is that since he identifies regal rule with monarchy, his logic should compel him to reject monarchy itself. Obviously he cannot do this, not least because he is a subject of the French king and supports monarchy. The result is an insoluble contradiction at the heart of his theory, and in many parts of the treatise Buridan writes of a king limited as in a mixed constitution. However, his only direct mention of the mixed constitution comes in his analysis of the sixfold schema. He asks whether there are exactly six forms; are there not many more since there are also mixed polities? His answer is that he is only speaking of the simple forms. Interestingly enough Buridan treats the mixed constitution as if it were a development of Plato's not really taken up by Aristotle: he asks whether Plato's idea of a mixed constitution is really an objection to Aristotle's sixfold classification.[38]

Buridan gives some of the usual arguments favoring the rule of the

---

[36] Buridan, *Questiones super Libros Politicorum*, 4, q.16, f.60ra, 61ra. "Queritur decimo sexto utrum in regimine politico seu civili solus rex vel princeps habeat vim legis coercitiva. Et arguitur non. Quia . . . in principatu timocratio quilibet de populo habent vim coercitiva legis non ergo rex solus . . . negatur consequentia. Quia totus populus ille in policia reputatur pro una rege vel pro uno principe."

[37] Buridan, *Questiones super Libros Politicorum*, 3, q.13, f.40vb. "Quia principatus regalis principalissimo assimilatur scilicet monarchie totius universi et ideo dicit philosophus pluralitas principantium mala . . . principatus regalis est melior et perfectior quam principatus politicus." (4, q.16, f.60rb) "Unde inter omnes principatus regalis est magis voluntarius."

[38] Buridan, *Questiones super Libros Politicorum*, 3, q.13, f.40vb.

many, employing Peter of Auvergne's distinction of a bestial and a well-ordered multitude: If the many are virtuous, they should rule; in this case they are better suited to judge than one where the law is indeterminate.[39] Like Peter and others who employ this distinction, Buridan argues that the best regime combines the advantages of a virtuous king and a well-ordered or nonbestial multitude. "That a polity is governed by one," he writes, "can be understood in two senses. In one way by one operating alone by that one's own sense and head without the counsel of others and not from the power and council of other magnates and prudent persons. In the other way not using that one's own counsel but by the counsel of other wise persons."[40] Buridan argues for this participation on the basis of expediency: the nonbestial multitude will profit the regime. But nowhere does he imply that the multitude has a right to participate. On the other hand, he is talking not just of counsel as such, as perhaps Giles of Rome intended, but of actual share in power. The function of the nonbestial multitude is manifold: it elects and corrects the king if he is delinquent or scorns the laws,[41] it gives council, and it participates in the making or changing of law.

Buridan insists that law of some sort is necessary for any right polity. What is not needed in all circumstances is written law—law internal to the ruler suffices. Even in a regal polity there is law, probably even written law, but the king is above it and can dispense from it for expediency. In any case the multitude, if it is not bestial, collaborating with the king is the best source of either written or unwritten law in any form of government. Even if the multitude is bestial the king needs the collaboration of the wise. In either case the nonregal element provides the prudence necessary to make the best law, and the king provides the coercive force necessary to make the law binding. Once established the law can only be overturned and changed in important matters through the convocation and consent of the

[39] Buridan, *Questiones super Libros Politicorum*, 3, q.3, f.33vb–34ra; 3, q.22, f.46va. See also 3, q.12, f.40ra.

[40] Buridan, *Questiones super Libros Politicorum*, 3, q.3, f.34ra. "Quod policiam regi ab uno potest intelligi dupliciter. Uno modo ab uno solo operante de proprio sensu et capite sine consilio aliorum et non ex potestate ac consilio aliorum magnatum et prudentum. Alio modo non utente proprio consilio sed consilio aliorum sapientum."

[41] Buridan, *Questiones super Libros Politicorum*, 3, q.12, f.40rb. Elsewhere he cites Giles of Rome's distinction that although election may be better per se, heredity may be better *per accidens* (3, q.22, f.47rb). But the two men intend different things by this statement, I believe. Giles intended his argument to be a justification for hereditary succession as best in all cases for fallen humanity. Buridan means it more relatively; specifically heredity is better if the multitude is bestial, and possibly for other unspecified reasons of practicality. And he very strongly insists that the multitude has the right to remove, even to kill, a tyrant regardless of the legitimacy of the tyrant's acquisition of power by either election or succession. See, for example, 4, q.17, f.68va or 3, q.12, f.40rb. The latter, however, refers specifically only to a tyrant elected by the people.

whole people.[42] To some extent Buridan is able to keep his king, ruling with the nonbestial multitude, regal. The king personally is not bound to the law, nor is he forced to apply it in particulars. Above all the law only becomes valid (in the sense of a coercive command) because of his assent to it, whereas a political ruler would be bound in every case to a law made by an agency outside himself. In this sense a king would rule in a different manner than, say, a podesta, who would be more of an administrator than a monarch. This is why Engelbert of Admont, for example, called the government of a podesta an aristocracy.

Considering the roles he assigns to the wise few and the multitude, I conclude that Buridan favors a mixed constitution of the one, the few, and the many when the many is capable, and of the one and the few when it is not. But though he describes a limited monarchy, his emphasis is not at all on limitation, but on collaboration; that is, on the virtues which each group can contribute to the common good. There is no sense, as in Thomas Aquinas and those in his tradition of the mixed constitution, that the arrangement is to ensure a balance of powers. Like Peter of Auvergne, Buridan only allows persons or groups to participate insofar as they are capable. As with Peter the corollary is that the many is seen positively, at least in some cases. Whereas Thomas must neglect or refute Aristotle's arguments for the proposition that the many is better than one, Buridan can incorporate it into his scheme by saying that it is better for certain functions and can best exercise these functions in a monarchy.

Buridan tries, not without a good deal of tension, to combine a regal monarch with the real power of the wise and the well-ordered multitude. Buridan's mixed constitution is the first that could reasonably be described in Fortescue's words as a "political and regal government." Although he does not use the words, he anticipates the usage in his discussion of law. The two requisites, Buridan writes, for the proper institution of laws are

[42] Buridan, *Questiones super Libros Politicorum*, 4, q.13, f.58vb–59ra. "Duplex est lex nam quedam est scripta. . . . Alia est lex mentalis et est debita intentio cum prudentia et recta ratiocinatione principantis circa subditos scilicet quando princeps habet debitam prudentiam sufficit ad regimen bone policie." 2, q.4, f.31ra. "Si iudex est superior ut rex vel imperatur retento casu eodem ipse licite revocare iudicium quia princeps est supra legem." 4, q.2, f.52ra. "Vir politicus . . . non habet leges constituere. Sed princeps habet ista curare . . . vir politicus habet legem considerare quantum ad constitutionem scilicet dando principia et consilia circa ista tria." 3, q.3, f.34rb. "Melius est simpliciter loquendo policiam regi ab uno solo quam a pluribus . . . sed sit associatus a pluribus prudentibus et aliis bonis viris." 2, q.3, f.29rb–29va. "In casu in quo bona que sequuntur ad novem legem non sint multum meliora quam mala que sequuntur ex lege antiqua. Isto casu stante non est antiqua lex ei incompossibilis abolenda sine convocatione et consensu tocius populi. . . . In casu quo bona que sequuntur ad novam legem sunt multum maiora quam alia sint mala que consequuntur ad antiquam legem paulatim meliori lege nova inventa antiqua incompossibilis ei cum consensu et convocatione populi est abolenda."

prudence and knowledge on the part of those making the laws and the coercive power necessary to enforce it. The political person, he continues, has the first requisite, but it is only the ruler [prince] who can provide the second.[43] In the case of his best mixed constitution the nonbestial multitude represents "political persons" and the king a regal ruler.

Finally, I want to say a few words about Buridan's idea of sovereignty, which is more highly developed than any other writer's theory of this period, with the exception of Marsilius of Padua's. Buridan argues that only the king or ruler [prince] has the coercive force of law; in a timocracy, "the whole people is reckoned as one king or as one ruler [prince]."[44] The point is that there must be one supreme and undivided repository of sovereignty, and it is this sovereign that determines the form of government: the king in a monarchy, the few in an aristocracy, and the many in a timocracy. It is for this reason that Buridan describes the mixed constitution as a monarchy: the king is sovereign, and as sovereign is necessarily regal—it would be a contradiction in terms to have a nonregal monarch. Notice that Buridan defines a political ruler as one who depends upon a superior. The nature of this superior determines the species of polity regardless of the day-to-day powers of the ruler or whether the ruler is one person or many.

I have saved Marsilius of Padua for the last, not because he wrote last (which he did not) but because I said that I would first give arguments for kingship and then proceed to popular sovereignty and the mixed constitution. The fact is that Marsilius has practically nothing to say about kingship. What he does favor is quite controversial. Most debate focuses on the question of whether he is in any sense of the word a democrat. Successive waves of scholarship have evaluated and reevaluated this question and have produced no firm conclusion. In the early years of this century the then corrupt standard text of the *Defender of Peace* strongly suggested that Marsilius indeed favored rule by absolute majoritarian principles.[45] The restoration of the true text initiated a swing in the other direction: scholars labelled Marsilius a traditionalist, an aristocrat, a monarchist, even a total-

---

[43] Buridan, *Questiones super Libros Politicorum*, 4, q.2, f.51vb–52ra. "Ad rectam legis institutionem et ordinationem primo requiritur prudentia at scientia ex parte imponentis. Secundo requiritur virtus coerciva rebellium et nolentium legibus obedire . . . quantum ad primum requisitus ad leges instituendas politicus . . . habet . . . quantum ad secundum requisitum . . . princeps habet ista curare." Peter of Auvergne said just the opposite—that it is the multitude that provides power, the few wisdom, and the one virtue or reason.

[44] Buridan, *Questiones super Libros Politicorum*, 4, q.16, 61ra.

[45] Earlier editions imply that "the weightier part" of a community, which has sovereignty, is a democratic majority. Early works largely viewing Marsilius as a democrat include: Richard Scholz, "Marsilius von Padua und die Idee de Demokratie"; Gierke, *Political Theories*; C. W. Previtè-Orton, "Marsiglio of Padua, Part II. Doctrines"; F. Battlagia, "Marsilio de Padova e il Defensor pacis"; Ephraim Emerton, *The Defensor pacis of Marsiglio of Padua: A Critical Study*; and many others.

itarian.[46] In the late 1950s, Alan Gewirth's painstaking analysis of the *Defender of Peace* again reversed the prevailing opinion, and Marsilius was seen once again as a supporter of popular sovereignty and universal participation in government, even if he could no longer be put in the camp of those who favored all rule by a numerical majority.[47] Finally, in recent years Gewirth's position has been attacked and partially undermined.[48] And as mentioned in the last chapter there have always been those who maintained that Marsilius was indifferent to the actual form of government and the location of ultimate sovereignty.[49]

My own opinion combines several of these positions and adds a new element: like Condren, I admit that Marsilius treated governmental institutions as relative and local problems; like Gewirth, I believe that he intended the participation of all or most citizens as parts of the legislator. Also like Gewirth, I see an analogy between Marsilius's legislator and Aristotle's polity. I have argued that Aristotle's polity can be consistently interpreted as a mixed constitution, and this is equally true of Marsilius's legislator, although the precise nature of the mixed constitution is different in the *Defender of Peace*, since Marsilius does not envision the liquidation of all classes into the middle class.

Any attempt to answer the question of what, if any, political organization Marsilius considered to be ideal must begin with two chapters of the First Discourse of the *Defender of Peace*: the first classifies all polities, the second defines and discusses the "legislator." In the first Marsilius sets forth the familiar sixfold schema of polities, making, however, a significant departure from Aristotle's and other medieval definitions. In both the distinction between well-tempered and diseased polities and those between the three good and three bad species, Marsilius appends to the Aristotelian criterion of the common good the necessity for the will or consent of the subjects. Unless a polity satisfies both criteria it is by nature diseased.[50]

---

[46] Carlyle and Carlyle, *Medieval Political Theory*; McIlwain, *Growth of Political Thought*; and Alessandro Passerin d'Entreves, *The Medieval Contribution to Political Thought*, all treat Marsilius as a traditionalist or an aristocrat. E. F. Jacob, *Essays in the Conciliar Epoch* and others see him as a totalitarian, P. Sorokin, *Contemporary Sociological Theories* as a protomarxist. Others who deny that Marsilius had democratic leanings include de Lagarde, "Marsile de Padoue," and *La Naissance de l'esprit laique*; and Leo Strauss, "Marsilius of Padua."

[47] Gewirth, *Marsilius of Padua*. See also Hyde, *Padua*; McGrade, *William of Ockham*, pp. 82–83, 108–9; Morrall, *Political Theory*, pp. 112–13; Rubenstein, "Marsilius of Padua"; Skinner, *Modern Political Theory*, pp. 61–65; and Ullmann, *History of Political Thought*.

[48] Condren, "Democracy."

[49] Condren and also Lewis, "Natural Law and Expediency" and "The Positivism of Marsiglio of Padua."

[50] Marsilius of Padua, *Defensor pacis*, 1.8.2, p. 37. "Voco autem 'bene temperatum' genus cum Aristotele 3° Politice, capitulo 5°, in quo dominans principatur ad commune conferens secundum voluntatem subditorum; 'viciatum' vero, quod ab hoc deficit."

Moreover, Marsilius links the two in such a way that it is clear that no polity can truly be said to strive for the common good unless it be by consent of the citizens: "These two [criteria] separate temperate from vicious rule, as appears from the clear statement of Aristotle; simply, however, or in greater degree it is the consensus of the subjects."[51]

Marsilius also calls the good rule of one regal monarchy and he also makes some important qualifications concerning the ruling class in aristocracy and polity. In aristocracy, he writes, the honorable class rules; in a polity, "every citizen participates in some way in rule or in the consultative function in turn according to that citizen's rank and ability or condition."[52] Marsilius defines the ruling class in a democracy in accord with the usual medieval understanding as the *vulgus* or multitude of the needy ignoring the good of the other classes.

At the end of this chapter Marsilius comments that he is not at present concerned with the relative goodness or badness of these forms or with the question of which is best or worst. Nowhere in his work does he take up these questions, and in fact he rarely mentions the names of the species again. He does say that regal monarchy is, "perhaps the more perfect,"[53] but when he writes of the legislator he makes what seems to me to be a prima facie case for viewing the legislator as analogous to the species of "polity," that is, all citizens form a part of the legislator, which acts for the common good with the consent of the citizens. I wish to propound this case, then see if the arguments of modern scholars can upset it.

I must begin by quoting the Marsilius's familiar definition of the word *legislator*:

Let us say, then, in accordance with the truth and the council of Aristotle in the *Politics*, Book III, c.6 that the legislator, or the first and proper effective cause of the law is the people or the corporation of citizens or its weightier part, through its election or will in the general congregation of citizens ordering or determining through its express speech that something should be done or not done concerning human civil acts under temporal punishment or penalty. I say "weightier part" taking into consideration the quantity and quality

---

[51] Marsilius of Padua, *Defensor pacis*, 1.9.5, p. 44. "Hec igitur duo predicta principatum temperatum et viciosum separant, ut apparet ex Aristotelis aperta sentencia, simpliciter autem aut magis subditorum consensus."

[52] Marsilius of Padua, *Defensor pacis*, 1.8.3, p. 38. "Civis quilibet participat aliqualiter principatu vel consiliativo vicissim iuxta gradum et facultatem seu condicionem ipsius." See Gewirth, *Marsilius of Padua*, vol. 2, p. 52, n. 12, for an explanation of Marsilius's and other medieval misunderstanding of the word "honoribilitas," understood by them as "honorable class," but really a mistranslation of Aristotle's word for "assessed property, τίμημα. Aristotle, of course, did not use this word with reference to aristocracy.

[53] Marsilius of Padua, *Defensor pacis*, 1.8.4, p. 38; 1.9.5, p. 31. "Una specierum bene temperati principatus, et fortasse perfeccior, est regalis monarchia."

of the persons in that community over which law is made, whether that corporation of citizens mentioned or its weightier part makes it immediately by itself, or whether it entrusts that which is to be done to someone or ones, who is not nor can it be the legislator simply, but only for some purpose and for a time, and according to the authority of the first legislator.[54]

In the next section Marsilius tries to explicate some of the more ambiguous terms in this passage:

A citizen I call, according to Aristotle in the *Politics*, Book III, chapters 1, 3, and 7, one who participates in the civil community, in the rule, or the consultative or judicial functions according to one's rank. By which description boys, servants [slaves, serfs], foreigners, and women are separated from citizens, although according to different ways. For sons of citizens are citizens in proximate potentiality, on account only of their defect in age. But the weightier part of the citizens ought to be seen according to the honorable custom of polities or be determined according to the opinion of Aristotle in VI *Politics*, c.2.[55]

These two passages have caused much of the controversy about Marsilius's position. But what does he say? Let us separate the question into two parts: what does he mean by saying "citizen"? And what does he mean by "weightier part"?

Marsilius's specific exclusions from the ranks of citizens are those with which all medieval writers agree (and, I might add, modern "democracies" have also excluded all these groups until very recently, and continue to exclude two of them): children, servants [slaves, serfs], aliens, and women. From this passage alone it is impossible to determine whether Marsilius would allow other exclusions, but elsewhere he is more forthcoming. Con-

---

[54] Marsilius of Padua, *Defensor pacis*, 1.12.3, pp. 63–64. "Nos autem dicamus secundum veritatem atque consilium Aristotelis 3° Politice, capitulo 6°, legislatorem seu causam legis effectivam primam et propriam esse populum seu civium universitatem aut eius valenciorem partem, per suam eleccionem seu voluntatem in generali civium congregacione per sermonam expressam precipientem seu determinantem aliquid fieri vel omitti circa civiles actus humanos sub pena vel supplicio temporali: valenciorem inquam partem, considerata quantitate personarum et qualitate in communitate illa super quam lex fertur, sive id fecerit universitas predicta civium aut eius pars valencior per seipsum immediate, sive id alicui vel aliquibus commiserit faciendum, qui legislator simpliciter non sunt nec esse possunt, sed solum ad aliquid et quandoque, ac secundum primi legislatoris auctoritatem."

[55] Marsilius of Padua, *Defensor pacis*, 1.12.4, pp. 64–65. "Civem autem dico, secundum Aristotelem 3° Politice, capitulis 1°, 3° et 7°, eum qui participat in communitate civili, principatu aut consiliativo vel iudicativo secundum gradum suum. Per quam siquidem descripcionem separantur a civibus pueri, servi, advene ac mulieres, licit secundum modum diversum. Pueri namque civium cives sunt in propinqua potencia, propter solum etatis defectum. Valenciorem vero civium partem oportet attendere secundum policiarum consuetudinem honestam, vel hanc determinare secundum sentenciam Aristotelis 6° Politice, capitulo 2°."

sidering the subdivisions of the multitude, he gives the common people a role in counseling and mentions specifically as members of this group: "the farmers, artisans, and others of that sort."[56] In still another passage he comments that any citizen can propose law, but this function (as opposed to approving law or giving counsel) is done better by the wiser who have the necessary leisure than by, "mechanics who must bend all their efforts to acquiring the necessities of life."[57] But in both cases the implication is clear—the mechanics and the *vulgus*, or poor, have a role in government and thus are citizens by Marsilius's definition. It seems indisputable that he intended that this term comprise all free adult males.

Does the weightier part allow an aristocratic substitution for the whole citizen body, as so many have claimed? On the surface, no. Marsilius continually asserts that the multitude is more capable of making law than the one or the few—clear references to monarchy and aristocracy.[58] In several places Marsilius uses the word *weighty* to refer to the overwhelming majority of the people—those who desire good government and laws. Quoting, albeit misconstruing, Aristotle, Marsilius writes:

> "By nature, therefore, there is in all humans an impulse toward such a community," that is, the civil community. From this truth there necessarily follows another . . . namely that "that part of the city which wishes the polity to endure must be weightier than the part which does not wish it." . . . Indeed, those who do not wish the polity to endure are reckoned among the servants, not among the citizens . . . [why "must"] is obvious; for [otherwise] it would mean that nature errs or is deficient. . . . If, therefore, the weightier multitude of humans wants the polity to endure, as seems to have been well said, it also wishes that without which the polity cannot endure . . . therefore, the weightier multitude of the city wants law, or else there would occur a deformity in nature and art in most cases, the impossibility of which is assumed from natural science.[59]

[56] Marsilius of Padua, *Defensor pacis*, 1.13.4, p. 73. "Vult dicere, quod omnium collegiorum policie seu civilitatis simul sumptorum amplior est multitudo sive populus, et per consequens iudicium securius iudicio alicuius partis seorsum; sive pars illa sit vulgus, quam hic nomine 'consilii' signavit, veluti agricole, artifices et huius modi."

[57] Marsilius of Padua, *Defensor pacis*, 1.12.2, pp. 62–63. "Legem sumptam quasi materialiter et secundum terciam significacionem, videlicet scienciam iustorum et conferenncium civilium, inverire potest ad quemlibet civem pertinere, licet inquisicio hec conveniencius fieri potest et compleri meliius ex observacione potencium vacare, seniorum et expertorum in agilibus quos prudentes appellant quam ex mechanicorum consideracione, qui ad acquirenda vita necessaria suis operibus habent intendere."

[58] E.g., Marsilius of Padua, *Defensor pacis*, 1.12.5, p. 66; 1.12.6, pp. 66–67; 1.13.3, p. 72; 1.13.2, p. 71; 1.13.4, pp. 73–74; 1.13.5, p. 74.

[59] Marsilius of Padua, *Defensor pacis*, 1.13.2, pp. 70–71. "'Natura quidem igitur in omnibus impetus est ad talem communitatem,' civilem scilicet. Ex qua siquidem veritate per necessitatem sequitur alia quedam . . . videlicet quod 'oportet valenciorem esse partem civitatis vo-

Immediately following this statement Marsilius identifies this "weightier multitude" with the weightier part by using the former term in a restatement of the nature of the latter: "the whole corporation of the citizens, or its weightier multitude, which must be taken for the same thing."[60] He then makes it even more clear that he does not just mean stronger: most citizens, he says, are usually not vicious or undiscerning; all or most of them are sane and can reason; each one of them can judge proposed law. Therefore, it seems indisputable that the weightier part is to comprise the vast majority of citizens, which group in turn comprises all free adult males.[61]

If the legislator acted directly as the government, what form would it represent? Clearly, since it comprises the many it would be either democracy or polity, and since the honorable class as well as the *vulgus* is represented it would be a polity. Indeed, Marsilius describes the two in very similar terms. The controversial words that the weightier part must take into account the quantity and quality of persons seems to echo and differ little from his stricture that in a polity each citizen participates according to rank, ability, and condition. Marsilius's suggestion that the composition of the weightier part be determined by reference to the *Politics* 6.2 (6.3 in modern editions) supports my interpretation. The reference is to Aristotle's discussion of democracies (used there as rule of many in general and not just the degenerate form alone) and how they are best established. Aristotle's solution is rather obscure, but one thing is certain: Aristotle wants to give more weight to the upper classes in order to prevent the *vulgus* from dominating and oppressing them. The idea is that a weighted majority will be more equitable than a pure numerical majority, which would reflect the views of the poor class alone (in the following quotation it should be remembered that Moerbeke mistranslated "property qualification" as "honorable class"):

---

lentem non volente manere policiam. . . .' Quinimo non volentes manere policiam computantur inter servos, non inter cives . . . apparet: quoniam hoc esset naturam peccare vel deficere. . . . Si ergo valencior hominum multitudo vult policiam manere, quenmadmodum bene dictum videtur, vult idem eciam, sine quo policia manere non potest. . . . Vult ergo valencior multitudo civitatis legem, aut contingeret orbacio in natura et arte, secundum plurimum; quod impossibilium supponatur ex sciencia naturali." For Marsilius's misinterpretation of Aristotle, turning what for Aristotle was a condition of good government into an absolute necessity, see Gewirth, *Marsilius of Padua*, vol. 2, app. 1, pp. 433–34.

[60] Marsilius of Padua, *Defensor pacis*, 1.13.2, p. 71. "Universitatem civium aut ipsius valenciorem multitudinem, que pro eodem accipienda sunt."

[61] Marsilius of Padua, *Defensor pacis*, 1.13.3, p. 72. "Nam civium pluralitas neque prava nequa indiscreta est quantum ad pluralitatem suppositorum, et in pluri tempore; omnes enim aut plurimi sane mentis et racionis sunt et recti appetitus ad policiam et que necessaria sunt propter eius permanenciam." Gewirth, *Marsilius of Padua*, pp. 166–225 and elsewhere comes to much the same conclusion with many excellent and lengthy arguments that I do not here reprise.

If whatever the few [decide is defined as just, there is] a tyranny (and if one should have more than the other wealthy, according to oligarchic right it is just for that one alone to rule), but if whatever those who are many according to number [decide is defined as just], they unjustly will ravage the possessions of the rich and few, as was said before . . . whatever seems [right] to the most citizens ought to be dominant . . . but since there are two parts . . . wealthy and poor, whatever seems [right] to both or to the most ought to be dominant, but if they seem opposed, whatever [they decide] who are more and of whom there is greater honorability.[62]

The last line seems to be yet another rephrasing of the idea of taking into account both quantity and quality, and seems to be perfectly in line with the idea of a weighted majority in a polity. Condren's contention that Marsilius is simply citing a meaningless authority seems preposterous.[63] There seems little doubt to me that Marsilius's legislator and the particular form of polity, as Marsilius defines it, are analogous in every respect, and that my prima facie case has been established.

In much the same way that Renna attacks as meaningless the dualistic statements of John of Paris, Condren attempts to discredit the pluralistic implications of the *Defender of Peace*: Marsilius, he says, like John in his time, has an overriding interest in weakening the papacy. The concept of legislator was developed as an ad hoc theoretical obstacle to the secular claims of the pope and was purposely designed to be ambiguous and have little content so that it could apply to any local government.[64] This, I believe, is indeed one of the reasons Marsilius endorses no particular form of government, but on the level of the legislator and the weightier part I do not believe that Condren's criticisms hold up. Let us examine his arguments.

Condren says that the content of the legislator or weightier part is solely the concern of each community that wishes to apply the concept to itself. Condren, as I have already noted, rejects Marsilius's appeal to Aristotle for the determination of the weightier part and concentrates on the words, "in

---

[62] Aristotle, *Politics*, 6.3.1318a.22–34. "Si quidem enim quodcunque qui pauci, tyrannis (et enim si unus habeat plura aliis divitibus, secundum oligarchium iustum principari solum iustum), si autem quodcunque qui plures secundum numerum, inusta agent depopulantes quae divitum et pauciorum, sicut dictum est prius . . . quodcunque videbitur pluribus civium, hoc oportet esse dominans . . . sed quoniam duae partes existunt . . . divites et pauperibus, quodcunque utrisque videatur vel pluribus, hoc sit quod dominans, si autem contraria videantur, quodcunque qui plures et quorum honoribilitas amplior." Thomas Aquinas interpreted this somewhat differently: "[If there is disagreement] then this should not be determined in the former way, but according to some other excellence, either of virtue or of desire for the common good." (*In Libros Politicorum*, 6.3.971, p. 317.) His idea is that if both classes agree numbers should decide, otherwise quality of some sort.

[63] Condren, "Democracy," p. 306.

[64] Condren, "Democracy," pp. 311–12.

accordance with the honorable custom of politics."[65] But I do not think that there is any substantial difference between the two criteria. In the *Politics* Aristotle proposes a specific weighting of influence; all Marsilius is saying is that this particular scheme need not be used, that local custom can determine the exact weight to be given to the various groups and the way this is done. Certainly, he wants to be flexible, but if he meant what Condren says he would contradict himself.

Condren gives a specific example of what he sees as Marsilius's equation of the weightier part with whatever group customarily dominates—the princes of the Roman Empire. Gewirth also thinks that many passages in the Second Discourse, including the one to which Condren refers, are at odds with Marsilius's usual ideas and he refers to Marsilius's "serious absolutist divergencies."[66] Marsilius writes, referring to the election of the Emperor:

> For he [the pope] is ignorant of what is the virtue and reason of an election, and why its power depends upon the weightier part of those who have the right to choose; and that its effect ought not and can not depend on the will of some one person, if it is to be reasonably instituted, but on the legislator alone, over whom the ruler [prince] ought to be instituted, or on those whom the same legislator has conferred such authority, as was certified through a demonstration in the First Discourse, chapters 12 and 13.[67]

Condren claims that Marsilius "comes close to equating the electoral princes of the Holy Roman Empire with the *valentior pars* of Christendom."[68] But Marsilius says no such thing. The weightier part in this context refers to the weightier part of those who have the right to elect, that is, the imperial electors, and there is no attempt to equate this group with the legislator or with the weightier part of the legislator. On the contrary Marsilius implies that the right of election comes to the electors from the legislator alone, and his reference to the First Discourse is presumably for the purpose of identifying this legislator with the whole body of citizens or its weightier part and of justifying its transfer of authority to a smaller group of people, "which is not nor can it be the legislator simply, but only for some purpose and for a time."[69]

[65] Condren, "Democracy," p. 306.

[66] Condren, "Democracy," pp. 308–9; Gewirth, *Marsilius of Padua*, vol. 1, p. 251.

[67] Marsilius, *Defensor pacis*, 2.26.5, pp. 491–92. "Ignorat enim ipse, que sit eleccionis virtus et racio, et propter quid in valenciore parte debencium eligere consistat potestas ipsius; et quoniam eius effectus ab alicuius unius voluntate solius dependere non debet nec potest, si fuerit racionabiliter instituta, sed a solo legislatore, super quem principans debet institui, vel ab hiis tantummodo, quibus idem legislator talem auctoritatem concesserit, quemadmodum certificatum per demonstracionem 12° et 13° prime."

[68] Condren, "Democracy," p. 308.

[69] Marsilius of Padua, *Defensor pacis*, 1.12.3.64.

To say that in the Roman Empire actual power is in the hands of a few says nothing about the composition of the legislator, but it may say something about whether Marsilius demands an active role for all citizens. To this extent Condren may be justified in seeing the concept of legislator simply as a prop for existing government. But Marsilius, especially when he is not directly supporting the emperor against the pope, argues repeatedly for the concept that the whole body of citizens is more trustworthy and more capable than any proper subset for ruling and for making law.[70] This seems to imply that by preference and certainly in the best situation the legislator would rule directly, or at least actively oversee the state.

I will not reprise all of Marsilius's arguments, but Condren so distorts one of them that I must comment on it. Marsilius writes: " 'Every whole is greater than its part,' which is true with respect both to magnitude or mass and to practical virtue and action. From this it clearly follows of necessity that the corporation of citizens, or its weightier multitude, which must be taken for the same thing, can better discern what must be elected and what rejected than any part of it."[71] This statement is given in the context of a refutation of those who want a few wise ones to rule. Gewirth reasonably interprets it to mean that the many rather than the few should rule, and thus that the whole community should have residual control over the parts of the community.[72] Condren completely misunderstands this. He says, "This reading would be correct but for the fact that there is no indication in Marsilius that the *valentior pars* is one of the parts Marsilius has in mind. On the contrary . . . he asserts the *valentior pars* and the *legislator* to be the same thing. That is, the use of the maxim has no bearing on the ratio of quality to quantity in the composition of the *legislator* as a whole."[73] He is correct in saying that Marsilius does not mean that the weightier part is a part. It is indeed to be taken as the same thing, as I have shown. Nor, I agree, does the maxim have anything to do with quantity and quality. But what does this have to do with a denial of rights to the whole community? Gewirth himself never claimed that the weightier part was a part, or that Marsilius was saying something here about quantity or quality. Condren is thus attacking straw people, and he advances no arguments against Gewirth's actual conclusions.

---

[70] Marsilius of Padua, *Defensor pacis*, 1.12.5, p. 66; 1.12.6, pp. 66–67; 1.13.2, p. 71; 1.13.3, p. 72; 1.13.4, pp. 73–74; 1.13.5, p. 74. See also Gewirth, *Marsilius of Padua*, vol.1, pp. 167–221.

[71] Marsilius, *Defensor pacis*, 1.13.2, p. 71. " 'Omne totum maius esse sua parte,' quod verum est tam in magnitude sive mole, quam eciam in activa virtute et accione. Unde satis evidenter per necessitatem infertur, universitatem civium aut ipsius valenciorem multitudinem, que pro eodem accipienda sunt, magis posse quid eligendum et quid sperendum discernere, quacumque sui parte seorsum."

[72] Gewirth, *Marsilius of Padua*, vol.1, p. 187.

[73] Condren, "Democracy," p. 308.

Marsilius very cleverly invents a metagovernment, the legislator, upon which he can project his ideals, yet he keeps this metagovernment separate from the actual government. In this way he can declare his idea of the best government and yet remain flexible enough to defend any existing government against the claims of the papacy. With regard to the metagovernment Marsilius equates the legislator with an Aristotelian polity in which there is near universal participation but in which the various classes are not represented purely in proportion to their numbers, but in a way designed both to balance the various interests and to assure that quality is properly represented. This form, a polity in Marsilius's terminology, is in all respects a mixed constitution and incorporates all the ideas about the mixed constitution that had been developing over the previous seventy-five years. Everyone has a share and the classes balance and restrain each other (as in Thomas Aquinas and John of Paris), but on the other hand the role of the people is positive (as in Peter of Auvergne and Engelbert of Admont) and not just a way to ensure its contentment. Like Peter of Auvergne, Marsilius requires a minimum of virtue for participation, but unlike anyone else of this school, before or after, he seems to believe that as a matter of course virtually all free adult men will satisfy this condition. There is thus no division between those places and times suited for the best government and those that are not. The particular form the best government may take is indeed subject to local customs and traditions, but the people everywhere is capable of a share in its own political destiny.

Above all is the emerging idea of popular sovereignty. The forms of government are all valid so long as they are in accord with the people's will. The legislator can temporarily give up its power to any kind of ruler, and any extant government can be interpreted as the rule of a temporary and limited legislator. The differences between this view and relativism are obvious. The people has a right to choose any government, but there is only one best choice—the mixed constitution.

Chapter 12

NICOLE ORESME AND THE SYNTHESIS OF
ARISTOTELIAN POLITICAL THOUGHT

NICOLE ORESME (c. 1320–82) wrote at the end of the century of intense study of Aristotle's *Politics* with which I have been concerned. Around 1371–74 he produced the "earliest viable translation of the *Politics* in any modern language": *The Book of Politics of Aristotle*, together with an extensive and exceptionally original commentary on it.[1] Oresme was one of the most fascinating of fourteenth-century thinkers, best known as an important scientist, mathematician, and economist, even though he studied theology at Paris and became grand master of the College of Navarre around 1356. He argued for a heliocentric theory of the solar system and developed with his teacher, Jean Buridan, an advanced physics of motion that was accepted until Newton and included the notion of relativity of motion. In mathematics he developed the notion of fractional powers and rules for using them and anticipated the field of analytical geometry. He also wrote the first coherent analysis of the origin and nature of money. He did write on theology, and possibly his Ockhamist views on the contingency of the universe left him open to nonstandard cosmology. He also held various church positions—canon and dean of the Cathedral of Rouen, chaplain to King Charles V, and, after 1378, Bishop of Liseaux.

With such a fertile mind Oresme would obviously not be content merely to gloss the meaning of passages in the *Politics*. Like earlier commentators he does explain the words of the text, but often he expands his comments into essays on topics raised by the discussion.[2] In these sections Oresme is

---

[1] Albert Menut, in his introduction to Nicole Oresme, *Le Livre de Politiques d'Aristote*, p. 3. In this chapter only, translations from and references to Aristotle's *Politics*, unless otherwise noted, will be from Oresme's version. I will also give standard references in parentheses. Apparently Pierre de Paris made an earlier, vastly inferior translation, also in French, that is now lost (Menut, p. 11). Menut has also published a partial "translation" into English of this work: *On Aristotle's Politics*. This version is inadequate. It is more a paraphrase than a translation, and it is often difficult to distinguish Oresme's words from Aristotle's and both of these from Menut's interpolations. The translation is often wrong, and occasionally it attributes sentiments to Oresme not found in the original. Moreover, indications of foliation do not always match those in Menut's own edition of Oresme.

[2] Susan Babbitt, *The "Livre de Politiques" of Nicole Oresme and the Political Thought and Development of the Fourteenth Century*, pp. 68–69, gives a list of the subjects of the longest of these digressions. Even within his translation, Oresme tends to expand the text in order to

clearly expressing his own opinion and not simply explicating Aristotle. In contrast to the earlier commentators, Oresme treats Aristotle's historical examples extensively, especially on the subject of Aristotle's mixed constitutions—Carthage, Crete, and especially Sparta. This last serves as the inspiration and partial subject of one of his longest glosses, which argues that limitation of the royal power is an overriding necessity for the well-being of the community.[3] Oresme also writes at length about Roman and contemporary history and about the structure of the Church.

But the main difference is one of tone. In Oresme there is a freshness and spontaneity not found in any of the earlier commentaries. One reason, no doubt, is the use of the vernacular, both because it was the author's native language and because by using it Oresme was able to free himself from the conventions of the Latin scholastic form, which almost demanded the continual repetition of certain stock phrases and structures. Also, by commenting on each sentence or short passage of the *Politics* as it came up rather than on whole sections, Oresme was freed from the organizational convention of dividing and subdividing the text and repeating initial words to indicate the passage under discussion. These organizational reforms may be as significant as the use of the vernacular, since we do find equally stimulating passages in Latin political treatises that are not commentaries.

This translation and commentary was not an academic exercise but a commission from King Charles V, who also enlisted him for the same task for the *Ethics, On the Heavens*, and the pseudo-Aristotelian *Economics*, for the purpose of educating the king and his advisors and of assisting in the improvement of actual governmental practice. Naturally, then, Oresme would tend to include as many historical, ecclesiastical, and contemporary examples as possible and would try to give practical political advice. Almost at once certain tenets of *The Book of Politics* were incorporated into the French government: starting in 1372, for example, Charles altered the selection procedures for certain high officials to include election by his council.[4]

For all of these reasons Oresme's commentary is also more useful to us than the earlier *Questions*. Above all, the less formal logical apparatus, especially when compared to Oresme's teacher Buridan, allows us more clearly to identify Oresme's own opinion. The confusion that Menut alleges results from Oresme's occasional defense for the sake of argument of

---

clarify the meaning. Thus the text sections themselves are partially gloss. Since it is more complete for my purposes I use this unpublished work of Babbitt rather than the published version of it, *Oresme's "Livre de Politique" and the France of Charles V*. Many of the same points are contained there as well.

[3] Oresme, *Le Livre de Politiques*, 5, chap. 25, p. 242–44.

[4] Menut in Oresme, *Le Livre de Politiques*, pp. 19–20, 31. It seems, however, that this practice was soon discontinued. See Menut in *On Aristotle's Politics*, p. 5.

a position he did not support is minimal since Oresme is always careful to come finally to his own determination and to identify it as such.[5]

There are two possible exceptions. First, when writing about the Church, Oresme frequently includes a disclaimer: power in the Church is from God, and so Aristotelian principles do not apply to it. Otherwise, we would be able to treat it like a polity and come to certain conclusions. Even so, applying natural reason to the Church might lead to some useful results.[6] Is Oresme serious in this disclaimer, or is he simply protecting himself? One's reading is very much a matter of one's subjective interpretation of Oresme's tone. Babbitt grants some veracity to Oresme's qualifications, stating that he "respectfully acknowledged the difference between the quality of secular and spiritual powers, but suggested that natural philosophy . . . might yet have something useful to say about the choices."[7] My own feeling is that Oresme very much believes that the Church can and should be treated as any other polity, and therefore that his disclaimers are for the sake of form only. His application of political theory to the Church leads to conclusions in accord with his views of the state, his own political position in France, and with a Gallican view of the Church. And he never insists on the disclaimer—he states it, then ignores it in his analysis and never at the end says that, of course, his conclusions are faulty because of it.

The second apparent ambiguity about Oresme's own opinion occurs in a few instances in which he writes, after a lengthy argument, that he put his conclusions forward not to determine anything, but simply to relate his best interpretation of what Aristotle meant.[8] These instances might indeed pose a problem were it not for the fact that in every case the views expressed accord with others put forth elsewhere with no such disclaimer. For this reason I am inclined to believe that Oresme is not distancing himself from the opinions expressed, but is merely expressing his lack of confidence that they accurately reflect Aristotle's position. Fortunately these instances are rare.

Oresme's commentary is also distinguished by its critical attitude toward earlier commentators and sometimes even toward Aristotle himself.

[5] Menut in Oresme, *Le Livre de Politiques*, pp. 31–32.

[6] See, for example, Oresme, *Le Livre de Politiques*, 5, chap. 25, p. 243. "Je respon a ce et di que posté qui est baille de l'auctorité de Dieu sans moien et par divin miracle ou policie est gouvernee par grace especial du Saint Esprit, teles choses ne sunt pas sousmises a ceste regle. Et discuter ou determiner de elles transcende et passe ceste science, fors par aventure en tant comme se aucunes choses profitables a tele policie povoient estre advisees par ceste philosophie en lumiere naturele, par raison et par prudence humaine." See also 3, chap. 24, p. 159; 3, chap. 17, p. 137; 3, chap. 21, p. 148; 6, chap. 12, p. 274; 7, chap. 19, p. 308; 7, chap. 21, pp. 311, 313; 3, chap. 3, p. 120; 4, chap. 9, p. 176; 4, chap. 16, p. 189; 5, chap. 14, p. 225.

[7] Babbitt, "*Livre de Politiques*," pp. 348–49.

[8] E.g., Oresme, *Le Livre de Politiques*, 5, chap. 25, p. 244.

Oresme recognizes that the text is often obscure and that the commentators often contradict themselves and the text. He sometimes points out that another commentator's opinion is wrong.[9] He is more respectful toward Aristotle, but nevertheless subjects his arguments to critical analysis and is quite capable of suggesting that Aristotle's conclusions are incomplete; for example, when he points out that Aristotle's cycle of polities represents only one possible of many courses of events.[10] His attitude is surprisingly empirical. Many fourteenth-century writers stressed expediency, but by a priori methods and with little consideration of the actual material conditions. *The Book of Politics* argues this way too, but occasionally transcends it: "One should not suppose something beyond that which is fact. And it is proper to take such things as they are commonly." Oresme takes this attitude so seriously that he sometimes reverses the usual meaning of the words *simply* and *absolutely*, which traditionally refer to the conclusion reached by pure reason and are contrasted to that reached by consideration of actual conditions and events—but Oresme says, for example, that election of a dynasty is best "simply and absolutely" since it is most suitable in practice.[11]

Taking all this into consideration, it is shocking that no general work on medieval political theory even mentions Oresme's contribution. Those few scholars who have written on *The Book of Politics*—recently only Babbit and Mario Grignaschi[12]—tend to minimize its importance and rank it as inferior to earlier commentaries. Their point seems to be that Oresme deviates from Aristotle's meaning. But surely it is precisely the degree to which writers creatively reinterpret or go beyond their sources that to a large extent determines their importance. By this criterion, Oresme is the most important of the commentators.

Babbit and Menut also minimize the influence of *The Book of Politics* on later thought.[13] But it survives in eighteen manuscripts (more than those of Marsilius of Padua's *Defender of Peace*, though less than those of Walter Burley's commentary) and in an incunabulum.[14] In one case the influence may have been seminal, if unnamed. Jean Gerson not only read the work

[9] Oresme, *Le Livre de Politiques*, 3, chap. 19, p. 144. "Et nul ne doit merveiller se je ne ensui toujours les expositeurs, car je les treuve souvent contraires l'un a l'autre et discordans au texte." See also 4, chap. 7, p. 174. At 6, chap. 12, p. 274 and 4, chap. 3, p. 168, he criticizes Albertus Magnus.

[10] Oresme, *Le Livre de Politiques*, 3, chap. 22, p. 152.

[11] Oresme, *Le Livre de Politiques*, 3, chap. 22, p. 154. "Ne doit l'en supposer fors ce qui est de fait. Et convient prendre les choses teles comme elles sunt communement. Et pour ce, je di secundement que la voie de succession par lineage bien eslu est absoluement et simplement la plus expediente."

[12] Grignaschi, "Nicole Oresme et son commentaire a la Politique d'Aristote."

[13] Babbitt, *"Livre de Politiques,"* p. 256; Menut, *Le Livre de Politiques*, p. 30.

[14] Menut, in Oresme, *Le Livre de Politiques*, p. 33.

but probably used it in his capacity as tutor to the dauphin Louis. And so, helping to shape Gerson's (and possibly Pierre d'Ailly's) theory of Church government, it may have been influential in the very area in which we are interested—the theory of the mixed constitution.[15] It is also probable, considering a number of similar formulations, that he also influenced several early modern defenders of the mixed constitution.

In a sense beyond his mere chronological position Oresme stands at the culmination of the century-long development of the Aristotelian theory of limited kingship and the mixed constitution. He brings together the various strands of thought and applies them to contemporary France, historical polities, the Church, and the Roman Empire. And in creatively combining and transmuting these elements, Oresme produces a synthesis of great power. *The Book of Politics* is an important milestone between Thomas Aquinas and the conciliar, Florentine, and English theories of limited government and mixed constitution to be developed in the next several centuries.

Oresme differs from all other medieval Aristotelian writers in that for him law, not the common good, is the central criterion for good government. Without it there can be no true polity, and once rulers begin to ignore the laws the polity is gradually undone.[16] Most others preferred the rule of law, but like Thomas Aquinas admitted the possibility of one virtuous enough to wield full power and released any king from the coercive force of law. Oresme supports the law in every case and without qualification.[17] "A thing which can be determined by law," Oresme writes, "is not to be left to the will of a man. For this reason, the more these things remain in the will of rulers, the less good is the polity, and the nearer to tyranny . . . there where the laws do not have dominion there is not properly a polity, but it is a corruption of polity. . . . And then in a good polity laws should be about all things which can be determined by laws."[18] Even an

[15] Menut, in Oresme, *Le Livre de Politiques*, p. 30. Menut mistakenly asserts that Francis Oakley in *The Political Thought of Pierre d'Ailly* claims Oresme as the source of much of d'Ailly's conciliar thought. I believe the conclusion to be partially true, but in fact Oakley never even mentions Oresme's name. Could Menut have read "Ockham" as "Oresme"?

[16] Oresme, *Le Livre de Politiques*, 3, chap. 24, p. 159. "La ou les lays ne ont domination ce ne est proprement policie, mes est corruption de policie." 5, chap. 14, p. 225. "Prevarication est quant aucune bonne lay, coustume ou ordenance est delessié ou cassee ou rompue. Et ce doivent soigneusement eviter les gouverneurs de la policie, car autrement toute la policie se deffait peu a peu."

[17] Oresme, *Le Livre de Politiques*, 6, chap. 12, p. 274. "Tout prince est sous la lay selon droit." See also 3, chap. 14, p. 137.

[18] Oresme, *Le Livre de Politiques*, 3, chap. 24, p. 159. "Ne est pas bien de lessier en volunté de homme chose qui puisse estre determinee par lay. Et pour ce, de tant comme pluseurs de teles choses demeurent en la volenté des princes, de tant est la policie moins bonne et plus proceine a tirannie . . . la ou les lays ne ont domination ce ne est pas proprement policie, mes est corruption de policie. . . . Et donques en bonne policie doivent estre lays de toutes choses

evil law must prevail. Jurists, he writes, mistakenly equate law and right; on the contrary, they should always question laws and try to change or appeal them if necessary. But, so long as a law is law they must abide by it: "They ought to take the laws as their legislator framed them and use them in their judgments."[19]

Oresme bucks the medieval consensus in his answer to Aristotle's question of whether it is better to be ruled by the best man or the best law, by stressing law's passionless nature. "[Aristotle] says that law is intellect because it is according to pure reason, without mixing from the sensitive appetite. And then it is more expedient to be governed by law than by the will of a man."[20] In a sense law for Oresme is the real lord in a good polity. As he puts it: "It is not that one citizen or many should not hold the rule, but they should be under the law . . . and they should govern according to the law. And therefore the law is as the sovereign ruler."[21]

What if the law itself puts the ruler above the law, as was the case in Roman Law? Oresme rejects this situation out of hand:

> By the false opinion and evil suggestion of such adulators and flatterers some
> laws have been made in times past which say that rulers are above the law: that

---

qui pevent estre determinees par lay." On several occasions he quotes Aristotle (slightly mistranslated by Moerbeke and therefore by Oresme): "Whoever orders that intellect have rule or dominion, it seems that he orders that God and the laws should have rule. But he who orders that a man should have rule and dominion, he proposes that a beast should have rule." (*Politics*, 3, chap. 24, p. 158 [3.16.1287a.28–30]) Aristotle actually wrote: "Who orders the law to rule orders God and reason to rule." See also Oresme's comments at 4, chap. 10, p. 178 and 5, chap. 25, p. 243.

[19] Oresme, *Le Livre de Politiques*, 5, chap. 25, p. 243. "Il doivent recevoir les lays teles comme leur legislateur leur bailla, et en doivent user en leur escoles et en jugements. Mes se par raison naturel, il leur apparoit que aucune tele lay ne fust pas juste ou expediente pour le bien publique, il le devroient monstrer par bonne prudence en lieu et en temps et en maniere licite."

[20] Oresme, *Le Livre de Politiques*, 3, chap. 24, p. 158. "Il dit que la lay est un entendement pource qu'elle est selon pure raison, sans mixtion de appetit sensitif. Et donques est il plus expedient de estre gouverné par lay que par volenté de homme." See also 3, chap. 22, p. 151.

[21] Oresme, *Le Livre de Politiques*, 3, chap. 24, pp. 157–58. "Non pas que ce ne soit bien qu'un citoien ou pluseurs tiennent le princey, mes il dovient estre soubs la lay. . . . Et ainsi la lay est aussi comme le souverain prince." Oresme's use of the words *souverain* and *souveraineté* is ambiguous. Babbitt points out (*Livre de Politiques*, p. 240) that often he uses the adjective to mean only "extreme" or "greatest," and that although he is not consistent with respect to the noun it most frequently refers to the highest public power, which is in some sense absolute—in contrast to *seigneurie*, which is feudal lordship, that is, power as a private possession. But she adds that these two terms often overlap (p. 243). Here he implies that the law is or should be the highest power in a state. His usage here is in distinction to his identification of *souverain* with Aristotle's *politeuma*—the highest office in a state. For example, he generally refers to the true king as *souverain*, yet still subjects him to the law and even to the citizen body. I will show later that by *sovereign* he often just means the person or group that exercises day-to-day authority.

"the ruler is free from the laws," and "what pleases the ruler has the force of law." Such a thing is contrary to the doctrine of this science . . . such things Aristotle would call not royal but tyrannical.[22]

The point is not that there is a logical paradox, but that a law can be valid only if it accords with reason, which demands that all rulers be under law. For this reason such precepts of Roman Law are not valid laws. "Aristotle would call fools," he writes, "those who give such power and the ruler who takes it—if he loves the rule. And, nevertheless, some are so perverse and so like beasts that they choose to believe of the ruler that all is his . . . as if he were God on earth."[23]

Yet Oresme champions regal (as opposed to political) rule. To do this he must distort both Aristotle's distinction and Aquinas's interpretation of it, which Oresme actually incorporates into his translation of Moerbeke: "When a man has sovereign precedence, this is royal rule, but when he governs according to the rules of the discipline, that is, the laws of the city, and he is in part holding rule and in part subject under the king, then this is political rule."[24] At first this definition seems to contradict everything Oresme has written, but his gloss to the previous passage clarifies matters: "Political and royal rule are over a great multitude or community, and they differ because royal rule is sovereign and political rule is under royal rule, over one city or region, and is according to the customs and the laws of the region."[25]

Oresme was familiar with Thomas Aquinas/Peter of Auvergne's commentary, but he chooses to redefine the key words. He distinguishes between the royal ruler who has no superior and local rulers who are subject

[22] Oresme, *Le Livre de Politiques*, 5, chap. 25, p. 243. "Item, par la fausse opinion et malvese suggestion de telz adulators et flateurs ont esté faites ou temps passé aucunes lays lesquelles attribuent as princes qu'il sunt par desus les lays: Et quia princeps est solutus legibus, et quia principi placuit, legis habet vigorem [Menut comments, unbelievably, "(unidentified)"]. Laquelle chose est contre la doctrine de ceste science. . . . Lesquelles choses Aristote diroit estre non pas royals mes tiranniques." For attacks on the *lex regia*, the law by which the Roman people supposedly gave up its political rights to the emperor, see also 3, chap. 14, p. 138; 4, chap. 10, p. 178; and 7, chap. 10, p. 293.

[23] Oresme, *Le Livre de Politiques*, 4, chap. 9, p. 178. "Et diroit Aristote que ceulz furent folz du donner et le prince du recevoir, se il amoit le princey. Et nientmoins, aucuns sunt si pervers et si bestes que il funt croire au prince que tout est in proprieté et que ce que un subject tient justement . . . aussi comme se il fust Dieu en terre."

[24] Aristotle, *Politics*, 1, chap. 1, p. 45 (1252a.15–17). "Car quant un homme a la souveraine presidence, ce est princey royal; mes quant il gouverne selon les paroles de la discipline, ce est a dire selon les lais de la cité et il est en partie tenant princey et en partie subject sous le roy, adonques ce est princey politique." The equation of "sermones disciplinae" (Moerbeke) with law was Thomas Aquinas's contribution.

[25] Oresme, *Le Livre de Politiques*, 1, chap. 1, p. 45. "Princey politique et royal sont sus une grande multitude ou communité; et different, car princey royal est souveraine et princey politique est sous princey royal, sus une cité ou païs, et est selon les coustumes et les lais du païs."

to the king. But both are equally under law—he manages to interpret the bit about the political ruler being subject to law as a mere recognition of the fact that local laws exist, and not as a contrast with the situation of a regal ruler. In fact, it is precisely because the political ruler administers the city according to its laws that he governs at all, just as the king is a ruler because he rules according to the laws of the kingdom. The political ruler is subject, not because he is bound by laws but because there is a higher power—the king.

Throughout his treatise Oresme uses *regal* to mean the rule of one not subject to a superior governmental organ. But he specifically attacks the view of Giles of Rome and others that attempts to preserve both law and the power of the monarch by declaring that the best rule gives full power to the king, who then rules by his own will according to laws that he himself has made. For the most part, even those who favored rule by law agreed that the ruler instituted and gave coercive force to the law. Oresme is the first to reject completely this view. Others like Ptolemy of Lucca rejected full power, but no one previously denied that a king could be an appropriate source of law.

Full power to the ruler is, according to Oresme, the principal property of corrupt polities. This is true regardless of the composition of the ruling class. Discussing three particular types of monarchy, aristocracy, and democracy, Oresme writes: "Each of these three polities is the worst of all those of its type," because the rulers "govern to their will with full power without laws." Elsewhere, Oresme characterizes tyranny as the situation in which a king wields full power, and in commenting on Aristotle's variety of kingship in which a king has full power over the army adds that in peacetime and in the city he rules royally according to the laws.[26]

Most startling is his rejection of law that the ruler makes: "But it seems to me that there is little difference if some govern according to their will or if they govern according to laws which they themselves have made, without the consent of the multitude, in their own favor and to their own profit."[27] At one stroke Oresme upsets the synthesis of regal rule and rule

---

[26] Oresme, *Le Livre de Politiques*, 4, chap. 10, p. 178. "Pleniere puissance . . . est la principal proprieté de teles transgressions ou corruptions." 4, chap. 19, p. 194. "Car chescune de ces .iii. policies est la tres plus malvese de toutes celles de son gerre. Et ces .ii. policies sunt quant un petit nombre, en comparoison de l'autre multitude ou, un seul gouvernent a leur volenté de plaine posté sans lays." 5, chap. 25, p. 243. "Plenitude de posté . . . Aristotle diroit estre non pas royals mes tiranniques." 3, chap. 20, p. 146. "Telz roys gouvernoient seulement les osts de princey royal de pleine posté. Et en la cité en temps de paiz il avoient autre maniere de princey royal selon les lays."

[27] Oresme, *Le Livre de Politiques*, 4, chap. 11, p. 178. "Mes il me semble que peu a de difference se aucuns gouvernent selon leur volenté ou se il gouvernent selon lays lesqueles eulz meismes ont faictes sans le consentement de la multitude en leur faveur et a leur profit ou propre conferent et contre le bien publique."

by law elaborately established by Giles of Rome and other proponents of a king with full power. Rule by self-made law becomes tyrannical, and in this manner Oresme completes the assault on it begun by Ptolemy of Lucca, while preserving the term *regal* for the good king who rules by an external and independent law. Oresme also upsets the idea that the only human law to which the king is bound is customary law, that he is consequently above the positive law. A passage in the *Politics* bolstered this opinion. In Moerbeke's version, Aristotle wrote

> Hence, those laws which are according to customs are more principal and of more principal things than those which are according to letters. Whence if a human ruler is more secure than those things which are according to letters; nevertheless, this ruler is not more secure than those things which are according to custom.[28]

Oresme's translation distorts the meaning:

> Likewise the laws confirmed and approved according to custom are more principal and of more principal things than those which are according to letters. And for this reason, if the man who is ruler according to letters is more sure; nevertheless, he is not so sure as he who is ruler according to custom.[29]

The gloss to this passage confirms that Oresme has changed the order and puts rule of a man below both written and customary law:

> He wants to say that to judge according to written laws or rules not confirmed by custom is a more sure thing than to judge according to will, but it is more sure to judge according to written laws confirmed by custom, and less sure in such a matter to judge according to will.[30]

Another passage in the *Politics* poses a problem for Oresme's interpretation of law and regal rule. Aristotle wrote:

> that one who is called king according to the law, that is to say who governs according to the law [does not rule a] kingdom properly speaking . . . the rule

---

[28] Aristotle, *Politics* (Moerbeke), 1287b.6–8. "Adhuc principaliores et de principalioribus quam hec secundum litteras leges sunt quae secundum consuetudines. Quare si iis quae secundum litteras homo princeps est securior, sed non iis quae secundum consuetudinem." Thomas Aquinas follows this reading—see *In Libros Politicorum*, 3.15.516, p. 181.

[29] Aristotle, *Politics*, 3, chap. 24, p. 159. "Item les lays qui sunt confirmees et aprouvees selon coustume sunt plus principalz et de pluz principalz choses que ne sunt celles qui sunt selon les lettres. Et pour ce, se le homme qui est prince selon les lettres est plus seur, toutesvoies encore ne est il pas si seur comme est celui que est prince selon coustume."

[30] Oresme, *Le Livre de Politiques*, 3, chap. 24, p. 159. "Il veult dire que jugier selon les lays ou regles escriptes et non confermees par coustume est plus seure chose que jugier selon volenté, mes encor est plus seur jugier selon lays escriptes et confermees par coustume, et moins seur en tele maitere jugier selon volenté."

which is entirely and simply called kingdom [is one] in which the king holds the rule over all according to his will.[31]

This surely implies that true regal rule is above the law, but Oresme again finds an explanation which preserves his view:

> And because of this, such a one is not properly a king; because a king disposes completely according to his will all things which are not determined by the laws . . . [that the king rules by will] is to be understood with respect those things which are not determined by the laws.[32]

Thus Oresme twists the text to defeat the prevalent opinion that a true king rules by will. His point is that the king can deal with particulars and with things not covered by law. It is not that he is not bound by law or that he orders everything by his will, but that he is not king if he can do nothing except by law. The example that he mentions shows that this is an important characteristic of a king, separating him from a political ruler of even great authority. A democracy or an aristocracy can have a war leader, he writes, but he is not a king since he is under the power of the many or the few. The point is that such a one is completely restricted by the law and governing body of the polity.[33]

Oresme is clear that law is not only to be supreme but also relative to each particular polity. Commenting on Aristotle's statement to this effect (which Oresme repeats frequently), he writes:

> The polity or the health of the polity is the reason why the law exists. For this reason, that one who institutes a polity ought to regard which polity he institutes. And according to this, he should frame suitable laws and conform them and apply them to the polity. And if he has his primary regard to the laws and according to them institutes the polity, he perverts natural order, because one ought primarily to have regard for the end.[34]

[31] Aristotle, *Politics*, 3, chap. 24, p. 157. "Car celui qui est dit roy selon la lay, ce est a dire qui gouverne selon la lay, ce ne est pas proprement royalme . . . princey qui est tout et simplement appellé royalme, auquel le roy tient le princey sus touz selon sa volenté."

[32] Oresme, *Le Livre de Politiques*, 3, chap. 24, p. 157. "Et pour ce, tel ne est pas proprement roy; car roy fait a sa pleine volenté de toutes choses qui ne sunt determinees par les lays. . . . Il est a entendre quant as choses qui ne sunt determinees par les lays."

[33] Oresme, *Le Livre de Politiques*, 3, chap. 24, p. 157. "En royalme le roy est souverain et en democracie le peuple tient le souverain princey et en aristocracie aucuns vertueus et non pas le prince ou le duc de l'ost, car son princey est soubs l'autre, qui est souverain." In a few passages Oresme does seem to attribute the dread full power to a king, but usually that can be interpreted simply as an imprecise statement of universal jurisdiction. In most of these cases he is following Thomas Aquinas's wording very closely. See 3, chap. 21, p. 148–49; 1, chap. 15, p. 71; 3, chap. 9, p. 128. Cf. Thomas Aquinas, *In Libros Politicorum*, 1.10.152, 154.

[34] Oresme, *Le Livre de Politiques*, 4, chap. 2, p. 166. "Et la policie ou le salut de la policie est la fin pourquoy est la lay. Et pour ce, celui qui institue une policie doit resgarder quele policie il institue. Et selon ce, il doit metre lays convenables et les conformer et appliquer a la

Although no positive law is good absolutely, this is not at all to say that a given law is morally neutral—it is good if and only if it advances the ends of a good polity. If it does not, it should be changed:

> After the time of Noah, when the peoples separated themselves and began to inhabit diverse regions, it is likely that several established ordinances and polities and laws rudely and less well composed, and it was well done to change them afterward . . . [singulars] are innumerable and cases unforseeable. And one can not make written laws except as a universal. For this reason it is proper sometimes to make new laws and to change ancient laws according to the quality of the facts, the times, the customs, the peoples.[35]

These views put Oresme in sharp opposition both to the contemporary proponents of Roman Law, such as Bartolus of Sassoferrato, and to those who used precisely the same argument to attack the supremacy of law. He rails against the Roman Lawyers, saying that they ignorantly identify Roman and natural law:

> Commonly our legists are introduced to the laws that Justinian compiled and to other Roman Laws, and it seems to them that there is no other written law and that it ought to be followed everywhere, saving local customs, etc. But even though in their books there be some natural laws or some almost natural to the human community and which are to pertain everywhere; nevertheless, the greatest part is positive laws. And though they are mostly reasonable; nevertheless, no one is obliged to follow them by the virtue or authority of the rule of Rome except those who are of that rule—if it still exists. Because each rule, each polity has its positive laws and its written or non-written law, and if some such laws are similar to those of Rome or if they are not, it has no force, because they have no authority in a rule outside of that rule itself. And to say that all ought to be under that rule and under the laws of Rome, this is a great folly and error against natural reason. . . . And then neither in the schools nor in judgments is a legist constrained or obliged to use the Roman Laws outside of the authority of its legislator.[36]

---

policie. Et se il avoit son premier resgart as lays et selon elles il instituit sa policie, il pervertiroit ordre naturele; car l'en doit premierement resgarder a la fin." Here Aristotle is discussing the laws of different varieties of polity, for example, monarchies, aristocracies, etc. But in his many allusions to this principle Oresme refers also to different peoples in different regions with different customs, etc. See also 2, chap. 16, p. 99, 5, chap. 25, p. 243, 7, chap. 10, p. 293.

[35] Oresme, *Le Livre de Politiques*, 3, chap. 15, p. 98. "Apres le temps de Noé, quant les gens se espartirent et commencerent habiter diverses regions, il est vraisemblable que pluseurs establirent ordenances et policies et lays rudement et moins bien composees, et fu bien fait de les muer apres . . . [singulares] sunt innombrables et les cas inopinables. Et ne peut l'en faire lays escriptes fors en universal. Et pour ce convient il aucunes foiz faire en de nouveles et muer les anciennes selon la qualité des faiz, des temps, des meurs, des gens."

[36] Oresme, *Le Livre de Politiques*, 5, chap. 25, p. 243. "Communement nos legistes sunt

The original framers of Roman Law were not similarly deluded, Oresme writes, for they clearly understood the distinction between natural and positive law.[37]

Since positive law is not absolute it is only reasonable that it be subject to change when better law comes along or when customs and such change. Oresme includes the usual medieval cautions about such change—that it causes danger and uncertainty and might make the law less respected—but he concludes that law should always be examined to determine its goodness and expedience. Although jurists must judge according to the law, they should not be blinded, as they usually are, by its authority. Rather, they and others should separate themselves from the authority of law and think of it "as if it were newly proposed":

> One ought in just balance to weigh the reason for the law and the reason against it. And to consider who made it and for what end and for what polity . . . and afterwards according to this, one ought to judge not as a legist submissive to that law, but as one who has in himself political prudence.[38]

In the end caution should prevail; law can be changed, but only if a good would ensue that would outweigh all the disadvantages, and if the change reflects the consent or assent of the people.[39]

With an understanding of the nature of the law that must underlie all

---

introduiz es lays que Justinian compila et en autres lays romaines; et leur semble que il ne est nul autre droit escript et que il deust estre tenu partout, salvés les coustumes locaus, etc. Mes combien que en leur livres soient aucuns droiz naturelz ou presque naturelz a communitaté humaine et qui sunt a tenir partout, toutesvoies la plus grande partie sunt droiz positis. Et combien que il soient raisonnables quant au plus, nientmoins nul ne est obligié a les tenir par la vertu ou auctorité du princey de Romme excepté ceulz qui sunt de cellui princey se il dure encore. Car chescun princey, chescune policie a ses lays positives et ses droiz escrips ou non escrips, et se aucuns telz droiz sunt semblables a ceulz de Romme ou non, il n'i a force; car toutesvoies ne ont il auctorité en un princey fors par cellui princey meisme. Et dire que tous deussent estre sous le princey et sous les lays de Romme, ce est grande simplece et erreur contre raison naturele. . . . Et donques ne en escoles ne en jugemens, nul legiste ne est abstraint ne obligié a user les lays romains fors de l'auctorité de son legislateur." See also 7, chap. 10, p. 293.

[37] Oresme, *Le Livre de Politiques*, 4, chap. 1, p. 166.

[38] Oresme, *Le Livre de Politiques*, 5, chap. 25, p. 244. "Mes le remede est que l'en se abstraie sans soy adherdre a la lay pour l'auctorité de elle, mes comme se elle fust de nouvel proposee a mettre. L'en doit en juste balance peser la raison de la lay et la raison contraire. Et considerer qui la fist et pour quelle fin et a quelle policie. . . . Et apres, selon ce, l'en doit jugier non pas comme legiste sousmis a celle lay, mes comme celui qui a en soy prudence politique."

[39] Oresme, *Le Livre de Politiques*, 2, chap. 15, p. 99. "Les malveses lays anciens sunt a muer et les autres aussi ou cas que il s'ensuiroit plus grant bien que n'est le mal contraire a la fermeté et reverence des lays anciennes. Et convendroit que tel bien fust tres grant et aussi comme desire de tout le peuple et pour necessité ou pour evidente utilité." See also 3, chap. 24, p. 158; 3, chap. 14, p. 138. "Il [le prince] ne peut la lay enfreindre ne muer sans l'assentement du peuple."

good polities, we are now ready to see how Oresme analyzes the various forms of government. His definitions follow Aristotle's description of the sixfold schema, though to avoid confusion Oresme prefers to use *common polity* or *timocracy* instead of *polity* for the good rule of the multitude for the common good.[40] Although Marsilius of Padua influenced Oresme, he does not explicitly require consent in his definition of the good forms, but it is certainly essential. The people must assent to law; he writes, for example, that "a tyrant rules for his own profit and against the will of his subjects, whereas the reverse is true in a kingdom."[41]

Despite his formal adherence to Aristotle, Oresme really views the forms of government differently and far more fluidly than any medieval writer. Glossing Aristotle's definition of citizen he makes an important distinction between active and potential citizens and restricts the meaning of the term *multitude*:

> [A citizen], that is to say, one who has authority to be in the council of affairs [that is, the deliberative council] or in judgments. And one who has such authority in fact, he is a citizen simply, and one who does not have it in fact and is of such a condition that he is able and can be elected to it, he is a citizen after a fashion but not properly. And for this reason in a democracy all are citizens simply, excluding children, the old, serfs, foreigners, and those of vile condition or of vile employment, and also in a timocracy. But in other polities some are citizens simply and others after a fashion.[42]

Most of these exclusions are typical, but usually in democracy at least the poor are included—indeed this is often given as the failing of the form. The last sentence raises the possibility that the citizen body could be identical in an aristocracy and in a common polity. The difference would be that the entire citizenship participates actively in the latter, whereas a smaller group is elected for a limited time in the former.

[40] Oresme, *Le Livre de Politiques*, 2, chap. 10, p. 89; 3, chap. 9, p. 128. In this chapter I will use the terms interchangeably.

[41] Oresme, *Le Livre de Politiques*, 3, chap. 20, p. 146. "En vraie tirannie sunt .ii. choses; une est que le prince gouverne a son propre profit; l'autre est qu'il opprime ses subjects par force et par violence et tient en servitute contre leur volenté. Et en vrai royalme sunt .ii. choses contrairs as dessus dictes; une est que le roy gouverne ou profit es subjects; autre est que il lui sunt subjects de leur volenté."

[42] Oresme, *Le Livre de Politiques*, 3, chap. 2, p. 116. "Ce est a dire, qui a auctorité de estre au conseil des besognes ou es jugemens. Et celui qui a tele auctorité de fait, il est citoien simplement, et celui qui ne l'a pas de fait et est de tele condition qu'il est habile et peut estre esleu a ce, il est citoien aucunement et non pas proprement. Et pour ce, en democracie tous sunt citoiens simplement, exceptés les enfans, les passé de eage, les serfs, les estranges et ceulz de ville condition ou de vile office, et aussi en timocracie. Mez es autres policies aucuns sunt citoiens simplement et les autres aucunement."

Elsewhere is made the distinction between a citizen in a democracy and a citizen in a common polity:

> And in democracy the popular multitude holds the sovereignty, as was said before. But in the common polity and in aristocracy not the popular multitude but the multitude and universal congregation of all the rules or offices and of the principal citizens has sovereign dominion and the correction or alteration of particular rules or offices and the jurisdiction or cognizance of the greatest questions, and to it pertains the reform of the polity, and to compose or change the laws . . . and such a thing is in some ways similar to the Assembly General of the Masters of the University of Paris.[43]

The example is informative. Menut says that this assembly is "approximately equivalent to an American University Faculty meeting of full professors only, but with all the separate schools and colleges included."[44] Thus, the citizen body in a timocracy, as in an aristocracy, is restricted to the most important people. The distinction is that a democracy includes skilled workers and those from the lower middle class as citizens, whereas a common polity or an aristocracy does not. Timocracy would then differ from aristocracy only in having wider participation of the upper classes, as frequently happened at an earlier period in the Northern Italian communes. Oresme confirms this when he states that of the five kinds of people who live in a city—the free who do not do physical work, the free who do for necessity work, serfs, vile laborers, and those who work for wages (such as house builders and vintners)—only the first can be citizens in a good polity.[45] Although the distinctions among the three types of workers are not clear, he plainly intends to exclude more than just the lowest manual laborers. In other glosses he also explicitly excludes sailors, tradesmen, and artisans from citizenship in a good polity.[46]

---

[43] Oresme, *Le Livre de Politiques*, 6, chap. 12, p. 274. "Et en democracie la multitude populaire tient la souvereineté, si comme souvent est dit. Mes en commune policie et en aristocracie la multitude non pas la populaire mes la multitude et congregation universele de tous les princeys ou offices et des principalz citoiens a la souvereine domination et la correction ou alteration des particuliers princeys ou offices et le ressort ou cognoissance des tres grandes questions, et a elle appartient la reformation de la policie, et composer ou muer ou approver et accepter les lays, si comme il appert par ce que fu dit ou xiiiie et ou xviie chapitres du tiers; et monstrer evidenment par raison naturele. Et tele chose est aucunement sembalble a l'assemblee general des Maistres de l'Etude de Paris."

[44] Menut in Nicole Oresme, *On Aristotle's Politics*, p. 227, n. 1.

[45] Oresme, *Le Livre de Politiques*, 3, chap. 6, p. 124. "Il touche .v. manieres de gens, ce est assavoir les frans, qui ne sunt pas occupés en oeuvres corporeles; item les frans qui se occupent en telez oeuvres pour leur neccessité; item, les sers; item, les bannauses, qui sunt ordes gens comme dit est; item, les mercenaires qui labourent pour loier, comme sunt recouvreurs de maison, vignerons et teles gens. Et de ces .v. manieres les premiers pevent estre citoiens en bonne policie, et les autres non."

[46] Oresme, *Le Livre de Politiques*, 7, chap. 12, p. 296. "Et aussi comme les servans ne les

The similarity of the citizen bodies in an aristocracy and in a timocracy suggests that the two forms may shade off into each other depending on the size of the citizen body and the degree of participation. Indeed, this is how Oresme treats all polities. He restates Aristotle's position that aristocracy and monarchy are close because they are both based on virtue and develops the similarity of aristocracy and polity and polity and democracy. He uses Aristotle's idea of many species of each simple form to argue that the series of all polities forms a linear continuum, segments of which can be conveniently labeled with names such as polity, aristocracy, and democracy, but that the boundaries of such segments are ill-defined. For example, the more virtuous or restrictive the citizen body of a timocracy is (Oresme believes it will be more virtuous if all have moderate wealth) the closer it is to aristocracy; the less restrictive and less purely based on virtue aristocracy becomes the more it approaches timocracy. Likewise, timocracy and democracy can overlap in the extreme form of each.[47] Although Oresme does not mention such relationships with regard to democracy and oligarchy or oligarchy and tyranny it seems as if a similar argument could be made for them, thus establishing an alternative mode of transformations of polities from the more common one which describes the decline of a good polity into its opposite degenerate form.

Oresme states repeatedly that monarchy is the best form of all: it is the "most divine" and "best in excellence"; it serves as a model and as a measure of the virtue of other regimes; under it is the "most perfect felicity of political life according to human possibilities," and thus other polities are good to the extent that they approach it.[48] Remarkably, he gives no argu-

---

laboureurs ne sunt pas citoiens, non sunt telz mariniers." 7, chap. 17, p. 305. "Il ne convient pas querir citoiens qui mainent vie bannosique ou non honeste, ne vie de negotiation. Et par 'bannauses' il entent gens de vils artifices et mercennaires. Et par 'negotiation' il entent gens qui communelment estudient a gaing par marcheandise."

[47] Oresme, *Le Livre de Politiques*, 4, chap. 2, p. 166. "L'une et l'autre estre selon vertu large et parfecte." 4, chap. 3, p. 168. "Aristocracie . . . elle est proceine a royalme." See also 4, chap. 12, p. 181; 4, chap. 15, p. 185. "Car peu de gens ou peu de cités pourroient tenir les aristocracies de la premiere espece qui sunt simples et selon vertu purement. Mes celles qui sunt des autres especes mises en le xie chapitre et qui sunt composees, elles sunt plus communes. . . . Et donques la policie en laquelle plus de gens sunt riches moiennement a quant a ce plus grant similitude a vertu et est miex fortunee et miex disposee a bien vivre." 4, chap. 12, p. 181. "Car toutes .ii. sunt bonnes et aussi comme aristocracie est proceine de royalme, policie est pres de aristocracie." 3, chap. 22, p. 152. "Democracie et timocracie sunt proceines et different en peu de choses." See also 4, chap. 2, p. 167; 4, chap. 7, p. 175.

[48] Oresme, *Le Livre de Politiques*, 2, chap. 10, p. 90. "Royalme, lequel est princey premier d'ancienneté . . . premier en dignité et in bonté." 3, chap. 20, p. 145. "Policie royal est la tres melleur." 7, chap. 10, p. 291. "Se tele monarchie estoit juste, ce seroit policie royal laquele est tres bonne et tres divine." 7, chap. 29, p. 324. "Et ce est policie royal tres bonne en excellence." 3, chap. 20, p. 145. "Policie royal . . . est aussi regle et mesure des autres." 4, chap. 15, p. 185. "Ici est felicité de vie politique tres parfecte selon possibilité humaine." 3, chap.

ments for this judgment; it seems that kingship is so natural to him that he does not feel called upon to justify it even to the extent that other writers did—as a microcosm, or as natural, for example. Nevertheless, he writes much about the nature of kingship and the proper character of kings and how they should be chosen.

For one thing, Oresme clarifies the distinction between a king and a single ruler in an aristocracy. This had always been a problem, especially in regard to Northern Italian podestas. Oresme explains that in a democracy or aristocracy there may be a leader or a general who rules alone and permanently, but although he may be called a king, he is not, for "in a kingdom the king is sovereign and in a democracy the people hold the sovereign rule and in aristocracy some virtuous [have sovereign power] and not the power of the ruler or the leader of the army, because his rule is under the other, which is sovereign."[49] This makes the underlying structure of a polity more significant for its classification than its apparent structure. It also means that just as the citizen bodies may be identical for timocracy and aristocracy—the two being distinguished by whether the whole body of virtuous citizens holds sovereignty or whether a part of it does—so may they be for kingdom and aristocracy. Indeed, Oresme writes that many exercise rule in any good polity,[50] including a kingdom, but in a kingdom one alone has sovereignty. This concept, that all good polities coincide in the composition of their ruling classes and differ only in the way they choose to distribute power among this class, is original with Oresme. In due course I will examine how this affects the theory of the mixed constitution and arguments in favor of popular participation.

This ultimate authority of the king, however, does not give him the rights of an owner of property. The king must have ability and his people must be free.[51] To illustrate this point Oresme uses the standard example of early Israelite kingship and the discrepancy between the monarchy pre-

---

20, p. 145. "Et tant plus en approchent et il valent miex." See also 3, chap. 21, p. 149 and 3, chap. 27, p. 164.

[49] Oresme, *Le Livre de Politiques*, 3, chap. 24, p. 157. "En royalme le roy est souverain et en democracie le peuple tient le souverain princey et en aristocracie aucuns vertueus et non pas le prince ou le duc de l'ost, car son princey est soubs l'autre, qui est souverain." Ptolemy of Lucca and Giles of Rome give arguments similar to Oresme's in substance, the former specifically refering to podestàs and Roman consuls (*De Regimine Principum*, 4.1.67, p. 13) and separating them from kings on the basis of the fact that they depend on the many. Giles of Rome makes the same point about podestàs.

[50] Oresme, *Le Livre de Politiques*, 7, chap. 10, p. 292. "Car en toute bonne policie, selon Aristote, sunt pluseurs princeys ou officez."

[51] Oresme, *Le Livre de Politiques*, 2, chap. 21, p. 109. "Royalme ne est pas comme une possession propre seroit ou une rente familiare, mes est dignité et une seigneurie et honourableté." 3, chap. 21. p. 149. "En vray royalme les subjecs sunt citoiens et frans, non pas sers." See also 3, chap. 23, pp. 153–55; 7, chap. 5, p. 283; 3, chap. 20, p. 148; 3, chap. 23, p. 155.

dicted in Deuteronomy and in I Kings. In part, Oresme follows Ptolemy of Lucca's argument—that the king of I Kings was a despot and not a true king, unlike that of Deuteronomy. They differ, however in that Ptolemy of Lucca used this example to identify kingship with despotic rule and thereby discredit it, and he called Samuel a political ruler, whereas Oresme wishes to exalt true kingship. Oresme describes how the Israelites demanded that Samuel, a good ruler, give them a king "as all nations had." God treated this request as a rejection of him, and Samuel portrayed the king to come as an oppressor who would seize property and impress children to his service. Oresme comments:

> It seems to me that the right above is the right which the ruler in the monarchy called "barbarian" has, and that this is not the right of a true king. Both text and reason accord. . . . Aristotle says . . . that such barbarian monarchies are in Asia . . . and the people of Israel, who were in that region, demanded a king as other nations had—and this must be understood as neighboring nations. . . . Likewise, Aristotle says . . . that such rulers are tyrants because they govern to their own profit. . . . But they have a similarity to a king in that their subjects are voluntary . . . the above right is to the profit of the ruler, and it also appears that the people of Israel wanted such a king. . . . Likewise, in a true kingdom the subjects are citizens and free. . . . Scripture says that all the children of Israel will be serfs to such a king. Likewise, Scripture does not say simply and generally, "this will be the right of a king," but it says twice, "this will be the right of the king who will rule over you" . . . he will not be a king except in name. . . . Likewise, the rights of a true king are not exactions . . . the gloss says on "this will be the right of the king," "by exaction and dominion." . . . Likewise, a true kingdom is the best polity, and then it is not evil to ask for and have a true and a good king. And it is certain that it would not displease our Lord if his people demanded this king. . . . And then they cannot have demanded a true king. . . . And then he who uses the above right would not be a true king. But to speak of a king according to that which Aristotle presents, and not of a barbaric king, it is certain that Samuel governed the people of Israel as a king, and that he was a true king . . . how was it that he was called "Judge"? Perhaps because in that country and in that time they did not call those kings except those who held barbaric monarchy.[52]

---

[52] Oresme, *Le Livre de Politiques*, 3, chap. 21, pp. 149–50. "Il me semble que le droit dessus dit est le droit que se dit avoir le prince en monarchie appellee barbarique et ne est pas le droit de vray roy. Et l'une et l'autre, texte et raison si acordent . . . Aristote dit . . . que telz royalmes barbariques sunt en Asye. . . . Et le peuple d'Israel qui estoit en celles parties demandoit tel roy comme ont toutes nations. Et est a entendre dez nations voisins. . . . Item, Aristote dit . . . que telz princes sunt tirans, car il gouvernent a leur profit. . . . Mes il ont une similitude a roy en tant comme leur subjecs sunt volontaires . . . le droit dessus dit est ou profit du prince et appert aussi que le peuple d'Israhel vouloit avoir tel roy. . . . Item, en vray royalme les subjecs sunt citoiens et frans. . . . Et l'Escripture dit que tous les filz d'Israel seroient sers a tel

The difference between Oresme's treatment and Ptolemy of Lucca's reveals their disparate conceptions of kingship. Having rejected Thomas Aquinas's idea of political kingship as a contradiction in terms, Ptolemy of Lucca must identify Samuel as a political nonmonarch and therefore presumably as an aristocratic ruler, and he can really find no place for the good king of Deuteronomy. Oresme has restored Thomas Aquinas's conception, if not his terminology (or rather he diverges from him at the other extreme in that he does not recognize a king according to will), and therefore can classify Samuel as a king according to law. This makes for a more consistent distinction between regal and despotic rule, and as a consequence a more coherent interpretation of I Kings. Likewise, he is able with more assurance to integrate the *Politics* and the Bible.

Thus we see that although Oresme, Ptolemy of Lucca, and Thomas Aquinas share the ideal of a single ruler ruling according to law for the good of his people—what Thomas calls a political king, Ptolemy of Lucca a political ruler, and Oresme a regal king—they differ on some of the details. Ptolemy and Thomas are equivocal as to how to choose a king. Oresme concludes that there are three ways to become king. One is by pure succession, which is not right since it violates the premise that kingship is not a possession; another way is by election, but this is not expedient; but "the third is a mean in that it participates in the two others and is thus, as it were, composed of election and succession."[53] Oresme essentially follows the line found first in Peter of Auvergne and Giles of Rome that while election is better simply, heredity is better *per accidens* but concurs with John of Paris and others that consent to the line is necessary. And, as we shall see, succession by heredity does not at all imply that the people cannot depose an unsatisfactory king. It is interesting that here too he seeks the

---

roy. Item, l'Escripture ne dit pas simplement et generalment "ce sera le droit du roy"; mes dit par .ii. fois 'ce sera le droit du roy qui regnera sus vous' . . . ne seroit roy fors seulement de nom. . . . Item, les droiz de vrai roy ne sunt pas exactions . . . et la ou l'Escripture dit, 'ce sera le droit du roy,' la glose dit, 'par exaction et par domination'. . . . Item, vrai royalme est tres bonne policie, et donques ne est ce pas mal de demander et avoir vrai roy et bon. Et est certain que il ne despleust a Nostre Sire, se son peuple demandast ce roy. . . . Et donques ne avoient il pas demandé vrai roy. . . . Et donques celui qui useroit du droit dessus dit ne seroit pas vrai roy. Mes a parler de roy selon ce que Aristote le prent, et non pas de roy barbarique, il est certain que Samuel gouverna le peuple de Israel comme roy et que il fu vray roy . . . combien que il fust appellé juge? Car peut estre que en ce païs et en ce temps, il ne appelloient roys fors ceulz qui tenoient monarchie barbarique."

[53] Oresme, *Le Livre de Politiques*, 3, chap. 23, pp. 154–55. "Il me semble que .iii. voies sunte touchees comme l'en peut venir a tenir royalme. Une est par pure succession . . . mes . . . royalme ne est pas de tele nature comme sunt heritages que l'en peut eschangier ou vendre . . . ce ne est pas vrai royalme. . . . Une autre voie . . . est par election, et ceste voie ne est expediente. . . . La tierce est moienne en participant as .ii. autres et est ainsi comme composee de election et de succession." See 3, chap. 20, p. 147 for his theory of how the kings of England and France fit this model. See also 3, chap. 23, p. 153 and 2, chap. 21, p. 109.

best solution as the mean of two extremes or, as he almost puts it, as a mixture of the two.

Most of the medieval theorists were interested in interpreting the *Politics* as a defense of kingship. Although there were a number of passages that could be used for this purpose, there were far more that promoted the idea of popular participation. Two ways were used to avoid contradiction. Thomas Aquinas developed the first: the theory that the multitude should share in government with the king as part of a mixed constitution. He relied solely on this explanation and advocated such an arrangement even if the multitude was not virtuous. To Peter of Auvergne this seemed to be nonsense—how could a nonvirtuous mob hope to govern effectively? His theory proposed the participation of the people only if it were "reasonable" or "nonbestial." Most of those who wrote in the following century accepted this explanation and usually combined it with an explicit or an implicit defense of a mixed constitution among a virtuous people. Even Marsilius of Padua, who came the closest to suppport of universal participation, provided the concept of the "weightier part" to exclude the unworthy.

Oresme also follows this distinction. He thinks that regal rule—which implies popular participation—can exist only if the people is good enough. He assumes that there is a periodic degeneration and regeneration of people; for example, in discounting Aristotle's idea that heroic kingship could exist only in the past, he writes that it might exist at any time since the world goes through cycles—at any time the people might be good enough for true kingship.[54] Commenting on I Kings, Oresme bases his conclusion that the king Samuel predicted was unjust precisely on the nature of the ancient Jews—they were not slaves and lived civilly, and therefore despotism could not be expedient to them.[55] The changeability of the masses, he feels, is the greatest drawback in allowing them to participate. Further, the people is often divided, and it can be easily deceived by "false seducers." On the other hand, since a nondespotic city is a community of free people,

---

[54] Oresme, *Le Livre de Politiques*, 3, chap. 20, p. 147. "Et pour ce dit Maximian du viellart: 'Laudat preteritos, presentes despicit annos' [*Eligiae* 1, 197]. 'Il loe les ans pasés et blasme les presens.' Toutesvoies, il ne est pas tousjours ainsi, mes aucune fois le monde quant as gens va en empirant et autres foiz en amendant, si comme il peut assés apparoir par les hystoires. . . . Et doit l'en savoir que la monarchie royale desus dite peut estre en touz temps."

[55] Oresme, *Le Livre de Politiques*, 3, chap. 21, p. 150. "Apres je di que le peuple d'Israel ne estoit pas tele [bestiale] multitude, car Aristote ne dit pas universelement que tous ceulz d'Asye fussent proprement sers . . . il appert assés par l'hystoire du livre des Roys et alleurs en l'Escripture que lez filz d'Israel ne estoient pas telz sers et qu'il vivoient civilement." In this he differs from Ptolemy of Lucca, for example, who assumed that the despotic kingship was the deserved penalty of a people become evil. Elsewhere (5, chap. 25, p. 244) Oresme does suggest that in some periods of their history the Israelites were what he calls a "bestial multitude," and as such did not deserve to have a king.

all citizens should in some way, Oresme writes, share in rule. Besides this principled reason, participation is expedient since it inculcates love of the polity, which gives stability, and since the judgment of many is often better than that of one.[56]

These arguments are decisive if the people is virtuous. If a reasonable multitude is more virtuous than any subgroup, a bestial one is worse:

> In distribution of rule one ought not to have regard for one sole propriety or dignity of persons, but for all which are pertinent . . . such a multitude comprehends and contains better in itself all the good qualities pertaining to good rule. And it is to be noted first that Aristotle did not say universally that in every city the multitude ought to have such sovereignty, but he says that it could happen some times. Because . . . some multitudes are bestial and vile, and such multitudes in which perhaps a small number are virtuous and the greater part are more unreasonable than reasonable, even though all together are more rich than one part, nevertheless according to virtue one part is weightier than all together, and virtue pertains more to rule than riches, and then the above argument does not demand that such a multitude should have rule.[57]

With regard to material things the whole is always greater than the parts, Oresme says, but with regard to virtues this is true only if each element, or at least most, possesses a minimum of the quality. Otherwise, the bestial part will poison the rest. But given the minimum, the relationship holds; since the few with great virtue and prudence are part of the multitude the whole must be greater than the part: "Many eyes see what one does not. And for this reason, in the city, although a small number might be virtuous and prudent; nevertheless, some of the multitude have had certain experiences and have in their work certain things profitable to the council that the more prudent do not have." Just as the Apostles together wrote the

---

[56] Oresme, *Le Livre de Politiques*, 3, chap. 14, p. 136; 3, chap. 17, p. 142; 3, chaps. 7–8, pp. 127–28. "Teles policies sunt despotiques, et cité est communité de gens qui sunt frans' . . . tous les citoiens doivent aucunement participer en princey." Oresme is here using *citizen* in the loose but common sense. See also 3, chap. 25, p. 161; 5, chap. 31, p. 251; 6, chap. 12, p. 274.

[57] Oresme, *Le Livre de Politiques*, 3, chap. 17, pp. 141–42. "En distribution de princeys l'en ne doit pas resgarder a une seule bonne propreté ou dignité de personnes, mes a toutes celles qui sunt appartenantes . . . tele multitude comprent et contient miex en soi tous les bons accidens appartenans a bon princey. Et est noter premierement que Aristote ne dit pas universaliment qu'en toute cité la multitude doie avoir tele souveraineté, mes il dit qu'il peut estre aucune foiz. Car . . . aucune multitude est comme bestial et ville, et tele multitude en laquele par aventure un petit nombre sunt vertueus et la plus grande partie sunt plus desraisonnablez que raisonnables, combien que tous ensemble soient plus riches que une partie, toutesvoies selon vertu une partie est plus vaillant que tous ensemble et vertu appartient plus a princey que richeces, et donques la raison dessus dite ne conclut pas pour tele multitude que elle doie avoir princey." See also 3, chap. 22, p. 151.

Creed, Oresme argues, each individual can find something to profit the city, and no part can have as much prudence and experience as the nonbestial multitude as a whole.[58]

In the passages just cited, the words "one part is weightier" immediately bring to mind Marsilius of Padua's "weightier part." Marsilius also required that only the reasonable portion of the multitude participate in government and identified the weightier part with this portion. Yet, at least in the interpretation I have proposed for the *Defender of Peace*, Marsilius assumed that in any polity reasonable individuals comprise the vast majority of the adult, free, native, male population, whereas for Oresme, Peter of Auvergne, and his tradition it is a very variable matter—some polities may produce none or one or only a few suitable citizens. Remember also that Oresme is more restrictive than Marsilius of Padua in the composition of the citizen body.

Marsilius of Padua did influence Oresme, who cites his work on a number of occasions, all having to do with the role of the people. Commenting on Aristotle's statement that one who lives in a house is the best judge of it, Oresme writes:

> In a book entitled *Defender of Peace* this argument is alleged to show that human positive laws ought to be made, promulgated, corrected, or changed on the authority and consent of all the community or the weightier part . . . in such a manner the wise know how to compose and make the laws and statutes and all the multitude of wise and other common people know which laws are profitable to all. . . . Similarly, with respect to the correction or the mutation of laws and to the reform of the polity, no one can know so well what is expedient to all as can all the multitude together. And also one can say with respect to the correction and election of rulers . . . [Marsilius says] that the multitude ought to have dominion over the greatest persons and the best . . . the whole is greater than the part . . . the whole is weightier than the part. And dominion is due to the weightier part and consequently all the multitude should have dominion over correction and election of the rulers. And this must be understood concerning a reasonable multitude.[59]

[58] Oresme, *Le Livre de Politiques*, 3, chap. 13, pp. 134–35. "Pluseurs oeulz voient ce que qu'un oeul ne voit pas. Et pour ce, en la cité combien que un petit nombre soient vertueus et prudens, toutesvoies aucuns de la multitude ont veu aucunes experiences et ont en eulz aucunes industries profitables au conseil que les plus prudens ne ont pas . . . chescun de pluseurs treuve aucune chose bonne pour la cité. Et tout ensemble est tres bon, et l'en dit qu'en ceste maniere les Apostelz composerent le Credo . . . un petit nombre de gens ne a pas tant de prudence ne de experience comme ce qui est concuilli de toute la multitude, mes il monstre apres quele multitude est et quele non."

[59] Oresme, *Le Livre de Politiques*, 3, chap. 14, p. 137. "En un livre intitulé *Defensor pacis* ceste raison est alleguee a monstrer que lays humains positives doivent estre faictes, promulguees, corrigees ou muees de l'auctorité et consentement de toute la communité ou de la plus

These roles for the multitude—election, correction, making and changing laws, and judging—which Oresme has adapted from Marsilius of Padua, are its by right in any form of government. I have already shown that Oresme envisioned the same citizen body in both timocracy and aristocracy, and he extends it to kingdom as well, for even there the nonbestial multitude deserves to exercise these functions:

> And with regard to royal polity, again perhaps it is expedient that such a reasonable multitude or part of it should have this power. . . . Especially because all this multitude of which the king and his familiar council are one small part knows better how to consider and order all that which is good for the republic. And also, that which all approve is more firm and more stable, more acceptable and more aggreeable to the community, and gives less occasion for murmuring or for rebellion than if it were otherwise.[60]

Notice that Oresme includes the king and his council as elements of the multitude, and therefore that in giving the multitude power he is not necessarily setting up an organ opposed to or balancing the king, just as canonists had traditionally said that the General Council was stronger than the pope but meant to include the pope as the leading element of the General Council. On this occasion and several others Oresme interprets Aristotle to mean that the ruling element—the king in a monarchy or the few in an aristocracy—ought to be stronger than individuals but weaker than the multitude or its weightier part.[61] Just how this limits the king's power has

---

vaillant partie . . . en tele maniere les sages scevent composer et faire les lays et estatus et toute la multitude de sages et d'autres communs scevent quelles lays sunt profitables pour touz. . . . Semblablement, quant a la correction ou mutation des lays et a la reformation de la policie, nul ne peut si bien savoir que est expedient a touz comme peut toute la multitude ensemble. Et aussi peut l'en dire quant a la correction et election des princes . . . il expose ainsi que la multiitude doit avoir la domination des plus grans personnes et des melleurs. . . . Car le tout est plus grant que la partie . . . le tout est plus vaillant que la partie. Et domination est deue au plus vaillant et par consequent, toute la multitude doit avoir domination sus la correction et election des princes. Et est a entendre de multitude raisonnable."

[60] Oresme, *Le Livre de Politiques*, 6, chap. 12, p. 274. "Et quant est en policie royal, encor par aventure est il expedient que tele multitude raisonnable ou partie de elle ait ceste puissance. . . . Meisement car toute ceste multitude de laquele le roy et son familier conseil sunt une petit partie scet miex considerer et ordener tout ce qui est bon pour la chose publique. Et aussi, ce que tous funt et appreuvent est plus ferme et plus estable, plus acceptable et plus aggreable a la communité, et donne moins de occasion de murmere ou de rebellion que se il estoient autrement."

[61] Oresme, *Le Livre de Politiques*, 3, chap. 23, p. 157. " 'Mes sa puissance doit estre moindre que celle de la multitude.' Ou de la plus vaillant partie. Et la cause est car autrement il pourroit grever la cité et tourner son gouvernement en tirannie." Aristotle, *Politics*, 3.15.1286b.34–37, wrote that in a monarchy according to law the king should be greater than individuals but less than the whole multitude. For Oresme all monarchies are according to law. See also 5, chap. 24, p. 241. Oresme makes an interesting misconstruction of another of Aristotle's texts on this point. Aristotle had written that it is impossible that the rulers should be more

to do with the mixed constitution, which I will get to soon. In short, a nonvile people deserves to rule, and there cannot be a good government over a vile people, for a vile people deserves despotic rulers.[62]

Where does this leave sovereignty, if the multitude is to have such powers? Recall that Oresme distinguished among kingdom, aristocracy, and common polity on the basis of the numerical content of the sovereign. Oresme himself sees no conflict, nor has he developed a complete theory of sovereignty as we know it. The multitude has certain functions and rights, but the sovereigns, or greatest powers, are those who exercise the greatest power on a regular basis:

> Likewise if the multitude is reasonable and honorable, again it seems to me that he [Aristotle] does not intend that it ought to hold the day-to-day rule and government with respect to judgments, but there ought to be one sovereign or many who hold the rule and exercise it according to the laws. . . . But the multitude can have dominion in three things . . . election . . . correction of rulers in the case that they abuse their dignity . . . establishment or mutation and acceptation of laws. . . . Because it is said that that which touches all ought to be approved by all. And perhaps Aristotle by "politeuma" intended these three things.[63]

In this Oresme clearly intends to distinguish between Aristotle's *politeuma*, which for Aristotle was the arrangement of offices in government, and sovereign, which to Oresme was that governmental organ superior to all others. Now this interpretation differs from any previous one. Marsilius of Padua, for example, identified the *politeuma* with the "principal part," that is, with what Oresme calls the sovereign. This is what William of Ockham also meant when he equated the *politeuma* with the ruling class.[64] For

---

powerful than the whole multitude. He meant by this only that the multitude is physically stronger than the few rulers, but Oresme understands Aristotle to say that the multitude should have power if it is not bestial (7, chap. 29, p. 324). Marsilius also misread this passage, but whereas he took the impossibility to stem from the natural and general impulse of humans toward political community, Oresme takes it to refer to the particular and contingent existence of a reasonable multitude.

[62] Oresme, *Le Livre de Politiques*, 5, chap. 25, p. 244. "Un autre cas seroit se la multitude subjecte devenoit ou fust faite vilz, bestial et servile. . . . Et que elle ne fust plus digne de gouvernement royal, et que par sa misere eust deservi soustenir princey despotique."

[63] Oresme, *Le Livre de Politiques*, 3, chap. 18, p. 142. "Item, se la multitude est raisonnable et honorable, encor me semble que il ne entent pas qu'elle doie tenir le princey et le gouvernement cotidian quant a distribution d'offices et quant a jugemens, mes doit estre un souverain ou pluseurs qui tiennent le princey et l'excercent selon les lays. . . . Mes tele multitude peut avoir domination quant a .iii. choses . . . l'election dez princes . . . la correction des princes ou cas que il abuseroient de leur dignité . . . la constitution ou mutation et acceptation des lays. . . . Car l'en dit que ce que touche tous doit estre approuvé de tous. Et par aventure, Aristote par 'policeme' entent ces .iii. choses." See also 4, chap. 10, p. 178.

[64] See also McIlwain, *Growth of Political Thought*, p. 306.

Oresme sovereignty as we understand it is divided between two elements: first, the ruling element (king, aristocrats, or multitude), which he calls the sovereign because it is its task to exercise the highest power in all matters according to the law and according to its own discretion in matters not covered by the law; and second, the reasonable multitude, identical for all the good polities, which elects the ruling element (and is the ruling element in a timocracy) and makes and changes the laws but which does not except in timocracy and democracy itself exercise the highest power. The law itself, although it is supreme and binding on all, is nevertheless completely subject to the reasonable multitude and is not therefore an element of the sovereign. This division of sovereignty suggests a mixed constitution. It is to this topic that I finally turn.

Oresme does not often refer directly to the mixed constitution—though whenever he does he has only good things to say about it. His primary emphasis is on limitation of power by legal and institutional means. By linking restraints in the Spartan polity—the primary Greek example of a mixed constitution—to those in the French monarchy and in his ideal government he demonstrates his preference for a mixed monarchy.

Glossing Aristotle's statement "and some say that it is suitable to the best polity that it should be mixed and composed of all [forms] or of all citizens," Oresme comments: "Because one polity [that is, form] is moderated and restrained by the other. And also when almost all the citizens have some dominion they have less material for sedition, as if the people have authority in some things, and the great in another, and the king in another."[65] These are the exact reasons Thomas Aquinas gives in support of a mixed constitution. Similarly, Oresme explains Aristotle's advocacy of power for the multitude in an aristocracy as a device to prevent its degeneration into an oligarchy.[66] This goes along with his oft-repeated principle that too much power in the hands of the ruling group is a step toward tyranny, by which he commonly means any of the degenerate forms.

At one point Oresme introduces the mixed constitution to rationalize what he sees as a contradiction in Aristotle, who wrote that the change of a polity from monarchy to aristocracy is a change from a good form to a better one. Oresme's first thought—that Aristotle is just arguing a point

[65] Aristotle, *Politics*, 2, chap. 10, p. 90. "Et aucuns dient que a tres bonne policie il convient que elle soit mixte et composee de toutes ou de tous citoiens." Oresme, *Le Livre de Politiques*, 2, chap. 10, p. 90. "Car une policie est attrempee et refrenee par l'autre. Et aussi quant presque tous les citoiens ont aucune dominacion il ont moins matiere de sedicion, si comme se le peuple a auctorité en aucune chose et les grans en une autre et le roi en une autre." Oresme takes this description of the mixed constitution directly from Thomas Aquinas, *In Libros Politicorum*, 2.7.245.

[66] Oresme, *Le Livre de Politiques*, 3, chap. 14, p. 136.

without implying a conclusion—does not satisfy him, and he makes the following suggestion:

> But in order to see how the above argument is true, one ought to know that he speaks of rule with respect to judgments and shows that the judgment of many wise men is of more value than that of one alone. And then if there should be a king who wanted to judge and condemn by himself, such rule or such a kingdom would not be the best polity. . . . But if a king makes his judgments by the deliberation of the many wise . . . this is well done. And as a mixture of kingdom and of aristocracy, which is more desirable than kingdom alone in the first manner, or than aristocracy alone.[67]

This argument is in line with Peter of Auvergne's support of the mixed constitution as the union of good qualities and with Thomas Aquinas's statement that since monarchy and aristocracy are the two best simple forms the best form includes both.

Oresme also recognizes a type of mixed constitution that does not result from the balancing or juxtaposition of forms but from taking their mean. This is his explanation for Aristotle's assertion that the common polity is a mixture of oligarchy and democracy. That view posed a problem for medieval writers that Aristotle did not face since he used the words democracy and oligarchy loosely, but they could not help but think that he meant the perverted forms of polity and aristocracy. How could a good form be a combination of two bad forms? How could a form contain as a proper part of itself its own opposite? How can a simple form be mixed? In spite of his less strict terminology Aristotle himself had to face some of these questions, and as I have interpreted him he probably meant exactly what Oresme takes him to mean. Oresme alone of all medieval writers, and almost alone of modern writers, interprets Aristotle in this way:

> Of two harmful and contrary things one middle thing is composed which is good and profitable, as one makes medicine of two things of which one is too cold and the other too hot, or of which one is too bitter and the other too sweet. And similarly . . . oligarchy and democracy are also contraries . . . oligarchy is . . . too harsh and too rigid and the other is too remiss and too soft. And then of these two can be composed one middle polity well moderated. . . . It is not composed of these two in such a manner that they should be in it in their proper forms, but it has qualities in some points similar to

---

[67] Oresme, *Le Livre de Politiques*, 3, chap. 22, p. 152. "Mes pour veoir combien la raison dessus mise conclude verité, l'en doit savoir que il parle de princey quant as jugemens et monstre que le jugement de pluseurs sages vault plus que de un seul. Et donques se il estoit un roy qui vousist jugier et condempner lui seul, tel princey ou tel royalme ne seroit pas tres bonne policie. . . . Mes se un roy fait ses jugemens par la deliberation de pluseurs sages . . . ce est tres bien fait. Et aussi comme une mistion de royalme et de aristocracie, qui est plus eslisible que royalme selon la premiere maniere, ne que aristocracie seule."

these two polities . . . nevertheless it is simple in substance. And it is thus as
one says that the air, which is a simple element, is composed of humidity and
dryness, which qualities are . . . more sensible in water or fire than in air. And
thus as the dryness of fire and of the air are of a another nature and of diverse
species, similarly the rigor or harshness of oligarchy and that of this polity
differ in species. And then this polity can be called simple with respect to its
form, but with respect to the matter, it is composed of poor and rich . . . this
polity is not composed of democracy as of its integral part and which resides
in it in its proper form.[68]

Like Aristotle, Oresme sees the common polity as a mixture of rich and
poor in the sense that they are blended into a middle class which predominates in this form: "And then the people of middle estate who are neither
very rich or very poor hold the rule in this polity."[69]

Interesting as this interpretation is, this kind of mixture is not the usual
kind in either Aristotle or Oresme. For both men the mixed constitution
as such referred to the mixture of some and usually all of kingdom, aristocracy, and timocracy. Aristotle gave three principal examples: Crete, Carthage (translated by Moerbeke as Chalcedonia), and Sparta. Oresme mentions Crete and Carthage in their places but devotes most of his attention
to Sparta. With Aristotle, he attributes its endurance to the limitation of
the power of its kings. In fact, Aristotle's comments to this effect inspired
one of Oresme's longest glosses, in which he defends the idea that the more
restricted a king is the longer his polity will last. Historically Sparta went
through two stages, according to Oresme. Limited from the outset, the

[68] Oresme, *Le Livre de Politiques*, 4, chap. 12, p. 180. "De .ii. choses nuisibles et contraires
est composee une chose moiennne, bonne et proficable, si comme l'en fait selon medicine de
.ii. choses dont l'une est trop froide et l'autre est trop chaude ou dont l'une est trop amere et
l'autre trop douce. Et par semblable . . . olygarchie et democracie sunt aussi comme contraires
. . . olygarchie est . . . trop aspre et trop dure et l'autre est trop remisse et trop molle. Et
donques de ces .ii. peut estre composee une moienne policie bonne attrempee . . . elle ne est
composee de ces .ii. en tele maniere que il soient en elle en leur propres formes; mes elle a
qualités et propretés aucunement semblables a ces .ii. policies . . . nientmoins elle est simple
en substance. Et est ainsi comme l'en diroit que l'aer, qui est un simple element, est composé
de humidité et de chaleur, lesquelles qualités sunt plus congneues et plus sensibles en l'eaue
et ou feu que il ne sunt en l'aer. Et aussi comme la chaleur du feu et de l'aer sunt d'autre nature
et de diverse espece, semblablement la rigeur ou aspreté de olygarchie et celle de ceste policie
different en espece. Et donques ceste policie peut estre dicte simple quant est a sa forme; mes
quant a la matiere, elle est composee de povres et de riches . . . ceste policie ne est pas composee de democracie comme de sa partie integral et qui demeure en elle en sa propre forme."
See also 4, chap. 13, p. 182, where Oresme writes that democracy and oligarchy are mixed in
the sense of similarity of qualities. At 2, chap. 10, p. 90, Oresme states that a good polity
cannot result from the mixture of two bad forms—here referring to Socrates' advocacy of a
mixture of democracy and tyranny. But here he is referring to mixture in the usual sense.

[69] Oresme, *Le Livre de Politiques*, 4, chap. 13, p. 182. "Et donques gens de moien estat qui
ne sunt tres riches ne tres povres tiennent le princey en ceste policie."

kingship was further weakened by King Theopompe, whom Oresme treats as a hero. Aristotle wrote that Sparta lasted since from the beginning rule was divided into two parts. Oresme comments:

In such a manner that the kings had the sovereignty but in many great things they could do nothing without the other rule, which would be perhaps as is the *parlement* in France, or as was sometimes the Senate of Rome. And from this it appears clearly that this regulation [that is, limiting the king's power] is most excellent, because the Spartans had many unsuitable things in their polity . . . and nevertheless their polity lasted long on account of this regulation alone . . . what power Theopompe gave to that ruler or chamber or college which he calls the ephorate I do not know how to determine beyond that which appears in the text, that with regard to certain great things in which it could judge and order or give and distribute according to its will, it could abridge and lessen this power [kingship] and restrain it with regard to him [King Theopompe] and his successors. And concerning this there was made a law by which a great part of the power which he had was transferred, transported, and given to these masters called ephors. And Valerius Maximus [*Memorabilia*, 4.1.8] relates this example and says that . . . [Theopompe] instituted in Sparta the ephors so that they would be in opposition to the royal power in the manner that in Rome the tribunes of the people were in opposition to the consular rule. . . . But it could be that the Spartans did not maintain this ephorate in the manner that he had ordained, because it is in some parts criticized in *Politics* II.27. . . . And then it appears clearly that in this case King Theopompe was wiser than King Solomon . . . because if Solomon had done as Theopompe, his son Roboam would not have overlooked the voice of the people of Israel . . . and Roboam would not have lost four of the five parts of his kingdom.[70]

[70] Oresme, *Le Livre de Politiques*, 5, chap. 25, p. 242. "En tele maniere que les roys avoient la souveraineté, mes en pluseurs grandes choses il ne povoient rien sans l'autre princey, lequel estoit par aventure comme seroit parlement en France, ou comme fu aucune foiz le senat de Romme. Et par ce appert clerement que ceste regle est tres excellent; car les Lacedemones avoient en leur policie pluseurs choses inconvenientes. . . . Et nientmoins, leur policie dura longuement pour ceste seule regle. . . . Mes quele puissance Theopompe bailla a ce prince ou college ou chambre que il appelle 'efforie' je ne scay pas determineement, fors tant que assés appert par le texte que de aucunes grandes choses desquelles il povoit jugier et ordener ou donner et distribuer a sa volenté, il retrencha et lessa de ceste puissance et la restraint quant a lui et a ses successeurs. Et de ce fu faite lay par laquelle grande partie de la posté que il avoit devant fu translatee, transportee et baillié a ces maistres appellés 'effores.' Et tel exemple recite Valerius Maximus [*Memorabilia* 4.1.8] . . . et dit que . . . [Theopompe] instituta en Lacedemone les effores afin que il fussent opposites a la posté royal en la maniere que a Romme les tribuns du peuple estoient opposites au princey consulaire. . . . Mes peut estre que les Lacedemones ne maintindrent pas ceste efforie en la maniere que il avoit ordenee; car elle est en aucuns poins blasmee ou xviie chapitre du secunt. . . . Et donques appert clerement que en cest cas le roy Theopompe fu plus sage que le roy Solomon. . . . Car se Salomon eust fait si

Oresme shows some uncertainty about the structure of the Spartan mixed constitution, in particular about the nature of the kings. At most times he treats them as if they were true kings, for example, he criticizes the Spartans because they "change their kings often, and for this reason the royal power would be less esteemed and less feared."[71] Even ignoring the use of the word *royal*, this is a criticism which could only apply to a king, for in Oresme's view a king should be chosen for life, but all other offices should change. (In the same chapter he also reproaches the Spartans for giving a life tenure to the Ancients.) Again, when he argues that in a royal polity a reasonable multitude should have power, he gives as an example Theopompe and his establishment of the ephorate.[72] On the other hand he occasionally calls the two kings an aristocratic element: "The aristocratic rulers," he writes, "are called kings because aristocracy and kingdom are near polities."[73] And he lets pass Aristotle's remark that Sparta chooses its officials only with regard to virtue and the people, commenting only that "by virtue he means aristocracy."[74] Most of these examples are from very short explanatory glosses on the *Politics*; it may be that Oresme in these places was merely trying to make sense of the text, and was not expressing his own opinion. In the longer glosses he nearly always treats the Spartan kings as true kings. One possible exception is his implied comparison of the kings and the Roman consuls, when he says that the ephorate was designed to oppose the kings just as the tribunes opposed the consulate. Oresme may consider the consulate to be an aristocratic office, in which case perhaps by implication the kingship is also.[75] On the other hand perhaps he is simply making an analogy of structural arrangements without reference to the actual nature of components. The idea of a double mon-

---

comme fist Theopompe son filz Roboam ne eust pas oÿe la voiz de tout le peuple d'Israel. . . . Et ne eust pas Roboam perdu de .v. parties de son royalme les .iiii."

[71] Oresme, *Le Livre de Politiques*, 2, chap. 17, p. 103. "Et il muoient leurs roys souvent, et par ce l'auctorité et posté royal estoit moins prisié et moins doubtee."

[72] Oresme, *Le Livre de Politiques*, 6, chap. 12, p. 274. "Item, a cest propos . . . meisement l'example du roy Theopompe, qui pour la salvation de son royalme instituta .i. princey ou office appellé 'efforie'."

[73] Oresme, *Le Livre de Politiques*, 5, chap. 12, p. 222. "Les princes aristocratiques estoient appellés roys, car aristocracie et royalme sunt policies proceins."

[74] Oresme, *Le Livre de Politiques*, 4, chap. 11, p. 179. "En la policie des Lacedemones il resgardent en election de princes a vertu et au peuple.' Par vertu il entent aristocracie." He had already at this point identified regard for the people as democratic and called Chalcedonia, which had regard for virtue, riches, and the people a mixture of three polities—aristocracy, oligarchy, and democracy.

[75] Oresme, *Le Livre de Politiques*, 3, chap. 22, p. 152. "Se le roy commençoit a tirannizer . . . lors seroit mué royalme en tirannie. Et se l'en povoit resister et qu'un petit nombre vertueux obtenissent la domination, il seroit mué en aristocracie, comme fu le royalme des Romains." Of course, since he does not mention the consulate directly here he may be referring to the senate.

archy is one that always gave some trouble, and Oresme does not confront it directly.

Neither is he clear with some of his other correspondences. His reference to *parlement* and Senate is ambiguous. Coming as it does immediately following Aristotle's statement that the Spartan rule was from the beginning divided into two parts, one would think he must be alluding to some aspect of the double kingship since the ephorate was not established until later. His sense would then be that in ordinary matters the two act independently as kings, but in important matters they check each other much as the Senate and *parlement* check the consuls and the French king respectively. Kingship would function, then, both as monarchy and aristocracy, and the ephorate would fulfill a democratic function comparable to the tribunate in Rome. Elsewhere, however, Oresme makes a comparison of the ephorate with the Senate and *parlement*.[76] In still another passage Oresme considers Sparta more clearly and traditionally as a mixture of the three good polities: "The Spartans have three rulers or types of rulers. The ones were called ephors, others were called ancients or the wise, and still others were called kings. And it seems as if their rules and offices were separated in such a way that only in a few things would one be under the other . . . perhaps the kings were sovereigns over the other rules."[77] Here the correspondences are clear. The kings, as sovereigns, were the royal element, the ancients, as wise ones, were the aristocratic element, and the ephors, "taken or elected indifferently from all those of the people,"[78] were the democratic element. The actual correspondences are not as significant as the fact that Oresme considers that the institutions of these three polities are analogous: Sparta, the classical Greek example of a mixed constitution; Rome, the polity which was to Polybius (of whose work Oresme was ignorant) and was again to be a prime exemplar of the mixed constitution; and medieval France. All three developed, in his view, governmental bodies that effectively balanced the power of the king.

Speaking of Aristotle's idea that there must be one highest office, Oresme writes: "The ephorate is one most principal rule as is the Senate of Rome or as is the *parlement* of France."[79] Now, clearly the king of France,

[76] Oresme, *Le Livre de Politiques*, 6, chap. 12, p. 274.

[77] Oresme, *Le Livre de Politiques*, 2, chap. 17, p. 102. "En Lacedemone avoit .iii. princes ou manieres de princes. Les uns estoient appellés effores, les autres estoient diz anciens ou sages et les autres estoient diz roys. Et semble que leur princeys et offices fussent separees sans ce que l'un fust soubz l'autre fors en peu de choses . . . les roys . . . estoient il souverains par sus les autres princeys."

[78] Aristotle, *Politics*, 2, chap. 17, p. 102. "Et nientmoins, il estoient faiz et pris ou esleus indifferentement de tous ceulz du peuple." This is a text passage following closely the gloss just quoted.

[79] Oresme, *Le Livre de Politiques*, 6, chap. 12, p. 274. " 'Efforie' est .i. princey ou office tres principal, si comme estoit le senat de Rome ou si comme le parlement de France."

as the sovereign, is in Oresme's opinion a greater power than *parlement*. His point must be twofold. First, when he speaks of office he must refer to offices under the king, of which the *parlement* can be regarded as the most important. Second, as the arbiter of law, *parlement* is the highest office and is not subject to correction even by the king. And yet he does not regard *parlement* as having authority over the other offices in all matters; for example, he remarks that as with other democratic institutions, neither the *parlement* nor the Chamber of Accounts is to be regarded as over the other.[80] His emphasis, then, is on division of function or separation of powers, and *parlement* is highest in that it deals with the highest affairs, that is, the law, and has no superior, even the king.

While the king is sovereign, in some sense the whole body of citizens must, as Oresme writes many times, be stronger than the king. This suggests another possible mixed constitutional arrangement. So far with respect to France Oresme has been making analogies between mixed constitutions and one set of French institutions. But he immediately moves from this statement on the supremacy of *parlement* to take up the issue of how and when representative councils can be called. The transition is curious, as if *parlement* itself were more on the order of the English Parliament. The problem is that Aristotle has enforced such an approach; he begins by saying that the ephorate is such a supreme body, and then immediately asks how councils can be formed. Rather than grapple with this problem Oresme chooses to treat the adjacent comments as unrelated. Although Oresme never unites these two types of mixed constitution (king and *parlement*; king, council, and general assembly) he does make several clear statements about the role of the assembly of citizens in restraining the king, the most interesting of which imposes a mixed constitution on the Olympian gods:

> Seneca recites in his book *Natural Questions* [2.33] that the ancient philosophers said that there were nine kinds of lightning, and they divide them into three groups of three, and thus there were three general types. And they say that the first does no harm, the second does harm, and the third destroys everything. The first Jupiter or Jove can hurl all alone on his authority, the second he cannot use without the council of the twelve gods chosen and ordained to this, the third he cannot use without the council of all the gods—the sovereign ones as well as the others. Afterwards Senaca says that these philosophers who were most wise did not intend that the truth would be such, but

[80] Oresme, *Le Livre de Politiques*, 6, chap. 2, pp. 258–59. "Aussi comme l'en diroit que la Chambre des Comptes ne eust a resgarder sus le Parlement, ne le Parlement sus elle. Et aussi du grant conseil et des autres offices; ce est condition democratique." Historically, *parlement* and the Chamber of Accounts originated as a division of the king's council under the reign of St. Louis. *Parlement* had regard to justice and the Chamber of Accounts to finance.

through poetry they wanted to signify that the king could help by himself, but that he should not injure without council. Thus says Seneca. And it seems that he wanted to say that to the example of Jupiter, whom they thought to be king of the sky, the earthly king can on his own authority admonish, threaten, and lightly correct. But he ought not sentence any to death without the council of many. And he should not destroy a people or country without the council of all the wise of his kingdom. And perhaps, but I do not know, the twelve peers of France were anciently ordained to the similitude of the twelve gods mentioned. Afterwards it appears by this where it is said that the council of all the gods is more powerful and greater than the council of twelve, and it appears also that the council of such a multitude is better than that of a small number; because it is the multitude of gods which is reasonable according to the ancients.[81]

The general assembly of citizens is in Oresme's view an essential concomitant of any of the good polities. These, in order to exist, presuppose the existence of a reasonable multitude, which has a right to rule and is by nature greater than the possibly smaller ruling group—what he calls the sovereign, which is the greatest power in the state only in the sense that it exercises ordinary jurisdiction.[82]

A king who tries to rule without such a council is more a tyrant than a king. Oresme makes this clear in a comment about the Church: "If the

---

[81] Oresme, *Le Livre de Politiques*, 3, chap. 13, p. 135. "Senaque recite ou livre des Questiones naturelez [2.33] que les philosophes anciens disoient que de foudres sunt ix manieres et les partoient et mettoient .iii. et .iii. et ainsi estoient .iii. en general. Et disoient que la premiere ne fait mal, la secunde fait mal et la tierce gaste tout. La premiere Jupiter ou Joves la peut envoier ou jectet tout seul de son auctorité; la seconde il n'en peut ferir sans le conseil de .xii. diex a ce esleus et ordenés; la tierce il n'en peut user sans le conseil des diex tant dez souverains comme dez autres. Apres dit Senaque que ces philosophes qui furent tres sages n'intendirent pas que la verité fust tele, mes par maniere de poëtrie il vouloient par ce signifier que le roy peut tout seul aider, mes il ne doit pas nuire sans conseil. Ce dit Senaque. Et semble que il vueille dire que a l'example de Jupiter, lequel il disoient estre roy du ciel, le roy terrien peut de son auctorité admonester, manacier et legierement corriger. Mes il ne doit pas aucun mettre a mort sans le conseil de pluseurs. Et si ne doit pas gaster une gent ou un païz sans le conseil de tous les sages de son roialme. Et par aventure, mes je ne le sei pas, que les .xii. pers de France furent jadis ordenés a la similitude dez .xii. dieux a esté faicte mencion. Apres il appert par ce que dit est que le conseil de tous les diex est plus pesant et plus grant que le conseil de .xii., et appert aussi de quele multitude le conseil est melleur que de un petit nombre; car c'est de multitude de diex qui sunt raisonnables selon les anciens." Oresme is led to give this example by a misunderstanding of Aristotle's interjection "by Jupiter!" Oresme assumes that Aristotle means "by the example of Jupiter," that is, that the government of the gods is a model for humans.

[82] Oresme, *Le Livre de Politiques*, 5, chap. 24, p. 241. See also 3, chap. 13, p. 135, where Oresme writes in generalizing the theory of Jupiter's lightening that the few or the one have sovereign rule but that the multitude judge in councils great works which touch the common good.

polity of the Holy Church were not governed by supernatural influence and by the special grace of the Holy Spirit, to say that the pope is above the laws and above the General Council, this would not be honor for this polity according to this doctrine; because by this one would make it more similar to tyranny than to kingdom."[83] The implication is clear that at least a regal king in a secular monarchy should be subject to law and council. And despite his disclaimer it is also clear to me that Oresme envisioned the perfect Church government as a mixed constitution under law, combining the papal monarchy, the aristocracy of the cardinals, and the timocracy of the many assembled in the General Council.

Babbitt argues that unlike John of Paris and Pierre d'Ailly Oresme does not advocate a mixed constitution for the Church but rather a limited monarchy. She is not clear on the distinction; her position seems even more unclear in the light of her favorable quotation of Figgis who identifies the mixed constitution and limited monarchy: "The belief of the Conciliar writers . . . was that this constitution was a πολιτέια, a limited monarchy, in which while the monarchical principle is preserved the danger of tyranny should be removed by the power of a small body of permanent advisors, a continual council, and ultimately checked by a large representative assembly."[84] This is precisely what Oresme advocates for the Church: he argues for a papal monarchy limited by the College of Cardinals and the General Council. This is exactly the kind of mixed constitution that he repeatedly supports in Sparta, Rome, and France. One could imagine a limited monarchy restrained only by law or a limited polity in which another group representing the same interests, for example, two opposed kings or aristocratic councils, restrains the ruling group; in these cases the limited government would not properly be a mixed constitution. But this is not the case here. Babbitt's reference to Oresme's distaste for a Church run by Cardinals and to his neglect to mention the congregation of the faithful as the final source of authority in the Church does not prove that Oresme did not regard it as a mixed constitution. The first only shows that Oresme opposed a pure aristocratic form for the Church, and the second does not deny a role, if not the sovereign role, to the whole body of the faithful. But in fact Oresme does imply that this group, or rather the subgroup of the reasonable multitude, does have ultimate power, if not to dispense with God's plan, at least to legislate in those areas left to humans.

In his most positive (in the sense that it contains no disclaimer) state-

---

[83] Oresme, *Le Livre de Politiques*, 6, chap. 12, p. 274. "Et donques par les choses desus dictes appert que se la policie de Sainte Eglise ne estoit gouvernee par influence supernaturele et par grace especiale du Saint Esperit, dire que le pape est par desus les drois et sus le Concile General, ce ne seroit pas honneur pour cest policie selon ceste doctrine; car par ce, l'en la feroit plus semblable a tirannie que a royalme."

[84] Babbitt, *"Livre de Politiques,"* p. 370, n. 54, p. 338, n. 11; J. N. Figgis, Political Theory *From Gerson to Grotius*, p. 44.

ment about the Church Oresme insists that it must be considered as a polity in the Aristotelian sense despite its special status and unequaled extent: "The community of those whom we call the 'people of the Church' can be called a city. And they have a polity which is universal and general in many countries and kingdoms. And it should be a mirror and exemplar for other polities, and it should direct them." His opinion is that as it stood in his day the Church failed to come up to this ideal; not only was it not the simply best polity, it was more similar to "tyranny than to a kingdom."[85]

Why was this? Well, in the first instance because of the pope's assumption of a plenitude of power, whereas he should be restrained both by law and other powers, as is any other king. Oresme begins by addressing the corruption of the Roman Republic and then switches to the Church:

> But since the people transported or gave all power to the ruler, and they put the ruler over the law, it soon appeared that their polity went into corruption and their dominion into decline. . . . And if some should say that according to Aristotle in the following Seventh Book, the sacerdotal polity of the Church is as a royal polity and then that the sovereign mortal ruler of this polity should have moderated power under the subjects in the manner above said, and should be under the law, or that the above inconveniences would follow, especially if his power were greatly extended or be far from the mean beyond the above regulation, I answer that . . . to discuss or determine of these transcends and goes above this science, but perhaps some profitable things could be advised for such a polity by this philosophy in natural light, by reason and by human prudence.[86]

In many other places Oresme attacks the idea of plenitude of power, stating, for example, that full power without laws is wrong, and adding that the Church especially should take note of this and guard against it.[87]

[85] Oresme, *Le Livre de Politiques*, 4, chap. 16, p. 189. "La communité de ceulz que nous appellons 'gens d'Eglise' peut estre dicte cité. Et ont une policie qui est universale et generale en pluseurs païs et royalmes. Et doit estre miroer et exemplaire des autres policies et les adrecier." 3, chap. 24, p. 160. "Il ne seroient pas dignes de estre gouverneés par policie tres bonne simplement." 6, chap. 6, p. 274. "L'en la feroit plus semble a tirannie que a royalme."

[86] Oresme, *Le Livre de Politiques*, 6, chap. 25, pp. 242–43. "Mes depuis que le peuple transporta ou bailla toute posté au prince et que il mist le prince sus la lay, assés tost apparut que leur policie ala en empirance et leur prosperité en deffaillant et leur domination en declinant. . . . Et se aucun disoit que selon Aristote ou .vii. livre ensuiant, la policie sacerdotal ou de l'Eglise est aussi comme policie royal et donques le souverain prince mortal de ceste policie doit avoir sus les subjects posté moderee en la maniere desus dicte, et doit estre sous la lay, ou autrement s'ensuiroient les inconveniens desus mis; meisement se sa posté estoit grandement esloingnee ou loing du moien et hors la regle desus dicte; je respon . . . discuter ou determiner de elles transcende et passe ceste science, fors par aventure en tante comme se aucunes choses profitables a tele policie povoient estre adivisees par ceste philosophie en lumiere naturale, par raison et par prudence humaine."

[87] Oresme, *Le Livre de Politiques*, 4, chap. 19, p. 194. "Tres plus malvese . . . quant un petit nombre . . . ou, un seul gouvernent a leur volenté de plaine posté sans lays. . . . Et pour ce,

It is not simply a question of law. The Church, according to Oresme, has too great inequality in it; that is, share in rule and honors is too severely restricted.[88] The acceptance of plenitude of power represents a gradual and regretable change from the early rule of the Church, when it had timo-cratic, and possibly aristocratic aspects: "Each of many finds something good for the city. And all assembled is best, and one says that in this man-ner the Apostles composed the Credo. . . . And similarly, in the Holy Church at the beginning and afterwards when it proceded in prosperity and in belief, all notable things were ordained by the General Councils."[89] Whether or not the assembly of apostles is a separate aristocratic group or identical with the General Council is not obvious, but the point is clear: when the Church was at its best the many limited the pope. And elsewhere he does identify the gerousia, the aristocratic element of the Carthaginian polity, as the "Sacred College," suggesting that the cardinals play a similar role in the Church.[90]

Finally, the General Council has the power to control the pope and make law for the Church independently of the pope, in the sense that his assent or order was not necessary for its summoning. In the early Church, law regulated assemblies, which met regularly and whenever necessary. Even without such a mechanism they could be summoned by secular rulers—if the papacy became a tyranny or an oligarchy, such a method would be necessary. As in a secular state the composition of the General Assembly would be limited to the elite many.[91]

---

les souverains de l'Eglise devroient plus que autres prendre garde a grant sollicitude que leur gouvernement ne tournast ou fust tourné en semblable policie.." See also 4, chap. 11, p. 178; 3, chap. 24, pp. 159–60; 3, chap. 14, p. 137.

[88] Oresme, *Le Livre de Politiques*, 3, chap. 24, p. 160. "Inequalité bien proporcionee selon ceste regle ne a pas assés esté gardee en la policie de le Eglise."

[89] Oresme, *Le Livre de Politiques*, 3, chap. 13, p. 134. "Chescun de pluseurs treuve aucune chose bonne pour la cité. Et tout ensemble est tres bon, et l'en dit qu'en ceste maniere les Apostelz composerent le Credo. . . . Et semblablement, en Sainte Eglise au commencement et apres quant elle procedoit en prosperité et en croissance, toutes choses notables estoient ordinees par les conciles generals." See also 4, chap. 9, p. 176.

[90] Oresme, *Le Livre de Politiques*, 2, chap. 21, p. 108. "Il est dit de 'geros,' qui est 'saint' ou 'sacre'; car ce estoit .i. saint college selon les Calcedones."

[91] Oresme, *Le Livre de Politiques*, 6, chap. 12, p. 274. "Comment ceste multitude doit estre assemblee. Premierement, il est possible que par la lay est ordené et assigné temps determiné quant ceste assemblee doit estre faite; si comme anciennement fu establi que les conciles de Sainte Eglise fussent de an en an a certain terme. Item, peut estre que par la lay sunt deter-minés et designés certains cas lesquelz quant il aviennent, il convient faire ceste assemblee. Si comme en Sainte Eglise pluseurs conciles furent faiz jadis pour discuter et determiner de divisions et divers opinions de la foy." 3, chap. 24, p. 161. "Et pluseurs conciles . . . furent faiz du commandement des empereurs et des roys, et eulz presens et autres seculiers . . . le princey de la court de Romme se trasist a la similitude de princey olygarchique ou tirannique." In this regard Oresme takes one of several swipes at the mendicants. 4, chap. 16, p. 189. "Such people of the Church should be citizens and not laborers or craftsmen . . . they should

There are some differences between the Church and a secular state. The reasonable multitude, institutionalized in a General Assembly, is, as I have shown, what we would call the sovereign power. It has the right and, indeed, at times the responsibility to institute varying types of government—something not possible for the Church. "Naturally," Oresme writes, "some multitudes want to be governed by a king and some by a small number of virtuous people and some by all the citizens or by themselves. And the government which is suitable by nature and is expedient to one multitude is not suitable to another according to the variety of customs and the size of the region and the times and other circumstances." The simply best polity (that is, a mixed monarchy) may not suit a particular people.[92] In any case the reasonable multitude has ultimate control; if this group consists of only one or a few, no good polity can be achieved.

This being the case, any good polity except for the common polity, which I have already noted, Oresme considers to be a nonstandard mixture of oligarchy and democracy, is by its very nature a mixed constitution. Peter of Auvergne and Engelbert of Admont took a similar position. In this, as in so much, Oresme blends the views of Thomas Aquinas and Peter of Auvergne. Thomas felt that a mixed constitution was especially necessary for a corrupt people—indeed, this was one argument he used in suport of what he saw as the Old Testament mixed constitution of Moses. Peter of Auvergne rejected the notion that a "bestial" people could serve a useful role in government, but thought that a good king or a good few could exist even if their people were bestial. Oresme partially follows Peter of Auvergne; he also feels that a certain minimum virtue should be required for a share in government, but he also feels that a virtuous people is necessary for any good government. On the other hand, Oresme goes beyond the assignment of a purely contributory role for the multitude; as it was for Thomas its primary function is to limit the power and thereby balance the ruling element, be it king or aristocracy. Also, like Thomas, Oresme saw the value of giving all a share in power to ensure that everyone is satisfied with the polity. In addition to the examples already cited Oresme mentions that in the French monarchy offices like *parlement* or the Chamber of Accounts are loved more if they incorporate both rich and poor.[93]

---

have honorable estate. And then to establish or approve that some people of the Church should be poor simply, would be unsuitable according to this science."

[92] Oresme, *Le Livre de Politiques*, 3, chap. 26, p. 163. "Naturelement aucune multitude veult estre gouvernee par roy et aucune par un petit nombre de gens vertueus et aucune par tous les citoiens ou par soy meismes. Et le gouvernement qui est convenable par nature et expedient a une multitude ne est pas convenable a l'autre selon la varieté des meurs et de la quantité de la region et du temps et des autres circumstances." 4. chap. 1, p. 165. "Ce est assavoir supposé que ceste multitude soit tele qu'elle ne pourroit actaindre a policie tres bonne simplement, le legislateur doit savoir quele policie est la mell[e]ur ou la tres bonne a quoy ceste multitude pourroit actaindre."

[93] Oresme, *Le Livre de Politiques*, 5, chap. 31, p. 251.

But limitation of power is the essence of Oresme's theory—it is the one theme to which he always returns. The less limited a government is, the more it is similar to tyranny. He even manages to impose this idea on those sections of the *Politics* most supportive of absolute kingship—passages accepted as such and approved even by Thomas Aquinas. There are a series of mistranslations involved. Aristotle wrote that if there exists one of transcendently superior virtue he deserved to rule absolutely and permanently as king and that the citizens should not rule in turn but always be subject to him. Moerbeke translated this passage to read that such a superior man should not be subject "according to a part," which Thomas Aquinas and following him most medieval theorists took to mean that he should not be subject to the law. Oresme translates this in yet another way: "And it does not appear that the multitude should be subject to him according to a part." Now, Thomas Aquinas did not believe that such a theoretically perfect absolute monarchy could exist, but he approved it in principle if the right king could be found. Oresme does not want to accept it even theoretically. Therefore, he interprets the passage in a way that allows him to keep his limited king even in this case: "This [that the multitude should not be subject to him according to a part] is to say, it seems to me, that no one of this polity should be exempt from his dominion and jurisdiction."[94]

Limitation thus exists in all good governments—which the reasonable multitude exercises by means of law and through correction and even deposition of rulers who rule unjustly or beyond their jurisdiction. The last claim is controversial. Babbitt alleges that Oresme waffles on the issue but ultimately rejects actual sedition even for the common good. If she means by this that it is always wrong for individuals to take action against a ruler, even a tyrannical one, and even if good results, she is correct. But Oresme does allow the reasonable multitude to overthrow the ruler. He poses the problem as a conflict of authorities—Peter of Auvergne, who approved sedition for just cause, and the Bible, which always treated sedition as an evil—but concludes:

> Because, according to Aristotle . . . all the multitude together has the ordinary power to correct rulers. And when all together or those deputed to this make such corrections by one will, this is not sedition and they do not "resist the power" because they have sovereign power. And thus the Romans did concerning Nero and those of Jerusalem concerning Queen Athaliah. . . . And especially when the oppressions and the tyrannies are very excessive, the mul-

---

[94] Aristotle, *Politics*, 3.17.1288.a.30 (Moerbeke). "Quare relinquitur solum obedire tali et dominum esse non secundum partem, sed simpliciter." 3, chap. 26, p. 163. "Et ne appartient pas que la multitude lui soit subjecte selon partie." Oresme, *Le Livre de Politiques*, III, c.26, p. 163. "Ce est a dire, ce me semble, que nul de celle policie ne doit estre exempte de sa dominacion et jurisdicion."

titude can do this justly if it is not bestial and servile . . . all the multitude can
repel this violence if it be outrageously grave.[95]

Thus it is only individual action against a ruler that Oresme opposes—
rulers who opposed the reasonable multitude would themselves be com-
mitting sedition. On the other hand, an unreasonable multitude may not
legitimately oppose even an evil king, who must be an agent of God's punishment. In this way Oresme is able to combine the ideas of people's sovereignty and the Augustinian idea of government as punishment for sin.
Like Ptolemy of Lucca, however, he ignores Augustine's idea that all peoples by virtue of original sin deserve the punishment of government. For
Augustine all multitudes are by nature bestial; for Oresme reasonable multitudes seem to be the general rule or at least quite common.

Even sedition, though evil, may serve God's purpose—as in the case of
the sedition against Julius Caesar and David.[96] One might question the
difference between the revolts against Nero and Caesar. His thought may
be that Nero was overthrown by the army, which in the medieval understanding of Roman Law was the body which made emperors, and thus
could be interpreted as being the reasonable multitude. On the other hand
individuals, albeit well-intentioned individuals, assassinated Julius Caesar.
The difference between the cases of Athaliah and David is more clear:
Athaliah was deposed by the rightful king with the support of the people;
David was attacked by individuals.

Oresme found models for his perfect kingship, which is in a sense the
most limited government, in Aristotle's examples of mixed constitutions,
in the government of the ancient Jews, in the Roman Republic,[97] and most

[95] Babbit, "Livre de Politiques," pp. 242–45; Oresme, Le Livre de Politiques, 5, chap. 1, p.
204. "Car selon Aristote. . .toute la multitude ensemble a posté ordinaire de corriger les
princes. Et quant tous ensemble ou les deputés a ce funt teles corrections d'une volenté, ce ne
est pas sedition et si ne resistent pas a la posté, car il ont puissance souveraine. Et ainsi firent
les Romains de Neron l'empereur, et ceulz de Jherusalem de la reine Athalie. . . . Et meisement quant les oppressions et tirannies sunt tres excessives ce peut faire justement la multitude
se elle ne est bestial et servile . . . toute la multitude peut bien repeller ceste violence se elle est
grevee outrageusement."

[96] Oresme, Le Livre de Politiques, 5, chap. 1, pp. 204–5. See also 3, chap. 23, p. 154; 2,
chap. 22, p. 112; 7, chap. 29, p. 323; and 3, chap. 24, p. 157.

[97] Oresme, Le Livre de Politiques, 2, chap. 21, p. 108. Oresme compares the organization of
the Chalcedonian state, one of Aristotle's mixed constitutions, with that of the Jews and the
Romans. In particular he equates the Council of 104 in Chalcedonia with the Roman Council
of 320 described in I Machabees, and mentions that these are like the council of the Jews
described in Exodus. Oresme's approval of the Roman Republic is yet another blow to Baron's thesis that no reasoned opposition to the Empire and support of the Republic based on
an analysis of the decline of virtue existed in this period or country. Oresme's analysis is
precisely in these terms: the Republic flourished because of the virtue and participation of the
reasonable multitude and was only transformed into the despotic Empire because of the loss
of reason among the multitude.

significantly in the France of his own day under his patron Charles V. His identification of all these examples makes it clear that he regarded France as a mixed constitution, even though he is not completely successful in making a strict correspondence of parts. This is undoubtedly a result of the fact that the institutional structure was not yet completely in place in France. But as a supporter of the mixed constitution Oresme wanted to find such a structure, and in one of his attempts presents France as a classical blend of monarchy, aristocracy, and democracy represented by king, peers, and general assembly (the nascent Estates General), each part with a function and power limiting the others.

Oresme was undoubtedly elitist in his conception of which people could be admitted to the reasonable multitude and thus to the general assembly. But his theory of the mixed constitution is the most thorough and the most universal of application of any in our period. Although its wide influence is questionable, it stands on its own as an independent treatment of a type of government which had exercised a fascination on medieval political theorists in the centuries following the rediscovery of the *Politics*, and did exert an influence on European political theory at least by means of the theories of Church government promoted by Jean Gerson and Pierre d'Ailly.

PART 4

The Fifteenth Century and the Early Modern Period

Chapter 13

CONCILIARISM

NICOLE ORESME is a natural stopping point for the medieval Aristotelian discussion of mixed constitutionalism and limited government, but he in no way represents the end of this mode of thought. The purpose of this chapter and the next two is to make connections between medieval and early modern mixed constitutionalism without dwelling on any one thinker. It will no longer be so intimately tied to close analysis of Aristotle, but it will nonetheless be present in much of the political thought of the fifteenth and sixteenth century. At the same time, especially in the sixteenth century, some writers, whom I will rarely mention, turn to theories of absolute kingship existing by divine right, the very antithesis of mixed constitutionalism or any other medieval political theory. But the older arguments persist, remain important, and tie directly into the flowering ideas of limited government in the seventeenth and eighteenth centuries. What is more, these arguments persist in forms very similar to the medieval ones, though increasingly dressed up in classical, and especially Polybian, garb—particularly in Italy where humanists loathed and deprecated scholasticism and medieval thought in general, not realizing just how dependent they were upon it. It is not my intention, nor is it within the scope of this book, to trace all the lines of transmission of medieval mixed constitutional theory in any comprehensive way through the early modern period. I may return to this in a future work, but for now my purpose is simply to demonstrate that the mixed constitutional ideas and modes of thought that I have shown to have developed in the thirteenth and fourteenth centuries persisted and played a major part in the thinking of a wide variety of later and influential political theorists. Thus, early modern mixed constitutionalism is not primarily the result of a new revival of classical ideas, but rather a development of medieval thought.

The political and ecclesiastical near-anarchy that characterized late medieval society had much to do both with the desire for strong monarchies, which resulted in the nationalism and emergence of the so-called New Monarchies of England, France, and Spain around 1500 and the post-Schism papacy, and the desire to restrain irresponsible kings, popes, and nobles bent on self-aggrandizement and enrichment. So for the most part the fifteenth- and sixteenth-century writings are more in the nature of treatises on particular governments—usually monarchies in Northern Europe and Republics in Italy—than general works on government as a whole.

This is nowhere more true than in the Church. By the end of the "Babylonian Captivity" (1305–78) and the Great Schism (1378–1415) many clerics came to believe that peace and unity could be preserved only by a fundamental restructuring of Church government. The conciliar movement sought to establish the principle that a General Council (which was not in itself a new body but could be traced to the early Christian centuries) was the authoritative legislative and doctrinal organ for the entire Church, superior even to the pope. The authority of a General Council had never been questioned, but always before the pope himself called and presided over it, personally sanctifying and ratifying its decrees. Now, to end the Schism it had to act in opposition to the two (and later three) popes simultaneously claiming canonical legitimacy. To defend such an action theorists looked back to the canon lawyers of the previous three centuries and to political theorists such as John of Paris, William of Ockham, and Marsilius of Padua.[1] None of the conciliarists was so radical as to suggest, as had Ockham and Marsilius, that the members of the Church were free to establish any government that might please them—several popes, no pope, or equal rule of bishops, for example. All accepted the papal monarchy. The only alternatives then were either to vest electoral and correctional sovereignty in the congregation of the faithful, which would be obligated by divine commission to establish a pope or to argue for some sort of coordinate power among the pope, General Council, and possibly the College of Cardinals. In practice, most writers did both to some extent, placing ultimate sovereignty in the whole Church as represented by a General Council, but insisting on a necessary constitutional role for the pope and cardinals.

An obvious defense of this position would be to argue that the Church is an Aristotelian mixed constitution established by God as the best form for His people and taking its positive laws and officials from the consent of its members. This is exactly what two of the most important conciliarists— Pierre d'Ailly (1350–1420) and Jean Gerson (1362–1428?)—maintained. Both men were French and associated with the University of Paris. Both, therefore, came from the tradition of John of Paris, Jean Buridan, and Nicole Oresme. The influence of John of Paris (and Thomas Aquinas) is most evident in their work, but Nicole Oresme undoubtedly exercised a seminal influence on both, especially on Gerson, who actually used Oresme's translation and commentary in his role as tutor to the dauphin. Perhaps because of this circumstance Gerson goes beyond a narrow concern with reforming the Church to draw conclusions affecting the French monarchy and, by implication, all secular governments.

[1] This whole development of conciliar ideology from earlier medieval thought is admirably developed by Tierney, *Foundations of the Conciliar Theory*.

In contrast, D'Ailly focuses entirely on the Church and, as a cardinal himself, is especially interested in establishing a definite constitutional role for his peers. He introduces the mixed constitution in a treatise written at the Council of Constance just after the deposition of Pope John XXIII, a pontiff whose line was established at the Council of Pisa, in whose deliberations d'Ailly himself participated. D'Ailly gives many justifications for the Council's actions, but begins this line of argument by explaining why it does not contradict God's ordination to act against a pope: Although the papal dignity is from God, whence it can be neither made greater or less by humans, nevertheless, the use of plenitude of power can be restricted by authority of a General Council to exclude its abuse.[2]

By what authority can the Council do this? Others, and d'Ailly himself, often resort to a purely pragmatic answer summed up in the Roman Law maxim that "necessity knows no law." In other words, the Church (and any society) must be able to protect itself against schism and heresy, and therefore must be able to do whatever is necessary to avoid them. In particular, God has promised that his Church can never fail, and this promise would be hollow if a schismatic or heretical pope could not be controlled. But this argument gives authority to a council or the cardinals only in extreme circumstances. Here, d'Ailly is concerned with establishing ongoing participation in Church government and so resorts to general political principles:

> But for regulating the use of plenitude of power and to exclude its abuse, it is proper to consider that it is not expedient for the Church (which is said to have a regal [rule] of priests) to be governed by a purely regal government, but by one mixed with aristocracy and democracy, and I mean democracy in the general sense as the rule of the people and not strictly, as one contrary to polity, which is a certain species of government or of temperate rule according to virtue, as Aristotle says in his *Politics* . . . although the government of kings, in which one singularly rules the multitude according to virtue is better than any other simple rule, as Aristotle shows in III *Politics*, nevertheless if it be mixed with aristocracy, in which many exercise dominion according to virtue; and with democracy, in which the people rules, such a government is better, in so far as in a mixed government all have some part in rule, and even because although regal government is the best in itself, if it is not corrupted; nevertheless, on account of the great power that is conceded to a king, the government

---

[2] Pierre d'Ailly, *Tractatus De Ecclesiae, Concilii Generalis, Romani pontificis, et Cardinalium Auctoritate*, cols. 945–46. "Licet Papalis dignitas a Deo sit, unde ab homine nec major nec minor fieri potest; tamen, usus plenitudinis Potestatis, ad excludendum abusum, potest Concilii Generalis authoritate restringi." Oakley's *Pierre d'Ailly* is an excellent book about d'Ailly's political thought in general.

easily degenerates into tyranny, unless there be perfect virtue in the king, which is found rarely and in few.[3]

D'Ailly immediately proceeds to show that the form approved by the political thinkers was sanctified by God for his Church:

> As a sign of this thing, God instituted among the people of Israel, to whom the Christian people succeeds, a king in a certain way, although not with full power, as is clear in Moses, Joshua, and their successors, who had precedence over that people, as Numbers 27 and Judges 2 makes clear. Moreover, although there was a regal government among them, in so far as one principally had precedence over all, nevertheless there was something of aristocracy, in that under that one seventy-two elders were chosen, as Deuteronomy 1 makes clear. But there was also something of democracy in that the seventy-two were chosen from all the people and by all the people, as is said in the same place. Thus it seems manifest that it would be the best rule of the Church, if under one pope many were chosen from and by each province, and such ought to be Cardinals, who ought to govern the Church with the pope and under him, and ought to temper his use of plenitude of power.[4]

The sources for d'Ailly's argument are evident. The majority of his exposition on simple forms, the mixed constitution, and the best form of Church government is directly, and in most places word for word, from John of Paris, but there are some small but significant modifications. First,

---

[3] d'Ailly, *De Ecclesiae*, col. 946. "Sed ad regulandum usum plenitudinis Potestatis et excludendum abusum eiusdem, considerare convenit, quod non expedit Ecclesiae (quae habere dicitur Regale Sacerdotium) quod ipse regatur regimine Regio puro, sed mixto cum Aristocratia et Democratia, et capitur hic Democratia generaliter, pro Principatu populi, et non stricte, prout contrariatur Politiae quae est species quaedam regiminis, vel Principatus temperati, secundum virtutem, ut capit Aristoteles, *in Politicis*. Pro cuius declaratione, sciendum est, quod licet regimen Regium, in quo singulariter principatur multitudini, secundum virtutem sit milius [sic] quolibet alio regimine simplici, ut ostendit Philosophus, 3 Politicorum, tamen si fiat mixtum cum Aristocratia, in qua plures dominantur secundum virtutem; et cum Democratia, in qua populus principatur, tale regimine melius est, in quantum in regimine mixto omnes aliquam partem habent in Principatu: et etiam quia licet regimen regale sit optimum in se, si non corrumpatur; tamen propter magnam Potestatem quae Regi conceditur, de facili regimen degenerat in tyrannidem, nisi sit in Rege perfecta virtus, quae raro et in paucis reperitur."

[4] d'Ailly, *De Ecclesiae*, col. 946. "In cuius rei signum, in populo Israël, cui succedit populus Christianus, Deus instituit quodammodo Regem, licet non cum plena Potestate, ut patet in Moïse, et Josue, et eorum successoribus, qui toti illi populo praeerant, ut patet Numer. 27 et Judicum 2. Licet autem in eis esset regimen Regale, in quantum unus principaliter praeerat omnibus, erat tamen aliquid de Aristocratia, in quantum sub illo uno, septuaginta duo seniores eligebantur de omni populo, et ab omni populo, ut ibidem dicitur: sic etiam manifeste videtur, quod esset optimum regimen Ecclesiae, si sub uno Papa eligerentur plures de omni, et ab omni Provincia, et tales deberent esse Cardinales, qui cum Papa et sub eo Ecclesiam regerent, et usum plenitudinis Potestatis temperarent."

he takes out all references to the particular nature of the Israelites. Both John and Thomas Aquinas had said that the mixed constitution was best "at least for that people," and had stressed that the danger of degeneration into tyranny was especially real for the Jews who were cruel and avaricious by nature. I have argued that both did not mean thereby to imply that the mixed constitution was not universally best, but their words have been so read even today. D'Ailly wants to eliminate the possibility that someone might deny the applicability to the Church on the basis that this form is suited only to the Jews. On the other hand, he does not really care about applying the mixed constitution to secular government (although it is clear from his presentation that he believes that this also is best) and so he can take a step deliberately avoided by John and make a typological argument—the ancient Jews are a type for the Church, and so God intended by instituting a mixed constitution for the Jews to give a sign to the Church as to its proper ordering. The Church is a natural political community subject to Aristotelian analysis, but it is also the divinely established congregation of the faithful. John says that such "would be the best rule of the Church," as if it were up to us to organize it as we wish (the only necessity being to preserve papal monarchy in some form); d'Ailly uses the same words, but by preceding them with a typological statement implies that only one way is at all in line with God's will.

D'Ailly is a conciliarist, but insofar as possible he wants to give the greatest authority to the College of Cardinals. This explains his third addition to John—the identification of the many chosen by and from each province with the cardinals and not with the General Council itself. Immediately following the passages just quoted, d'Ailly goes on at length about the utility and necessity of the cardinals and about their role according to canon law as coadjutors of the pope. It is they, he says, who are to "temper" the pope's use of the plenitude of power vested in the Church. This is his fourth addition to John, and in this case he takes the idea of tempering not from John of Paris, but from Thomas Aquinas, who used the same word to explain why a mixed constitution is best.[5] As one would expect from one involved in deposing a monarch, d'Ailly supports the mixed constitution as a way to balance the ruling elements, particularly the monarchical one that normally has the greatest power.

By his support of the Cardinals d'Ailly does not thereby eliminate or

[5] Thomas writes about tempering in *On the Government of Rulers*, a work certainly available to d'Ailly since he refers to it in another regard in the very next passage (albeit to Ptolemy of Lucca's portion). If he had *Summa Theologiae* at hand, however, d'Ailly almost certainly would have appended Thomas's assertion (dropped by John of Paris in the passage that d'Ailly got from him) that because monarchy and aristocracy are the best simple forms their combination with democracy is best of all. This would have been even more support for the aristocratic cardinalate.

trivialize the role of the General Council. He writes that the plenitude of ecclesiastical power belongs separably to the pope, inseparably to the whole Church, and representatively to the General Council.[6] The General Council, then, has the right, as representative of the whole Church to meet and enact legislation for the good of the Church and limit the plenitude of power of and bind the pope. In fact, d'Ailly wants to institutionalize the General Council by having it meet every thirty or fifty years with or without the pope's approval.[7] The pope and General Council is as it were a second mixed constitution within the Church that further assures that it acts for the common good of the faithful. In many ways d'Ailly's conception is similar to that of Oresme, who also described France as a mixed monarchy limited by *parlement* on the one hand and council and General Assembly on the other. He even echoes Oresme when he states that "properly" the pope alone possesses plenitude of power since it is he who regularly uses it.[8] Oresme said the same about sovereignty in France, but did not mean to deny that the king's powers could and should be limited.

Jean Gerson also, and in many of his works, supports a mixed constitution for the Church, and he gives some of the same reasons. However, he places much less emphasis on the cardinals, and, what is more interesting, he also compares the Church to the French monarchy. While d'Ailly implies that parallels exist between temporal and ecclesiastical rule (something developed especially in John of Paris and William of Ockham, who greatly influenced them both) only Gerson draws out and employs these parallels.

On 21 July 1415, at about the same time that d'Ailly was writing his *Treatise on the Church*, after the deposition of John XXIII in May 1415, Gerson delivered a sermon at Constance in which he sets forth an application of a mixed constitution to the Church. In this he explicitly compares the governments of the Church and of France; both are mixed constitutions, but the Church is better in that it mixes all three good polities:

> The tradition of Aristotle of three polities could be considered in this place, namely a regal and monarchical [polity], in which one beneficially has precedence, to which a tyranny is opposed. Another is aristocracy, where a few and good [ones] exercise dominion, to which oligarchy is opposed. He places timocracy third, in which the people exercise dominion well, which has democracy as an opposite. Moreover, there is in between these polities that one that is better than any singular one, which is composed from regal and aristocracy, as in the kingdom of France, where the king instituted *parlement*, from which he does not shrink from being judged. But it would be the best and most

---

[6] d'Ailly, *De Ecclesiae*, col. 950.

[7] d'Ailly, *Tractatus de Materia Concilii Generalis*, p. 317.

[8] d'Ailly, *De Ecclesiae*, col. 950.

salubrious of all polities which embraced these three good [forms]: regal, aristocracy, timocracy. Moreover, the General Council is such a composite polity, having its direction more from the special assistence of the Holy Spirit and promise of Jesus Christ than from nature or from human industry. Hence it is that which we previously said, that it is the most salubrious and most efficacious regulation either for preserving or reforming or discovering the tranquil rule of the whole Church, as it were the supreme and sufficient legislator universal and potent in equity, and also legitimate and secure, and not rationally suspect by any Christians, since it proceeds from all, or as it were by the common consent or assent of all.[9]

This passage is not very clear. Gerson seems to be saying that it is the General Council itself that is the mixed constitution of three elements, but this can only be reasonable if it is seen as including the pope as monarch and possibly the cardinals (or bishops) as an aristocratic element. I say possibly because it would be more in line with the Mosaic model, which Gerson also cites (although not word for word from John of Paris as did d'Ailly),[10] to consider the council itself as the aristocratic element, democratic only in that it is chosen from and by all the faithful. D'Ailly did not apply this model to the General Council; for him the mixed constitution consisted of pope and cardinals taken from the people; the General Council was an extra-constitutional body representing the whole Church. But when Gerson is being most precise, the Council itself is the democratic element:

Conforming to the already-mentioned three polities of Aristotle distinguished in natural government we can divide the ecclesiastical polity into papal, collegial, and synodal (that is, of the general council). Papal [rule] imitates regal, the collegial [rule] of the Lord Cardinals imitates aristocracy, general synodal

[9] Jean Gerson, "Sermo super Processionibus Faciendis pro viagio Regis Romanorum," in *Opera Omnia*, 3ª pars, 2ª directio, col. 279. "Considerari posset in hoc loco Arestotelis traditio de triplici Politia, Regali scilicet et Monarchica, in qua unus bene praeest, cui Tyrannis opponitur. Altera est Aristocratia, ubi dominantur pauci et boni, cui opponitur Oligarchia. Tertiam ponit Timocratiam, in qua populus bene dominatur, quae oppositam habet Democratiam. Esset autem inter istas Politias illa melior quam aliqua singularis, quae ex Regali et Aristocratia componeretur, ut in Regno Franciae, ubi Rex instituit Parlamentum, a quo judicari non refugit. Esset vero omnium optima et saluberrima Politia, quae triplicem hanc bonam complecteretur, Regalem, Aristocratiam, et Timocratiam. Est autem Generale Concilium Politia talis composita, habens suam directionem magis ex assistentia speciali Spiritus Sancti, et promissione Jesu Christi, quam ex natura vel ex humana industria. Hinc est illud quod praediximus, quod ipsum est saluberrima et efficassima regula ad regimen totius Ecclesiae tranquillam vel conservandum vel reformandum vel inveniendum, tanquam supremus et sufficiens Legislator universalis et potens Epekeies: praeteres legitimus et securus, nec suspectus rationabiliter ab aliquibus Christianis: cum procedat omnium, vel quasi omnium consensu vel assensu."

[10] Gerson, *De Potestate Ecclesiastica*, in *Oeuvres Complètes*, vol. 6, no. 282, pp. 224–25.

[rule] imitates polity or timocracy; or rather it [the ecclesiastical polity] is a perfect polity that results from all.[11]

For Gerson and d'Ailly, both of whom were embroiled in the Schism, it is obvious that the main purpose of a mixed constitution is to restrain the monarchical element. In this regard Gerson approvingly quotes Thomas Aquinas on the tempering effect of other elements in avoiding tyranny, and both Thomas and Nicole Oresme on the necessity for a public authority in restraining a tyrant.[12] On this point Gerson echoes Oresme in seeing limitation of monarchy as the key to good government; it is this which distinguishes France—although in Gerson's view it is less than optimal in that it has no democratic element—from Germany and Italy and gives it peace and stability.[13]

For the most part Gerson feels comfortable applying secular political principles to the Church. The mixed constitution is best for the Church because it is the best form of government; Gerson feels no necessity to bring in a typological argument as did d'Ailly. The only real difference between the two spheres is that the Church must be some sort of monarchy, because Christ so ordained it, whereas all other polities are mutable:

The monarchy or regal [power] of any civil polity is removable or changeable by enacting a law, so that it might become aristocratic, but it is not thus concerning the Church, which was founded by Christ with one supreme monarch over all. . . . Christ instituted no other polity that is immutably monarchic, and in a certain way regal except for the Church. . . . It is otherwise where a community is ruled solely by natural and traditional human laws, which are laudably and usefully varied according to the variety of times and places.[14]

[11] Gerson, *De Potestate Ecclesiastica*, in *Oeuvres Complètes*, p. 248. "Possumus conformiter ad praedictam Philosophi politiam tripliciter distinctam in naturali regimine, politiam ecclesiasticam dividere, quod alia est papalis, alia est collegialis, alia synodalis seu concilii generalis. Papalis imitatur regalem, collegialis dominorum cardinalium imitatur aristocratiam; synodalis generalis imitatur politiam seu timocratiam; vel potius est perfecta politiae quae resultat ab omnibus."

[12] Gerson, *Contra les VII Assertions*, in *Oeuvres Complètes*, vol. 10, no. 514, pp. 191–92.

[13] Gerson, *Discours au Roi contre Jean Petit* (also known as *Oratio ad Regem Franciae*), in *Oeuvres Complètes*, vol. 7, no. 389, pp. 1017–18. "Sire, c'est la plus principale garde de vostre royaulme ce que vous n'avez qu'un cour de justice souveraine, c'est vostre parlement auquel vous meme répondes et tous autres subjets le doivent mieulx faire. Par deffaut d'une telle cour vont a perdition autres pays comme Allemanie et Italie ou plus fort vaint et vive qui vainche."

[14] Gerson, "De Auferabilitate papae," in *Opera Omnia*, v.ii, consideratio 8ª, col. 213. "Auferibilis est aut mutabilis, lege stante, quaelibet Politiae Civilis Monarchia seu Regalis ut fiat Aristocratica, et non sic de Ecclesia quae in uno Monarcha Supremo per universum fundata est a Christo . . . nullam aliam Politiam instituit Christus immutabiliter Monarchicam, et quoddammodo Regalem nisi Ecclesiam. . . . Secus ubi Communitas regitur Legibus solis naturalibus et traditionibus humanis, quae pro varietate temporum et locorum laudibilius et

Even in the Church the pope should not try to enforce positive canons or customs everywhere and in the same manner. Gerson believes, for example, that the schism with the Greek Church resulted from papal insensitivity to local conditions in the East. And in the Church as in secular polities the whole community possesses an inalienable right and power to correct or depose its rulers:

> And this power cannot be taken or given away by a free community, which can deal with its own affairs according to its desires, nor can it be suspended through appropriation or through some law: how much more will the Church hold this? . . . The rational power of limiting the plenitude of papal power through the Council of Holy Men is founded on this, not indeed that it should take away or diminish that power, but in its own virtuous, proper, licit, and expedient use on behalf of the whole Church in itself or in its parts; by taking the virtuous mode of this kind of power in its own use, according as the Church or the Council of Holy Ones representing it will judge.[15]

Like d'Ailly, Gerson uses the example of Moses, but to support the council, not the cardinals. After relating Jethro's advice about the Jewish government, Gerson continues:

> If Moses, who spoke famliarly to God as a friend to a friend, listened obediently to the counsel of a gentile concerning the government of the whole synagogue, how much more ought this Supreme Pontif [listen obediently] to the dictate of the whole Church or the General Council [acting] in its name. . . . Finally we conclude from the given counsel of Moses and the precept of the law in Exodus xvii, and from the institution of Christ in Matthew xviii, that nothing was previously nor will be in future a more pernicious plague on the Church than the omission of General or Provincial Councils, either in not having them or in ignoring their authority. . . . The ecclesiastical polity remains with the best government just as it was under Moses; since it was mixed from three polities: regal in Moses, aristocratic in the seventy-two elders, and timocratic since the rectors were chosen under Moses from the people and from single tribes.[16]

---

utilius variantur." See also *De Potestate Ecclesiastica*, in *Oeuvres Complètes*, vol. 6, no. 282, pp. 226–27.

[15] Gerson, "De Auferabilitate papae," in *Opera Omnia*, v.ii, consideratio 8ᵃ, cols. 213, 216. "Et haec potestas inauferibilis vel inabdicabilis est a Communitate libera, quae de rebus suis facere potest ad libitum, nec per appropriatorem vel aliquam Legem potest suspendi quanto magis hoc habebit Ecclesia? . . . fundatur in hac radice potestas rationalis limitandi plenitudinem Papalis potestatis per Sanctorum Concilium, non quidem ut tollatur vel diminuatur ipsa potestas, sed in usu suo virtuoso, decenti, licito et expedienti pro tota Ecclesia in se vel in suis partibus; accipiendo modum virtuosum huiusmodi potestatis in suo usu, pro ut Ecclesia, vel Sanctorum Concilium representans judicabit."

[16] Gerson, *De Potestate Ecclesiastica*, in *Oeuvres Complètes*, pp. 224–25. "Si Moyses loquens

Notice that Gerson's identification of the governments of the Old and New
Testament churches is not exact. Under Moses there were two parts to the
state: one monarchic and the other aristocratic; democracy had a part only
in the selection of aristocratic officials. In the Catholic Church, in contrast,
there are three bodies, each representing one of the good forms of government. Nevertheless, the democratic General Council is aristocratic in its
actual membership, and Gerson's point seems to be not that the ancient
Jews and modern Christians have the same government, but that both
combine all three good polities. This is what we would expect, taking into
consideration Gerson's rejection of typology and his support of relativism
and the validity of analogical argument. Since times have changed, it is
only reasonable that there would be a somewhat different constitutional
arrangement that preserved only the monarchical element (since God requires this) and the mixture in one way or another of the three simple
forms (since such a combination is best).

Finally, like Nicole Oresme, Peter of Auvergne, and Engelbert of Admont before him, Gerson believes that all, or almost all, polities are in fact
mixed; that, for example, there is no such thing in reality as pure monarchy. The names of the simple forms are given simply to identify the dominant element. The question is whether there is a proper balance of the good
forms and the elimination so far as possible of the bad forms of democracy,
oligarchy, and tyranny. These perversions assert themselves especially
when the polity does not effectively limit the various powers, which then
tend to become corrupt. Gerson suggests that this may be one of the ills of
the Church, commenting cryptically (and possibly echoing Oresme) that
in the bad forms rulers seek their own good, want their subjects to be
ignorant, impotent, and divided and adds, "the studious reader may know
if such can be found in the Church."[17]

Although Constance was the high point of the conciliar movement and
Gerson and d'Ailly most influential for later political thought, conciliar
thought continued throughout the fifteenth and sixteenth centuries, and

Deo familiariter sicut amicus ad amicum obedienter audivit consilium gentilis hominis in
regimine totius Synagogae, quanto magis debet hoc Summus Pontifex ad dictamen totius
Ecclesiae vel generalis concilii suo nomine. . . . Concludimus tandem ex dato Moysi consilio
et praecepto legis Exod. xvii, et ex institutione Christi, Matth. xviii, quod nulla fuit hactenus
nec erit in posterum perniciosior pestis in Ecclesia quam omissio generalium conciliorum et
provincialium vel in re ipsa vel in auctoritate . . . maneat ecclesiastica politia optimo regimine
quale fuit sub Moyse gubernata; quoniam mixta fuit ex triplici politia: regale in Moyse, aristocratica in lxxii senioribus, et timocratica dum de populo et singulis tribubus sub Moyse
rectores sumebantur."

[17] Gerson, *De Potestate Ecclesiastica*, in *Oeuvres Complètes*, pp. 248–49. "Cognoscet ex hiis
studiosus lector si possit in ecclesiastica politia tale aliquid tripliciter et proportionabiliter
inveniri . . . fere nulla est quae mixtionem excludat, sed a praedominanti talis vel talis nimi-
natur."

much of it was also influential. Many of the later conciliar writers do not mention the mixed constitution by name, but they incorporate its essential features. The Council of Basel, begun in 1431 in accordance with the decree *Frequens* issued by the Council of Constance to institutionalize General Councils, attempted to assert its authority against Pope Eugenius IV, although eventually it was to succumb to the general perception that it was overstepping the bounds of moderation. It is interesting that Joannes de Turrecremata, who supported the papal position at Basel, gives explicit support to the idea of a mixed constitution (which none of the conciliarists at Basel did), in his commentary on Gratian's *Decretum*. There he repeats Aquinas's description of the simple polities and concludes that the best form is composed of all three, where law is made by "those noble by birth together with the people" (a quotation from Isidore of Seville).[18] Turrecremata, of course, did not write with conciliarism in mind, and the most important work to come out of the Council of Basel was Nicolaus of Cusa's *On Catholic Concordance*, which he presented to the council in late 1433 or early 1434.[19] Nicolaus eventually defected to the papal side, and his respect for the papacy is evident in all his writing. In this work, however, he vigorously supports the conciliar theory. He is most celebrated for his unyielding insistence on consent as the basis of all rule, but he also presents a strong case for a balanced government in both Church and state. This is true despite the fact that Nicolaus usually follows up radical sounding principles with conservative applications that stress natural subordination and serve to limit the day-to-day role of the people to passive consent.

In his argument Nicolaus assumes a complete dualism between Church and state, so that even those things, such as infallibility, that were specifically given to the Church by God, have their parallels in the secular order. Thus, he carries the conciliar theory over to the state and consent theory from the state to the Church, which by reason of its direct institution by God would seem not to need it. There is a major shift in the formulation of his ideas, though not so much in their content at the end of book 2 and especially at the beginning of book 3. It was as he was finishing book 2 that Nicolaus read for the first time Marsilius of Padua's *Defender of Peace*. Before this time he had probably not even read Aristotle's *Politics*, for there are no earlier references to it in *On Catholic Concordance*, and all later references are demonstrably taken from Marsilius.[20] Although the theories of

[18] Joannes Turrecremata, *Commentary on Gratian's* Decretum, d.2, as reported in Carlyle and Carlyle, *Medieval Political Theory*, vol. 6, pp. 167–68.

[19] Nicolaus of Cusa, *De Concordantia Catholica Libri Tres*. See Paul E. Sigmund, *Nicholas of Cusa and Medieval Political Thought*, for a good summary and analysis of this work.

[20] See Sigmund, *Nicholas of Cusa*, p. 189. Book 3 was written later than book 2, and it omits all direct reference to Marsilius, presumably because of his image as a heretic. Cusanus does frequently mention his name at the end of book 2.

the two are generally similar, Nicolaus is often more conservative and less open to variety in government.

Nicolaus says repeatedly that consent is the basis of all government. By this, of course, he means good government. In his definition of the six forms of government, for example, he inserts Marsilius of Padua's criterion for the three good forms that they be by the will of the subjects. He justifies this by appeal to natural rights and the social contract:

> Whence since all are free by nature, all rule, whether it consists in written law or law living in the ruler . . . comes solely from the concordance and consent of the subjects. For if by nature humans are equally powerful and equally free, the true and ordained power of one naturally equal of common power can not be established except by the election and consent of the others, just as law is established by consent. . . . By a general pact human society has agreed to want to obey kings.[21]

He echoes many of the earlier writers, such as John of Paris, by grounding rule (in this case papal rule) in God through the people and councils by elective consent.[22] The question is what exactly Nicolaus means by consent, and what part the various elements of society are to have in the ordering of society. Cusanus follows Marsilius in giving ultimate power to the greater or weightier part of the citizens, and astonishingly he equates this procedure with Christ's promise that his Church can never fail:

> Since . . . according to Saint Cyprian by Christ's promise the greater part of the priesthood will not fall away from the true law, so in like manner, when things for the conservation of the republic are treated by common consent, the greater part [*maior pars*] of the people, citizens, or heroic [ones] will not fall away from the path that is right and useful for the time. Otherwise it might happen that natural desire would be frustrated, as is held as most unsuitable among the philosophers in many things. For we see that humans are political and civil animals and are naturally inclined to civility. Hence it is necessary that the weightier part [*valentior pars*] of a polity be on behalf of the remainder, as Aristotle concludes in *Politics* I.1.[23]

---

[21] Nicolaus of Cusa, *De Concordantia Catholica*, 3, *Prooemium*, 279, pp. 319–20; 2.14.127, pp. 162–63. "Unde cum natura omnes sint liberi, tunc omnis principatus, sive consistat in lege scripta sive viva apud principem . . . est a sola concordantia et consensu subiectivo. Nam si natura aeque potentes et aeque liberi homines sunt, vera et ordinata potestas unius communis aeque potentis naturaliter non nisi electione et consensu aliorum constitui potest, sicut etiam lex ex consensu constituitur . . . pacto generale convenit humana societas velle regibus oboedibus." See also 3, *Prooemium* and 3.4.

[22] Nicolaus of Cusa, *De Concordantia Catholica*, 2.34. "Principatus sit a deo per medium hominis et conciliorum, scilicet mediente consensu electivo."

[23] Nicolaus of Cusa, *De Concordantia Catholica*, 3, *Prooemium*, 270, p. 314. "Quoniam . . . secundum sanctum Cyprianum ex Christu promissione major pars sacerdotii a vera lege non

In both Church and state these things done to preserve the polity consist especially of legislation and election of officials. In the few pages following the previous quotation Nicolaus repeats many of Marsilius's arguments for the primacy of law and the ability of the weightier part to make the best law, but his is a more elitist concept than Marsilius's. It stresses the equation of the weightier part and the wise, who are better able to choose rightly than the mass of foolish people. This takes somewhat away from his sweeping combination of Roman Law and Aristotelianism to defend popular sovereignty and the primacy of law:

> Moreover, the laying down of law ought to be done by all those who ought to be bound by it or by the greater part of them by election since it ought to be for the common [good], and what touches all, ought to be approved by all, and a common definition is elicited only from the consent of all or of the greater part. . . . Thus it is even better for the republic to be governed by laws than by the best person . . . for where laws do not rule there is no polity.[24]

Just how this is to be implemented is demonstrated in some comments on the Church:

> I think that one thing ought to be added to the above, namely so that law [*lex*] can be made, or more truly ancient law [*ius*] can be renewed through that holy council, the pope can not do anything in difficult matters, especially against its canons or the canons of other universal councils, without [the consent] of the lord cardinals, who are judged to be clerics of the universal Church deputed in the above-mentioned mode; if he should do otherwise, that would be without effect. . . . And it is the ultimate resolution, that in those things touching the universal Church, it is true that the pope can do nothing without the cardinals. But I believe that to come and dispense against the canons, even in whatever particular case, this can rationally be said to concern the universal Church on account of a canon of the universal Church, which [canon] seems to be injured through a dispensation of this kind. . . . Even if the whole Church should be subjected as it were to one monarch by papal disposition, nevertheless the things of the Church, among which I believe especially to be

---

deficiet, ita pariformiter, dum communi consensu res pro conservatione rei publicae tractantur, maior pars populi, civium aut heroicorum a recta via ac pro tempore utili non deficiet. Alioquin contingeret naturalem appetitum frustrari, ut in plutibus, quod pro inconvenientissimo apud philosophantes hebetur. Videmus enim hominem animal esse politicum et civile et naturaliter ad civilitatem inclinari. Hinc oportet valentiorem partem pro remanentia politae esse, ut Aristoteles primo Politicae primo capitulo concludit."

[24] Nicolaus of Cusa, *De Concordantia Catholica*, 3, *Prooemium*, 276–77, p. 318. "Legis autem latio per eos omnes, qui per eam stringi debent, aut maiorem partem aliorum electione fieri debet, quoniam ad commune conferre debet, et quod omnes tangit, ab omnibus approbari debet, et communis diffinitio ex omnium consensu aut maioris partis solum elicitur. Quare etiam melius pro re publica exstitit legibus quam optimo viro regi . . . Ubi enim non principantur leges, ibi non est politia."

the holy canons, can [singular] not be changed or alienated according to the things said above without the consent and subscription of the clergy. For the cardinals come in the name of the clergy of the Roman Church, in so much as the Roman Church signifies monarchy, as is said above. . . . Moreover, I believe that the pope with the cardinals cannot do away with the canons of universal councils without the consent of a universal council.[25]

Nicolaus is clearly describing a mixed constitution of papal monarchy limited by the aristocracy of the cardinals and ultimately the democracy of the General Council. The very term *difficult matters* are the ones medieval Aristotelians used commonly to bind kings to the legislative supremacy of a parliament or other secular councils. Equally important is the fact that Cusanus views the cardinals not as in fact they are and were as the apointees of the pope, chosen for political expediency, but as the representatives of the ecclesiastical provinces. It is in this capacity that they serve as electors of the pope.[26] This idea, of course comes from d'Ailly and Gerson, who in turn got it from John of Paris. It is only as representatives that the cardinals have an elective power since this power ultimately resides with the people who have authorized the electors to act in their behalf but have never relinquished the right to take it back and exercise it directly. And they never even bind themselves permanently to the official elected either directly or through representatives—they can depose the pope, the emperor, or any other secular ruler, and not just for ruling badly, but even if they are motivated solely by political expediency.[27]

With regard to the Empire, Nicolaus sets up an analogous arrangement of election and limitation of rule. The privy council serves the emperor as the cardinals the pope, and an assembly of princes, electors, and delegates from the cities is like a General Council—it should meet at least for one

---

[25] Nicolaus of Cusa, *De Concordantia Catholica*, 2.21.191–193, pp. 233–35. "Ad superiora unum adiciendum esse censeo, scilicet quod per istud sacrum concilium lex fieri aut verius ius antiquum posset innovari papam in arduis negoriis maxime contra canones huius et aliorum universalium conciliorum causis urgentibus absque dominorum cardinalium, qui clerici censentur universalis ecclesiae modo supradicto deputati, non posse quidquam; alias si fecerit, quod tunc illud irritum sit. . . . Et est ultimo resolutio, quod in tangentibus universalem ecclesiam verum est papam sine cardinalibus nihil posse. Ego autem credo, quod contra canones venire et dispensare etiam in quocumque particulari casu, rationabiliter dici posset hoc concernere universalem ecclesiam propter canonem universalis ecclesiae, qui laedi per huiusmodi dispensationem videtur . . . etiam si dispositioni papali tota ecclesia subiaceret tamquam monarchae unico, tamen res ecclesiae, inter quas maxime sacros conones esse credo, iuxta superiora mutare vel alienare non potest sine sui cleri consensu et subscriptione. Nomine enim cleri Romanae ecclesiae, in quantum monarchiam significat Romana ecclesia, cardinales veniunt, ut superius quodam loco dicitur. . . . Tollere autem canones universalium conciliorum absque consensu universalis concilii credo papam cum cardinalibus non posse."

[26] Nicolaus of Cusa, *De Concordantia Catholica*, 2.18.163–65, pp. 199–203.

[27] Nicolaus of Cusa, *De Concordantia Catholica*, 2.18, 3, *Prooemium*, 3.4.

month a year and when needed to deal with difficult matters and legislation. Just as in the Church the emperor needs permission of the privy council to dispense from law and the approval of the council of both estates to change it or make any innovation concerning the entire polity. Again, this is what most medieval Aristotelians demanded. Like Aristotle, Marsilius, Oresme, and others, Nicolaus describes a well-constructed polity in biological terms: laws are the nerves of the imperial body and bind all the parts together. If the body is ill the head (emperor) should call in physicians (wise ones) to concoct an efficacious prescription, let the teeth (privy council) test it, then send it to the stomach (greater council) for final approval, and finally send the perfected medicine to the liver (judges) for distribution to each member according to its needs. The emperor, like the pope, is a judge and executor of law, not a legislator. Referring specifically to the pope Nicolaus states that a judge interprets law but does not make it, for otherwise instability would result.[28]

Nicolaus is one of the first to combine what is in all important respects a mixed constitution with the social contract and the doctrine of separation of powers. All but the last of these comes from Marsilius of Padua, who also insisted on government as an expression of the will of the people. Nicolaus also shares a Marsilian attitude toward how popular participation should be regulated, but is, as I have said, much more suspicious of their capacity. This is why his council is more elitist than that of the earlier conciliarists and Ockham. It is also why Nicolaus puts such great emphasis on Marsilus's "weightier part," which he interprets as a weighted majority even within the already restricted Church or secular council—he states this specifically with regard to the Church.[29] The masses of people express their consent passively to the decisions of their representatives who are to make law and elect the ruler. But at least he argues unambiguously for the individual election of each monarch (as in the Church and Empire) instead of the election of a dynasty (as in the national monarchies), as had most medieval thinkers, who thereby put the idea of consent one step more removed from actual political process. There is a hint that Nicolaus, like Marsilius, considers the mixed constitutional monarchy equivalent to the simple form of polity—he repeats Marsilius's statement that in a polity each citizen participates "according to his grade." As in Marsilius this suggests the weighted majority model of mixed constitution. Although Nicolaus mistrusts the people and tends to think of monarchy as the only form fully approved by God, and although at times he seems more interested with the proper hierarchy and ordained relationships of parts in any polit-

[28] Nicolaus of Cusa, *De Concordantia Catholica*, 3.35; 3.12; 3.41; 2.14, 2.20.
[29] Nicolaus of Cusa, *De Concordantia Catholica*, 2.16.

ical entity, his principles provide the basis for a full mixed constitutional theory.

Conciliar theory fell into disrepute following the defeat of the Council of Basel in the context of the general humanist tolerance of despots, but it was revived at the beginning of the sixteenth century, again in the wake of an ultimately unsuccessful Church Council—the so-called Conciliabulum of Pisa, which began in 1511. Jacob Almain and later John Mair wrote in support of the council, and both were influenced by the earlier conciliarists, especially d'Ailly and Gerson, although they did not agree with them about everything. Mair, for example, explicitly rejected the mixed constitutional model of d'Ailly and Gerson, but in reality both men essentially accepted such a model implicitly. Mair is insistent that his precepts preserve full monarchy; he writes that the king has full authority in most matters, unlike an aristocratic leader, but he adds that "he can be compelled in difficult matters to consult the peers of his kingdom who stand in the place of the whole community, or the three estates."[30] Mair uses the traditional mixed constitutional phrases of popular participation in important matters and the representative function of an aristocratic council. Although they prefer election of a dynasty and great monarchical power, Mair and Almain insist that the people never surrender the right to depose the king, nor actually (although not in the Church) to change the form of government and even, if they wish, to dispense with monarchy altogether.[31] So even though they are more conservative than the earlier conciliarists, Mair and Almain defend a limited monarchy with ultimate sovereignty vested in the whole people.

Harold Laski's statement that "the road from Constance to 1688 is a direct one" (explicitly mentioning Nicolaus of Cusa and Gerson in this regard), has been much quoted and argued, as has John Neville Figgis's assertion that *Haec Sancta*, the decree of the Council of Constance that claimed ultimate power for the General Council, is a watershed between the medieval and modern world.[32] What cannot be disputed is that later opponents of absolute monarchy and supporters of mixed constitutions frequently turned to and cited the conciliarists, particularly d'Ailly, Gerson,

[30] John Mair, *In Secundum Sententiarum* (Paris, 1510). For the place of the council representing the three estates, see also *A History of Greater Britain, as well England as Scotland*, Archibald Constable, ed. and trans. (Edinburgh, 1892), pp. 213–19.

[31] John Mair, *In Mattheum ad Literam Expositio* (Paris, 1518), 18; Jacob Almain, *Quaestio Resumptiva, de Domino Naturali, Civili, et Ecclesiastico*, in Jean Gerson, *Opera Omnia*, col. 964.

[32] Harold Laski, "Political Thought in the Later Middle Ages," p. 638; Figgis, *From Gerson to Grotius* , p. 41. See especially Francis Oakley, "On the Road from Constance to 1688: The Political Thought of John Major and George Buchanan," and "Almain and Major: Conciliar Theory on the Eve of the Reformation."

Almain, and Mair. These include the Gallicans of the seventeenth and eighteenth century and the British mixed constitutionalists and monarchomachs of the sixteenth and seventeenth centuries. I will cite a number of these in the next chapter, where I take up secular theories of mixed government.

Chapter 14

LATER THEORIES OF MIXED GOVERNMENT IN ENGLAND AND NORTHERN EUROPE

CRITICAL TO THE LATE medieval development of English constitutionalism was John Fortescue (1394?–1476?), a jurist and for almost twenty years Lord Chief Justice of the King's Bench under Henry VI. Fortescue was not explicitly a supporter of mixing monarchy, aristocracy, and democracy as such, but his theory of regal and political power provides one of the most important bridges between medieval and early modern mixed constitutionalism. He was one of the most influential writers for the theoreticians of the Tudor and Stuart monarchies.

Fortescue revived the distinction between regal and political rule that was so important to Thomas Aquinas and made a combination of the two the basis of good government. Like Thomas, Fortescue applies his definitions only to kingship and distinguishes two modes by how law is made. However, he does not normally consider political rule independently but only in combination with regal rule:

> Ther bith ii kyndes of kingomes, of the wich that on is a lordship callid in laten *dominium regale*, and that other is callid *dominium politicum et regale*. And thai diuersen in that the first kynge mey rule his peple bi suche lawes as he makyth hym self. And therfore he mey sett vppon thaim tayles and other imposicions, such as he wol hym self, withowt thair assent. The secounde kynge may not rule his peple bi other lawes than such as thai assenten unto. And therfore he mey sett vpon thaim non imposicions withowt thair owne assent. This diuersite is wel taught bi Seynt Thomas, in his boke wich he wrote *ad regem Cypri de regimine principum*.[1]

What Fortescue calls regal and political rule seems to be exactly that which Thomas defined as political rule. Felix Gilbert has explained the discrepancy by showing that Fortescue's source is actually Ptolemy of Lucca's portion of *On the Government of Rulers*, in which Ptolemy used the same words to describe the Roman Empire; regal in that the emperor is supreme judge and lawgiver, but political in that he is elective. Fortescue originally used

[1] John Fortescue, *The Governance of England: Otherwise Called The Difference between an Absolute and Limited Monarchy*, chap. 1, p. 109. This work, the first theoretical political treatise written in English, is in many places simply an adaptation of Fortescue's earlier *De Laudibus Legum Angliae*.

the phrase to refer to any system that had some features in common with regal rule and some with political—specifically mentioning the Empire in this regard—but eventually gravitated to the more common association with law only. Gilbert argues that this usage came about because of Fortescue's need to defend the hereditary but limited Lancastrian monarchy.[2]

Although Fortescue sometimes treats both modes as legitimate, if not equally good, he sometimes rejects regal rule altogether. Aristotle may say that the best person is better than the best law, "but because it does not always happen, that the person presiding over a people, is so qualified, St. Thomas . . . wishes, that a kingdom be instituted, so that the king might not be at liberty to tyrannize over his people; which only comes to pass in the present case; that is, when the sovereign power is restrained by political laws." This is a common medieval argument, that pure regal rule might be better if it were not for the probability of a corrupt ruler. Most medieval writers, however, also felt that if people were not degenerate they would not need any kind of regal rule. For Fortescue, though, regal and political rule is always the best. According to Aquinas, he writes, all humanity would have been ruled eternally in Paradise regally and politically had it not been for sin (actually, Aquinas implied that simple political rule existed in Eden).[3] The only difference is that after sin such rule becomes more difficult to institute and maintain. But the people would never establish purely regal rule by their compact and consent, and without such an establishment no king can have a legitimate claim to power. Pure regal rule, therefore, could arise only in a government imposed by force. The capacity to do harm is the only privilege the regal king holds that the regal and political one does not, and this, Fortescue writes, is more impotency than potency.[4] So pure regal rule is never justified and never legitimate. Even Ptolemy of Lucca never went so far. Even though the latter was passionately

[2] Gilbert, "Fortescue's 'Dominium.' "

[3] Fortescue, *De Laudibus Legum Angliae*, chap. 9. "Sed quia non semper contingit Praesidentem Popolo hujusmodi esse Virum, Sanctus Thomas . . . optare cencetur, Regum sis institui, ut Rex non libere valeat Populum Tyrannide gubernare, quod solum fit, dum Potestas Regia Lege Politica cohibetur. . . . Tali lege, ut dicit idem Sanctus, regulatum fuisset totum Genus humanum, si in Paradiso Dei Mandatum non praeteriisset."

[4] Fortescue, *De Laudibus*, chap. 14. "Non alio Pacto Gens aliqua, proprio Arbitrio, unquam se in Regnum corporavit, nisi ut per hoc se et sua, quorum Dispendia formidabant, tutius quam antea possiderent . . . non potuit revera Potestas hujusmodi ab ipsis [populis] erupisse; et tamen si non ab ipsis, Rex hujusmodi super ipsos nullam obtineret Potestatem. E regione, aliter esse concipio de Regno, quod Regis solum Auctoritate et Potentia incorporatum est, quia non alio pacto Gens talis ei subjecta est, nisi ut ejus Legibus, quae sunt illius Placita, Gens ipsa, quae eodem Placito Regnum ejus effecta est, obtemperaret et regeretur. . . . Potestas, qui, qua eorum alter perperam agere liber est, Libertate hujusmodi non augetur, ut posse languescere morive, Potentia non est, sed propter Privationes in Adjecto, Impotientia potius denominandum."

antimonarchic, he felt that most peoples were so corrupt that only oppressive regal rule could restrain them.

What is important is that Fortescue's formulation of regal and political rule describes a situation in which power is divided between a king and the people—a mixed constitution. He even uses the Thomist terminology of restraining the regal king with political power. Michael Mendle discounts Fortescue's importance in mixed constitutional thought. He feels that Fortescue had not really absorbed Aquinas's republicanism and that what he really describes was a king limited by a body of largely traditional law and not a mixed constitution.[5] This was, of course, a standard view of the English monarchy, made famous by Bracton's dictum that "the king is under God and the law." In this view, regal and political rule describes two modalities of royal action depending on whether or not the king could act on his will alone, and consent is relegated to the domain of tradition or passive acceptance. Mendle also objects that Fortescue did not use what was to become the classical three-part division of government, but rather a two-part one, leaving room for the traditional three estates of clergy, lords, and commons within Parliament.

Since the House of Lords had not yet been established, Fortescue cannot outline what was to become the classical model of English mixed monarchy, but he does perceive a three-fold division of king, privy council, and Parliament. The privy council is to meet every day and give counsel on all difficult cases: "And the wise man saith '*vbi multa consilia, ibi salus.*' And trewly such a contenuall counsell mey wel be callid, '*multa consilia*,' for it is ofte, and euere day counsellith."[6] This is clearly an aristocratic body: the king determines its composition, but he should choose twelve each of the wisest clerics and lay persons of the kingdom and, in addition, every year four each of the greatest spiritual and temporal lords, the greatest part of whom can remove any unsuitable member.[7]

And although Fortescue does favor the monarch as the dominant element in government, he also describes an active role for at least the upper classes in determining legislation, changing existing law, and, by limiting the king's actions, preventing him from becoming a tyrant. The king can administer law with the aid of his privy council, but he needs Parliament for making or changing law or levying taxes:

> But, it is not thus that the statutes of England arise: since they are by no means enacted by the will of the Prince, but also by the assent of the whole kingdom by which the people are unable to effect injury by that or not procure their own convenience. By necessity it is judged that they be formulated by pru-

[5] Mendle, *Dangerous Positions*, p. 42.
[6] Fortescue, *Governance*, chap. 14, p. 144.
[7] Fortescue, *Governance*, chap. 15, pp. 145–46.

dence and wisdom, since they are produced not by the prudence of one or a hundred counsellors alone, but by that of more than three hundred elected persons, by which number the state of the Romans was once ruled. Such are those who make up the English Parliament. And if these statutes, produced with such great prudence and solemnity, do not answer the intentions of the founder, they can be immediately changed; but not without that assent of the community and of the leading persons of the kingdom, in the same way that they were earlier put forth.[8]

Fortescue's conception is rather close to and undoubtedly influenced by the conciliar ideas discussed in the preceeding chapter: the pope needs the approval of the College of Cardinals for day-to-day business and application of the law in particular cases and consent of a General Council for important matters or for changing law. It is also close to Nicole Oresme's idea of a French mixed constitution with a king limited by council and the Estates General. Indeed, although Fortescue reviles the current French government—calling it tyranny and not even regal rule—he says that it was not always thus. St. Louis and his predecessors, "sette neuer tayles or other imposicion vppon the peple of that lande with owt the assent of the iij estates, wich whan thai bith assembled bith like to the courte of parlement in Ingelonde." France continued as a regal and political state until the Hundred Years' War made it impossible for the Estates-General to meet, with the result that of necessity the king took taxation upon himself. Even worse, Fortescue continues, he chose to impose taxes unequally, overburdening the commons (which has not yet rebelled), and exempting the nobles for fear of their rebellion. So France degenerated first to regal rule, then to tyranny. The current poverty of France proves the bankruptcy of such government. "Yf the reaume of Englonde," he writes, "were rulid vnder such a lawe, and vnder such a prince, it wolde be than a pray to all other nacions that wolde conqwer, robbe, or deuouir it." In contrast, any country with regal and political rule has freedom and prosperity.[9]

Fortescue gives several other examples of regal and political rule—Scot-

---

[8] Fortescue, *De Laudibus*, chap. 18. "Sed non sic Angliae Statuta oriri possunt, dum nedum Principis Voluntate, sed et totius Regni Assensu, ipsa conduntur, quo Populi Laesuram illa efficere nequeunt, vel non eorum Commodum procurare. Prudentia, etiam et Sapientia necessario ipsa esse referta putandum est, dum non unius, aut centum solum consultorum Virorum Prudentia, sed plusquam trecentorum electorum Hominum, quali Numero olim Senatus Romanorum regebatur, ipsa edita sunt, ut ii, qui Parliamenti Angliae Formam. . . . Et si Statuta haec tanta Solemnitatae et Prudentia edita, Efficaciae tantae, quantae Conditorum cupiebat Intentio, non esse contingant, concito reformari ipas possunt; et non sine Communitatis et Procerum Regni illius Assensu, quali ipsa primitus eminarunt." For the necessity of "the whole kingdom expressing its assent or consent in Parliament" for taxation, see chap. 36.

[9] Fortescue, *Governance*, chap. 4, p. 117; chap. 3, pp. 113–14.

land, Egypt, and Lybia, for instance—but most significantly the situation in ancient Israel and Rome. Not coincidentally these are the governments that medieval writers most often praised for their mixed constitutional structures. He also mentions, without elaboration, the governments of Athens and Sparta, another common example of the mixed constitution, as examples of states that flourished because of the excellence of their councils.[10] Fortescue does not use the arguments of Thomas Aquinas or John of Paris concerning Israel, but rather modifies a few comments in Ptolemy of Lucca's portion of *On the Government of Rulers*. But whereas Ptolemy had emphasized the purely human political aspect of the rule of the Judges, Fortescue labels it a regal and political regime, a political theocracy to be exact.[11] What he has in mind is not exactly clear, but perhaps God ruled as king through the human agency of the Judges, while the councils, described in Deuteronomy as by and from all the people, made laws. If so, this is quite close to Savonarola's scheme for Florence in the 1490s, a scheme also greatly influenced by Ptolemy of Lucca.

He writes more of ancient Rome, again basing his account on Ptolemy's, and his reference to the Roman Senate, to which he compares the English Parliament, as the council of over 300 men suggests the frequent medieval citations, by Ptolemy and many others, of the Book of Machabees to support the mixed constitution. The major difference is that Ptolemy treated the Empire as tyrannical, and most often the early kingship as well, although he did make a puzzling reference to political rule from the kings on, a comment happily picked up by Fortescue. Fortescue, on the other hand, glorifies the whole history of Rome with the exception of a few periods of bad government, until Nero destroyed the Senate:

> The Romaynes . . . wer firste gouerned by kinges; but whenne thoo kingis throughe insolence, folowing thair passions, laste the counsell of the Senate, the Romaynes roose uppon theyme, and put away their kinges for evermor. And thane thei wer reuled by the Senatours and by Consuls politikly many yeres. . . . But after their grete welthe, by division that fille betwene the consuls for lakke of an hed, they hadde amonges them civile battailles. . . . And after that they wer governed by oon hed called an Emperour, whiche using in all his reule the counsell of the Senate, gate the monarchie of the worlde. . . . Whiche lordship and monarchie themperour kepte all the while thei were reuled bi the counsele of the Senate. But after that, whan themperour laste the counseill of the Senate, and somme of theime, as Nero, Dommacion, and other, had slayne gretche partey of the Senatours, and were ruled by their privat counsellours, thastate of themperour fill in dekeye, and their lordship woxe

[10] Fortescue, *Governance*, chap. 16, p. 150; chap. 1, pp. 110–11.
[11] Fortescue, *De Laudibus*, chap. 9.

alwey sythen lasse and lasse; so as now themperour is not of such mighte as is oone of the kinges whiche sumtyme were his subgiettes.[12]

Fortescue is worried because he believes that the same thing has happened to the English monarchy during the War of the Roses, and he calls for the abolition of private councils and a return to well-chosen ones. He has not yet come around to a Polybian conception of the Roman consuls as kings. Instead he treats them, as had Ptolemy of Lucca for different reasons, as aristocrats moderated by the power of the Senate. Despite his preference for monarchy he approves of this government, but is able to show that it was precisely the lack of a king that ultimately led to its downfall during the period of civil wars and its transformation into an even better mixed constitution of Emperor and Senate.

At the beginning of the sixteenth century we begin having to sort out the Aristotelian and Polybian influences, for it was at this time that the sixth book of Polybius's *Histories* first became available in Latin. Hexter has argued that Claude de Seyssel (1450?–1520) and Niccolò Machiavelli (1469–1527) were the first two political theoreticians to use it in their works. In fact, Machiavelli's and Seyssel's writings are the only evidence that it was known before the 1520s. There was a fifteenth century Latin translation of the first five books, but it omitted the sixth book, the only one to describe Rome as a mixed constitution and theorize about the nature of mixed constitutions.[13] Seyssel was a Savoyard educated in civil law at Turin and Pavia and a bishop who served in the *parlement* of Paris, as chancellor, and as ambassador to England, and who later became a member of the Grand Council under King Louis XII. He published *The Monarchy of France* in 1515. Like Machiavelli, whom I will discuss later, Seyssel does not name Polybius. But unlike him, Seyssel's language is not so close as to make Polybius's influence a certainty. Hexter bases his conclusion on certain similarities, such as the design of the work, the use of a cycle of constitutions, the assumption that decay results from the demoralizing effect of power on rulers, and the emphasis on checks and balances as the essence of a mixed constitution.[14] While this is merely suggestive, and while I do not doubt that Seyssel did use Polybius to some extent, I believe the medieval Aristotelian influences are greater. In fact, the points of similarity between Seyssel and Polybius are also found in medieval thought to some

---

[12] John Fortescue, "Example What Good Counseill Helpith and Advantageth, and of the Contrare What Folowith," app. A in *The Governance of England*, pp. 347–48. See also *Governance*, chap. 16. Plummer, the editor, p. 347, says that "Good Counsseill" "reads like an alternate version of chap. 16."

[13] Polybius, *Polybii Historiarum Libri Superstites in Latinum Sermonem Conversi a N. Perotto*. See J. H. Hexter, "Seyssel, Machiavelli, and Polybius VI: the Mystery of the Missing Translation," pp. 75–76.

[14] Seyssel, *The Monarchy of France*. See J. H. Hexter, "Seyssel," pp. 78–80.

extent. Seyssel directly cites Aristotle, Thomas Aquinas, and Giles of Rome and seems to be influenced in his mixed constitutional ideas by Nicole Oresme and perhaps John Fortescue.

Just as Fortescue argued that both a regal and a political king possess the same power, Seyssel insists that even though a king should be bridled by the law (as well as by religion and the judiciary) his royal power and dignity remains entire, though not absolute. With Thomas Aquinas and many others he concedes that if a perfect king could be found there would be no need for any restrictions since the king would always do what was right, but even if this were to happen, even so his successors would not necessarily be suitable rulers.[15] To explain how best to restrict the monarch, Seyssel describes several mixed constitutional models for the French government.

In a minor work, "Proem to Appian," Seyssel discusses the relative value of the various forms of government in the framework of Herodotus's account of the debate of the Persian nobles over the proposed organization of their government after the defeat of pseudo-Smerdis (Polybius did not mention this debate). He begins by approving in general their conclusion that monarchy is best of the three usual good forms in light of the natural dissention and ambition that is always present among humans, although he is careful to acknowledge that each form could be best for a particular people. Monarchies normally are more peaceful and last longer than the other two, but even they eventually decay. Unlike Herodotus, Seyssel concludes that a better system would combine all three good forms, and gives as a good example France, which, he says, has avoided tyranny for a long time:

> I find it [France] so reasonable and so civilized that it is altogether free from tyranny. That is the reason, in my opinion, why this regime, among all others . . . has endured so long and prospered and is now at the height of its prosperity. For looking at this French empire as a whole, it partakes of all three forms of political government. First of all there is the king . . . [who] is nonetheless ruled and limited in the exercise of this great and sovereign liberty by good laws and ordinances and by the multitude and great authority of officials.[16]

This is definitely more medieval than Polybian. In particular, Seyssel does not follow Polybius in his praise for Rome; on the contrary he attacks it for being at once too monarchical—in the beginning and end, of course, but also during the Republic, when he says that the Roman people yielded

---

[15] Seyssel, *Monarchy*, 1, chap. 8, p. 51; 2, chap. 1, p. 68.

[16] Claude de Seyssel, "Proem by Messire Claude de Seyssel, Councillor and Master of Ordinary Requests of the Household of the Most Christian King of France, Louis the twelfth of that name, to the translation of the history by Appian of Alexandria entitled *The Deeds of the Romans*, pp. 170–73.

their authority to a single man in periods of extreme danger and in very important matters—and also too democratic at times. Unlike France, Rome was continually torn by strife—a result of excessive power being given to the people as a whole.[17]

Seyssel is clearly hostile to the masses of people; he praises Venice, for example, for successfully mixing monarchy and aristocracy in the institutions of the doge and the Great Council, and for subordinating the lower classes, though scrupulously preserving their rights and liberties. By these means, he feels, Venice has instituted the most perfect Republic to date.[18] These comments serve as a warning when we encounter others that seem to support a role for the multitude. For example, Seyssel refers on several occasions to the role of the three estates, by which he means the nobility, the middle class (or rich), and the "lesser folk":

> Thus the goods and honors, responsibilities, and administration of the commonweal being divided and parceled out in this manner among all the estates proportionately, according to their condition and preeminence and the equality of each maintained, there ensues a harmony and consonance which is the cause of the preservation and augmentation of the monarchy.[19]

The harmony of the parts working smoothly together suggests both Ptolemy of Lucca, whom Seyssel undoubtedly read, and Walter Burley, who at least was widely available. Participation according to station and merit recalls both Aristotle's distributive justice—about which Seyssel discourses in another context[20]—and Marsilius of Padua's weightier part, in the interpretation that I have given it. It is likely he came to this idea by way of Nicole Oresme.

When Seyssel writes in the *Monarchy* about the institutional nature of the restraints on the king, however, he leaves little role for the masses and speaks only of aristocratic bodies. Judicially the *parlements* bridle any attempt of the king to wield absolute power—he must submit to them and he is even unable to depose those who sit in a *parlement*. As sovereign powers they are a true Roman Senate. Likewise, the legislative powers of the king are subject to bridles of aristocratic councils and disposal of public lands is possible only in emergencies and only then with the approval of the *parlements* and Chamber of Accounts.[21] When he comes to describe the structure of councils in the French mixed constitution Seyssel, like others, finds biblical models, one the usual Moses and councils (though with no

[17] Seyssel, "Proem to Appian," pp. 172, 179.
[18] Seyssel, *Monarchy*, 1, chap. 3, pp. 42–43.
[19] Seyssel, *Monarchy*, 1, chap. 13, p. 58. See also "Proem to Appian," p. 177.
[20] Seyssel, *Monarchy*, 1, chap. 10, p. 54.
[21] Seyssel, *Monarchy*, 1, chap. 10, p. 54; "Proem to Appian," p. 174.

mention of a popular element as in Aquinas or John of Paris), but also one that is unique to him. The French king should be like Christ:

> And to satisfy everybody it seems to me necessary that a great prince have three kinds of councils just as our redeemer Jesus Christ had, according to whose example we ought to do all things so far as possible. For besides the twelve apostles He had first his Great Council, the seventy-two disciples. He did not often assemble them, for He sent them into various places to preach and to carry out his Commandments, but in several matters He spoke to them altogether, apart and separate from the crowd. The second council was the twelve apostles, to whom He ordinarily communicated all secret affairs. The third comprised three of the twelve, St. Peter, St. John, and St. James, to whom he communicated the innermost matters and highest mysteries, such as the Transfiguration.[22]

In the next few chapters Seyssel explains how this model should be applied in France. These three councils are separate from the ordinary offices of government—*parlements* and the Great Council. He is not always precise in keeping his terminology straight, referring, for example both to the ordinary Great Council and the first of these three councils as the General or Great Council. He is clear, however, that they are separate bodies. The first, or General Council, is an extraordinary council summoned only for something of great consequence to the kingdom—war, broad laws, and the like. The Great Council of the ruler should, in contrast, meet frequently for all matters of importance. The General Council should include the most important clerical and secular officials, important nobles, and good and notable persons from various estates. In no way, however, does Seyssel suggest that it should be representative. The second council should meet frequently, as much as every day or at least three times a week. The third council, composed of a few members of the second, is the secret council with which the king should consult every day.[23]

In sum, Seyssel explicitly supports a mixed monarchy in which the king's power is bridled by law, an independent judiciary, and a series of councils of state. He asserts the primacy of law and the necessity of government to serve the common good of its citizens. The mixed constitution is to combine the good qualities of monarchy and aristocracy and, more importantly the various institutions serve to prevent any one faction (especially the king) from attaining too much power and degenerating into tyranny. Seyssel has little confidence in the abilities of the masses, but allows them some role to make them satisfied, as did Thomas Aquinas, and explicitly states that democracy is a part of the best polity. In other words he is a fairly

---

[22] Seyssel, *Monarchy*, 2, chap. 4, pp. 72–73.
[23] Seyssel, *Monarchy*, 2, chap. 5–7, 73–77.

typical medieval proponent of mixed government. Granted there are a few features and examples used in his writings that could come only from Polybius, and in some areas he has adapted Polybius's ideas to his own. But there is no discontinuity, and there is no feeling that Polybius has come as a revelation to him breaking through all the medieval murkiness and the rigidity of scholastic thought. On the contrary, Seyssel does not even deem it necessary to mention Polybius, and all he really does is assimilate some parts of the *Histories* to his fully medieval Aristotelian conceptions. As I have said on several occasions Aquinas and others had already independently come up with some of Polybius's ideas, especially the idea of checks and balances and the necessity to temper monarchy. So when Seyssel read Polybius he was reading simply one more formulation of a theory with which he was already familiar.

The great Christian humanist Desiderius Erasmus (c. 1466–1536), a close contemporary of Seyssel who wrote his *Education of a Christian Prince* in 1516, also emphasizes the ideas of balance and tempered monarchy but shows absolutely no trace of Polybian influence. He never once mentions Polybius, but his book abounds with references to Aristotle (and Plato), and his outlook is typically medieval. He repeats the common arguments for monarchy, saying that it would be best if the best man could be found, but that this is a futile hope. In the real world the best is a limited monarch checked and lessened by aristocracy and democracy. This arrangement, he writes, will prevent tyranny since the elements will balance each other. Young princes especially should not be allowed to make any decisions without the approval of many wiser men, at least until their judgment proves worthy. Erasmus bases government upon "common agreement" and insists that no Christian should have "full power" over any other Christian since Christ did not want his people to be slaves. He even alludes to the Thomist distinction of regal and political power, saying that magistrates rule in part and obey in part. This is exactly how Thomas defined political rule, so the implication is that the best state, as it is in Fortescue, is a combination of regal and political power. Also, he concurs with Fortescue and Seyssel that limitation of a king in a mixed constitution does not diminish a king's power in any way, since it only prevents him from doing evil.[24] In short, Erasmus, one of the key figures in the Northern Renaissance and one whose influence persisted for centuries, places his discussion of the best government in a medieval Aristotelian context. His conclusions about balance and consent are compatible with Polybius's, but they and especially his comments on modal characteristics of rule and the

[24] Desiderius Erasmus, *Education of a Christian Prince*, b446, p. 173; b458, p. 183; b447–48, pp. 177–79; b466, p. 236.

ideal superiority of pure monarchy are clearly derived from the medieval discourse.

Somewhat later the Protestant leader John Calvin (1509–64) devoted the last chapter of his monumental and influential *Institutes of the Christian Religion* (first edition, 1536) to the question of the nature and authority of civil government. Calvin is not much interested in abstract questions of ideal government (and, in any case, he believes that the best form depends upon circumstances). He wants for the most part to defend the idea of government, Christian participation in it, and especially the obligation of Christians to obey any government, but he does express a personal preference for aristocracy, especially if mixed with democracy:

> If you compare the different states with each other, without regard to circumstances, it is not easy to determine which of these has the advantage in point of utility, so equal are the terms on which they meet. Monarchy is prone to tyranny. In an aristocracy, again, the tendency is not less to the faction of a few, while in popular ascendency there is the strongest tendency to sedition. When these three forms of government, of which philosophers treat, are considered in themselves, I, for my part, am far from denying that the form which greatly surpasses the others is aristocracy, either pure or modified by popular government, not indeed in itself, but because it so rarely happens that kings so rule themselves as never to dissent from what is just and right. . . . Owing, therefore to the vices or defects of men, it is safer and more tolerable when several bear rule, that they may mutually assist, instruct, and admonish each other, and should any one be disposed to go too far, the others are censors and masters to curb his excess. This has already been proved by experience, and confirmed also by the authority of the Lord himself, when he established an aristocracy bordering on popular government among the Israelites, keeping them under that as the best form, until he exhibited an image of the Messiah in David.[25]

It is interesting to see how the medieval argument for limiting monarchy on the grounds that a king is rarely perfect is here turned against monarchy itself. Calvin's personal preference may be for a mixture of aristocracy and democracy, but he also praises institutional checks on kings by aristocratic and democratic organs of government. For instance, he condemns any kind of individual action against even a tyrannical government but makes it clear that he is not talking about public authorities constituted to check the power of kings, such as the Ephors in Sparta, the Tribunes in Rome, or the Demarchs in Athens. These, in fact, he greatly approves, and he enjoins them to vigilance. He speculates that the Three Estates in Euro-

---

[25] John Calvin, *Institutes of the Christian Religion*, 4.20.8, pp. 656–57.

pean monarchies perform a function similar to these when they assemble.[26] Although Calvin himself is not very interested in these questions, his few comments provide a basis for much later theorizing by Protestants reluctant to base themselves on Catholic sources, particularly in England. Calvin wrote this before the disasters that would soon engulf France, and that would make resistance to authority more desirable for the Calvinists. In any case Calvin always allowed at least passive resistance if the secular authority ordered things against God.

One of those who expanded Calvin's theory of resistance was François Hotman (1524–90), who wrote much later than his countryman Seyssel and was strongly influenced by him in his *Francogallia* (1573). Hotman earned a doctorate of law at Orléans, practiced at Paris, and in 1546 became a professor of Roman Law there. He was a member of the French school of Romanists who against the post-Glossators and in line with contemporary humanism tried to recover the authentic classical legal texts. His political views were undoubtedly influenced by his religious experience—converted to Calvinism in 1347 he spent most of the rest of his life as a wandering exile, teaching in Lyon, Geneva, Lausannne, Strassbourg, and in his last years in Basel. In 1563 he was able to come back to France to teach at Valence and Bourges, but he again had to flee after the St. Bartholemew's Day Massacre in 1573. He published *Francogallia* in Geneva after the massacre, but he had actually written it in the six months before. Thus, it is not simply a reaction to that disaster but was a major contribution to the developing Calvinist theory of resistance.

Although Hotman cites Polybius, he also acknowledges a more significant debt to Aristotle, as well as Plato and Cicero, stating that these authors favored a mixed constitution. Hotman argues that the French constitution is, or at least was in more tolerant times, that most distant from tyranny, which is characterized by its involuntary nature, mercenary foreign bodyguards for the ruler, and the subordination of all things to the convenience of the ruler, not of the subjects or republic. In contrast,

> that supreme administration of the kingdom of Francogallia was vested in the annual public council of the nation, which was later called the Assembly of the Three Estates. The constitution of this kingdom then is the one which the ancient philosophers—including Plato and Aristotle, whom Polybius followed—declared to be the best and most excellent, a constitution, namely, which is a blend and mixture of all three simple types: the royal, the aristocratic, and the popular. . . . For since royal and popular dominion are antithetical by nature, a third component should be introduced which is between them and common to them both, and this is the nobility, or leading men. . . . This tempered mixture of three elements is, thus, the commonwealth adopted

[26] Calvin, *Institutes*, 4.20.32, p. 675.

by our forefathers, and they wisely decreed that a public council of the entire kingdom should be held each year on the first of May, in which council all the major business of the commonwealth would be settled by the common counsel of all the Estates. And the wisdom and usefulness of this institution can be seen mainly in these three considerations: First, there is much wisdom in a large number of experienced men. . . . Secondly, it is an essential part of liberty, that affairs should be administered by the advice and authority of those who have to bear the risk, as in the common saying that "what concerns all should be approved by all." And finally, those who have great influence with the king and hold great offices can be kept within the bounds of duty through fear of that council in which the remonstrations of the cities are freely voiced. For, as Aristotle very rightly observes in his *Politics* (III), kingdoms governed at the discretion and pleasure of the king alone are not governments of men who are free and have the light of reason, but rather of sheep and brute beasts who have no judgment. . . . A multitude of men should be ruled and governed, not by some one individual among them, who may be among the least discerning of their number, but by men approved and selected by the consent of everyone as being more eminent; and by mutual counsels; and by one mind compounded out of many, as it were.[27]

Hotman also gives other examples of mixed constitutions: classical Sparta, England, and Spain, but also the German Empire, ruled by an assembly of the three estates consisting of emperor, princes, and provincial delegates. He not only believes that the parliamentary (he uses this word in reference to the Estates-General of France too) mixed constitution is best and widespread, but also that any true royal government is of this form or it is tyrannical.[28] Clearly this has as much to do with Aristotelian concepts of distributive justice as with Aristotelian or Polybian ideas of balance. For Hotman it is an attempt to prove that the Valois kings had usurped the proper authority of the people, thus becoming tyrants, and that therefore the people had every right to depose them and install another, more tolerant king. It is his hope and belief that a return to the proper and traditional constitutional procedures in France would prevent the persecutions to which he and his coreligionists were then subject.

Most of the sixteenth-century French and English works advocating limited government remain within the medieval Aristotelian framework, even if they do occasionally use Polybius, and they increasingly bring in Venice as a mixed constitutional model. Corinne Weston has written on the development of mixed constitutionalism in England in the century before the famous "Answer to the Nineteen Propositions" (1642), in which Charles I formally accepted the notion. In her *English Constitutional Theory and*

[27] François Hotman, *Francogallia*, pp. 65–68.
[28] Hotman, *Francogallia*, pp. 69–70.

the House of Lords, 1556–1832, she argued that the classical concept of England as a mixed monarchy of king, lords, and commons developed in this period. Recently, Michael Mendle has challenged her conclusions and her later work, arguing that the decisive period was later and that the Tudor and Stuart monarchies could in no way be seen as institutionalizing such a concept.[29] While in many ways Mendle corrects erroneous conclusions on Weston's part, particularly on the actual structure of the government, he does not really have an effect on her arguments about the development of ideas, and still less my argument. He is simply arguing for the exact roots of a certain mixed constitutional configuration represented by the "Answer to the Nineteen Propositions." This does correct Weston's idea that it came directly out of Tudor kingship, but it really has nothing to do with the transmission of mixed constitutional ideas from the Middle Ages to the Early Modern Era, although Mendle often acts as if it did. He falls into the common trap of defining a mixed constitution in some very specific way and then failing to find it anywhere before he wants to. Also leading to the same conclusions are Mendle's attempts to show that whatever anyone said there was not an actual mixed constitution in practice until later—but again this really has nothing to do with the circulation of the ideas, nor even with contemporary perception of the government.

Thomas Starkey (late 1400s–1538), who is just a little early for Weston (Mendle discounts him), but whom Thomas Mayer has treated extensively in a recent book,[30] was influenced by a number of medieval and contemporary Italian authors. Starkey spent much of the 1520s and early 1530s traveling and living in Italy, primarily in Padua, with Cardinal Pole, whom he met when he was studying at Oxford. He and Pole also spent time in Paris in 1529–30 and on his own he took up the study of civil law in Avignon in 1532. He wrote his *Dialogue between Cardinal Pole and Thomas Lupset* between 1529 and 1532. His intention initially was to advance both his own and Pole's career by promoting Pole as the leader of an aristocratic reform party and enlisting King Henry VIII in this cause. Later, when Pole did not take up the role of a party leader, Starkey attempted to curry the favor of those around the king and succeeded in winning a position with Thomas Cromwell. However, at the end of his life Starkey fell out of favor and had he not died he may have been indicted for treason.[31]

One can understand why his views might be suspect, especially when, after long negotiations, Cardinal Pole did not go along with Henry's divorce. In Starkey's dialogue, Pole brings forth most of the medieval argu-

---

[29] Weston, *House of Lords*; Weston and Greenberg, *Subjects and Sovereigns*; Mendle, *Dangerous Positions*.

[30] Thomas Mayer, *Thomas Starkey and the Commonweal: Humanist Politics and Religion in the Reign of Henry VIII*.

[31] Mayer, *Thomas Starkey*, pp. 1–3.

ments against pure monarchy and for the mixed constitution. He is concerned that English king's power is becoming too great and that something must be done to curb it:

> Hyt ys not vnknown to you, Master Lvpset, that our cuntrey hathe byn gouernyd and rulyd thes many yerys vnder the state of pryncys, wych by theyr regal powar and pryncely authoryte, haue jugyd al thyngys perteynyng to the state of our reame to hange only apon theyr wyl and fantasye . . . wych ys, wythout dowte, and euer hath byn, the gretyst destructyon to thys reame, ye, and to al other, that euer hathe come therto.[32]

This might be acceptable if the king were always worthy, but especially when his title comes by inheritance this seldom happens, and giving him full power is disastrous. Thus, "bettur hyt ys to the state of the commyn wele, to restreyne from the prynce such hye authoryte, commyttyng that only to the commyn counseyl of the reame and parlymente assemblyd here in our cuntrey."[33]

This has been seen many times before. Starkey also specifically advocates a mixed constitution:

> The most wyse men, consyderyng the nature of pryncys, ye, and the nature of man as hyt ys indede, affyrme a myxte state to be of al other the best and most conuenyent to conserue the hole out of tyranny. For when any one parte hath ful authoryte, yf that parte chaunce to be corrupt wyth affectys, as oft we se in euery other state hyt dothe, the rest schal suffur the tyranny therof . . . the authoryte of the prynce must be temperyd and brought to ordur.[34]

Starkey goes on to describe how the mixed constitution should work in England: a council of the chief men of England and representatives of London, which, acting as a "lytyl parlyament," "schold represent the hole body of the pepul without parlyament and commyn counseyl geddryd of the reame," should choose the king's council and summon Parliament when necessary. Thus the king's power is severely limited and he cannot even pick his own cronies as advisors.[35] Starkey establishes the elements of a typically medieval threefold mixed constitution of monarchy, aristocracy, and democracy under the supremacy of law.

Starkey mentions Venice as his example of an existing polity in which a mixed constitution works well, since the doge is sufficiently bridled by an aristocratic council. This reflects his experience in humanist circles in Padua and especially the influence of both Contarini and Giannotti, the latter of whom influenced the form and some of the content of his dia-

---

[32] Thomas Starkey, *Dialogue between Cardinal Pole and Thomas Lupset*, pp. 100–101. See also Carlyle and Carlyle, *Medieval Political Theory*, vol. 6, pp. 259–63.

[33] Starkey, *Dialogue*, p. 102.

[34] Starkey, *Dialogue*, p. 181.

[35] Starkey, *Dialogue*, pp. 182–84.

logue.[36] I will show in the next chapter that these men also derived their concept of mixed constitutions from medieval Aristotelians. Mayer also proves that the fifteenth-century conciliarists and Seyssel influenced Starkey. Pole had Gerson and conciliarist writings in his library, and Starkey stated that he always followed "Gerson and the Parisian school" on the constitution of the church.[37] It is difficult to trace all of Starkey's sources; some similarities to Marsilius of Padua, who was enjoying a renewed popularity in England at the time, have led many scholars to assert a direct influence. Mayer, however, argues rather persuasively that the similarities are slight and may result merely from common Aristotelian roots and ideas that were currently widely available.[38]

John Ponet (1516?–56) continues the development of the theory of the mixed constitution in England in *A Shorte Treatise of Politike Power* (1556). Ponet was educated at Cambridge and under the patronage of Archbishop Thomas Cranmer rose to the position of bishop of Winchester and Rochester and influence in government circles. When the Catholic Mary became queen in 1553 Ponet was stripped of his bishoprics and, after participating in an abortive rebellion against Mary in 1554, fled to the continent. It is not surprising that he then wrote a treatise against tyranny and in favor of limited government. His epigram to this work is from Psalms 118: "It is better to trust in the Lord, than to trust in Princes." He is the first to bring together explicitly Fortescue's theory of a regal and political monarchy with mixed constitutional theory, and he was probably influenced by Thomas Starkey, as well as Marsilius of Padua, John Mair, Desiderius Erasmus, and John Calvin. It is with Ponet that Weston begins her *English Constitutional Theory and the House of Lords, 1556–1832.*

Ponet makes no break with medieval Aristotelian thought, but argues more strongly for mixed constitutions in that he considers them not only the best but also the only good kind of government. He writes that there are two kinds of ruler, but both base their power upon the whole body of the people. The first, corresponding to Fortescue's regal king, makes positive law by himself by a grant of the people (even so he is bound by the law). The second, corresponding to Fortescue's regal and political king, has received no such grant; the people have reserved lawmaking to themselves. Ponet points out that this second situation is a mixed state. What is even more interesting is that only this situation is legitimate at all; even though the regal ruler rules by the authority of the people he "nevertheless is rather to be compted a tiranne than a king."[39]

---

[36] Mayer, *Thomas Starkey*, p. 43.

[37] Mayer, *Thomas Starkey*, pp. 79–89.

[38] Mayer, *Thomas Starkey*, pp. 139–46. The classic article on Marsilian influence is Franklin le van Baumer, "Thomas Starkey and Marsilius of Padua."

[39] John Ponet, *A Shorte Treatise of Politike Power*, pp. 25–26.

Elsewhere, he describes the mixed constitution in more traditional terms:

> And these diverse kyndes of states or policies hade their distincte names, as wher one ruled, a Monarchie: wher many of the best, Aristocratie: wher the multitude, Democratie: and wher all together, that is, a king, the nobilitie, and commones, a mixte state: which men by long continuaunce have iudged to be the best sort of all. For wher that mixte state was exerciced, ther did the common wealthe longest continue.[40]

God sees to it that tyranny cannot exist among those that love God, and he does this by the institutional safeguards of the mixed constitution. Without explaining why pagans would be included, Ponet includes the ancient states of Rome and Sparta among those so divinely favored:

> And the state of the policies and common wealthes have ben disposed and ordained bi God, that the headdes could not (if they wolde) oppresse the other membres. For as among the Lacedemonians certain men called Ephori were ordayned so see that the kinges should not oppresse the people, and among the Romaynes, the Tribunes were ordayned to defende and mayntene the libertie of the people from the pride and iniurie of the nobles: so in all Christian realmes and dominiones God ordayned meanes, that the heades the princes and gouernours should not oppresse the poore people after their lustes, and make their willes their lawes. As in Germany betwene themperour and the people, a Counsail or diet: in Fraunce and Englande, parliamentes, wherin ther mette and assembled of all sortes of people, and nothing could be done without the knowledge and consent of all.[41]

While some of Ponet's ideas, such as the endurance of mixed constitutions, conceivably could have come from Polybius, there is nothing here that is not medieval, and some of his phrases, such as "nothing could be done" and other examples are clearly medieval.

It is shortly afterward, in 1559, that John Aylmer (1521–94), for the first time made a full-fledged identification of the English constitution of king, House of Lords, and House of Commons with the classical mixed constitution of monarchy, aristocracy, and democracy. Like Ponet, Aylmer had been an exile from England during Mary's reign, and he was now trying to defend Queen Elizabeth's right to rule, partially by convincing misogynists that a woman ruler is tolerable. His reason is that although an absolute Queen may be unthinkable, "Where mixed rulers be, women's government can not be dangerous." And this, he writes, is the situation in England: "The thinge in deed, is to be sene in the parliament hous,

---

[40] Ponet, *Shorte Treatise*, p. 9.
[41] Ponet, *Shorte Treatise*, pp. 11–12.

wherein you shal find these 3 estats. The kinge or Quene, which representeth the Monarche. The noblemen, which be the Aristocratie. And the Burgesses and Knights the Democratie." Explicitly acknowledging his debt to Aristotle, he compares England to the Sparta of kings, senate, and Ephors, explaining in typically medieval terms that as in Sparta so in England all three are needed for any important matters, and that the king could ordain nothing without the houses of Parliament.[42]

Thomas Smith (1513–77), a law professor who served as secretary of state, vice chancellor, and diplomat during Elizabeth's reign and who much earlier had been Ponet's teacher, implies the same conception of mixed government of kings, lords, and commons in his influential *On the Republic of the English*, originally written in 1565, revised until Smith's death, and finally printed in 1583. He also acknowledges his debt to Aristotle and goes on to repeat the common medieval (but not classical) idea, espoused by Engelbert of Admont and Nicole Oresme among others—and even using some of their words—of all government as mixed: "Seldome or never shall you finde common wealthes or government which is absolutely and sincerely made of any of them above named, but always mixed with an other, and hath the name of that which is more and overruleth the other alwayes or for the most part."[43]

With Aylmer and Smith all the elements of what Weston calls the "Classical Theory of the English Constitution" are in place. During the next century various authors developed and embellished the theory further, culminating in the pragmatic and formal acceptance of this mixed constitutional model by Charles I in 1642 and the flowering of mixed constitutionalism during and after the Civil War and throughout the eighteenth century. It is this development that Corinne Weston outlines; there is no need to repeat it here. The point is that all these authors were influenced by medieval political theory, particularly that of Fortescue, the conciliarists, and also the other late medieval and Early Modern English authors that I have discussed in this chapter, but also by Thomas Aquinas, Marsilius of Padua, and others. By the time the Constitutional Convention of the United States was discussing the mixed constitution, the debate had become centered upon Polybius, and the medieval mixed constitutionalists had been forgotten. But developmentally the origin of all the major ideas of Early Modern mixed constitutionalism were indisputably medieval and Aristotelian.

[42] John Aylmer, *An Harborowe for Faithfull and Trewe Subjects*, pp. 26–28, as reported in Weston, *House of Lords*, pp. 16–18 and Mendle, *Dangerous Positions*, pp. 48–49.

[43] Thomas Smith, *De Republica Anglorum*, 1.6. See Weston, *House of Lords*, p. 16.

Chapter 15

THE MIXED CONSTITUTION AND ITALIAN
REPUBLICANISM

IN ITALY, when the theory of the mixed constitution began to flourish in the sixteenth century, especially in Florence, it was closely tied to Polybius. Machiavelli in particular framed his ideas in classical terms and ignored his medieval predecessors; it was his presentation of the ideas that became normative for later Italian mixed constitutionalists. Yet there is no question but that such ideas developed in the Italian city-states before the translation of Polybius and particularly in regard to the so-called "myth of Venice," which in its ultimate form attributed that city's unique success to a mixed constitution of monarchic doge, aristocratic Senate, and democratic Great Council. "This assertion," Pocock writes, "was to be expressed in the language and assumptions of Polybian theory, but in the *quattrocento* Polybius's sixth book was insufficiently known to be listed among the sources of the Venetian myth, and it is rather to the grand tradition of Athenian philosophy and civic humanism that we should direct our attention."[1] For the most part, this is correct when talking about Florentine writers, but I will argue that the fifteenth-century civic humanists were in turn concealing their sources and that we should look rather to medieval Aristotelians. In the Venetian writers themselves the lines of transmission are clear, although not universally recognized—Venetian theory is indisputably Aristotelian and the original idea of Venice as a mixed constitution is medieval.

As an exceptionally stable state amid the chaos of Northern Italy, Venice had long aroused admiration. Even before the *Politics* was available writers praised it for its stability, prosperity, and good government, though obviously not in Aristotelian terms of simple forms of government and mixed constitutions. For example, Bartholomaeus Anglicus, an Englishman who taught in Paris and Magdeburg, describes it in the 1230s in his encyclopedia *On the Properties of Things* in a manner much like the later standard "myth," except for the analysis of its institutions, which Bartholomaeus mentions only generally and with regard to the city's "just laws" and its refusal to allow sectarian divisiveness.[2] That such a description originated in Northern Europe, from someone who so far as we know never went to

---

[1] Pocock, *Machiavellian Moment*, p. 102.

[2] From the excerpt edited by David Robey and John Law, "Venetian Myth and the 'De republica veneta' of Pier Paolo Vergerio," p. 51.

Italy shows how early the myth became widespread. About the same time the Florentine writer Boncompagno attributed Venice's success to its climate. A few generations later even Ptolemy of Lucca, who generally despised monarchies, praises Venice and excuses the monarchical attributes of the doge since his is a "temperate rule."[3]

Felix Gilbert, the author of one of the most important studies of the Renaissance concept of a Venetian mixed constitution and the influence of the myth of Venice on Florence, and others argue that even if there was early appreciation of the success of Venice, it was only in the early fifteenth century that writers, particularly Venetian humanists such as Francesco Barbaro (c. 1398–1454) and Pier Paulo Vergerio the Elder (1370–1444) and Florentine civic humanists, began to attribute Venice's unique prosperity and stability to the perfection of its governmental institutions—usually perceived as a perfect aristocracy, although they did write of a mixture of aristocracy and monarchy and mentioned the division of powers into doge, Senate, and Great Council. Sometime later, perhaps in the early sixteenth century, this argument continues, other writers, such as the Florentine Guicciardini, described Venice's mixed constitution more explicitly as a mixture of all three good simple forms and identified each of the powers with one of the forms. More commonly even then, however, analysts saw Venice as an aristocracy, and as such both in the fifteenth and sixteenth centuries it appealed to Florentine optimates around the Medici who were anxious to assert their own power.[4] Pocock attributes the eventual dominance among Florentine writers of the formulation involving a threefold mixture to the tradition of a politically active *popolo* in Florence combined with the necessity to use the one-few-many terminology in light of the actual structure of Venetian government and classical usage.[5]

More recently, David Robey, sometimes in collaboration with John Law, has proven that the description of Venice as a mixed constitution dates back at least to the early fourteenth, perhaps the late thirteenth century, and that there is a direct line between these early descriptions and the more famous classical formulations of the myth of Venice in the fifteenth through the seventeenth centuries. Robey and Law build on and extend the work of Gina Fasoli, who has long argued that the myth of Venice flourished in and out of Venice in the High Middle Ages, achieving its mature form by the fourteenth century. She, however, did not recognize that the introduction of mixed constitutional thinking also went back to this same period. Recently Quentin Skinner has taken up Robey and Law's

---

[3] Ptolemy of Lucca, *De Regimine Principum*, 2.8.

[4] Felix Gilbert, "The Venetian Constitution in Florentine Political Thought," to which I am indebted for much of the material for this section.

[5] Pocock, *Machiavellian Moment*, p. 101.

opinion, at least to the extent of admitting that the full-fledged myth of
Venice dates back to around 1300.[6]

Most significantly, Robey and Law trace the later influence of Henry of
Rimini, a Thomist, a Dominican, and a sometime Venetian resident about
whom little is known other than that in 1308 he was granted permission
to visit Serbia to promote ecclesiastical union, and that in the same year
Venice sent him on a conciliatory mission to the papal Curia, which was
infuriated because of Venice's attack on Ferrara.[7] Henry wrote only two
surviving works: a treatise on the four cardinal virtues and another on the
seven deadly sins. The latter was not, apparently, very popular; it survives
in only one manuscript and was never printed. The former, on the other
hand, in which Henry's political comments appear, was widely circulated—there survive many fourteenth and fifteenth-century manuscripts, it
was quoted by many other writers, and there are two fifteenth-century
printed editions. Robey and Law argue for internal reasons that Henry
must have written this treatise after 1268, before which the general assembly of citizens elected the doge, and not too many years after 1297, when
the Great Council expanded beyond 400 members.[8]

In his analysis of the three good simple forms of government and why
although monarchy is the best of the three it is doomed to decay into tyranny, Henry follows closely Thomas Aquinas's argument in the *Summa
Theologiae*. He likewise follows Thomas in his solution of a mixed government of all three forms as best and in his description of the structure of
such a mixed government and the role of election, at times using Thomas's
exact words. Since the peace is best preserved when everyone has some part
of rule, he writes, the mixture of all three forms is best. Therefore some
wise ones should be chosen from the people who would then also elect a
king over all. The result is democratic since rulers are elected, aristocratic
since the optimates rule, monarchic since there is a king. This is directly
from Thomas, as is Henry's analysis immediately following of the Jewish
government under Moses. Like Thomas, Henry expresses no confidence in
the ability of the many and includes a democratic element only so that all
shall have a part and be content. What is unique about Henry is that he
then applies these principles to Venice:

[6] Robey and Law, "Venetian Myth"; David Robey, "Pier Paolo Vergerio the Elder: Republicanism and Civic Values in the Work of an Early Humanist." To the former are appended Pier Paulo Vergerio's "De republica veneta," an anonymous letter to Louis of Hungary, and excerpts from Bartholomaeus Anglicus, Henry of Rimini, and Benzo d'Alessandria.
Much of what follows I owe to Robey and Law's work and to the key Latin texts of the
important writers that they edit. See Quentin Skinner, "Political Philosophy."

[7] Robey and Law, "Venetian Myth," p. 52.

[8] Robey and Law, "Venetian Myth," pp. 11–12.

Among all polities that exist among the Christian people in our time, the polity of the nation of Venetians seems to come closest to that mixed government. For in it about 400 from the nobles and even from the honorable people are admitted to a public Council, by whom some of the more prudent are elected to create their own ruler. These elect someone from the nobles of their own nation whom they place in authority over all as leader [doge]. Moreover, this leader thus elected by the greater men, together with six, whom they call Counselors, and 40, whom they consider as it were the Ancients of the people, exercise governance over the polity. And those who exercise governance over the polity with the leader do not always remain the same, but individuals from the council are elevated for established times to the already mentioned offices of Counselors or Ancients by the election of all. And thus each of those mentioned who are elected to the council has some part in the polity, which as it were participates somewhat from three governments. For in so far as one is placed in authority over all, it can be called the government of a kingdom; but in so far as some greater ones elect the leader himself, and they themselves or others elected for this in various times rule the polity with him, it can be called the government of the best; but in so far as the said greater ones, electors of the leader, Counselors, or the 40, are elected from the whole council, it participates somewhat in the polity of the people. For there are in the said council not only greater nobles, but also many of the honorable people. Moreover, this nation of Venetians enjoys such great peace and security. . . . All are secure. . . . They do not follow the Common Laws [i.e., the Roman Law] but live in a wonderful way according to their own statutes accommodated to the affairs of the polity; and nevertheless when the laws fail they turn themselves not to foreign law but to paternal customs. They are most faithful to the republic, which everyone strives to maintain in opulence and honor; but also the republic itself conserves and preserves carefully its citizens, even the plebians, in great liberties and singular immunities.[9]

[9] Henry of Rimini, *Tractatus de Quattuor Virtutibus Cardinalibus*, tr. 2, chap. 4, pt. 15; pt. 16, pp. 54–55. "Inter omnes politias que nostris temporibus in populo Christiano fuerunt politia gentis Venetorum ad hoc regimen mixtum videtur approprinquare. In ipsa namque circiter quadringenti tam ex nobilibus quam etiam ex honorabili populo ad consilia publica admittuntur, per quos aliqui prudentiores in creationi principis eliguntur. Ei hi aliquem ex sue gentis nobilibus eligunt quem in ducem omnibus preficiunt. Predictus autem dux sic a maioribus electus una cum sex, quos consiliarios vocant, et quadraginta, quos quasi populi antianos habent, politiam gubernat. Nec hi qui cum duce civitatem gubernat idem semper permanent, sed singuli de consilio statutis temporibus ad predicta officia consiliarie vel antianarie per electionem omnium assumuntur. Et sic quilibet de predictis ad consilium electis partem habet aliquam in politia, que quasi ex tribus regiminibus aliquid participat. Nam in quantum unus omnibus est prefectus, regimen regni dici potest; in quantum vero aliqui maiores ipsum ducem eligunt, et cum ipso politiam regunt ipsi vel alii diversis temporibus ad hoc electi, regimen optimatum dici potest; in quantum vero predicti maiores, ducis electores, consiliarii, vel quadraginta, a toto consilio eliguntur, aliquid de politia populi participat. Sunt enim in dicto consilio non solum maiores nobiles, sed etiam multi de populo honorabili. Hec

The only substantial difference between the Venetian government and the ancient Jews is that the wise men did not elect the king of the Jews, rather he was directly appointed by God (a point that Thomas did not emphasize, but which Henry does). In this description Henry not only fits Venice into Thomas's mixed constitutional schema and assimilates it to the divinely preferred government, but implicitly compares it with other Northern Italian republics, where in many places "ancients" and analogous officials, such as the priors in Florence, were ruling public officials during the period of the *popolo*. By the time Henry is writing, the "antimagnate" legislation many cities passed defining and then restricting the hereditary nobility had failed. Many of these cities had fallen to despots representing the magnates, and most of the rest were unstable. Henry apparently feels that Venice has greater stability and less to fear from the magnates because the ancients and other public officials are elected by the nobles and guildsmen (that is the "honorable people") acting together. This is in a way yet another aspect of mixing the government. He also implicitly compares the Venetian doge, a Venetian citizen elected for life with the common institution in other cities of a foreign podesta elected for a limited period. Again, he apparently feels that the Venetian institution, which later inspired the Florentine gonfalonier for life, was more admirable because it strengthened the monarchical element and made it independent of the other components of government.

In the light of the future development of the myth of Venice, one thing in particular stands out in Henry's theory—his obvious preference for aristocracy over the other simple forms, even though he admits that if it were as good as possible monarchy would be absolutely best. In his description of the mixed constitution aristocracy predominates—not only because the counsellors, ancients, the 40, and so forth are the key governmental institutions, but also because the democratic element is only a slightly extended aristocracy. While it is true that no medieval writer with the possible exception of Marsilius envisioned universal adult male participation when they wrote about democracy, it is also true that few so limited it as Henry to the upper eschelons of the guild movement—not just the *popolo* but a few of the more honorable *popolo*. And, in addition, most at least required the consent of the multitude. The most Henry will allow is that even the plebs have a great degree of freedom, and that no one in Venice is born the slave of another. This is significant because the praise of aristocracy was

---

autem Venetorum gens tanta pace et securitate fruitur. . . . Secura sunt omnia. . . . Leges communes non sequuntur, sed secundum statutapropria vivunt miro modo politie negotiis accomoda; nec tamen ad iura aliena ubi statuta desunt sed ad patrias consueditudines se convertunt. Fidelissimi sunt reipublicie, quam unusquisque in opulentia et honore tenere studet; sed et ipsa reipublica suos cives etiam plebeios magnis libertatibus et singularibus immunitatibus conservat et contuetur."

always one of the most prominent characteristics of the myth of Venice. It seems likely that this feature of later thought also comes from medieval mixed constitutionalism.

Writing a few years later, around 1320, Benzo d'Alessandria, who is mostly known for his description of Milan, mentions Venice in passing in his *Chronicle*, in the course of a survey of the world's principal cities. He appropriates Boncompagno's idea about the climate, but goes on to analyze Venice's government in terms quite similar to Henry's, suggesting that it thrives because of its good institutions and specifically because of its mixed constitution:

> Moreover, their institutions by which the community lives are most outstanding, but more in this, because on their account the citizens love the good of the republic. They rejoice in lasting peace and cultivate the highest justice. For, led healthfully by a certain innate discipline, they submit themselves strenuously to their highest leader [doge], in whose election not a foreign person but a citizen is chosen. Nor does nobility have greater influence, but the suffrage of all. . . . Who [the doge], although he may be regarded by customs and prefer great equity, nevertheless can not will everything. For 40 Counselors, who are called wise men, are deputed by whose counsels it is judged.[10]

Note that Benzo also takes care to point out the difference between the doge and the typical Italian podesta, and the fact that it is not only the nobility that has a say in his election but the people as a whole. In this last, at least superficially, Benzo has a more democratic bias than Henry, or for that matter any other analyst of the Venetian constitution. Despite the similarities, there may well be no direct influence, since the institutions are described rather differently—in particular there is no mention of the Great Council (though this is probably what Benzo has in mind when he refers to the "sufferage of all") and because he calls counsellors what Henry calls ancients. In any case, this shows that the mixed constitutional explanation of Venice's success was well known by the early fourteenth century.

The sources are fairly thin for most of the fourteenth century, but in the very late fourteenth and fifteenth centuries, that is, during the early years of the humanistic development of the myth of Venice and civic humanism, Henry's influence is apparent in several works and possible in another— Pier Paolo Vergerio the Elder's fragmentary "De Republica Veneta." Ver-

---

[10] Benzo d'Alessandria, *Chronicon*, p. 56. "Eorum autem instituta quibus vivat communitas prestantissima sunt, sed in hoc magis, quod ex illis rei publicae bonum amplexi cives. Diutina pace gaudent et iustitia summe colunt. Nam summo duce eorum, ex quadam innata disciplina salubriter ducti, obnixe se submittunt, in cuius eleccione non extranea, sed civis persona admittitur. Non nobilitas prevalet, sed universorum suffragium. . . . Qui licet spectaturus [spectatus] sit moribus et magnam preferat equitatem, ei tamen totum licere nolunt. Nam xl consiliari, qui sapientes dicuntur, deputantur, quorum consiliis iudicatur."

gerio (1370–1445), an important humanist, especially in the development
of ideas on education, lived in Venice only for brief periods, but he was of
Venetian parentage and was closely connected with humanist circles in
Venice, Florence, Padua, and the papal Curia. After the end of the Council
of Constance in 1417 he left Italy for the last time in the service of the
Emperor Sigismund. The exact date of his incomplete treatise on Venice is
not known, but it must have been written between 1398 and 1403, probably after his visit to Florence in 1400.[11] In about the same period he also
wrote another political treatise, *On Monarchy*.

Gilbert sees Vergerio as the first proponent of the Venetian mixed constitution of doge, Senate, and Great Council. This obviously is not true,
and in fact Vergerio is less explicit on this point than Henry:

> The Republic of the Venetians is governed by the administration of the best
> [or optimates], which genus of civility may be called "aristocracy" in the Greek
> vocabulary, and which is half way between the rule of kings and a popular
> rule. But this [government] is even much better since because it participates
> in both of the laudable extremes it is mixed from all types of laudable polity at
> the same time. For the leader [doge] in Venice is elected for life, and affairs are
> conducted by his name and authority, and the supreme power of making law
> is with the people when the position of leader [dogeship] is vacant, which
> [law] can be abrogated by no college or person beyond the people itself.[12]

Later, Vergerio clarifies the structure of government in Venice, describing how "the power of the Great Council and the whole city" resides in the
Council of 100 (the Senate), and how most matters are referred to a subset
of this council, the four Great Wise Men, also known as the Heads of
Council.[13] Whether or not Henry is a direct influence, Vergerio shares his
preference for aristocracy and in fact makes it a more restrictive aristocracy.
The "people," as he explains, is not the whole body of people, what he calls
the "plebs," to whom he allows no power and only minor positions such
as that of scribe, but rather it is just another name for the nobility. He does,
however, recognize that nobility is not a hereditary status but a legal one
dependent upon membership in the Great Council. An interesting consequence of this is that if the democratic element is itself noble, the aristo-

[11] Robey and Law, "Venetian Myth," p. 29.
[12] Vergerio, "De Republica Veneta," pp. 38–39. "Venetorum respublica optimatum ad-
ministratione regitur, quod genus civilitatis greco vocabulo licet appellare, que inter regium
popularemque principatum media est. Hec vero tanto est etiam melior, quod quoniam
utroque laudabilium extremorum participat, ex omni genere laudabilis politie simul commixta est. Nam et Dux in ea constituitur perpetuus electione, cuius nomine auctoritatque res
gerantur, et penes populum suprema potestas est, cum vacat ducatus, condende legis, quam
nulli collegio aut homini preter populum ipsum licet abrogare." See Gilbert, "Venetian Constitution," p. 468.
[13] Vergerio, "De Republica Veneta," p. 44.

cratic element must represent an oligarchic elite within the nobility, an elite that the body of nobles finds necessary to restrain.[14]

The question of whether Vergerio drew directly on Henry of Rimini is difficult. It is probable—his treatise was available at this time—but the idea of a Venetian mixed constitution was widespread long before 1400. In the key passages on Venice, the two are not close enough to determine an influence. Robey and Law argue that the differences are a result of historical events—namely the admission of thirty formerly non-noble families to the Great Council after the War of Chioggia (1377–81), including Vergerio's patron Francesco Novello in 1392, and on the gradual narrowing of the base of Venetian government during the fourteenth century. By reflecting these changes, as Robey and Law write, "Vergerio adapts the principles employed by Henry to the political reality of the Quattrocento, and by so doing fills an important role as intermediary in the transmission of this aspect of the Venetian myth." In other passages, particularly in his treatment of kingship in the treatise *On Monarchy*, there is a close resemblance—one that can only be explained either by direct influence or by a common use of Aquinas. It is intriguing that both Henry and Vergerio select the same passages and points from Aquinas, suggesting that Vergerio may be getting his Thomist ideas via Henry. In any case there is no doubt that the humanist Vergerio's mixed constitutional ideas were derived from the medieval scholastic tradition—and that his treatment of the Venetian polity is the same in all important respects as in the more well known sixteenth-century treatises by Contarini and others.[15]

Two texts from the first half of the fifteenth century prove Henry of Rimini's continuing influence. Of minor importance in itself is a sermon that the popular preacher Leonardo of Utine delivered in Venice in 1446 that repeats Henry's analysis of Venice word for word.[16] More important is Lorenzo dei Monaci's *Chronicle*, written around 1420. Lorenzo (c. 1351–1428) wrote this work while serving as Chancellor of the Venetian administration of Crete (1388–1428), and was especially influential for early fifteenth-century humanists. He quotes a long section from "brother Henry" describing Venice but not its mixed constitution and later (without citing him) appropriates Henry's analysis of the government:

> There are three species of ruling. [The species] of a king, which for the most part is converted into tyranny. Of the few best, which is quickly corrupted either by hatred, or jealousy, or avarice. Of the people, which always either by ignorance or imprudence or furor or lightness of spirit acts foolishly in gov-

[14] Vergerio, "De Republica Veneta," p. 44 and Robey and Law, "Venetian Myth," p. 16.

[15] Robey and Law, "Venetian Myth," pp. 17–18, 34.

[16] Leonardus de Utino, *Sermones aurei de Sanctis*, as reported in Robey and Law, "Venetian Myth," p. 13.

erning and either slips into tyranny or external domination. The rule of Venice, mixed from these three, is fortified upon a more solid rock. It has a leader [doge] in similarity to [the species of] a king; it has a most healthful Council of Rogators [the Senate; this is the same term Henry used] in similarity to that of the few best; it has a Great Council in similarity to that of the people—moreover, each of these species is subject to its institutes and laws. But where laws rule, there is a true polity; and a political [rule] is nothing except what is good.[17]

Clearly deriving from Henry, this chronicle favors aristocracy less explicitly than the slightly earlier work of Vergerio. In fact, perhaps consciously, Lorenzo reverses Vergerio's statement that the whole republic depends on the Senate and says that it all depends on the Great Council. Of course, Lorenzo also sees the Great Council as composed only of aristocrats.

Robey and Law do not claim to have unearthed all of the medieval sources of the myth of Venice. As they write, "The conclusion to be drawn, we believe, is that the work of such as Contarini and Paruta can only be properly understood on the basis of a thorough study of their Quattrocento and medieval predecessors—a study which has yet to be completed."[18] This is not that study. I am merely trying to show the continuity between medieval and Renaissance theories.

As one example of this continuity I will look briefly at Gasparo Contarini (1483–1542), whose treatise *On the Magistrates and Republic of the Venetians* was published in 1543 but composed in the 1520s. Contarini came from a prominant and politically involved family of Venetian aristocrats and himself served in almost every important office in his city and was ambassador to Emperor Charles V (1520–25) and Pope Clement VII (1528–30). A skilled compromiser in these two hostile courts, he attempted, at Charles V's request, to mediate the dispute between Catholics and Lutherans at Regensburg in 1541 and there proposed the doctrine of double justification as one possibly acceptable to both sides. Neither, however, would accept it. One of the most influential propagators of the myth

[17] Lorenzo dei Monaci, *Chronici de Rebus Venetis*, pp. 276–77. "Tresque sint species principandi. Regis, quae pro majori parte convertitur in tyrannidem. Optimorum paucorum, quae cito corruit vel odio, vel invidia, vel avaritia. Populi, quae semper vel ignorantia, vel imprudentia, vel furore, vel animi levitate desipit in regendo, et aut in tyrannidem labitur, aut in dominationem externam. Principatus Venetus ex his tribus permixtus, super solidiori petra firmatus est. Habet ducem in similtudinem regis; habet Consilium sanissimum Rogatorum in similtudinem paucorum optimorum; habet majus Consilium in similtudinem populi; quaelibet autem harum specierum subjecta est suis institutis, et legibus. Ubi vero leges principantur, est vera politia, et politicum non est nisi quod bonum est." For the use of "political" in the last sentence see Nicolai Rubinstein, "The History of the Word *politicus* in Early Modern Europe," p. 46. On Lorenzo's influence, see Margaret L. King, *Venetian Humanism in an Age of Patrician Dominance*, p. 215, n. 28.

[18] Robey and Law, "Venetian Myth," p. 13.

of Venice, Contarini was soon translated into English (1599) and other European languages, everywhere stimulating and helping to shape the already existing mixed constitutional traditions.[19]

Very little is new in Contarini, or indeed in any of the sixteenth-century Venetian political writers. In these works, a panegyric on the virtue of the Venetians and the singular success, beauty, and prosperity of Venice is combined with praise of its government. The key elements come directly from the earlier writings of Henry of Rimini, Vergerio, Lorenzo dei Monaci, and others. There is no evidence of Polybian influence, but constant use of Aristotle's *Politics* and medieval Aristotelianism. Contarini divides the government into the usual three parts, an equally balanced mix of "princely sovereignty, the government of the nobility, and popular authority," but he especially praises the aristocratic portion. Like Vergerio he points out that the Great Council is itself a body of nobles and recognizes that the participation of such a wide group of nobles serves to check oligarchy. Like Lorenzo and the medieval Aristotelians, he places primary emphasis on government under law and recommends the mixed constitution as the best way to defend the laws against the encroachments of any one segment of society. He rehearses the usual virtues and failings of the three simple forms of government and shows how the Venetian balance ensures the former and avoids the latter. Even though he denies citizenship to workers, like Vergerio he allows the plebians certain offices in the community—the better ones can be secretaries and all can take part in companies in which they can elect their own officers—so that, as Aquinas and Henry say, all shall feel like they have a part. It is the perfect balance of the government that explains Venice's longevity: "Every mixture dissolveth, if any of the elements (of which the mixed body consisteth) overcome the other. . . . If you will have your commonwealth perfect and enduring, let not one part be mightier than the other."[20]

In Florence, because of the antipathy to Aristotle and even more to medieval Aristotelians, the later writers cover their tracks more thoroughly. Niccolò Machiavelli's analysis of the mixed constitution in the second chapter of *The Discourses*, written between 1512 and 1520, is taken directly from Polybius, and future discourse continued the Polybian emphasis.[21] Machiavelli, and Seyssel in France, were the first Westerners since classical times to apply Polybius's mixed constitutional theory. Yet the tradition that Machiavelli is drawing on and, in the form of the myth of Venice, reacting against developed in Florence in the fifteenth and first decade of the sixteenth century under medieval Aristotelian influences. This is true

[19] Gasparo Contarini, *De Magistratibus et Republica Venetorum*; *The Commonwealth and Government of Venice*.
[20] Contarini, *Commonwealth*, pp. 13, 15–16, 33; 141–42; 67.
[21] Niccolò Machiavelli, *The Discourses*.

especially in regard to the reformation of the Florentine government in the period of Medician exile, 1494–1512, the very period that shaped Machiavelli's outlook.

Leonardo Bruni (c. 1370–1444), the famous Chancellor of the Florentines (1427–44) and one of the founders of civic humanism, is also exceptionally important in the transmission of Aristotelian political ideas through his new, and for centuries definitive, translation of the *Politics*. Equally important is the fact that most of the early printed editions of this translation and some other translations that also appeared at this time included Thomas Aquinas's and Peter of Auvergne's commentary.[22] In the period before Cosimo de' Medici's assumption of power in 1434 Leonardo propounded a purely civic humanist philosophy of universal participation and the nurturing of civic virtue as the only means of self development and the preservation of liberty. Although he did not at first use mixed constitutional language, Bruni's early ideal is similar to Aristotle's ideal of a mixed government in which the component elements disappear and all citizens are assimilated to a single, middle class. Afterwards, Bruni turned toward the more common kind of Aristotelian mixed constitution so as to justify the new order.

This is most apparent in his short treatise "On the Polity of the Florentines," written in Greek in 1439 for the edification of the Greeks coming to the Church Council of Florence. As might be expected from one who was trying to use critical principles to recover the exact meaning of classical sources, Bruni stays fairly close in tone to Aristotle in the *Politics*, but he also adapts some medieval theory in his insistence that, however rarely this may be necessary, only an assembly of all the people can ratify great changes in the polity. For the most part, however, Bruni views Florence as a mixture of aristocracy and democracy with a bias toward aristocracy. Democracy plays a part more by the inclusion of democratic principles of selection by lot, short terms for officials, and respect for liberty and by the exclusion of magnates from participation than by any positive opportunities for universal civic activity.[23] In his actual description of the mechanics of Florentine government, however, Bruni comes close to the portrayal of Venice by Vergerio and others. Not only is there the same aristocratic preference, but also the idea of a larger group of aristocrats balancing potential oligarchs:

> The highest office in the city is that of the nine magistrates whom we call Priors. . . . First among these is the standard-bearer of justice, who is chosen

[22] Charles B. Schmitt, *Aristotle and the Renaissance*, p. 20; Ferdinand Edward Cranz, "The Publishing History of the Aristotle Commentaries of Thomas Aquinas," pp. 160, 170.

[23] Leonardo Bruni, "On the Polity of the Florentines," pp. 140, 143. I alter this translation slightly for consistency.

only from those prominent in honors and lineage. . . . These nine magistrates are assisted by . . . twenty-eight . . . councillors. . . . Nothing can be referred to the great councils that has not first been resolved upon by the Nine and the Councillors. There are two great councils in this city, one of the people with three hundred members, the other of the most prominent citizens, with two hundred. Those matters that come up are first considered carefully by the Nine and the Councellors and voted upon by them. They are then referred to the Council of the People; if they are approved there, they are brought before the Council of the Prominent. If they are passed by this council as well, they are then put into effect. . . . The great councils are like an assembly of the people, while the Nine and the Councellors are like a council, so that it is possible to say of laws approved in this manner . . . that they have been "decreed by the Council and the People of the Florentines."[24]

Despite the dominance of the aristocracy, Bruni does concede a veto power to the Council of the People, that is, of the guilds. Except for the much greater restriction on citizenship to at most the guildsmen, the constitutional structure Bruni describes is compatible with the theories of Marsilius of Padua: a few wise men propose laws that the many evaluate and approve or reject; consideration is given to quantity in the Council of the People and quality in the priorate and the Council of the Prominent; the ultimate sovereign, in the sense that only it can approve a change in the mode or strucure of the polity is the assembly of all the people, although, no doubt, Bruni did not intend this to be inclusive either.

According to Pocock, Bruni was ambivalent about an aristocratic mixed constitution—he states that the shift from democracy occurred only after the people gave up bearing arms on their own behalf (also the chief complaint of Machiavelli). He used the mixed constitutional model because he sought to explain and justify the Medicis' power, but also worried lest giving up power even to those of superior ability would make it impossible for the citizen to achieve the highest degree of civic virtue.[25] But as the Medici hold strengthened in the mid-fifteenth century, aristocratic political theory did as well with a concomitant decrease in concern for democracy. It was then that Florentines turned to and contributed to the myth of Venice. Gilbert shows, and Pocock repeats, that at first only Florentine aristocrats, who unanimously interpreted Venice as an aristocracy, were interested in the myth. They apparently were at first unconcerned with the common formulation of Venice as a balance of the one, the few, and the many because they were used to a complicated governmental structure of numerous councils, officials, and podestas and could regard the one, few, and many simply as various incarnations of aristocratic power. Because he

---

[24] Bruni, "Polity of the Florentines," pp. 140–42.
[25] Pocock, *Machiavellian Moment*, p. 90; Bruni, "Polity of the Florentines," p. 144.

was not familiar with the early Venetian material, Pocock assumes that Venetians themselves always looked at their government as an aristocracy and that it was the Florentines who first described it as a mix of monarchy, aristocracy, and democracy. But he is correct in his explanation of why they eventually did so; namely that in Florence there was a real tradition of popular participation, that belief in the value of such participation did not go away under the Medici rule, and that this already existing tendency was strengthened by the traditional equation of the many with democracy.[26]

All of these factors contributed to the appropriation of the myth of Venice by democratic forces after the expulsion of the Medici in 1494, and the eventual construction of a government in Florence patterned after Venice with a monarchical gonfalonier for life, an aristocratic Signoria, and a democratic Great Council. At its inception the Florentine Great Council represented the widest extent of popular participation in Florentine history, and indeed in that of medieval, Renaissance, or Early Modern Europe—3,200, or about one out of five adult males, qualified for membership. Aristocrats worked to change the democratic bias of this government by means of a proposed aristocratic Senate holding most real power both then and especially in the next period of Medicean exile, 1527–30, but the model of Venice, interpreted once again in the familiar way of Vergerio and other Venetian writers as a mixed constitution with an aristocratic bias, was dominant in their arguments.

The key figure in Florentine politics in the first years after 1494 was the Dominican Girolamo Savonarola (1452–98). Born in Ferarra, but a Florentine resident from 1482, Savonarola was an influential preacher and, after the revolution of 1494, in which he was a leader, the dominant force in Florentine politics and the inspiration for the reform of the government. He was not a public official, but he dominated the new republic until he fell out of favor and was executed for sedition and heresy in 1498. He was not originally much interested in practical secular politics, and the initiative for constitutional change in imitation of Venice may have come from a group of reform-minded aristocrats who went to him for backing.[27] Nevertheless, he took up the cause with enthusiasm and ultimately is responsible for the perception of the reform as democratic. In the 1480s Savonarola wrote in theoretical defense of monarchy and came to republicanism later in life only through his experience and through his idea of Christ as king in the virtuous republic, but one thing that is constant in his political writings is the influence of Thomas Aquinas and especially Ptolemy of Lucca by way of their *On the Government of Rulers*, all of which was at the time

---

[26] Gilbert, "Venetian Constitution," p. 472ff.; Pocock, *Machiavellian Moment*, pp. 99–101.

[27] Weinstein, *Savonarola and Florence*, pp. 151–53, 248–53. This excellent work is the basis of much of my discussion of Savonarola.

attributed to Thomas. In following Thomas and Ptolemy, Savonarola revives their distinction between regal and political power that had been modified or overlooked by many intervening writers. This is apparent in his earliest discussion of politics, the portion of his *Compendium of All Philosophy*, written in the 1480s, entitled "On the Polity and Kingdom." In this Savonarola repeats almost verbatim Ptolemy's view that those, such as the Italians, possessed of intelligence and an independent spirit are suited only for political rule and tends to equate despotism and regal rule. He even gives the same counterexample to the observation that in Italy all those who try to become permanent monarchs end up as tyrants—the doge of Venice.[28] To be sure, as is common, he modifies his republicanism with a general praise of monarchy as the best absolute form of government, but, as with Thomas, Savonarola is insistent that monarchy itself be political and not regal—that the community "temper" (Thomas's own word) the king's power so that he cannot become a tyrant.[29] In other words, the king can be effective as one element of a mixed constitution dependent upon the law and the people. Unlike Ptolemy, Savonarola never completely breaks with the idea of a monarch as compatible with a political regime, but tends later to relegate the monarchical element to a metaphysical plane with the concept of Christ as king of an earthly republic. Weinstein treats "On the Polity and Kingdom" as essentially a monarchist work and the theory of Christ as king a transitional stage to Savonarola's later republicanism.[30] I think, however, that as Weinstein's own evidence proves, Savonarola was always in favor of limited or mixed government, except for the most servile peoples, and republican government for the best—as in Italy. This view never really changed, although what was at first only a detached theoretical statement of Thomist political thought in a comprehensive summary of philosophy became a passionate plea for the perfect polity in the course of his experiences of the events of 1494 and after.

Savonarola wrote his last and most influential work of political theory, *Treatise on the Constitution and Government of Florence*,[31] not long before his downfall, but while he was still popular, at the behest of the Signoria to defend and explain the new arrangement of the Florentine government—the government that at his insistence had added a Great Council in imitation of Venice. This treatise goes beyond Savonarola's mentors, Thomas and Ptolemy, by tying the question of best government to God's

---

[28] Girolamo Savonarola, "De Politia et Regno," p. 585, as reported in Weinstein, *Savonarola and Florence*, pp. 292–93.

[29] Savonarola, "De Politia et Regno," p. 588. "Debet principatum eius ita temperare, ut non possit faciliter tyrannizare." See Weinstein, *Savonarola and Florence*, p. 291.

[30] Weinstein, *Savonarola and Florence*, p. 295.

[31] Savonarola, *Constitution of Florence*. Original Italian Version, *Trattato circa el reggimento e governo della città di Firenze*.

plans for Florence as the biblical "New Jerusalem," the chief city in a new order for the world. It is no longer simply a matter of whether a specific people succeeds or fails to develop in the most appropriate way—the virtue of Florentines and the particular constitutional arrangements of their city acquire cosmic, millennial significance.

Despite this, Savonarola's treatise is still basically Thomist and Aristotelian in orientation, even if the new outlook leads to some apparently contradictory or ambiguous statements. In his analysis of the three simple forms of government, though, what appears to be contradictory in fact comes directly from Thomas and Ptolemy and leads to a relativisim typical of fourteenth-century Aristotelians—the best regime is determined by the particular character of a people. Government is established for the common good, and in principle monarchy is best, aristocracy second best, and civil government (that is, polity) third best (for all the usual Thomist reasons). But in fact it is only in a cowardly, servile community that monarchy would be even acceptable. If a people is quarrelsome it would be the worst form, if especially intelligent and vital, as were the Florentines, it would be intolerable.[32] Except for the particular position of Florence here, this is exactly what Ptolemy wrote about any king and Thomas about a regal king. Similar arguments discredit aristocracy. The conclusion is inescapable—a virtuous people needs a civil government.

Even though he appealed to the Venetian model for Florentine reform, Savonarola did not refer either to the tradition of Venice as a mixed constitution nor advocate imitating Venetian aristocracy, as that polity was most commonly viewed. On the contrary, he distinguished carefully between the restricted nature of the Venetian government and the democratic requirements of Florence, and, after using Venice in his call for a Great Council, rarely referred to Venice again. Nevertheless, as Pocock points out, Savonarola and the events of 1494 "marked a decisive stage in the growth of the image of Venice as a perfect combination of all three forms of government, and the reasons are to be sought in the way political discussion was carried on after Savonarola's failure and death."[33] This is true especially in relation to the addition of Soderini as gonfalonier for life in 1502, in clear imitation of the Venetian doge, and the persistant arguments for an aristocratic Senate, again in imitation of Venice.

Niccolò Machiavelli (1469–1527) was an active participant in the Florentine Republic, from 1498 to 1512 as secretary to the Second Chancery and after 1502 as an associate of gonfalonier Piero Soderini. Bitter at his temporary arrest, torture, permanent exile after the restoration of the Medici in 1512, he sought to understand the causes of defeat. At first, in *The*

[32] Savonarola, *Constitution of Florence*, pp. 234–36.
[33] Weinstein, *Savonarola and Florence*, p. 308; Pocock, *Machiavellian Moment*, p. 112.

Prince, he sought to curry favor with his city's new masters, but returned to undisguised republicanism in *The Discourses*. In this work he explicitly rejects the Venetian model but uses Polybius to defend a mixed constitution in general. The question that I must address is to what extent Machiavelli is influenced also by the medieval and earlier Florentine Aristotelians. As with Seyssel (though to a lesser extent), who with Machiavelli was the first Renaissance writer to use Polybius's sixth book, some of the similarities with Polybius actually coincide with various positions of the medieval Aristotelians that ultimately stem from Aquinas's reinterpretation or misinterpretation of Aristotle in an unconsciously Polybian direction in his emphasis on balance of governmental forms. Clearly, Machiavelli follows Polybius closely in the second chapter of *The Discourses*. He names and approves the sixfold classification of polities—significantly without actually defining any of the simple forms—and discusses the evolution of government from the primitive life of people who lived like beasts and the inevitable cycle of simple forms from kingship to tyranny to aristocracy to oligarchy to popular government to licentiousness to kingship. Because they decay,

> all kinds of government are defective; those three which we have qualified as good because they are too short-lived, and the three bad ones because of their inherent visciousness. Thus sagacious legislators, knowing the vices of each of the three systems of government by themselves, have chosen one that should partake of all of them, judging that to be the most stable and solid. In fact, when there is combined under the same constitution a prince, a nobility, and the power of the people, then these three powers will watch and keep each other reciprocally in check.[34]

The particular cycle is from Polybius, but all the other ideas are ones available from the medieval tradition, and certainly ones Machiavelli would have been familiar with from the Florentine debates, if not directly from his reading. This is true particularly considering that the Soderini government, with which he was so closely associated, was an attempt to realize the stabilization of the Florentine government with just such a blend of monarchy, aristocracy, and democracy.

Machiavelli's objection to Venice is that its mixed constitution was biased in the direction of the nobility, giving the people little or no voice. Despite his frequent pessimism he manages also to have a confidence in the people that goes back to Aristotle, Marsilius of Padua, and other medieval commentators rather than to Polybius or Aquinas. These writers tolerated the people as a necessary evil to restrain the aristocrats and king, but Polybius at least agreed with most of the theoreticians of the Venetian myth

---

[34] Machiavelli, *Discourses*, 1.2, pp. 111–15.

in favoring a mixed constitution with an aristocratic bias. This is why, for example, he thought Rome defeated Carthage—although both had mixed constitutions, Rome leaned to aristocracy while Carthage was more democratic.[35] Like Marsilius, Machiavelli admits that the people may not be the best judges of universal principles, and that therefore they should perhaps neither hold high office nor propose laws. With regard to particulars, however, they are the best judge; as he writes, "No wise man should ever disregard the popular judgment upon particular matters, such as the distribution of honors and dignities; for in these things the people never deceive themselves," and again, "the people are more prudent and stable, and have better judgment than a prince." Though he does not define the simple forms, Machiavelli is clearly more concerned with the common good, an Aristotelian characteristic, than with voluntary submission to government, the Polybian criterion. Consent is important, but more in the way that it was presented by the medieval writers than by Polybius. And Machiavelli associates the common good with a strong popular voice: "It is not individual prosperity, but the general good that makes cities great; and certainly the general good is regarded nowhere but in republics, because whatever they do is for the common benefit." Ignoring this is the problem with the Spartan as well as the Venetian mixed constitution, and only with the establishment of the tribunate as a popular institution did Rome rise above these polities and perfect their constitution.[36] True, Machiavelli phrases his general description of the Roman evolution in Polybian terms, but Ptolemy of Lucca also presents a similar analysis, as well as the suggestion that a mixed constitution might lead to a perfectly stable polity. Machiavelli actually seems to combine elements of both.

It is clear to me that Machiavelli is clothing old ideas that had been in circulation for centuries in respectable classical terms. His experience in the Florentine government and in Florentine intellectual circles discussing these issues more or less constantly in a time of turmoil, revolution, and reaction shaped his attitude to the mixed constitution. Savonarola's influence was perhaps greater than usually conceded. The failure of the reform government could be blamed on a decline of virtue of the citizenry, on inadequacies and imbalances of the constitutional machinery, on aristocratic conspiracies, and perhaps most of all on powerful outside forces that a small city-state would find irresistable. Reflecting on these things, Machiavelli came across and was greatly impressed by Polybius, who as a bonus was infinitely more authoritative to a Renaissance thinker than the despised scholastics. In addition, Polybius provided yet another reason for the decline of even a mixed polity, while holding out hope for future great-

---

[35] Polybius, *Histories*, 6.51.
[36] Machiavelli, *Discourses*, 1.47, p. 237; 1.58, p. 263; 2.2, p. 282; 1.2, p. 116.

ness—the inevetable degeneration of all government in the cycle of decline and renewal. Putting all this together and adding radical new ideas and interpretations of his own, Machiavelli created a theory whose influence is still felt and whose ideas, sometimes praised but often vilified, are present in virtually all Early Modern political thought. His accomplishment may have been possible had Polybius never been recovered, but it certainly would never have happened without the medieval Aristotelian tradition or without the peculiar situation of early sixteenth-century Italy. Just as feudalism and the emergence of Northern monarchies and Italian city-states prepared the ground for acceptance of Aristotle's *Politics*, so medieval political theory and the later medieval state made possible the easy assimilation of Polybius's *Histories*.

In terms of his preference for a mixed constitution Machiavelli differs from other contemporary and later writers only in his dislike for Venice and Sparta, whereas almost all others, certainly aristocrats like Francesco Guicciardini (1483–1540), but even those like Donato Giannotti (1492–1573), who also advocate a popular bias, praise them as prime models of well-balanced polities. Coming from an optimate family who supported the Republic with reservations, Guicciardini never abandoned his preference for wide-scale participation and even a Great Council of sorts, but he felt that the Savonarolian and Soderinian governments put too much power in the hands of the masses, entrusting them with tasks suitable only for the very few. As Pocock notes, "Guicciardini's theory as regards both election and legislation rests upon an Aristotelian [or late medieval Aristotelian and Marsilian but clearly non-Polybian and non-Thomist] conception of decision-making by the many. Though not themselves capable of magistracy, they can recognize this capacity in others; though not themselves capable of framing or even debating a law, they are competent judges of the draft proposals of others."[37]

Guicciardini's ideal of a mixed constitution in his *Dialogue on the Government of Florence*, which Pocock reads as almost a response to Machiavelli's *Discourses*, and, as a defense of the Venetian paradigm, reflects this belief.[38] He considers his own class, the optimates, most capable of exercising power but is also well aware that it would abuse its position if allowed to rule unchecked. His proposal, then, establishes a small, elite, aristocratic Senate, preferably with a lifetime membership as in ancient Rome, but possibly with more limited membership, as in Venice, as the principal governing body. Combined with this would be a monarchic gonfalonier for life

---

[37] Pocock, *Machiavellian Moment*, p. 129. See Skinner, *Modern Political Theory*, vol. 1, p. 170.

[38] Pocock, *Machiavellian Moment*, p. 186. Francesco Guicciardini, *Dialogo e Discorsi del Reggimento di Firenze*. Most of the following description of Guicciardini's *Dialogue* is taken from Pocock, chapter 8, especially pp. 253ff.

and a Great Council limited to those citizens capable of holding office. This last restriction represents a shift from Guicciardini's earlier belief in a more widely based council and toward the actually quite narrow Venetian Great Council. Since the Senate is to be the actual governing body, the Great Council exists primarily to prevent it from degenerating into oligarchy by itself appointing all magistrates (by vote rather than by the more democratic and traditional Florentine practice of lot), by approving or vetoing legislation determined by the Senate, and above all by preserving the established constitutional structure.

Guicciardini approves the tradition of Florentine republicanism that extended the possibility of holding an office to a great number of citizens by limiting terms of office to a few months at most on the basis of the justice of such an arrangement, itself an Aristotelian and non-Polybian concept. But he also regrets that the experience and prudence necessary to govern effectively might require a longer tenure. Venice, he believes, has found the best compromise in the person of one magistrate, the doge, who serves for life, but who is monitered and restrained at all times by councils whose consent is necessary for him to act. Adapting this institution to Florence leads him to support a gonfalonier for life. The gonfalonier is an elected official who serves as the presiding officer of the Ten of War, the executive council of the Senate, but one whose only authority is his prestige within this council and its parent body.

In all important respects Guicciardini believes that this Florentine government and the Venetian one are identical; the fact that it is more difficult to enter the Great Council in Venice is a mere matter of form and not substance, for in each city the entire citizen body (admittedly more restricted in Venice) participates in council, and there is at least "formal equality of access to office; 'they make no distinctions of wealth or lineage, as is done where optimates rule,' and the Venetian system is as popular as the Florentine, the Florentine as optimate as the Venetian."[39] One may be skeptical about whether advancement in either polity actually depended on ability alone, but the important point is that Guicciardini is the first Florentine to take over the whole mixed constitutional component of the myth of Venice with its traditional aristocratic bias and apply it to Florence.

Although Guicciardini usually argues for this model of mixed constitution, at one early point in the *Dialogue* he defends the pre-1494 Medician state against the charge of tyranny, albeit rather tepidly. The Medici did not rule absolutely, he argues, rather they preserved and shared power with the aristocracy which in turn acted as a "bridle" on their actions. Unknowingly using the same word as had Henry of Bracton or his editor over three hundred years before, Guicciardini here comes close, as Pocock observes,

---

[39] Pocock, *Machiavellian Moment*, p. 258; Guicciardini, *Dialogo*, p. 106.

to outlining a theory of limited monarchy substantially different from his usual limited aristocracy, one similar to various conceptions of the English and French monarchies.[40] This argument underlines his belief that although there is one best form of government, at least for Florentines, any government can be serviceable if it prevents any one segment of society from dominating and if it allows those most knowledgeable and capable to contribute. This, and especially his provision that in a limited monarchy the ruler must seek the consent of his chief men, puts him squarely in the tradition of the medieval Aristotelians.

Finally, I will look briefly at Guicciardini's younger contemporary, Giannotti. His later date of birth (1492) made him less directly involved in the 1494–1512 republic, and his writing is generally more detached and academic than either Guicciardini's or Machiavelli's. In his youth he associated with Machiavelli and attended the political discussions in the Oricellari Gardens. From 1520–25 he was a professor, apparently of politics, at the University of Pisa, and before his return to Florence in 1527 he traveled to Venice and Padua. He was an active supporter of the 1527–30 republic and actually held the same position as Machiavelli twenty years earlier; like him he was exiled after the return of the Medici. Giannotti's experience and service both under the moderate but aristocratic gonfalonier Niccolò Capponi (1527–28) and later under the more radical popular government when the Florentine republic was under siege (1528–30) transformed his views from his earlier support of a limited aristocratic government to support of a more popular regime. This is reflected in his two major works: the unfinished *Book on the Republic of the Venetians* (1525–27, published in 1540), which was widely circulated, especially in Italy and England, and *On the Florentine Republic* (after 1530, but not printed until 1721).[41]

Giannotti intended his book on Venice to conclude with a third section on theory, but he never really got past the first part, which described the components of the Venetian government. In this he never explicitly refers to the mixed constitution nor to concepts, either Polybian or Aristotelian, of balance. On the other hand he does discuss the nature of the Venetian doge, Great Council, and smaller aristocratic councils, and when Englishmen such as Harrington read this treatise in the next century it inevitably suggested to them the mixed constitution that was already a commonplace of their political theory. It is not absolutely clear what his views were at this time, but in two short treatises written during the 1527–30 republic

[40] Pocock, *Machiavellian Moment*, pp. 236–37; Guicciardini, *Dialogo*, pp. 77–78.

[41] Pocock, *Machiavellian Moment*, pp. 272–73; Donato Giannotti, *Opere Politice*. As with Guicciardini, Pocock is my main source for Giannotti's political ideas, in this case pp. 272–320. Pocock uses an older edition of Giannotti, *Opere*, to which I will refer.

his thought is of an aristocratic mixed constitutional type quite similar to that of Guicciardini.[42]

In his later work about Florence, however, he not only takes up the mixed constitution at great length and theoretically, but also he becomes a partisan of a popular bias. Here he acknowledges his debt to Aristotle, and Machiavelli, as well as to Polybius, thus becoming the first Italian writer to mention the Polybian theories by name. Of these three he himself puts Aristotle in first place, "from whom, as from a superabundant spring that has spread through all the world overflowing streams of doctrine, I have taken all the fundamentals of my brief discourse."[43] Giannotti's theory is interesting for the way it combines his various sources, the way he develops Aristotle's idea of the middle class polity, and also for his original contribution respecting the relationship of the balanced elements. He declares, echoing Peter of Auvergne, Englebert of Admont, and Nicole Oresme, that although each of the three simple forms is good, each is an abstraction unreachable in practice, if for no other reason that in the world of corruption any of monarchy, aristocracy, or popular government will inevitably degenerate into its opposite. So any good regime must be mixed, and the only question is to determine the proper alignment of powers:

> In the form of government we are seeking it is necesssary that one man be prince, but that his principate is not dependent on himself alone; that the great command, but that their authority does not originate with themselves; that the multitude be free, but that their liberty involve some dependence; and finally that the middle class, as well as being free, can attain to honours [or "offices"], but in such a way as is not placed entirely at their will.[44]

As it stands this is a fairly typical medieval Aristotelian description of a mixed constitution based upon a broadly based but by no means universal participation. Where Giannotti differs is in his analysis of the blending. Plato and Aristotle had praised Sparta and Polybius Rome for an equal balance of the internal forces, commenting that outsiders could not decide whether they were dealing with a monarchy, an aristocracy, or a democracy. The medieval Aristotelians and Contarini followed suit, as did Machiavelli, despite his innovation of viewing internal strife as progressive. But Giannotti believes that an equal balance can lead only to chaos since the individual qualities of each group involved do not disappear in the mixture (perhaps echoing Aristotle's views on physical mixture) and that therefore "it is impossible to 'temper [Thomas Aquinas's terminology] a state so perfectly that the *virtù*—let us call it power—of each part is not

[42] Pocock, *Machiavellian Moment*, p. 286.

[43] Giannotti, *Opere*, 2, p. 12; Pocock, *Machiavellian Moment*, p. 295.

[44] Giannotti, *Opere*, 2, pp. 16, 20; Pocock, *Machiavellian Moment*, pp. 297, 299.

apparent,' and if these are equal, then the oppositions and resistances between them will be equal, and the republic will be full of dissensions which will bring about its ruin."[45]

In thus rejecting both Polybius and Aristotle, Giannotti poses the question of which element should dominate in the best mixed constitution: he rejects the monarchical out of hand and considers only the great men or the people. Largely following Aristotle, Machiavelli, and perhaps Marsilius of Padua, he defends the role of the people.[46] In so doing, I must note, he does not adopt Bodin's position that there can be only one sovereign and that therefore the mixed constitution is a contradiction in terms; on the contrary the whole purpose of his theory is to develop a true, workable balance of power. In fact, he is much closer in spirit here to the medieval Aristotelians, who in general did often emphasize one part of the mixture (though usually without stating this explicitly)—northern writers generally the king, Italian the people or aristocrats—than to Bodin or to any of the ancient writers. He concludes that the Great Council should exercise those "functions which are sovereign in the republic and embrace all the power of the state."[47] Venice, then, is Giannotti's ideal for a mixed republic; he attacks the Roman mixed constitution praised by Polybius and Machiavelli for arranging its parts too equally.[48]

Giannotti does follow Aristotle in basing the prospects of success of good government on a large middle class. This is because he believes only members of this class are at once capaple of exercising power by holding office and willing to obey those in authority over them. To make a mixed constitution viable, it must be as strong as the great individuals and the lower classes put together—and in this case only a mixed constitution can possibly succeed. The best case and purest and most stable would result if the entire population were of the middle class; this would be Aristotle's ideal middle-class polity describable either as a perfect democracy or perfect mixed constitution. Giannotti does not believe that such a place can actually exist, and so in the real world he entrusts the balance of power to the people—by which he means, of course, the middle class. Giannotti believes that Florence has the middle class required for a successful mixed constitution, largely because the Medici in the fifteenth century raised up many poor men to political office so as to lessen the power of the aristocracy. Referring to these ideas and to the similar idea of Harrington, who, influenced by Giannotti, ascribed a role analagous to the Medici to the Tudors in building up the English landowning class, Pocock comments: "One is tempted to say that both offered ways out of the Polybian cycle

---

[45] Pocock, *Machiavellian Moment*, p. 307; Giannotti, *Opere*, 2, 99–100.

[46] Pocock, *Machiavellian Moment*, pp. 309ff.

[47] Giannotti, *Opere*, 2, p. 122; Pocock, *Machiavellian Moment*, p. 313.

[48] Pocock, *Machiavellian Moment*, p. 308; Giannotti, *Opere*, 2, pp. 101–3.

and into the rotating spheres of ordered government; but in fact their causal vocabularies were so rich that they never had recourse to the Polybian model at all. The vocabulary of Aristotle was less stilted, and it is this that Giannotti is using."[49]

Thus we see that even as Polybius becomes important in sixteenth-century Italian political discourse, it is Aristotle, directly through the *Politics* and as filtered through medieval Aristotelians and civic humanists, who remains the dominant force.

[49] Pocock, *Machiavellian Moment*, pp. 300–303; Giannotti, *Opere*, 2, pp. 24, 45–48.

Chapter 16

CONCLUSION

IN THE INTRODUCTION I outlined two goals for my book. My first goal was to show that most thirteenth- and fourteenth-century Aristotelian political thinkers came to accept a mixed constitution, usually involving a king limited by the body of citizens, as the best political arrangement and to show that even those who did not go so far incorporated elements of mixed constitutional theory, consciously or unconsciously, into their models of ideal government. Their approaches toward the question of the best government and their conclusions were inevitably conditioned by their particular experiences and political needs and problems and thus necessarily resulted in a reciprocal relationship with Aristotle in which on the one hand they imposed their concerns and values on him, and on the other he molded and significantly altered their modes of thought. My second goal was to relate medieval mixed constitutionalism to the later flourishing of such theories in the late Middle Ages, the Renaissance, and the Early Modern period. This goal is undoubtedly more important for the history of political thought as a whole, and when I posed it in the introduction I indicated that it speaks to two separate issues; one, the late fourteenth- and fifteenth-century ideas of conciliarists like Jean Gerson and Pierre d'Ailly who advocated a mixed constitution for the Church and legists like John Fortescue who labeled the English system a "regal and political kingdom," and two, the Renaissance and Early Modern ideas of the mixed constitution in Italy, England, and the United States. I make this twofold division because in the first case medieval Aristotelian influence is indisputable, even if its significance is controversial, whereas in the second case traditional wisdom insists on the predominant influence of classical authors, and especially Polybius, who was translated into Latin for the first time at the beginning of the sixteenth century.

After outlining the ancient Greek origin of the mixed constitution, its persistence in the Roman world, and its effective disappearance in the early centuries C.E., the bulk of my book addressed the first goal. One important and somewhat surprising conclusion to come out of my investigation was that although, as I expected, most writers tended toward mixed constitutionalism, there was little uniformity, even among writers long regarded as almost indistinguishable, regarding either the reasons for supporting this form or the details of the government or the roles of the component elements or the composition of the elements themselves.

The most profound disjunction—and one that right at the beginning set the stage for the two major approaches to the mixed constitution—was between Thomas Aquinas and Peter of Auvergne, Thomas's devoted pupil and the continuer of his commentary on the *Politics*. Their combined commentary circulated widely under Thomas's name alone with many or most copies of the *Politics*, even after humanist translations of Aristotle replaced that of William of Moerbeke, and thus influenced all succeeding theorists. Thomas's emphasis was on rule by law, and so he developed the influential distinction between regal and political power, depending upon whether the ruler (assumed to be one man in either case) ruled with full power or was limited by the laws of the polity. He supported a political king "tempered" by the power of the wise few and of all the citizens. He chose this as the best government because he thought that, in general, it would best serve the common good, in that it would include the best forms of government, that is, monarchy and aristocracy, and it would ensure the loyalty of every citizen by giving each one some voice in government, while at the same time, and above all, deny sovereignty to any one element and thus guard against the tyranny of the one, the few, or the many. This would follow regardless of the virtues or vices of the particular people; in fact, it would be even more necessary for an evil people. In his emphasis on checks and balances, as in his disdain for the wisdom of the people, Thomas was accidentally closer to Polybius, who was unknown to him, than to Aristotle, who had little interest in restraining the various groups and was more concerned with equitably representing the classes of society. When Polybius was rediscovered, this affinity aided in the fusion of the Aristotelian and Polybian traditions.

Peter of Auvergne also identified the mixed constitution as best, but for him it could only prosper if the people were virtuous. It is superior to its components not because they check each other, as it was for Thomas, but because each element has something unique to offer: the king, unity; the few, wisdom; the many, power. The essence of the mixed constitution, then, was the uniting of the virtues of all the elements. In defending his argument Peter developed the influential distinction of the bestial and nonbestial multitude, the one worthy, the other unworthy of a share in government. For Thomas the political character of the ideal monarch was of first importance; for Peter it was not. His loose use of *regal* and *political*, which for Thomas were precise terms, has for centuries obscured the understanding of Thomas's theories. Because the ideal form was appropriate for only some peoples, Peter was more receptive than Thomas to Aristotle's relativism—the idea that we must be concerned in most instances with the best political solution for a particular time, place, and people than with any ideally best form. Beyond this, Peter initiated the medieval discussion of a number of other ideas that would prove important in the centuries to follow—the idea that all good government is mixed to some extent, the idea that the few should propose actions or rulers for the assent of the whole people, and most important of all the idea that the multitude, if it be not utterly degenerate, has something positive to offer and should not merely be given a sop to pacify it.

As with so many other medieval authorities, the presence within one document—in this case the Thomas/Peter commentary—of contradictory doctrines provided the opportunity for a wide range of interpretations and the material for numerous other theories. This opportunity was expanded by the fact that Thomas also did not complete his one independent political treatise, *On the Government of Rulers*. Although Ptolemy of Lucca, who finished this, was closer in many important ways to Thomas than has generally been recognized, his independent spirit and hostility to the institution of kingship provided another model for later writers and encouraged a more radical political approach. As with the commentary, Thomas's and Ptolemy's combined work circulated under Thomas's name alone.

Most other writers of the period, including Ptolemy, agreed with Peter that only the virtuous should take part in government, but some, also including Ptolemy, combined this with Thomas's idea of balance. Even Giles of Rome, who claimed to support an absolute king, in fact came close to advocating a mixed constitution, while at the same time, in a break with medieval tradition, laying the groundwork for later theories of divine right kingship. He described the medieval reality in which government was a mixture of monarchy and aristocracy resting on the passive consent of the people—the reality that others interpreted as an Aristotelian mixed constitution, but Giles himself never carried his ideas to this logical conclusion. Engelbert of Admont, one of the few in this period actually to use the classical terminology, described all the possible permutations in a mixed constitution and supported the mixture of as many good forms as possible. John of Paris was the first to advocate explicitly a mixed constitution for the Church and suggested that it would also be best for the state.

Expediency became the prime criterion for the early fourteenth-century scholars, but they still argued about what would be best in principle. Marsilius of Padua's "legislator" was in all essentials a mixed constitution, although the actual government could take on any form. William of Ockham and Jean Buridan further developed the concepts of expediency and limitation of power, Bartolus of Sassoferrato linked the best form to the size of the community, and Walter Burley described the English monarchy in terms suggestive of the mixed constitution. Finally, around 1375 Nicole Oresme produced a synthesis of these sources in which he set out a powerful defense of the mixed constitution, limited government, and law.

The antepenultimate and the first part of the penultimate chapter of my book took up the first part of my second goal—description of the medieval

Aristotelian influence on Schism and post-Schism conciliarism and fifteenth-century English political theory. The mixed constitutional theories
that Jean Gerson, Pierre d'Ailly, and others developed to end the Great
Schism and regulate a reformed Church derived largely from John of Paris,
Thomas Aquinas, and Nicole Oresme, but other medieval Aristotelians
also played a part. Both adapted John and Thomas's analyses of the ancient
Jewish constitution, but d'Ailly placed more emphasis on the role of the
cardinals and restricted his mixed constitutional thought to the Church.
Gerson in contrast argued that a properly mixed constitution should prevail in both spheres and, following Oresme and Engelbert of Admont, that
all government is inherently mixed in some way—the problem is to construct the best balance. Later conciliarists continued the arguments of Gerson and d'Ailly, although they seldom used the term *mixed constitution*.
Fifteen years after the Schism, Nicolaus of Cusa used these writers and
some earlier ones, above all Marsilius of Padua, to describe a papal and
imperial mixed constitution. He becomes one of the first to combine this
with the idea of a social contract and a doctrine of separation of powers.
Even after the effective demise of conciliar domination in the 1430s, conciliar thought continued throughout the fifteenth and sixteenth centuries,
most notably in the early sixteenth-century writings of Almain and Mair,
both of whom drew from Gerson, d'Ailly and others. Although conciliar
thought never again was able to dominate in the Church, the writers I have
mentioned became a major influence on later secular political thought and
were frequently cited by opponents of absolute monarchy, especially by
British mixed constitutionalists.

John Fortescue's conception of the relationship of king, privy council,
and Parliament is rather close to and undoubtedly influenced by these conciliar ideas, as well as being close to Nicole Oresme's conception of the
French mixed constitution and in some ways to Savonarola's scheme for
Florence in the 1490s. He did not explicitly support mixing monarchy,
aristocracy, and democracy as such, but his theory provides one of the most
important bridges between medieval and Early Modern mixed constitutionalism. In addition, he was one of the most influential writers for the
theoreticians of the Tudor and Stuart monarchies. Building on the ideas of
Ptolemy of Lucca and Thomas Aquinas he made a combination of regal
and political power the basis of good government—he even used the Thomist terminology of restraining the regal king with political power. He also
wrote approvingly of the standard medieval examples of mixed constitutions—Sparta, Rome, the Mosaic polity—and compared them to England.

By way of Fortescue and the conciliarists, as well as through the continuing influence of Thomas Aquinas and the other medieval Aristotelians,
medieval ideas of the mixed constitution made their way into Renaissance
and Early Modern thought. The last two chapters of my book take up the

remaining part of my second goal by bringing the story of the mixed constitution up to the mid-sixteenth century in both Northern Europe and Italy, and by showing how in every case medieval influence was prominent, even after Polybius became generally known, and even among humanists.

Claude de Seyssel, in his French mixed constitutional model, was one of the first to use Polybius, but the influence of Aquinas, Ptolemy of Lucca, Giles of Rome, Oresme, and perhaps even John Fortescue and Walter Burley was much stronger. There is no feeling that Polybius has come as a revelation to him; in fact, all he really did is bring in some parts of Polybius to his otherwise fully medieval argument. He apparently viewed Polybius as simply one more formulation of an already familiar theory. The same could be said of most of the other sixteenth-century French and English writers about mixed constitutions, including those like François Hotman, who developed the Calvinist theory of resistance. In England Thomas Starkey combined medieval, French, and conciliar ideas with Italian ones, particularly with the idea of Venice as a mixed constitution. In the mid- and late-sixteenth century John Ponet, John Aylmer, and Thomas Smith, influenced by Fortescue, Starkey, Marsilius of Padua, the conciliarists, and others, brought the "classical theory of the English constitution" to fruition and for the first time explicitly identified king, Lords, and Commons with the classical mixed constitution of monarchy, aristocracy, and democracy. In all of this Polybius played a very minor part.

Renaissance Italian humanist writers typically eschewed their medieval predecessors and imagined themselves to be rejecting them in favor of the revival of classical republicanism. Thus, more than in England or Northern Europe, Italian humanist discourse tended to be framed in classical terms. But in substance Italian mixed constitutionalism never strayed far from medieval ideas. In particular, the "myth of Venice," which explained that city's prosperity and longevity by its mixed constitution of doge, Senate, and Great Council, and which proved enormously influential in Florentine and other Italian political thought and even in the final description of England as a mixed constitution, first emerged around 1300 under the influence of scholastic Aristotelianism. The key figure in this development was Henry of Rimini, a follower of Thomas Aquinas, who applied his master's analysis of the Mosaic constitution to his own city. Henry also emphasized the aristocratic bias of the Venetian government, a characteristic element of most Renaissance applications of the Venetian myth. Henry's influence, directly or through the mediation of others, is apparent in fourteenth-, fifteenth-, and sixteenth-century Venetian writers such as Lorenzo dei Monaci, Pier Paolo Vergerio, and Gasparo Contarini.

In Florence, the Venetian myth enjoyed great influence, first among aristocrats anxious to defend the Medici, then by democratic forces after the Medici were expelled in 1494. Eventually it became the basis for a Florentine mixed constitution of gonfalonier for life, Senate, and Great Council. Savonarola, the most important influence in Florentine government from 1494–98, once again reinterpreted the myth of Venice, with the help of Ptolemy of Lucca and Thomas Aquinas. Machiavelli rejected Venice as a model, but retained a mixed constitutional ideal. He used Polybian language, but in many respects, such as the rejection of an aristocratic bias and his sometime confidence in the people, he goes back more to medieval writers like Marsilius of Padua and Ptolemy of Lucca than to Polybius or Aristotle. With respect to the mixed constitution, it is only in his dislike for Venice and Sparta and a differing emphasis on the balance of the particular groups that Machiavelli differs from the somewhat later mixed constitutionalists, the aristocratic Francesco Guicciardini, and democratic Donato Giannotti.

Historians traditionally point to a sharp break between humanism and Scholasticism, despite the fact that throughout the Renaissance Scholasticism continued to flourish in and dominate the universities. Pocock has stressed the disjunction of two modes of political thought—one based on law and another on republican virtue—that coexisted for a time in Italy, but which were essentially incommensurate. Some more recent work has shown that the interaction of humanists and Scholastic thinkers, especially conciliarists, was greater than previously thought.[1] But I am not disputing that there were many essential differences; I am only asserting that a number of concepts, including that of divided government and the mixed constitution, persisted in a variety of guises. It is not merely a question of influence—something that both Skinner and Pocock, for example, if not all Renaissance or Early Modern historians, accept. It is more the case of the ubiquity of certain ideas under a wide variety of means of expression. Both Skinner and Pocock speak in their own ways of vocabularies of political discourse, and both stress the necessity of understanding these dynamically in their historical settings and evolution so as, for example, not to mistake new ideas that employ antiquated terminology. No prudent person could dispute this, and, indeed, in my investigations I have shown the changing content of many words such as *political*, *mixture*, *democracy*, and the like. But I also have shown something quite different, that in many cases political writers, for a variety of reasons, use new language for old ideas. That fact and why they do this is equally important in understanding the mentalities of the writers and the outlook and fashions of the writers' times.

Renaissance humanist writers preferred not to base themselves on the

---

[1] See for example J.G.A. Pocock, "Virtues, Rights, and Manners," and David Peterson, "Conciliarism, Republicanism, and Corporatism: the 1415–1420 Constitution of the Florentine Clergy."

despised medieval Scholastics, but had unbounded respect for the ancients. Still more did Protestants hesitate to use explicitly the theories of the devilish papists. Both did in fact resort to such unsavory authorities on occasion, but more typically they clothed their essentially medieval ideas of divided government and mixed constitutions in Polybian or ancient Aristotelian garb. Eventually this charade was forgotten. John Adams, for example, probably had no knowledge of medieval mixed constitutionalism. But developmentally the origin of all the major ideas of Early Modern mixed constitutionalism were indisputably medieval and Aristotelian. It is true, but perhaps too weak, to say, as I have, that the medieval tradition made the enthusiastic reception of Polybius possible—it might be better to say that Polybius added a few concepts and some vocabulary to a thriving tradition. It was only later that the framework of medieval mixed constitutionalism disappeared and the Polybian superstructure alone remained visible.

BIBLIOGRAPHY

In general, medieval writers through the fourteenth century will be found under their first name and later authors under their surnames. Three exceptions are the fourteenth-century writers Jean Buridan, Nicole Oresme, and Walter Burley, who are listed by surname.

Aalders, G.J.D. "Die Mischverfassung und ihre historische Dokumentation in dem *Politica* des Aristoteles." In *La 'Politique' d'Aristote. Entretiens sur L'Antiquité Classique*, vol. 2, 199–244. Geneva: Vandoeuvres, 1965.

———. *Die Theorie der Gemischten Verfassung im Altertum*. Amsterdam: A. M. Hakkert, 1968.

Adler, Mortimer J. and Walter Farrell. "The Theory of Democracy." *The Thomist* 3 (1941): 397–449, 588–652; 4 (1942): 121–81, 286–354, 446–522, 692–761.

Albertus Magnus. *Commentarium in Decem Libros Ethicorum Aristotelis*. Vol. 14, *Opera Omnia*. Aschendorff: Monasterium Westfalorum, 1951–80.

———. *Commentarium in Octo Libris Politicorum Aristotelis*. Vol. 4, *Opera Omnia*. London, 1651.

Allan, Donald J. "Individual and State in the Ethics and Politics." In *La 'Politique' d'Aristote. Entretiens sur L'Antiquite Classique*, vol. 2, 53–96. Geneva: Vandoeuvres, 1965.

Allen, John William. "Marsilio of Padua and Medieval Secularism." In *The Social and Political Ideas of Some Great Medieval Thinkers*. Edited by J.F.C. Hearnshaw, 167–91. London, 1923.

———. *A History of Political Thought in the Sixteenth Century*. London: Methuen, 1957.

Almain, Jacobus. *Quaestio Resumptiva, de Dominio Naturali, Civili, et Ecclesiastico*. In Jean Gerson, *Opera Omnia*. Edited by Louis Du Pin. Antwerp, 1706.

Althusius, Johannes. *The Politics of Johannes Althusius*. Translated by Frederick S. Carney. Boston: The Beacon Press, 1964.

Aristotle. *Aristotle's Politics*. Translated by T. A. Sinclair. New York: Penguin Books, 1962.

———. *Ars Rhetorica*. Edited by Leonard Spengel. Vol. 1. Leipzig: B. G. Teubner, 1867.

———. *The Basic Works of Aristotle*. Edited by Richard McKeon. New York, 1941.

———. *Ethicorum Nichomacheorum libri decem*. Edited by Carolus Zell. 2 vols. Heidelberg: Mohr and Winter, 1820.

———. *Politicorum Libri Octo cum vetusta translatione Guilelmi de Moerbeke*. Edited by Franciscus Susemihl. Leipzig, 1872.

Aubert, J.-M. *Le droit romain dans l'oeuvre de Saint Thomas*. Paris: J. Vrin, 1955.

Augustine. *De Civitas Dei*. Vols. 47–48. *Corpus Christianorum Series Latina*, 1965.

———. *Epistolae. Patrologia Cursus Completus Patrum Latinorum*. Vol. 33. Paris, 1849.

Aylmer, John. *An Harborowe for Faithfull and Trewe Subjects*. Strasbourg, 1559.

Babbitt, Susan. *Oresme's Livre de Politique and the France of Charles V*. Vol. 75. Part 1 of *Transactions of the American Philosophical Society*. Philadelphia, 1985.

———. *The Livre de Politiques of Nicole Oresme and the Political Thought and Development of the Fourteenth Century*. Ph.D. diss., Cornell University, 1977.

Baethgen, F. "Die Entstehungszeit von Dantes Monarchia." *Sitzungsberichte der Bayischen Akademie der Wissenschaften: Phil.-Hist. Klasse*. (1967): fasc. 5.

Barker, Ernest. *The Dominican Order and Convocation*. Oxford: Clarendon Press, 1913.

———. *Greek Political Theory. Plato and his Predecessors*. London: Methuen, 1960.

———. *The Political Thought of Plato and Aristotle*. New York: Dover Publications, 1959.

Baron, Hans. "Cicero and the Roman Civic Spirit in the Middle Ages and Early Renaissance." *Bulletin of the John Rylands Library* 22 (1938): 72–97.

———. *The Crisis of the Early Italian Renaissance*. Princeton: Princeton University Press, 1966.

———. *From Petrarch to Leonardo Bruni*. Chicago: University of Chicago Press, 1968.

———. *Humanistic and Political Literature in Florence and Venice*. Cambridge: Harvard University Press, 1955.

Barraclough, G. *The Medieval Empire: Idea and Reality*. London: G. Philip, 1950.

Bartholomaeus Anglicus. Description of Venice from *De proptietatibus rerum*, appended to D. Robey and J. Law, "Venetian Myth and the 'De republica veneta' of Pier Paolo Vergerio." *Rinascimento*, 2d ser., vol. 15 (1975): 50–51.

Bartolus of Sassoferrato. *Opera*. Lucerne, 1590.

———. "Tractatus de Regimine Civitatis." In *Consilia, questiones et tractatus bartoli cum additionibus novis*, f.127r–128v. Venice, 1495.

———. "Tractatus de tirannia." In *Consilia, questiones et tractatus bartoli cum additionibus novis*, f.92v–94v. Venice, 1495.

Battlagia, F. "Marsilio de Padova e il Defensor pacis." *Rivista internazionale de filosofia del diritto* 4 (1924).

Baudry, L. "Le philosophie et le politique dans Guillaume d'Ockham." *Archives d'histoire doctrinale et litteraire du moyen âge* 12 (1939): 209–30.

———. "Les Rapports de Guillaume d'Ockham et de Walter Burleigh." *Archives d'histoire doctrinale et litteraire du moyen âge* 9 (1934): 155–73.

Baumann, J. J. *Die Staatslehre des heiligen Thomas von Aquino*. Leipzig: S. Hirzel, 1909.

Baumer, Franklin le van. *The Early Tudor Theory of Kingship*. New Haven: Yale University Press, 1940.

———. "Thomas Starkey and Marsilius of Padua." *Politica* 2 (1936–37): 188–205.

Bayley, Charles. "Pivotal Concepts in the Political Philosophy of William of Ockham." *Journal of the History of Ideas* 10 (1949): 199–218.

Beale, J. H. *Bartolus on the Conflict of Laws*. Cambridge: Harvard University Press, 1914.

Becker, Marvin B. "Dante and his Literary Contemporaries as Political Men." *Speculum* 41 (1966): 665–80.

————. "Some Aspects of Oligarchical, Dictatorial and Popular Signorie in Florence, 1282–1382." *Comparative Studies in Society and History* 2 (1960): 421–39.

Benzo d'Alessandria. Description of Venice from *Chronicon*, appended to D. Robey, and J. Law, "Venetian Myth and the 'De republica veneta' of Pier Paolo Vergerio." *Rinascimento*, 2d ser., vol. 15 (1975): 56–57.

Berber, Friedrich. *Das Staatsideal im Wandel der Weltgeschichte.* Munich: Verlag C.H. Beck, 1973.

Berges, W. *Die Fürstenspiegel des hohen und späten Mittelalters.* Leipzig: K. W. Hiersemann, 1938.

Black, Anthony. "The Conciliar Movement." In *Cambridge History of Medieval Political Thought c. 350–c. 1450.* Edited by J. H. Burns, 573–87. Cambridge: Cambridge University Press, 1988.

————. *Guilds and Civil Society in European Political Thought from the Twelfth Century to the Present.* London: Methuen, 1984.

————. "The Individual and Society." In *Cambridge History of Medieval Political Thought c. 350–c. 1450.* Edited by J. H. Burns, 588–606. Cambridge: Cambridge University Press, 1988.

————. *Monarchy and Community.* Cambridge: Cambridge University Press, 1970.

Bluhm, William T. "The Place of the Polity in Aristotle's Theory of the Ideal State." *Journal of Politics* 24 (1962): 743–53.

Blythe, James M. "Family, Government, and the Medieval Aristotelians." *History of Political Thought* 10 (1989): 1–16.

————. "The Mixed Constitution and the Distinction Between Regal and Political Power in the Work of Thomas Aquinas." *Journal of the History of Ideas* 47 (1986): 547–65.

Bodin, Jean. *Method for the Easy Comprehension of History.* New York, 1945.

————. *The Six Books of a Commonweal.* Cambridge: Harvard University Press, 1962.

Boehner, P. "Ockham's Political Ideas." *Review of Politics* 5 (1943): 442–68.

Booth, William J. "Politics and the Household. A Commentary on Aristotle's *Politics*, Book One." *History of Political Thought* 2 (1981): 203–26.

Born, Lester K. "Erasmus on Political Ethics." *Political Science Quarterly* 43 (1928): 520–43.

————. "The Perfect Prince: A Study in Thirteenth and Fourteenth Century Ideals." *Speculum* 3 (1928): 470–504.

Bouwsma, W. J. *Venice and the Defence of Republican Liberty.* Berkeley: University of California Press, 1968.

Bowe, Gabriel. *The Origin of Political Authority.* Dublin: Clonmore and Reynolds, 1955.

Bowle, J. *Western Political Thought.* New York: Oxford University Press, 1948.

Braun, E. "Aristokratie und aristokratische Verfassungsform in der Aristotelischen Politik." In *Politeia und Respublica.* Edited by P. Steinmetz, 148–80. Wiesbaden: F. Steiner, 1969.

————. *Das Dritte Buch der Aristotelischen "Politik."* Vienna: H. Böhlaus, 1965.

————. "Die Summierungstheorie des Aristoteles." *Jahreshefte des österisches Archäologisches Institut,* 157–84. Vienna, 1959.

Braun, E. "Die Theorie der Mischverfassung bei Aristoteles." *Wiener Studien* 80, N.F. 1 (1967): 80–85.

Bruni, Leonardo. *Historiarum Florentini Populi*. In *Rerum Italicarum Scriptores*. Edited by Emilio Santini, vol. 19. Bologna, 1926.

———. *Humanistisch-philosophische Schriften*. Edited by Hans Baron. Leipzig, 1928.

———. "On the Polity of the Florentines." Translated by Athanasios Moulakis. In *University of Chicago, Readings in Western Civilization*. Vol. 5, *The Renaissance*, 139–44. Chicago: University of Chicago Press, 1986.

Brynteson, W. "Roman Law and Legislation in the Middle Ages." *Speculum* 41 (1966): 420–37.

———. "Roman Law and New Law: The Development of a Legal Idea." *Revue internationale des droits de l'antiquité*. 3d Ser., vol. 12 (1965): 203–23.

Buridan, Jean. *Questiones super Decem Libros Ethicorum Aristotelis*. Reprint of the Paris, 1513 editon. Frankfort: Minerva, 1968.

———. *Questiones super Octo Libros Politicorum Aristotelis*. Reprint of the Paris, 1513 editon. Frankfort: Minerva, 1969.

Burley, Walter. *Expositio in octo libros Politicorum Aristotelis*. Manuscript. Cambridge University Library, ms 490/486, f.1r–74v.

Burns, J. H., ed. *Cambridge History of Medieval Political Thought c. 350–c. 1450*. Cambridge: Cambridge University Press, 1988.

———. "Fortescue and the Political Theory of Dominium." *Historical Journal* 28 (1985): 777–97.

———. "Politia Regalis et Optima: The Political Ideas of John Mair." *History of Political Thought* 2 (1981): 31–61.

Buschmann, Erna "Rex Inquantum Rex. Versuch Uber den Sinngehalt und geschichtlichen Stellenwert eines Topos in *De Regimine Principum* des Engelbert von Admont." *Miscellanea Mediaevalia* 7 (1970): 303–33.

Calvin, John. *Institutes of the Christian Religion*. Translated by Henry Beveridge. Grand Rapids, 1957.

Canning, J. P. "Introduction: Politics, Institutions, and Ideas." In *Cambridge History of Medieval Political Thought c. 350–c. 1450*. Edited by J. H. Burns, 341–66. Cambridge: Cambridge University Press, 1988.

Cappa-Legora, A. *La politica di Dante e di Marsilio da Padova*. Rome: Editrice Nazionale, 1906.

Carlyle, A. J. *Political Liberty: A History of the Conception in the Middle Ages and Modern Times*. London: F. Cass, 1963.

Carlyle, R. W. and A. J. *A History of Medieval Political Theory in the West*. 6 vols. Edinburgh and London: W. Blackwood, 1903–1936.

Carr, David R. "Marsilius of Padua and the Rule of Law." *Italian Quarterly* 28 (1987): 1–25.

———. "The Prince and the City: Ideology and Reality in the Thought of Marsilius of Padua." *Medioevo* 5 (1979): 279–91.

Cassirer, E. *The Myth of the State*. New Haven: Yale University Press, 1946.

Catto, Jeremy. "Ideas and Experience in the Political Theory of Thomas Aquinas." *Past and Present* 71 (1976): 3–21.

Ceard, Jean. "L'influence de Marsile de Padoue sur la pensée calviniste française de la fin du XVIᵉ siecle: Du Plessis-Mornay, Lecteur du 'Defensor Pacis'." *Medioevo* 6 (1980): 577–94.

Chambers, M. "Aristotle's 'Forms of Democracy.' " *Transactions of the American Philological Association* 92 (1966): 20–36.

Chaplais, P. "La Souveraineté du roi de France et le pouvoir législatif en Guyenne au début du XIVᵉ siècle." *Moyen Age* 59 (1963): 450–52.

Chenu, M. D. *Towards Understanding Thomas Aquinas.* Translated by A. M. Landry and D. Hughs. Chicago: Regnery, 1964.

Cheyette, Frederic. "Custom, Case Law, and Medieval Constitutionalism: a Reexamination." *Political Science Quarterly* 78 (1963): 362–90.

Chinard, Gilbert. "Polybios and the American Constitution." *Journal of the History of Ideas* 1 (1940): 38–58.

Chrimes, S. P. *English Constitutional Ideas in the Fifteenth Century.* Cambridge: Cambridge University Press, 1936.

Chroust, A. H. "The Corporate Idea and the Body Politic in the Middle Ages." *Review of Politics* 9 (1947): 423–52.

———. "The Function of Law and Justice in the Ancient World and the Middle Ages." *Journal of the History of Ideas* 7 (1946): 298–320.

Church, William Farr. *Constitutional Thought in Sixteenth Century France.* New York: Octagon Books, 1941.

Cicero, Marcus Tullius. *The Laws.* Translated by Clinton Walker Keyes. London, 1928.

———. *On the Commonwealth.* Edited by George H. Sabine and Stanley B. Smith. Columbus: The Ohio State University Press, 1929.

Clarke, M. V. *Medieval Representation and Consent.* London: Longmans, Green, and Co., 1936.

Coleman, Janet. "Dominium in Thirteenth and Fourteenth-Century Political Thought and Its Seventeenth-Century Heirs: John of Paris and Locke." *Political Studies* 33 (1985): 73–100.

Collins, Ardis B. *The Secular is Sacred: Platonism and Thomism in Marsilio Ficino's Platonic Theology.* The Hague, 1974.

Condren, Conal. "Democracy and the *Defensor pacis*: On the English Language Tradition of Marsilian Interpretation." *Il Pensiero Politico* 13 (1980): 301–16.

———. "George Lawson and the *Defensor Pacis*: On the Use of Marsilius in Seventeenth-Century England." *Medioevo* 6 (1980): 594–617.

———. "Marsilius of Padua's Use of Authority: A Survey of its Significance in the *Defensor pacis*." *Political Theory* 5 (1977): 205–18.

———. *The Status and Appraisal of Classic Texts: An Essay on Political Theory, Its Inheritance, and the History of Ideas.* Princeton: Princeton University Press, 1985.

Contarini, Gasparo. *Commonwealth and Government of Venice.* Translated by Lewes Lewkenor. London, 1599.

———. *Epistolae et Commentariolus De Potestate Pontificis.* In *Bibliotheca Maxima Pontifica.* Edited by J. T. Rocabertus, 177–87. Reprint of 1694 edition. Graz, Austria: Academische Druck- und Verlagsanstalt, 1969.

———. *De Magistratibus et Republica Venetorum.* In *Opera*, 259–326. Paris, 1571.

Coopland, G. W. "An Unpublished Work of John of Legnano: The 'Somnium' of 1372." Part 1 of *Nuovi studi medievali* 2 (1925–26): 65–88.

Copinger, W. A. *Supplement to Hain's Repertorium*. 2 vols. London, 1895–1902.

Costanzo, J. "The *De Monarchia* of Dante Algeheri." *Thought* 43 (1968): 87–126.

Cranston, Maurice. "Saint Thomas Aquinas as a Political Philosopher." *History Today* 14 (1964): 313–17.

Cranz, Ferdinand Edward. *Aristotelianism in Medieval Political Theory: A Study of the Reception of the Politics*. Ph.D. thesis, Harvard University, 1938.

———. *A Bibliography of Aristotle Editions 1501–1600*. Baden-Baden: V. Koerner, 1984.

———. "The Publishing History of the Aristotle Commentaries of Thomas Aquinas." *Traditio* 34 (1978): 157–92.

Czartorysky, P. "Gloses et commentaites inconnus sur la *Politique* d'Aristote d'après les mss. de la bibliothèque Jagellone de Cracovie." *Mediaevalia Philosophica Polonorum* 5 (1960): 3–44.

D'Ailly, Pierre. *De Emendatione Ecclesiae*. Basel, 1525.

———. *De Materia Concilii Generalis*. In Bernhard Meller, *Studien zur Erkenntnislehre des Peter von Ailly*. Freiburg, 1954.

———. *Tractatus de Ecclesiae, Concilii Generalis, Romani pontificis, et Cardinalium Auctoritate*. In Jean Gerson, *Opera Omnia*. Edited by Louis Du Pin. Antwerp, 1706.

Daly, Lowrie J. "Medieval And Renaissance Commentaries on the *Politics* of Aristotle." *Duquesne Review* 13 (1968): 41–55.

———. "The Conclusions of Walter Burley's Commentary on the *Politics*." *Manuscripta* 12 (1968): 79–92; 13 (1969): 142–49; 15 (1971): 13–22.

———. "Walter Burley and John Wyclif on Some Aspects of Kingship." Vol. 4, *Melanges Eugene Tisserant*, 163–74. Vatican City: Biblioteca apostolica vaticana, 1964.

———. "Some Notes on Walter Burley's Commentary on the *Politics*." In *Essays in Medieval History Presented to Bertie Wilkinson*. Edited by T. A. Sandquist and M. R. Powicke, 176–91. Toronto: University of Toronto Press, 1969.

Dante Alighieri. *Monarchia*. In *Le Opere di Dante Alighieri*. Vol. 5. Edited by Pier Giorgio Ricci (N.p., 1965).

David, Marcel. *La Souveraineté et les limites juridiques du pouvoir monarchique du IXᵉ au XVᵉ siècle*. Paris: Dalloz, 1954.

Davies, R. G. and J. H. Denton, eds. *The English Parliament in the Middle Ages*. Manchester: Manchester University Press, 1981.

Davis, Charles Till. "Brunetto Latini and Dante." *Studi Medievali*, 3d. ser., vol. 8 (1967): 421–50.

———. *Dante and the Idea of Rome*. Oxford: Clarendon Press, 1957.

———. "An Early Florentine Political Theorist: Remegio de' Girolamo." In *Proceedings of the American Philosophical Society* 104 (1960): 662–76.

———. "Ptolemy of Lucca and the Roman Republic." In *Proceedings of the American Philosophic Society* 118 (1974): 30–50.

———. "Roman Patriotism and Republican Propaganda: Ptolemy of Lucca and Pope Nicholas III." *Speculum* 50 (1975): 411–33.

De Wolf, H. "L'individue et le group dans le scholastique du XIIe siècle." *Revue Neoscholastique de Philosophie* 22 (1920): 341–57.

Demongeot, Marcel. *Le Meilleur regime politique selon saint Thomas.* Paris: Ancienne Librairie Roger et Chernoviz, 1928.

Dempf, A. *Sacrum Imperium: Geschichts- und Staats- Philosophie des Mittelalters und des Politischen Renaissance.* Munich: R. Oldenbourg, 1962.

Deslisle, Léopold. "Les Ethiques, Politiques et les Economiques d'Aristote traduites et copiés pour le roy Charles V." *Mélanges de paléographie et de bibliographie,* 157–82. Paris: Champion, 1880.

Devine, Francis Edward. "Stoicism and the Best Regime." *Journal of the History of Ideas* 31 (1970): 323–36.

Dickinson, John. "The Mediaeval Conception of Kingship and Some of Its Limitations, as Developed in the Policraticus of John of Salisbury." *Speculum* 1 (1926): 308–37.

Dondaine, H.-F. "Le Super Politicam de saint Thomas: tradition manuscrite et imprimée." *Revue des Sciences Philosophiques et Théologiques* 48 (1964): 585–602.

Donovan, G. M. and M. H. Keen. "The 'Somnium' of John of Legnano." *Traditio* 37 (1981): 325–45.

Dunbabin, Jean. "Aristotle in the Schools." In *Trends in Medieval Political Thought.* Edited by Beryl Smalley, 65–85. Oxford: Basil Blackwell, 1965.

———. "Government." In *Cambridge History of Medieval Political Thought c. 350– c. 1450.* Edited by J. H. Burns, 477–519. Cambridge: Cambridge University Press, 1988.

———. "The Reception and Interpretation of Aristotle's *Politics.*" In *The Cambridge History of Later Medieval Philosophy,* Edited by Norman Kretzmann. Cambridge: Cambridge University Press, 1982

———. "The Two Commentaries of Albertus Magnus on the Nichomachian Ethics." *Recherches de theologie ancienne et mediévale* 30 (1963): 232–50.

Eccleshall, Robert. *Order and Reason in Politics: Theories of Absolute and Limited Monarchy in Early Modern England.* Oxford: Oxford University Press, 1978.

Ehrenberg, Victor. *The Greek State.* Oxford: Basil Blackwell, 1950.

Elton, G. R. *The Body of the Whole Realm: Parliament and Representation in Medieval and Tudor England.* Charlottesville, Va., 1969.

———. "The Political Creed of Thomas Cromwell." *Transactions of the Royal Historical Society,* 5th ser., vol. 6 (1956): 84–86.

Elyot, Thomas. *The Boke Named the Governour.* 2 vols. London, 1883.

Emerton, Ephraim. *The Defensor Pacis of Marsiglio of Padua: A Critical Study.* Harvard Theological Studies 8. Cambridge: Harvard University Press, 1920.

———. *Humanism and Tyranny.* Cambridge: Harvard University Press, 1925.

Endres, Joseph A. "*De Regimine Principum* des hl. Thomas von Aquino." *Festschrift E. Baeumker,* 261–67. Münster, 1913.

Engelbert of Admont. "De providentia Dei." In *Bibliotheca Ascetica Antiquo-nova.* Edited by Bernhard Pez, vol. 3, 50–150. Reprint of the Regensburg, 1724 edition. Farnborough, England: Gregg Press, 1967.

———. *De regimine principum.* Regensberg, 1724.

Engelbert of Admont. *Speculum virtutum moralium*. In *Bibliotheca Ascetica Antiquonova*. Edited by Bernhard Pez, vol. 3, 1–498. Reprint of the Regensburg, 1724 edition. Farnborough, England: Gregg Press, 1967.

———. *Tractatus de ortu, et progressu statu et fine Romani Imperii*. In *Politica imperialia*. Edited by Melchior Goldast, 754–73. Frankfort: J. Bringer, 1614.

Erasmus, Desiderius. *Education of a Christian Prince*. New York: Octagon Books, 1973.

Eschmann, I. T. "Bonum commune melior est quam bonum unius." *Medieval Studies* 6 (1944): 62–120.

———. "Saint Thomas Aquinas on the Two Powers." *Medieval Studies* 20 (1958): 177–205.

———. "Studies on the Notion of Society in Saint Thomas Aquinas." *Medieval Studies* 8 (1946): 1–42; 9 (1947): 19–55.

———. "A Thomistic Glossary on the Principle of the Preeminence of the Common Good." *Medieval Studies* 5 (1943): 123–65.

Esmein, A. "La maxime *Princeps legibus solutus est* dans l'ancien droit public français." In *Essays in Legal History*. Edited by Paul Vinogradoff, 201–14. Oxford: Oxford University Press, 1913.

Faral, Edmond. "Jean Buridan. Notes sur le manuscrits, les éditions et le contenu de ses ouvrages." *Archives d'Histoire doctrinale et littéraire du Moyen Age* 21 (1946): 1–53.

Farrell, Walter. "The Natural Foundations of the Political Philosophy of Saint Thomas." *Proceedings of the American Catholic Philosophical Association* 8 (1934): 75–85.

Fasoli, Gina. "Nascita di un mito." In *Studi storica in onore di Gioacchino Volpe*. Vol. 1. Florence, 1958.

Fictenau, H. "Vom Verständnis der römischen Geschichte bei deutschen Chronisten des Mittelalters." *Festschrift Percy Ernst Schramm*, 401–19. Wiesbaden: F. Steiner, 1964.

Figgis, John Neville. "Bartolus and European Political Ideas." *Transactions of the Royal Historical Society* 19 (1905): 147–68.

———. *Political Theory from Gerson to Grotius*. Cambridge: Cambridge University Press, 1931.

Fink, Zera. *The Classical Republicans*. Evanston, IL: Northwestern University Press, 1945.

Flori, Ezio. "Il trattato 'De Regimine Principum' e le dottrine politiche di S. Tommaso." *Scuola cattolica*, Ser. 7 (1924): 134–69.

Folz, R. *L'idée de l'Empire en occident du V*ᵉ *au XIV*ᵉ *siècle*. Paris: Aubier, 1953.

Fortescue, John. "Example What Good Counseill Helpith and Advantageth, and of the Contrare What Folowith." Appendix A in *The Governance of England Otherwise Called The Difference between an Absolute and Limited Monarchy*. Edited by Charles Plummer. Oxford: The Clarenden Press, 1885.

———. *De Laudibus Legum Angliae*. Edited by A. Amos. Cambridge: J. Smith, 1825.

———. *De Laudibus Legum Angliae*. Edited by S. B. Chrimes. Cambridge, 1942.

———. *The Governance of England: Otherwise Called The Difference between an Ab-*

solute and Limited Monarchy. Edited by Charles Plummer. Oxford: The Clarendon Press, 1885.

Fowler, George B. "Additional Notes on Manuscripts of Engelbert of Admont." *Rechèrches de théologie ancienne et médiévale* 28 (1961): 269–82.

———. *Intellectual Interests of Engelbert of Admont*. New York: Columbia University Press, 1947.

———. "Manuscripts of Engelbert of Admont." *Osiris* 11 (1954): 484–85.

Franklin, Julian H. "Jean Bodin and the End of Medieval Constitutionalism." In *Jean Bodin: Verhandlungen der internationalen Bodin Tagung in München*. Edited by Horst Denzer, 151–66. Munich, 1973.

———. *John Locke and the Theory of Sovereignty: Mixed Monarchy and the Right of Resistance in the Political Thought of the English Revolution*. New York: Cambridge University Press, 1978.

Friedrich, Carl J. *The Philosophy of Law in Historical Perspective*. Chicago: University of Chicago Press, 1958.

———. *Transcendent Justice: The Religious Dimension of Constitutionalism*. Durham, N.C.: Duke University Press, 1964.

Galbraith, G. R. *The Constitution of the Dominican Order 1218–1360*. Manchester: The University Press, 1925.

Gebauer, Werner "Die Aufnahme der Politik des Aristoteles und die naturrechtliche Begründung des Staats durch Thomas von Aquino." *Vierteljahrsschrift für Sozial- und Wirtschaftsgeschichte* 29 (1936): 137–60.

Geerken, John H. "Pocock and Machiavelli: Structuralist Explanation in History." *Journal of the History of Philosophy* 17 (1979): 309–18.

George of Trebizond. *Praefatio in libros Platonis 'De Legibus.'* In *Studi in onore di Antonio Corsano*. Edited by F. Adorno. Manduria, 1970.

Gerson, Jean. *Oeuvres Complètes*. 10 vols. Paris: Desclée & Cie, 1973.

———. *Opera Omnia*. Edited by Louis Du Pin. Antwerp, 1706.

Gettell, R. G. *The History of Political Thought*. New York: Century, 1924.

Gewirth, Alan. "John of Jandun and the *Defensor pacis*." *Speculum* 23 (1948): 267–72.

———. *Marsilius of Padua. The Defender of Peace*. 2 vols. New York: Columbia University Press, 1951–56.

———. "Philosophy and Political Thought in the Fourteenth Century." In *The Forward Movement in the Fourteenth Century*. Edited by Francis Lee Utley. Columbus: Ohio State University Press, 1961.

———. "Republicanism and Absolutism in the Thought of Marsilius of Padua." *Medioevo* 5 (1979): 23–48.

Giannotti, Donato. *Opere*. Edited by G. Rosini. 3 vols. Pisa, 1819.

———. *Opere Politiche*. Milan: Marzurzti, 1974.

Gierke, Otto. *Natural Law and the Theory of Society*. Translated by Ernest Barker. Cambridge: Cambridge University Press, 1958.

———. *Political Theories of the Middle Ages*. Translated by Frederic W. Maitland. Boston: Beacon Press, 1958.

Gilbert, Allan H. "Had Dante read the *Politics* of Aristotle?" *Proceedings of the Modern Language Association* 43 (1928): 602–13.

Gilbert, Allan H. *Machiavelli's Prince and Its Forerunners*. Durham, 1938.

Gilbert, Felix. "Florentine Political Assumptions in the Period of Savonarola and Soderini." *Journal of the Warburg and Courtauld Institutes* 12 (1957): 187–214.

———. *Machiavelli and Guicciardini: Politics and History in Sixteenth Century Florence*. New York: Norton, 1984.

———. "Sir John Fortescue's 'Dominium Regale et Politicum,'" *Mediaevalia et Humanistica* 2 (1943): 88–97.

———. "The Venetian Constitution in Florentine Political Thought." In *Florentine Studies: Politics and Society in Renaissance Florence*. Edited by N. Rubinstein, 463–500. London: Faber and Faber, 1968.

Gilby, Thomas. *Principality and Polity: Aquinas and the Rise of State Theory in the West*. London: Longmans, Green, and Co., 1958.

Giles of Rome. *De ecclesiastica Potestate*. Edited by Richard Scholz. Stuttgart: Scientia Aalen, 1961.

———. *De Regimine Principum Libri III*. Reprint of the Rome, 1556 edition. Frankfort: Minerva, 1968.

———. *De Renunciatione Papae*. In *Bibliotheca Maxima Pontifica*. Edited by J. T. Rocabertus, vol. 2, 1–64. Reprint of the 1694 edition. Graz, Austria: Academische Druck- und Verlagsanstalt, 1969.

Gilmore, Myron P. *Argument from Roman Law in Political Thought, 1200–1600*. Cambridge: Harvard University Press, 1941.

Gilson, Etienne. *The Christian Philosophy of Saint Thomas Aquinas*. London: Victor Gollancz, 1957.

Goff, F. R. *Incunabula in American Libraries*. New York, 1964.

Goodenough, E. "The Political Philosophy of Hellenistic Kingship." *Yale Classical Studies* 1 (1928): 55–104.

Gough, J. W. *The Social Contract: A Study of Its Development*. Second Edition. Oxford: Clarendon Press, 1957.

Grabmann, Martin. "Hilfsmittel des Thomasstudiums aus alter Zeit." In *Mittelalterliches Geistesleben* II, 424–89. Munich, 1936.

———. "Die mittelalterlichen Kommentare zur Politik des Aristoteles." *Sitzungsberichte der Bayerischen Akademie der Wissenschaften* 2 (1941): Band 2, Heft 10, 1–83.

———. "Die Wege von Thomas von Aquin zu Dante." *Deutsches Dante-Jahrbuch* 9: 9–35.

———. "Studien über den Einfluss der aristotelischen Philosophie auf der mittelalterlichen Theorien über das Verhältnis von Kirche und Staat." In *Sitzungsberichte der Bayerischen Akademie der Wissenschaften zu München*. Part 2 of *Philosophische-Historische Abteilung*. Munich, 1934.

———. "Studien zu Johannes Quidort von Paris, O. P." *Sitzungsberichte der bayerischen Akademie der Wissenschaften, Phil.-Hist. Klasse*. Munich, 1922.

———. "Tolomeo von Lucca." in *Mittelalterliches Geistesleben*, vol. 1, 354–60. Munich: M. Huebner, 1926–56.

Granfeld, David. "The Scholastic Dispute on Justice: Aquinas versus Ockham." *Nomos* 6 (1963): 229–42.

Gray, Hanna H. "Valla's Encomium of St. Thomas Aquinas and the Humanist

Conception of Christian Antiquity." In *Essays in History and Literature Presented by the Fellows of the Newberry Library to Stanley Pargellis*. Edited by H. Bluhm. Chicago, 1965.

Grech, Gundissalvus. *The Commentary of Peter of Auvergne, the Inedited Part*. Rome: Desclée, 1967.

———. "The Manuscript Tradition of Peter of Auvergne's Inedited Commentary on Aristotle's *Politics.* " *Angelicum* 41 (1964): 438–49.

Greenidge, A.H.J. *A Handbook of Greek Constitutional Theory*. London: Macmillan, 1896.

Greenleaf, W. H. *Order, Empericism, and Politics: Two Traditions of English Political Thought 1500–1700*. London: Oxford University Press, 1964.

———. "The Thomasian Tradition and the Theory of Absolute Monarchy." *English Historical Review* 79 (1964): 747–60.

Gregory I. *Moralia in Job. Patrologia Cursus Completus Patrum Latinorum*. Vols. 75–76. Paris, 1849.

Griesbach, M. F. "John of Paris as a Representative of Thomistic Political Philosophy." In *An E. Gilson Tribute*. Edited by Charles J. O'Neill, 33–50. Milwaukee: Marquette University Press, 1959.

Grignaschi, Mario. "L'interprétation de la 'Politique' dans le Dialogue de Guillaume d'Ockham." In *Liber memoralis Georges de Lagarde*, 59–72. Louvain: Nauwelaerts, 1970.

———. "La definition du 'civis' dans la scholastique." *Anciens pays et assemblées d'Etats* 35 (1966): 70–100.

———. "La limitazione de poteri de principans in Guglielmo d'Ockham e Marsilio da Padova." *Atti del lo Congresso internazionale*, 35–51. Rome, 1958.

———. "La rôle de l'aristotelisme dans le *Defensor pacis* de Marsile de Padoue." *Revue d'histoire et de philosophie religieuses* 35 (1955): 301–40.

———. "Nicole Oresme et son commentaire à la Politique d'Aristote." *Album Helen Maud Cam*, vol. 1, 97–151. Louvain: Publications Universitaires de Louvain, 1960–61.

———. "Un commentaire nominaliste de la Politique d'Aristote: Jean Buridan." *Ancien Pays et Assemblées d'Etats* 19 (1960): 125–42.

Gugenheim, M. "Marsilius von Padua und die Staatslehre des Aristoteles." *Historische Vierteljahrschrift* 7 (1904): 343–62.

Francesco Guicciardini. *Dialogo e Discorsi del Reggimento di Firenze*. Edited by Robert Palmarocchi. Bari: Laterza, 1932.

Gwyn, W. B. *The Meaning of the Separation of Powers. Tulane Studies in Political Science*, Vol. 9. New Orleans: Tulane University Press, 1965.

Hain, Ludwig. *Repertorium bibliographicum*. 2 vols. Stuttgart, 1826–38.

Hamburger, M. *Morals and Law: The Growth of Aristotle's Legal Theory*. New Haven: Yale University Press, 1951.

Hamm, Marlis. "Elgelbert von Admont als Staatstheoretiker." *Studien und Mitteilungen zur Geschichte des Benediktiner-Ordensund seiner Zweige* 85 (1974): 343–495.

Hamman, A. *La doctrine de l'église et de l'état chez Occam*. Paris: Éditions Franciscaines, 1942.

Hamman, A. "La doctrine de l'église et de l'état d'après le Breviloquium d'Occam." *Franziskanische Studien* 32 (1950): 135–41.

——. "S. Augustin dans le Breviloquium de principatu tyrannico d'Occam." *Augustinus Magister* 2 (1954): 1019–27.

Hansen, Morgens Herman. "Initiative and Decision: the Separation of Powers in Fourth Century Athens." *Greek, Roman, and Byzantine Studies* 22 (1981): 345–70.

Hanson, Donald W. *From Kingdom to Commonwealth: The Development of Civic Consciousness in English Political Thought.* Cambridge: Harvard University Press, 1970.

Harding, Alan. "Political Liberty in the Middle Ages." *Speculum* 55 (1980): 423–43.

Häring, Nikolaus. "Commentaries and Hermeneutics." In *Renaissance and Renewal in the Twelfth Century.* Edited by R. L. Benson and G. Constable, 174–200. Cambridge: Harvard University Press, 1982.

Harrington, James. *The Commonwealth of Oceana.* London: Routledge, 1887.

Hawkins, D.J.B. *A Sketch of Medieval Philosophy.* New York: Sheed and Ward, 1947.

Hearnshaw, F.J.C. *The Society and Political Ideas of Some Great Medieval Thinkers.* London: G. G. Harrap, 1923.

Henry of Bracton. *De Legibus et Consuetudinibus Angliae.* Edited by Woodbine. 4 vols. New Haven: Yale University Press, 1915–42.

——. *On the Laws and Customs of England.* Translated by S. E. Thorne. Cambridge: Harvard University Press, 1968.

Henry of Rimini. Description of Venice from *Tractatus pulcherrimus de quatuor virtutibus cardinalibus,* tr. 2, chap. 4, part 16, appended to D. Robey and J. Law, "Venetian Myth and the 'De republica veneta' of Pier Paolo Vergerio." *Rinascimento,* 2d ser., vol. 15 (1975): 52–56.

——. *Tractatus pulcherrimus de quatuor virtutibus cardinalibus.* Strassbourg, 147?.

Henry Totting of Oyta. *Translatio super Politicam.* Manuscript, 14: f.158v–171v; 1445. 14/15: f.175r–243v. Leipzig: Karl-Marx-Universitäts Bibliothek, 1413.

Herodotus. *Histories.* In *The Greek Historians.* Edited by Francis R. B. Godolphin. Vol. 1. New York: Random House, 1942.

Hexter, J. H. "Seyssel, Machiavelli, and Polybius VI: the Mystery of the Missing Translation." *Studies in the Renaissance* 3 (1956): 75–96.

——. *Vision of Politics on the Eve of the Reformation: More, Machiavelli, and Seyssel.* New York: Basic Books, 1973.

Hinton, S. R. W. K. "English Constitutional Theories from Sir John Fortesque to Sir John Eliot." *English Historical Review* 75 (1960): 410–25.

Hocedez, E. "La vie et les oeuvres de Pierre d'Auvergne." *Gregorianum* 19, 3–36. Rome, 1933.

Hotman, François. *Francogallia.* In *Constitutionalism and Resistance in the Sixteenth Century.* Edited by Julian H. Franklin, 47–96. New York: Pegasus, 1969.

Hudson, Winthrop S. *John Ponet: Advocate of Limited Monarchy.* Chicago: University of Chicago Press, 1942.

Hyde, J. K. *Padua in the Age of Dante*. Manchester: Manchester University Press, 1966.

———. *Society and Politics in Medieval Italy*. New York: St. Martin's Press, 1973.

Jacob, E. F. *Essays in the Conciliar Epoch*. Manchester: Manchester University Press, 1943.

Isocrates. *Works*. Translated by Larue van Hook. 3 vols. Cambridge: Harvard University Press, 1945.

Isidore of Seville. *Etymologiarum sive Originum Libri XX*. W. M. Lindsay, ed. 2 vols. Oxford: Oxford University Press, 1911.

Jaffa, Harry V. *Thomism and Aristotelianism: A Study of the Commentary by Thomas Aquinas on the Nichomachean Ethics*. Chicago: University of Chicago Press, 1952.

Jenks, E. *Law and Politics in the Middle Ages*. New York: Holt, 1898.

John of Paris. *On Royal and Papal Power*. Translated by John A. Watt. Toronto: Pontifical Institute of Mediaeval Studies, 1971.

———. *Tractatus de Potestate Regia et Papali*. In *Johannes Quidort von Paris: Über königliche und päpstliche Gewalt*. Edited by F. Bleienstein. Stuttgart: E. Klett, 1969.

John of Salisbury. *Policraticus*. Edited by Murry F. Markland. New York: Frederick Ungar, 1979.

Jones, J. W. *Law and Legal Theories of the Greeks*. Oxford: Clarendon Press, 1956.

Kantorowicz, Ernst. *The King's Two Bodies*. Princeton: Princeton University Press, 1957.

Kayser, J. R. and R. J. Lettieri. "Aquinas's *Regimen bene commixtum* and the Medieval Critique of Classical Republicanism." *The Thomist* 46 (1982): 195–220.

Keen, M. H. "The Political Thought of the Fourteenth Century Civilians." In *Trends in Medieval Political Thought*. Edited by Beryl Smalley, 105–26. Oxford: Basil Blackwell, 1965.

Keohane, Nannerl O. *Philosophy and the State in France: The Renaissance to the Enlightenment*. Princeton: Princeton University Press, 1980.

Kern, Fritz. *Kingship and Law in the Middle Ages*. Translated by S. B. Chrimes. Oxford: Basil Blackwell, 1939.

King, Margaret L. *Venetian Humanism in an Age of Patrician Dominance*. Princeton: Princeton University Press, 1986.

Koebner, R. "Despot and Despotism." *Journal of the Warburg and Courtauld Institutes* 14 (1951): 275–302.

Kölmel, Wilhelm. *Regimen Christianum: Weg und Ergebnisse des Gewaltenverhältnisses und des Gewaltenverständnisses*. 8–14 Jahrhundert. Berlin: W. de Gruyter, 1970.

———. " 'Universitas civium et fidelium': Kriterien der Sozialtheorie des Marsilius von Padua." *Medioevo* 5 (1979): 49–81.

———. *Wilhelm Ockham und seine kirschen-politischen Schriften*. Essen, 1962.

Krause, H. "Consilio et iudicio. Bedeutingsbreite und Sinngehalt eines mittelalterlichen Formel." In *Speculum historiale. Geschichte im Spiegel von Geschichtsschreibungund Geschichtsdeuting*. Edited by C. Bauer, L. Boehm, and M. Müller, 416–38. Freiburg-Munich, 1965.

Kreitzer, Donald J. "Problems of the Origin of Political Authority." *Philosophical Studies*. (Maynooth) 10 (1960): 190–203.

Kretzmann, Norman, ed. *The Cambridge History of Later Medieval Philosophy*. Cambridge, 1982.

Kristeller, Paul O. "Humanism and Scholasticism in the Italian Renaissance." In *Studies in Renaissance Thought and Letters*. Rome, 1956.

Kurz, Hanns. *Volkssouveränität und Volksrepräsentation*. Cologne: C. Heymann, 1965.

Kuttner, Stefan. "Cardinalis: The History of a Canonical Concept." *Traditio* 3 (1945): 129–214.

Lachance, L. *L'humanisme politique de Saint Thomas*. Montreal: Éditions du Lévrier, 1965.

Lacombe, G. et al., eds. *Aristoteles Latinus. Codices*. 3 vols. Rome, 1939; Cambridge, 1955; Bruges-Paris, 1961.

Ladner, G. "Aspects of Medieval Thought on Church and State." *Review of Politics* 9 (1947): 403–22.

de Lagarde, George. "La philosophie de l'autorité impériale au milieu du XIV*e* siècle." *Lumière et vie* 9 (1960): 41–59.

———. "Comment Ockham comprend le pouvoir seculier." In *Scritti di sociologia e politia in onore Luigi Sturzo*, 593–612. Bologna: N. Zanichelli, 1953.

———. "L'Idée de représentation dans les oevres de Guillaume d'Ockham." *Bulletin of the International Committee of Historical Sciences* 9 (1937): 425–51.

———. *La Naissance de l'esprit laïque au declin du Moyen age*. 5 vols. Louvain: E. Nauwelaerts, 1956–70.

———. "Marsile de Padoue et Guillaume d'Ockham." In *Études d'histoire du droit canonique dédiees à Gabriel le Bras* 1, 593–605. Paris, 1965.

———. "Ockham et le concile général." In *Album Helen Maud Cam*, 83–94. Louvain: Publications universitaires de Louvain, 1960.

———. "Review of Conor Martin's *The Commentaries on the* Politics *of Aristotle in the Late Thirteenth and Early Fourteenth Centuries*." *Revue du moyen age latin* 6 (1950): 329–33.

———. "Review of Martin Grabmann." *Revue Historique de droit français et étranger*, ser. 4, vol. 15 (1936): 360–64.

———. "Sur l'interprétation d'un texte d'Aristote." *Mélanges Paul Fournier*. 375–93. Paris: Recueil Sireg, 1929.

———. "Un adaptation de la Politique d'Aristote au XIV*eme* siècle." *Revue Historique de Droit Français et Etranger*, 4th ser., vol. 11 (1932): 227–69.

de Laix, Roger A. "Aristotle's Conception of the Spartan Constitution." *Journal of the History of Philosophy* 12 (1974): 21–30.

Lajard, F. "Jean de Paris." *Histoire litteraire de la France* 25 (1869): 244–70.

Lane, F. C. *Venice and History*. Baltimore: Johns Hopkins Press, 1966.

Langmuir, Gavin I. " 'Per commune consilium regni' in Magna Carta." *Studia Gratiani* 15 (1972): 467–85.

Lapsley, G. "The Parliamentary Title of Henry IV." *English Historical Review* 49 (1934): 423–49, 577–606.

Laski, H. J. "Political Thought in the Later Middle Ages." *Cambridge Medieval History* 8. Cambridge: Cambridge University Press, 1936.

Latini, Brunetto. *Li Livres dou Tresor*. Berkeley: University of California Press, 1948.

Leclercq, Jean. *Jean de Paris et l'ecclésiologie du XIIIe siècle*. Paris: J. Vrin, 1942.

Leff, Gordon. "The Apostolic Ideal in Later Medieval Ecclesiology." *Journal of Theological Studies*, 18 (1967): 58–82.

———. *William of Ockham: The Metamorphosis of Scholastic Discourse*. Manchester: Manchester University Press, 1975.

Lenkeith, Nancy. *Dante and the Legend of Rome*. London: University of London, The Warburg Institute, 1952.

Leonardus de Utino. *Sermones aurei de Sanctis*. Venice, 1473.

"Letter to Louis of Hungary." Appended to D. Robey and J. Law, "Venetian Myth and the 'De republica veneta' of Pier Paolo Vergerio." *Rinascimento*, 2d ser., vol. 15 (1975): 57–59.

Levinson, R. B. *In Defense of Plato*. Cambridge: Harvard University Press, 1953.

Lewis, Ewart. "King above Law? 'Quod Principi Placuit' in Bracton." *Speculum* 39 (1964): 240–69.

———. *Medieval Political Ideas*. 2 vols. New York: Knopf, 1954.

———. "Natural Law and Expediency in Medieval Political Theory." *Ethics* 50 (1939–40): 144–63.

———. "Organic Tendencies in Medieval Political Thought." *American Political Science Review* 32 (1938): 849–76.

———. "The Positivism of Marsiglio of Padua." *Speculum* 38 (1963): 541–82.

Lewis, John D. and Oscar Jászi. *Against the Tyrant: The Tradition and Theory of Tyrannicide*. Glencoe, Il.: The Free Press, 1957.

Lewis, P. S. *Later Medieval France: The Polity*. New York: Macmillan, 1968.

Lewy, Guenter. *Constitutionalism and Statecraft during the Golden Age of Spain*. Geneva: E. Droz, 1960.

Liebeschütz, Hans. "Chartres und Bologna: Naturbegriff und Staatsidee bei Johannes von Salisbury." *Archiv für Kulturgeschichte* 50 (1968): 3–32.

Lohr, Charles H. "Medieval Latin Aristotle Commentaries." *Traditio* 23 (1967): 313–413 (A–F); 24 (1968): 149–245 (G–I); 26 (1970): 135–215 (Jacobus-Johannes Juff); 27 (1971): 251–351 (Johannes de Kanthi- Myngodus); 28 (1972): 281–395 (N-Richardus); 29 (1973): 93–197 (Robertus-W); 30 (1974): 119–43 (Supplemental).

———. "Renaissance Latin Aristotle Commentaries." *Studies in the Renaissance* 21 (1974): 228–89; *Renaissance Quarterly* 28 (1975): 689–741; 29 (1976): 714–45; 30 (1977): 681–741; 31 (1978): 532–603; 32 (1979): 529–80; 33 (1980): 623–734; 35 (1982): 164–256.

———. "Some Early Aristotelian Bibliographies." *Nouvelles de la république des lettres* 1 (1981): 87–116.

Lorenzo de' Monaci. *Chronicon de rebus Venetis*. Venice, 1758.

Luscombe, D. E. "State of Nature and the Origin of the State." In *The Cambridge History of Later Medieval Philosophy*. Edited by Norman Kretzmann. Cambridge: Cambridge University Press, 1982.

Machiavelli, Niccolò. *The Discourses*. In *The Prince and the Discourses*. Translated by Ricci and Vincent. New York: Random House, 1950.

Mackinnon, James. *A History of Modern Liberty*. London: Longmans, Green, and Co., 1906.

Maier, Anneliese. "Zu Walter Burleys Politik-kommentar." *Récherches de theólogie ancienne et mediévale* 14 (1947): 332–36.

Mair, John. *A History of Greater Britain, as well England as Scotland*. Edited and Translated by Archibald Constable. Edinburgh, 1892.

———. *In Secundum Sententiarum*. Paris, 1510.

———. *In Mattheum ad Literam Expositio*. Paris, 1518.

Major, J. R. "The Renaissance Monarchy as Seen by Erasmus, More, Seyssel and Machiavelli." In *Action and Conviction in Early Modern Europe*. Edited by Theodore K. Rabb and Jerrold Seigel, 17–31. Princeton, 1969.

Mansfield, Harvey C., Jr. *Machiavelli's New Modes of Order*. Ithaca: Cornell University Press, 1979.

Markus, R. A. "Two Conceptions of Political Authority: Augustine's *De Civitate Dei*, XIX, 14–15, and Some Thirteenth Century Interpretations." *Journal of Theological Studies*, N.S., 16 (1965): 68–100.

Marongiu, A. "The Theory of Democracy and Consent in the Fourteenth Century." In *Lordship and Community in Medieval Europe*. Edited by F. L. Cheyette, 404–21. Holt, Rinehart, and Winston, 1968.

Marsilius of Padua. *Defensor pacis*. Edited by Richard Scholz. Hanover: Hanische Buchhandlung, 1933.

Martin, Conor. "Some Medieval Commentaries on Aristotle's Politics." *History* 36 (1951): 29–44.

———. "The Vulgate Text of Aquinas' Commentary on Aristotle's Politics." *Dominican Studies* 5 (1952): 35–64.

———. "Walter Burley." In *Oxford Studies Presented to Daniel Callus*, 194–230. Oxford: Clarendon Press, 1964.

Massey, Hector J. "John of Salisbury: Some Aspects of His Political Philosophy." *Classica et Medievalia* 28 (1967): 357–72.

Mayer, Thomas. *Thomas Starkey and the Commonweal. Humanist Politics and Religion in the Reign of Henry VIII*. Cambridge: Cambridge University Press, 1989.

McCall, John P. "The Writings of John of Legnano with a List of Manuscripts." *Traditio* 23 (1967): 415–37.

McCulloch, D. and E. D. Jones. "Lancastrian Politics, the French War, and the Rise of the Popular Element." *Speculum* 58 (1983): 95–138.

McGrade, Arthur Stephen. "Rights, Natural Rights, and the Philosophy of Law." In *The Cambridge History of Later Medieval Philosophy*. Edited by Norman Kretzmann. Cambridge, 1982.

———. *The Political Thought of William of Ockham: Personal and Institutional Principles*. London: Cambridge University Press, 1974.

McIlwain, Charles H. *Constitutionalism: Ancient and Modern*. Ithaca: Cornell University Press, 1947.

———. *The Growth of Political Thought in the West*. New York: Macmillan Company, 1932.

McKeon, R. "Aristotle's Conception of Moral and Political Philosophy." *Ethics* 51 (1941): 253–90.

———. *Freedom and History.* New York: Noonday Press, 1952.

Mehl, James V. "The First Printed Editions of the History of Church Councils." *Annuarium Historiae Conciliorum* 18 (1986): 128–43.

Mendle, Michael. *Dangerous Positions. Mixed Government, the Estates of the Realm, and the Answer to the XIX Propositions.* University of Alabama Press, 1985.

Menzel, Ottokar. "Bemerkungen zur Staatslehre Engelberts von Admont." *Corona Quernea, Festgabe für Karl Strocker. Schriften der Reichsinstituts für altere deutsche Geschichtskunde, Monumenta Germaniae Historica,* 390–408. Leipzig: K. W. Hiersemann, 1941.

Merzbacher, Friederich. "Die Rechts-, Staats-, und Kirchenauffassung des Aegedius Romanus." *Archiv für Rechts- und Sozialphilosophie* 41 (1954): 88–97.

Meyer, H. "Lupold von Bebenburg: Studien zu seiner Schriften." *Studien und Darstellungen aus dem Gebiete der Geschichte* 7 (1909): 1–2.

Miller, S. J. T. "The Position of the King in Bracton and Beaumanoir." *Speculum* 31 (1956): 263–96.

Minio-Paluello, L. "Tre note alla 'Monarchia.' " In *Medioevo e Rinascimento. Studi in onore di Bruno Nardi.,* vol. 2, 511–22. Florence: G. C. Sansoni, 1955.

Molnar, Thomas. "The Medieval Beginnings of Political Secularization." *Modern Age* 26 (1982): 160–67.

Montesquieu, Baron de. *The Spirit of the Laws.* Translated by Thomas Nugent. New York: Hafner, 1949.

Moody, E. A. "Ockham and Aegidus of Rome." *Franciscan Studies* 9 (1949): 417–42.

———. "Ockham, Buridan, and Nicholas of Autrecourt." *Franciscan Studies,* new series 7 (1947): 113–46.

Morrall, John B. *Aristotle.* Boston, 1977.

———. *Gerson and the Great Schism.* Manchester: Manchester University Press, 1960.

———. *Political Theory in Medieval Times.* New York: Harper and Row, 1962.

———. "Some Notes on a Recent Interpretation of William of Ockham's Political Philosophy." *Franciscan Studies,* n.s. 9 (1949): 335–69.

Morrow, Glenn R. *Plato's Cretan City. A Historical Interpretation of the Laws.* Princeton: Princeton University Press, 1960.

Mosse, George L. "Sir John Fortescue and the Problem of Papal Power." *Medievalia et Humanistica* 7 (1952): 89–94.

———. "The Influence of Jean Bodin's *Republique* on English Political Thought." *Medievalia et Humanistica* 5 (1948): 73–83.

Most, R. "Der Reichsgedanke des Lupolds von Bebenburg." *Deutsches Archiv für Geschichte des Mittelalters* 4 (1941): 444–85.

Muir, Edward. *Civic Ritual in Renaissance Venice.* Princeton, 1981.

Mulcahy, D. G. "Marsilius's Use of St. Augustine." *Revue des Etudes Augustiniennes* 18 (1972): 180–90.

———. "The Hands of St. Augustine but the Voice of Marsilius." *Augustiniana* 21 (1971): 457–66.

Mulgan, R. G. "A Note on Aristotle's Absolute Ruler." *Phronesis* 19 (1974): 66–69.

———. "Aristotle and the Democratic Conception of Freedom." In *Auckland Classical Essays*. Edited by B. F. Harris, 95–112. Auckland: Aukland University Press and Oxford: Oxford University Press, 1970.

———. *Aristotle's Political Theory*. Oxford: Clarendon Press, 1977.

———. "Aristotle's Sovereign." *Political Studies* 18 (1970): 518–22.

Murray, Robert Henry. *History of Political Science*. Cambridge: W. Heffer, 1926.

Myers, Henry A. and Herwig Wolfram. *Medieval Kingship*. Chicago: Nelson-Hall, 1982.

Nederman, Cary J. "Bracton on Kingship Revisited." *History of Political Theory* 5 (1984): 61–77.

Newman, William Lambert. *The* Politics *of Aristotle*. 2 vols. Oxford: Clarendon Press, 1887.

Nicolaus of Cusa. *De Concordantia Catholica Libri Tres*. Edited by Gerhard Kallen. Hamburg: Felix Meiner, 1963.

O'Rahilly, A. "Notes on St. Thomas: II. The Commentary on the *Politics*." *Irish Ecclesiastical Record* 30 (1928): 614–22; "IV. *De Regimine Principum*" 31 (1929): 396–410; "V. Tholomeo of Lucca, Continuator of the *De Regimine Principum*" 31 (1929): 606–14.

Oakley, Francis. "Almain and Major: Conciliar Theory on the Eve of the Reformation." *American Historical Review* 70 (1965): 673–90.

———. "Celestial Hierarchies Revisited: Walter Ullmann's Vision of Medieval Politics." *Past and Present* 60 (1973): 3–48.

———. "Figgis, Constance, and the Divines of Paris." *American Historical Review* 75 (1969): 368–86.

———. "From Constance to 1688 Revisited." *Journal of the History of Ideas* 27 (1966): 429–32.

———. "Jacobean Political Theology." *Journal of the History of Ideas* 29 (1968): 323–46.

———. "Legitimation by Consent: The Question of the Medieval Roots." *Viator* 14 (1983): 303–35.

———. *Natural Law, Conciliarism, and Consent in the Late Middle Ages*. Variorum Reprints, 1984.

———. "Natural Law, the Corpus Mysticum and Consent in Conciliar Thought from John of Paris to Matthias Ugonius." *Speculum* 55 (1980): 786–810.

———. *Omnipotence, Covenant, and Order: An Excursion in the History of Ideas from Abelard to Leibnitz*. Ithaca: Cornell University Press, 1984.

———. "On the Road from Constance to 1688: The Political Thought of John Major and George Buchanan." *Journal of British Studies* 2 (1962): 1–31.

———. *The Political Thought of Pierre d'Ailly: The Voluntarist Tradition*. New Haven, 1964.

———. *The Western Church in the Later Middle Ages*. Ithaca: Cornell University Press, 1979.

Oliver, J. H. "Praise of Periclean Athens as a Mixed Constitution." *Rheinische Museum fur Philologie*, n.s., 98 (1955): 37–40.

———. "The Ruling Power." *Transactions of the American Philosophical Society* 43, vol. 4. Philadelphia, 1953.

Oresme, Nicole. *Le Livre d'Ethiques d'Aristote*. Edited by Albert Douglas Menut. New York: G. E. Stechert, 1940.

———. *Le Livre de Politiques d'Aristote*. Edited by Albert Douglas Menut. *Transactions of the American Philosophical Society*, n.s., vol. 60, pt. 6 (1970).

———. *On Aristotle's Politics*. Translated by Albert D. Menut. Lawrence, Ka.: Coronado Press, 1979.

Overfield, James H. *Humanism and Scholasticism in Late Medieval Germany*. Princeton: Princeton University Press, 1984.

Pagden, Anthony, ed. *The Languages of Political Theory in Early Modern Europe*. Cambridge: Cambridge University Press, 1987.

Parekh, Bikhu and R. N. Berki. "The History of Political Ideas: A Critique of Q. Skinner's Methodology." *Journal of the History of Ideas* 24 (1973): 163–84.

Pargellis, Stanley. "The Theory of Balanced Government." In *The Constitution Reconsidered*. Edited by Conyers Read, 37–49. New York: Harper and Row, 1968.

Parsons, W. "The Medieval Theory of the Tyrant." *Review of Politics* 4 (1942): 129–43.

Pascoe, L. B. *Jean Gerson: Principles of Church Reform*. Leiden, 1973.

Passerin d'Entreves, Alessandro. *Dante as a Political Thinker*. Oxford: Clarendon Press, 1952.

———. "La fortuna di Marsilio da Padova in Inghilterra." *Giornale degli economisti e annali d economia* 2 (1940).

———. *The Medieval Contribution to Political Thought*. Oxford: Oxford University Press, 1939.

———. *Natural Law: An Introduction to Legal Philosophy*. London: Hutchinson University Library, 1951.

———. *The Notion of the State*. Oxford: Clarendon Press, 1967.

Peter John Olivi. *De renuntiatione papae Coelestini*. Edited by V. P. Livarius Oliger. *Archivum Franciscanum Historicum* 11 (1918): 340–73.

Peter of Auvergne. *In Libros Politicorum Aristotelis Expositio*, Books 1–3.6. In *The Commentary of Peter of Auvergne, the Inedited Part*. Edited by Gundissalvus Grech. Rome: Descleée, 1967.

———. *In Libros Politicorum Aristotelis Expositio*. Books 3.7–8 of a work formerly attributed to Thomas Aquinas. Edited by R. M. Spiazzi. Turin: Marietti, 1966.

———. *Questiones super Politicum*. Manuscript. Paris BN 160.89, f.274r–319r.

Peterman, Larry. "Dante's *Monarchia* and Aristotle's Political Thought." *Studies in Medieval and Renaissance History* 10 (1973): 1–40.

Peterson, David S. "Conciliarism, Republicanism, and Corporatism: the 1415–1420 Constitution of the Florentine Clergy," *Renaissance Quarterly* 42 (1989): 183–226.

Piaia, Gregorio. *Marsilio da Padova nella Reformae nella Controriforma*. Padua, 1977.

Plato. *The Dialogues of Plato*. Translated by B. Jowett. 5 vols. Oxford: Oxford University Press, 1931.

Pleuger, Gunter. *Die Staatslehre Wihelms von Ockham*. Cologne University Inaugural Dissertation, 1966.

Plucknett, T.F.T. *Statutes and Their Interpretation in the First Half of the Fourteenth Century*. Cambridge: The University Press, 1922.

Pocock, J.G.A. *The Ancient Constitution and the Feudal Law: A Study of English Historical Thought in the Seventeenth Century*. Cambridge: Cambridge University Press, 1957.

———. "The Concept of a Language and the *métier d'historien*: Some Considerations on Practice." In *The Languages of Political Theory in Early Modern Europe*. Edited by Anthony Pagden, 19–38. Cambridge: Cambridge University Press, 1987.

———. *The Machiavellian Moment: Florentine Political Theory and the Atlantic Republican Tradition*. Princeton: Princeton University Press, 1975.

———. *Politics, Language, and Time: Essays on Political Thought and History*. New York: Athenium, 1971.

———. "Virtues, Rights, and Manners. A Model for Historians of Political Thought." *Political Theory* 9 (1981): 353–68.

Pollock, F. *History of the Science of Politics*. New York: J. Fitzgerald, 1883.

Polybius. *The Histories of Polybius*. Edited by Evelyn S. Shuckburgh. 2 vols. Bloomington: Indiana University Press, 1962.

———. *Polybii Historiarum Libri Superstites in Latinum Sermonem Conversi a N. Perotto*. Rome, 1473.

Ponet, John. *A Shorte Treatise of Politike Power*. In Winthrop S. Hudson, *John Ponet: Advocate of Limited Monarchy*. Chicago: University of Chicago Press, 1942.

Posch, Andreas. *Die Staats- und Kirchenpolitische Stellung Engelberts von Admont, Görres-Gesellschaft Veröffentl. d. Sektion für Rechts- und Sozialwissenschaft* 37. Paderborn: F. Schöningh, 1920.

Post, Gaines. Review of Alan Gewirth, *Marsilius of Padua*. *American Historical Review* 58 (1953): 338–40.

———. Review of Michael Wilks, *The Problem of Sovereignty in the Later Middle Ages*. *Speculum* 39 (1964): 365–72.

———. "A Romano-Canonical Maxim 'quod omnes tangit' in Bracton." *Traditio* 4 (1946): 197–251.

———. *Studies in Medieval Legal Theory*. Princeton: Princeton University Press, 1964.

———. "The Theory of Public Law and the State in the Thirteenth Century." *Seminar* 6 (1948): 42–59.

———. "Vincentius Hispanus, 'Pro Ratione Voluntas,' and Medieval and Early Modern Theories of Sovereignty." *Traditio* 28 (1972): 159–84.

Previté-Orton, C. W. "Marsiglio of Padua, Part II. Doctrines." *English Historical Review* 38 (1923): 1–18.

Ptolemy of Lucca. *De regimine principum ad regem Cypri*, Books 2.2.5–4 of a work formerly attributed to Thomas Aquinas. In Thomas Aquinas, *Opuscula Omnia necnon Opera Minora*. Edited by R. P. Joannes Perrier, 221–445. Tomus Primus: *Opuscula Philosophica*. Paris, P. Lethielleux, 1949.

———. *Determinatio Compendiosa de Juribus Imperii*. Edited by Marius Kramer.

Fontes Iuris Germanici Antiqui. Hanover and Leipzig: Bibliopolius Hahnianus, 1909.

———. *Exameron*, Edited by T. Masetti. Siena, 1880.

———. *Historia Ecclesiastica*. In *Rerum Italicarum Scriptores*, t.11. Edited by L. A. Muratori. Milan, 1727.

Quaglioni, D. " *'Regimen ad populum'* e *'regimen regis'* in Egidio Romano e Bartolo de Sassofarrato." *Bullettino dell' Istitutio Storico per il medio evo e Archivio Muratoriano* 87 (1978): 201–28.

Quétif, J. and J. Echard. *Scriptores Ordinis Praedicatorum.* Paris, 1719.

Quillet, Jeannine. "Community, Counsel, and Representation." In *Cambridge History of Medieval Political Thought c. 350–c. 1450*. Edited by J. H. Burns, 520–73. Cambridge: Cambridge University Press, 1988.

———. *La Philosophie Politique de Marsile de Padoue*. Paris: J. Vrin, 1970.

———. "Universitas populi et représentation au XIVe siècle." *Miscellanea medievalia* 8 (1971): 186–201.

Rager, John C. *The Political Philosophy of Blessed Cardinal Bellarmine*. Washington, D.C., 1926.

Reeves, Marjorie. "Marsiglio of Padua and Dante Alighieri." In *Trends in Medieval Political Thought*. Edited by Beryl Smalley. Oxford: Basil Blackwell, 1965.

Regan, Richard J. "Aquinas on Political Obedience and Disobedience." *Thought* 56 (1981): 77–88.

Reichling, D. *Appendices ad Hainii-Coperingi Repertorium bibliographicum*. 6 vols. and index. Munich, 1905–11.

Renna, Thomas J. "Aristotle and the French Monarchy." *Viator* 9 (1978): 309–24.

———. *Church and State in Medieval Europe: 1050–1314*. Dubuque, 1974.

———. "Kingship in the *Disputatio inter clericum et militem.*" *Speculum* 48 (1973): 675–93.

———. "The Populus in John of Paris' Theory of Monarchy." *Tjidschrift voor Rechtsgeschiedenis* 42 (1974): 243–68.

———. *Royalist Political Thought in France, 1285–1303*. Ann Arbor: University Microfilms, 1972.

Reynolds, Beatrice. *Proponents of Limited Monarchy in Sixteenth Century France: Francis Hotman and Jean Bodin*. New York: Columbia University Press, 1931.

Reynolds, Susan. "Medieval *Origines Gentium* and the Community of the Realm." *History* 68 (1983): 375–90.

Richardson, H. G. "The Commons and Medieval Politics." *Transactions of the Royal Historical Society*, 4th ser.,vol. 28 (1946): 21–45.

Riedl, G. *The Social Theory of Saint Thomas Aquinas*. Philadelphia, 1934.

Rivière, Jean. *Le problème de l'église et de l'état au temps de Philippe le Bel*. Louvain: Spicilegium sacrum lovaniese bureaux, 1926.

Robey, David. "Pier Paolo Vergerio the Elder: Republicanism and Civic Values in the Work of an Early Humanist." *Past and Present* 58 (1973): 3–37.

——— and John Law. "Venetian Myth and the *'De republica veneta'* of Pier Paolo Vergerio." *Rinascimento*, 2d ser., vol. 15 (1975): 3–59.

Roensch, F. J. *Early Thomistic School*. Dubuque, 1964.

Rouse, Richard H. and Mary A. "John of Salisbury and the Theory of Tyrannicide." *Speculum* 42 (1967): 693–709.

Rousseau, Jean Jacques. *The Social Contract*. Translated by G.D.H. Cole. In *Great Books of the Western World*. Chicago: Encyclopedia Britannica, 1952.

Rowe, C. J. "Aims and Methods in Aristotle's *Politics*." *Classical Quarterly* 71, n.s. 27 (1977): 159–72.

Rubinstein, Nicolai. "The History of the Word *politicus* in Early Modern Europe." In *The Languages of Political Theory in Early Modern Europe*. Edited by A. Pagden. Cambridge, 1987.

———. "Marsilius of Padua and Italian Political Theory of his Time." In *Europe in the Later Middle Ages*. Edited by J. R. Hale, J. R. L. Highfield, and B. Smalley, 44–75. Evanston: Northwestern University Press, 1965.

———. "Political Ideas in Sienese Art." *Journal of the Warburg and Courtauld Institutes* 21 (1958): 179–207

———. "Politics and Constitution in Florence at the end of the Fifteenth Century." In *Italian Renaissance Studies*. Edited by E. F. Jacob, 148–83. London, 1969.

Ruby, Jane E. "The Ambivalence of St. Thomas Aquinas' View of the Relationship of Divine Law to Human Law." *Harvard Theological Review* 48 (1955): 101–28.

Runkle, Gerald. *A History of Western Political Theory*. New York: Ronald Press, 1968.

Sabellico, Marco Antonio Coccio. *Historiae rerum Venetarum ab urbe condita libri XXXIII* in *Degl' istorici delle cose veneziane*. Vol. 1. Venice, 1718–22.

Sabine, George H. *A History of Political Theory*. New York: Holt, Rinehart and Winston, 1961.

Saenger, Paul. "John of Paris, Principal Author of the *Questio de potestate papae: Rex pacificus*." *Speculum* 56 (1981): 41–55.

Salvemini, Gaetano. *La Teoria del Bartolo da Sassoferrato sulle Constituzione Politiche*. Florence, 1901.

Savonarola, Girolamo. "De Politia et Regno." In *Compendium Totius Philosophiae*, 576–99. Venice, 1542.

———. *Trattato circa el reggimento e governo della città di Firenze*. Edited by Luigi Firpo, 435–87. Rome, 1965.

———. *Treatise on the Constitution and Government of Florence*. In *Humanism and Liberty*. Edited by R. N. Watkins. Columbia: University of South Carolina Press, 1978.

Sawada, P. A. "Two Anonymous Tudor Treatises on the General Council." *Journal of Ecclesiastical History* 12 (1961): 197–214.

Schilling, Otto. *Die Staats- und Sozialelehre des heiligen Thomas von Aquin*. Paderborn: F. Schöningh, 1923.

Schmidinger, Heinrich. *Romana Regia Potestas: Staats- und Reichsdenken bei Engelbert von Admont und Enea Silvio Piccolomini. Vorträge der Aeneas-Silvius-Stiftung an der Universität Basel*. Vol. 8. Basel and Stuttgart: Verlag Helbing und Lichtenhahn, 1978.

Schmitt, Charles B. *The Aristotelian Tradition and Renaissance Universities*. Cambridge: Harvard University Press, 1983.

———. *Aristotle and the Renaissance*. Cambridge: Harvard University Press, 1983.

Schochet, Gordon. *Patriarchalism in Political Thought*. Oxford: Basil Blackwell, 1975.

Schutte, Anne Jacobson. *Pier Paulo Vergerio: The Making of an Italian Reformer*. Geneva, 1977.

Scholz, Richard. *Aegidius von Rom*. Stuttgart: Druck der Union deutsche Verlagsgesellschaft, 1902.

———. *Die Publizistik zur Zeit Philipps des Schonen und Bonifaz VIII*. Stuttgart: F. Enke, 1903.

———. "Marsilius von Padua und die Idee de Demokratie." *Zeitschrift für Politik* 1 (1908).

———. *Unbekannte kirschenpolitische Streitschriften aus der Zeit Ludwigs des Bayern. 1327–1354*. 2 vols. Rome, 1911, 1914.

———. *Wilhelm von Ockham als Politischer Denker und sein Breviloquium de Principatu Tyranico*. Leipzig: K. W. Hiersemann, 1942.

Schulz, E. "Zur Beurteilung Engelberts von Admont." *Archiv fur Kulturgeschichte* 29 (1939): 51–63.

Schulz, Fritz. "Bracton on Kingship." *English Historical Review* 60 (1945): 136–76.

Scott, T. K. "Nicholas of Autrecourt, Buridan, and Ockhamism." *Journal of the History of Philosophy* 9 (1971): 15–41.

Sears, H. L. "Rimado de Palacio and the 'De Regimine Principum' Tradition of the Middle Ages." *Hispanic Review* 20 (1952): 1–27.

Seaver, P. W. "John of Paris, St. Thomas, and the Modern State." *Dominicana* 45 (1960): 305–27.

Segall, H. *Der Defensor pacis des Marsilius von Padua. Grundfragen der Interpretation, Historische Forschungen*, Band Z. Wiesbaden, 1959.

Seyssel, Claude de. *The Monarchy of France*. Translated by J. H. Hexter. Edited by Donald R. Kelley. New Haven: Yale University Press, 1981.

———. "Proem by Messire Claude de Seyssel, Councillor and Master of Ordinary Requests of the Household of the Most Christian King of France, Louis the twelfth of that name, to the translation of the history by Appian of Alexandria entitled The Deeds of the Romans." In *The Monarchy of France*. Translated by J. H. Hexter. Edited by Donald R. Kelley. New Haven: Yale University Press, 1981.

Shahar, Shulamith. "Nicolas Oresme, un penseur politique indépendant de l'éntourage du roi Charles V." *L'Information historique* 32 (1970): 203–9.

Sharvy, Richard. "Aristotle on Mixtures." *Journal of Philosophy* 80 (1983): 439–57.

Sheedy, Anna T. *Bartolus on Social Conditions in the Fourteenth Century*. New York: Columbia University Press, 1942.

Shepard, Max A. "The Political and Constitutional Theory of Sir John Fortescue." In *Essays in History and Political Theory in Honor of Charles Howard McIlwain*, 289–318. New York: Russell and Russell, 1936.

———. "William of Ockham and the Higher Law." *American Political Science Review* 26 (1932): 1005–24; 27 (1933): 24–39.

Sherman, Claire R. "A Second Instruction to the Reader from Nicole Oresme, Translator of Aristotle's *Politics* and *Economics*." *The Art Bulletin* 61 (1979): 468–69.

Sherman, Claire R. "Some Visual Definitions in the Illustrations of Aristotle's *Nichomachian Ethics* and *Politics* in the French Translations of Nicole Oresme." *The Art Bulletin* 59 (1977): 320–30.

Siegfried, W. *Untersuchung zur Staatslehre des Aristoteles*. Zurich: Schulthess, 1942.

Sigmund, Paul E. "The Influence of Marsilius on Fifteenth-Century Conciliarism." *Journal of the History of Ideas* 23 (1962): 393–402.

———. *Nicholas of Cusa and Medieval Political Thought*. Cambridge: Harvard University Press, 1963.

Silverstein, H. T. "On the Genesis of *De Monarchia* II, V." *Speculum* 13 (1938): 326–49.

Sinclair, T. A. *A History of Greek Political Thought*. Cleveland: World Publishing Company, 1968.

Skeel, C.A.J. "The Influence of the Writings of Sir John Fortescue." *Transactions of the Royal Historical Society*, 3d ser., vol. 10 (1916): 77–114.

Skinner, Quentin, ed. *The Cambridge History of Renaissance Philosophy*. Cambridge: Cambridge University Press, 1988.

———. *The Foundations of Modern Political Theory*. 2 vols. Cambridge: Cambridge University Press, 1978.

———. "Political Philosophy." In *The Cambridge History of Renaissance Philosophy*. Edited by Quentin Skinner. Cambridge: Cambridge University Press, 1988.

Smalley, Beryl. "Sallust in the Middle Ages." In *Classical Influences on European Culture 500–1500*. Edited by R. R. Bulgar, 165–94. Cambridge: Cambridge University Press, 1971.

———, ed. *Trends in Medieval Political Thought*. Oxford: Basil Blackwell, 1965.

Smith, Thomas. *De Republica Anglorum*. Edited by Mary Dewar. Cambridge: Cambridge University Press, 1982.

Sorokin, P. *Contemporary Sociological Theories*. New York: Harper, 1928.

Spitz, Lewis W. "The Course of German Humanism." In *Itinarium Italicum*. Edited by H. A. Oberman and Thomas A. Brady, Jr. Leiden, 1975.

Spörl, J. "Pie rex, caesarque future!" In *Festschrift H. Kunisch*. Berlin, 1961.

Stanka, Rudolf. *Die Politische Philosophie des Altertums*. Vienna and Cologne: Verlag A Sexl, 1951.

———. *Die Politische Philosophie des Mittelalters*. Vienna: Verlag A. Sexl, 1957.

Starkey, Thomas. *Dialogue between Cardinal Pole and Thomas Lupset*. In *England in the Reign of King Henry the Eighth*. Edited by Sidney B. Herrtage. Early English Text Society, nos. 12, 72. London: N. Trübner, 1878.

———. *Starkey's Life and Letters*. In Part 1 of *England in the Reign of King Henry the Eighth*. Edited by Sidney Herritage. London, 1878.

Stern, S. M. *Aristotle on the World State*. Columbia: University of South Carolina Press, 1968.

Stickler, A. Review of Walter Ullmann, *Traditio* 7 (1949–51): 450–63.

Stout, Harry S. "Marsilius of Padua and the Henrican Reform." *Church History* 43 (1973): 308–18.

Strauss, Leo. "Marsilius of Padua." In *The History of Political Philosophy*. Edited by L. Strauss and J. Cropsley. Chicago: Rand McNally, 1964.

Strayer, Joseph R. *Medieval Statecraft and the Perspectives of History*. Princeton: Princeton University Press, 1971.

Struever, Nancy S. *The Language of History in the Renaissance*. Princeton: Princeton University Press, 1970.

Struve, Tilman. *Die Entwicklung der Organologischen Staatsauffassung im Mittelalter*. Stuttgart: Anton Hiersemann, 1978.

Tejera, V. *The City-State Foundations of Western Political Thought*. Lanham, Md.: University Press of America, 1984.

Thomas Aquinas. *De Regimine Principum ad Regem Cypri*. In *Opera Omnia*. Edited by R. Busa, vol. 3, 595–601. Stuttgart-Bad Cannstatt, 1980.

———. *In Decem Libros Ethicorum Aristotelis ad Nichomachum Expositio*. Edited by R. M. Spiazzi. Rome: Marietti, 1949.

———. *In Libros Politicorum Aristotelis Expositio*. Edited by R. M. Spiazzi. Rome: Marietti, 1966.

———. *On the Governance of Rulers*. Translated by Gerald Phelan. London, 1938.

———. *Summa Contra Gentiles*. In *Opera Omnia*. Edited by Robertus Busa, vol. 2, 1–152. Stuttgart-Bad Cannstatt, 1980.

———. *Summa Theologiae*. In *Opera Omnia*. Edited by Robertus Busa, vol. 2, 184–926. Stuttgart-Bad Cannstatt, 1980.

Thomson, S. Harrison. "Walter Burley's Commentary on the *Politics* of Aristotle." In *Melanges Auguste Pelzer*, 557–78. Louvain: Bibliothèque de l'Université, 1947.

Thompson, W.D.J. Cargill. "The Sources of Hooke's Knowledge of Marsilius of Padua." *Journal of Ecclesiastical History* 25 (1974).

Thucydides. *The Peloponnesian Wars*. In *The Greek Historians*. Edited by Francis R. B. Godolphin, vol. 1, 567–1001. New York: Random House, 1942.

Tierney, Brian. "Aristotle, Aquinas, and the Ideal Constitution." In *Proceedings of the Patristic, Mediaeval and Renaissance Conference* 4 (1979): 1–11.

———. "Bracton on Government." *Speculum* 38 (1963): 295–317.

———. "The Canonists and the Medieval State." *Review of Politics* 15 (1953): 378–88.

———. *Church Law and Constitutional Thought in the Middle Ages*. London: Variorum Reprints, 1979.

———. "A Conciliar Theory of the Thirteenth Century." *Catholic Historical Review* 36 (1950–1951): 415–40.

———. " 'Divided Sovereignty' at Constance: a Problem of Medieval and Early Modern Political Theory." *Annuarium Historiae Conciliorum* 7 (1975): 238–56. Reprinted in Tierney, *Church Law and Constitutional Thought in the Middle Ages*. London: Variorum Reprints, 1979.

———. *Foundations of the Conciliar Theory*. Cambridge: Cambridge University Press, 1955.

———. " 'The Prince is not Bound by the Laws.' Accursius and the Origins of the Modern State." *Comparative Studies in Society and History*, vol. 5, no. 4 (1963): 378–400.

———. *Religion, Law, and the Growth of Constitutional Thought*. Cambridge: Cambridge University Press, 1982.

Troeltsch, Ernst. *The Social Teaching of the Christian Church*. Translated by Olive Wyon. 2 vols. New York: Harper, 1960.

Trompf, G. W. *The Idea of Historical Recurrence in Western Thought*. Berkeley: University of California Press, 1979.

Ullmann, Walter. "Bartolus and English Jurisprudence." In *Bartolo da Sassoferrato: Studi e Documenti per VI Centenario, ed. Universitá degli Studi di Perugia*, vol. 1, 47–73. Milan: Giuffrè, 1962–63.

———. "De Bartoli Sententia: Consilia representant mentem populi." In *Bartolo da Sassoferrato: Studi e Documenti per VI Centenario, Universitá degli Studi di Perugia*. Milan: Giuffrè, 1962–63.

———. "The Development of the Medieval Idea of Sovereignty." *English Historical Review* 64 (1949): 1–33.

———. *A History of Political Thought: The Middle Ages*. Baltimore: Penguin Books, 1965.

———. *The Individual and Society in the Middle Ages*. Baltimore: Johns Hopkins Press, 1966.

———. *Law and Politics in the Middle Ages: An Introduction to the Sources of Medieval Political Ideas*. Ithaca: Cornell University Press, 1975.

———. *The Medieval Idea of Law as Represented by Lucas de Penna*. London: Methuen, 1946.

———. "Personality and Territoriality in the 'Defensor pacis': The Problem of Political Humanism." *Medioevo* 6 (1980): 397–410.

———. *Principles of Government and Politics in the Middle Ages*. New York: Barnes and Noble, 1961.

van Steenberghen, F. *Aristotle in the West*. Louvain: Nauwelaerts, 1955.

Vélez-Sáenz, J. *The Doctrine of the Common Good of Civil Society in the Works of Saint Thomas Aquinas*. University of Notre-Dame Press, 1951.

Vergerio, Pier Paolo. *Epistolario di Pier Paolo Vergerio*. Edited by L. Smith. *Instituto Storico Italiano per il Medio Evo. Fonti per la Storia d'Italia* 74 (1934).

———. "De Republica veneta." Appended to D. Robey, and J. Law, "Venetian Myth and the 'De republica veneta' of Pier Paolo Vergerio." *Rinascimento*, 2d ser., vol. 15 (1975): 38–50.

Vile, M.J.C. *Constitutionalism and the Separation of Powers*. Oxford: Clarendon Press, 1967.

von Bezold, F. "Die Lehre von der Volkssouveranität während des Mittelalters." *Historische Zeitschrift* 36 (1876): 343–47.

von der Heydte, F. A. *Die Geburtsstunde des Souveränen Staates*. Regensburg: J. Habbel, 1952.

Von Fritz, Kurt. *The Theory of the Mixed Constitution in Antiquity: A Critical Analysis of Polybius' Political Ideas*. New York: Columbia University Press, 1954.

von Hertling, G. "Zur Geschichte der Aristotelischen Politik im Mittelalter." *Historische Beiträge zur Geschichte der Philosophie*. Kempten and Munich, 1911.

von Leyden, W. "Aristotle and the Concept of Law." *Philosophy* 42 (1967): 1–19.

Walbank, F. W. *Polybius*. Berkeley, 1972.

———. "Polybius on the Roman Constitution." *Classical Quarterly* 37 (1943): 73–89.

Walsh, James J. "Teleology in the Ethics of Buridan." *Journal of the History of Philosophy* 17 (1979): 265–86.

Weinstein, Donald. *Savonarola and Florence: Prophecy and Patriotism in the Renaissance*. Princeton: Princeton University Press, 1970.

Weston, Corinne Comstock. "Beginnings of the Classical Theory of the English Constitution." *Procedings of the American Philosophical Society* 100 (1956): 133–44.

———. *English Constitutional Theory and the House of Lords, 1556–1832*. London: Routledge and Kegan Paul, 1965.

———. "The Theory of Mixed Monarchy under Charles I and After." *English Historical Review* 75 (1960): 426–43.

——— and Janelle Renfrow Greenberg. *Subjects and Sovereigns: The Grand Controversy over Legal Sovereignty in Stuart England*. Cambridge: Cambridge University Press, 1981.

Whitfield, J. H. "Savonarola and the Purpose of the Prince." *Modern Language Review* 44 (1949).

Wicksteed, Philip H. *Dante and Aquinas*. New York: E. P. Dutton, 1913.

Wilkinson, Bertie. *Constitutional History of England in the Fifteenth Century*. London: Longmans, Green, and Co., 1964.

———. *Constitutional History of Medieval England, 1216–1399*. London: Longmans, Green, and Co., 1958.

———. "The Political Revolution of the Thirteenth and Fourteenth Centuries in England." *Speculum* 24 (1949): 502–9.

Wilks, Michael J. "Corporation and Representation in the *Defensor pacis*." *Studi Gratiani* 15 (1972).

———. *The Problem of Sovereignty in the Later Middle Ages*. Cambridge: Cambridge University Press, 1963.

William of Ockham. *Dialogus*. In *Monarchia Sancti Romani Imperii*. Edited by Melchior Goldast. Reprint of the 1614 Frankfurt editon. Graz: Akademische Druck- und Verlagsanstalt, 1960.

———. *Octo quaestiones de potestate papae*. In *Guillelmi de Ockham Opera Politica*. Edited by H. S. Offler. Vol. 1. Manchester: Manchester University Press, 1974.

Witt, R. "The Rebirth of the Concept of Republican Liberty in Italy." In *Renaissance: Studies in Honor of Hans Baron*, 173–99. Dekalb: Northern Illinois University Press, 1971.

———. "The *De Tyranno* and Coluccio Salutati's View of Politics and Roman History." *Nuova Rivista Storica* 53 (1969): 434–74.

Woolf, Cecil N. Sidney. *Bartolus of Sassoferrato: His Position in the History of Medieval Political Thought*. Cambridge: Cambridge University Press, 1913.

Wormuth, Francis D. "Aristotle on Law." In *Essays in Political Theory Presented to George H. Sabine*. 45–61. Edited by Milton R. Konvitz and Arthur E. Murphy. Ithaca: Cornell University Press, 1948.

———. *The Origins of Modern Constitutionalism*. New York: Harper, 1949.

Xenophon. *Hellenica*, In *The Greek Historians*. Edited by Francis R. B. Godolphin, vol. 2, 3–221. New York: Random House, 1942.

Zeiller, Jacques. *L'Idée l'Etat dans Saint Thomas d'Aquin*. Paris: F. Alcan, 1910.

Zillig, Paula. *Die Theorie der gemischten Verfassung in ihrer literarischen Entwickelung in Altertum und ihr Verhältnis zur Lehre Lockes und Montesquieusüber Verfassung.* Würtzburg: Stürtz, 1916.

Zuckerman, C. "Aquinas' Conception of the Papal Primacy in Ecclesiastical Government." *Archives d'histoire doctrinale et littéraire du moyen age* 48 (1973): 97–134.

INDEX